A WASHINGTON TRAGEDY

A WASHINGTON TRAGEDY

How the Death of Vincent Foster
Ignited a Political Firestorm

Dan E. Moldea

REGNERY PUBLISHING, INC.
Washington, DC

Library of Congress Cataloging-in-Publication Data

Moldea, Dan E., 1950–
    A Washington tragedy : how the death of Vincent Foster ignited a political firestorm / Dan E. Moldea.
        p.   cm.
    Includes bibliographical references and index.
    ISBN 0–89526–382–3
    1. Foster, Vincent W., d. 1993—Death and burial. 2. Clinton, Bill, 1946– —Friends and associates. 3. Homicide investigation—Virginia—Arlington—Case studies. 4. Suicide victims—Virginia—Arlington—Case studies.   I. Title.
    E840.8.F69M65 1998
    364.15'22'09755295—dc21   98–14634
                                        CIP

Published in the United States by
Regnery Publishing, Inc.
An Eagle Publishing Company
One Massachusetts Avenue, NW
Washington, DC 20001

Distributed to the trade by
National Book Network
4720-A Boston Way
Lanham, MD 20706

Book Design by Marja Walker

Printed on acid-free paper.
Manufactured in the United States of America

10 9 8 7 6 5 4 3 2 1

Books are available in quantity for promotional or premium use. Write to Director of Special Sales, Regnery Publishing, Inc., One Massachusetts Avenue, NW, Washington, DC 20001, for information on discounts and terms or call (202) 216-0600.

Books by Dan E. Moldea

The Hoffa Wars:
Teamsters, Rebels, Politicians, and the Mob
1978

The Hunting of Cain:
A True Story of Money, Greed, and Fratricide
1983

Dark Victory:
Ronald Reagan, MCA, and the Mob
1986

Interference:
How Organized Crime Influences Professional Football
1989

The Killing of Robert F. Kennedy:
An Investigation of Motive, Means, and Opportunity
1995

Evidence Dismissed:
The Inside Story of the Police Investigation of O.J. Simpson
(with Tom Lange and Philip Vannatter)
1997

A Washington Tragedy:
How the Death of Vincent Foster Ignited a Political Firestorm
1998

*To Mom
and in memory of
Carl Shoffler and Jack Tobin*

CONTENTS

"*No one can ever know why this happened. Even if you had a whole set of objective reasons, that wouldn't be why it happened.... What happened was a mystery about something inside of him.*"

—PRESIDENT BILL CLINTON,
on the death of Vincent Foster

PREFACE

MORE THAN JUST ANOTHER INDEPENDENT INVESTIGATION, this book is the story of the series of official and unofficial investigations of the same tragic event—the suicide of Vincent Foster—as well as the media reactions to and the political firestorms caused by these investigations.

This work is based on my numerous exclusive interviews with the top investigators, both official and unofficial, in the Foster case, as well as a close reading of the thousands of documents they authored. Key pieces of evidence are introduced through the characters who discovered them—by reprinting excerpts from the records they created.

When the writing of this book began, I was tempted to re-create scenes and conversations based on these existing documents—in order to massage some immediacy and additional drama into the text. However, because of all the controversy already present in the Foster case, I decided not to add to the confusion by placing my own personal spin on the actual words written and spoken between and among the characters—unless they re-created the conversations themselves.

In other words, I have attempted to write a straight narrative about the Foster investigations, organizing it into a chronology of events and using the present tense to create a sense of immediacy throughout the story. As a result, the reader learns as the investigators uncover the facts; the drama is inherent as the plot unfolds.

Simply speaking, this is a detective story, which details the detectives' and other investigators' work. It is neither a political history of the Clinton White House nor a revisionist's biography of the late Vincent Foster.

In addition, because the media are so important to this story, I have tried to be as scrupulous as possible in crediting those reporters who broke major news articles and wrote op-ed pieces about the events discussed in this book. As much as anything else, the work of these journalists was essential to the initial and continuing thrust of the Foster case.

Dan E. Moldea
Washington, D.C.
January 29, 1998

PART ONE
The Suicide—and Its Mysteries

"Vincent W. Foster, Jr., the one-time White House aide, still has not been murdered—not by the Clintons and not by anybody. This is the conclusion of Kenneth W. Starr, the Whitewater Independent Counsel for Life. Last week, he issued a report supporting his earlier finding—which was, as you may know, precisely the conclusion reached by a previous independent counsel, two congressional panels and the cops first on the scene. Now can we have an investigation into why there have been so many investigations?"

—RICHARD COHEN
THE *WASHINGTON POST*
OCTOBER 14, 1997

VINCENT FOSTER COMMITTED SUICIDE, and he acted alone.

Leaving the White House at a little after 1 PM on July 20, 1993, Foster—President Bill Clinton's deputy counsel, who appeared to be at the peak of his career—drove his 1989 gray Honda Accord to Fort Marcy Park in northern Virginia. He parked his car next to a trail that led to a large open grove.

Taking off his blue pin-striped suit coat and tie, he placed them on the front passenger seat of his car, along with his White House pass and his wallet, which contained, among other things, a list of three local psychiatrists.

After loosening the top button of his white shirt, Foster opened the glove compartment and reached for an oven mitt in which he had concealed an antique, black-colored, .38-caliber Colt revolver. Inside the cylinder were two live rounds of round-nosed lead ammunition.

He placed the gun in his left-front pocket, unknowingly transferring a portion of a sunflower-seed husk from the oven mitt. Leaving his car unlocked and the oven mitt in the glove compartment, Foster walked through the park, passing a Civil War cannon in the large grove, and eventually came to a second smaller grove nearly 250 yards from his car. Upon entering this heavily wooded area, he saw a second cannon.

He switched off his White House pager, sat in front of the cannon's barrel, and removed the gun from his left pocket. Bracketed by dense foliage, he was facing downhill.

He cocked the hammer of the revolver. Placing his right thumb on the trigger and steadying the weapon with his left hand, he put the gun in his mouth and fired a single shot.

The bullet perforated his brain and crashed out the back of his skull, killing him instantly; the backlash caused his eyeglasses to fall from his face and tumble down the hill. His hands fell limply down to his sides, with the gun still in his right hand; his thumb was trapped in the trigger guard. A stream of blood flowed from his mouth and nose, soaking the right shoulder of his shirt.

More blood flowed from a small exit wound in the back of his head and soaked the ground beneath him, as well as the back of his shirt.

Plain and simple, Foster, who left no suicide note, had taken his own life. But no one had seen him do it; no one had heard the shot. In fact, no known person had seen him alive in the park.

A mystery man in a white van, who had stopped in the park to urinate in the woods, stumbled across the body at about 6 PM. The mystery man quickly left the area, went to a nearby maintenance station for the National Park Service, and told an employee what he had found, asking him to call the police. Then, the mystery man vanished into rush-hour traffic.

The Park Service employee dutifully called the local rescue squad and then the U.S. Park Police, which had jurisdiction. Within minutes, two rescue teams and a lone Park Police officer, who had been stationed at an entrance to the nearby Central Intelligence Agency (CIA), arrived at the scene. The officer joined two of the rescue workers in their frantic search for the reported body, splitting off from them in the main grove and finding his way into the hidden grove. There, the officer located the unidentified body and called for the paramedics.

Within minutes, police investigators arrived at the crime scene and began a routine investigation, which found no evidence of a struggle and no reason to believe that Foster, who was identified after a search of his car, had been murdered.

However, during that routine investigation:

- No one could account for Foster's whereabouts for the five-hour period from the time he left the White House until his body was found.

- No fingerprints were found on the gun in Foster's right hand.

- The bullet that killed Foster could not be located.

- A blood transfer stain on Foster's right cheek could not be fully explained; the investigators found his head straight up, not resting on his right shoulder where blood had accumulated.

- A roll of 35 mm film that the police had used to memorialize the crime scene was underexposed and worthless.

- Two back-up Polaroid photographs taken at the scene were missing.

- None of the investigators at the crime scene was present at the autopsy.

- Foster's clothes were stacked in an unsegregated pile by a coroner's assistant, causing possible cross-contamination.

- No gunpowder was found on Foster's tongue.

- The mystery man in the white van could not be identified or located.

- Other visitors to the park reported seeing several unidentified men behaving suspiciously.

- No one from Foster's family could positively identify the gun, which had two serial numbers, as being his.

- Foster's friends and relatives, at first, denied that he had been depressed. In fact, President Clinton, who had just talked to Foster the night before his death and scheduled a meeting with him, had declared only twenty hours after Foster's body was discovered, "No one can ever know why this happened.... What happened was a mystery about something inside of him."

Also, in the midst of the Park Police probe, the White House Counsel's Office, which didn't order Foster's office sealed until the day after his death, initially stalled police investigators, preventing them from conducting interviews and searching the office. When the police were finally permitted to speak with four of the last known White House staffers to have seen Foster alive, the interviews were monitored and, in one case, disrupted by members of the Counsel's Office.

Earlier, the police had agreed to the White House Counsel's Office request to allow attorneys from the Department of Justice to serve as intermediaries during a review of the documents in Foster's office. The police understood the arrangement as this: If the White House declared a particular document privileged information and didn't want to show it to the police, the attorneys from Justice would view the material and decide on the merit of the claim.

But, instead, White House Counsel Bernard Nussbaum conducted the search unilaterally two days after Foster's death, refusing to allow either the Park Police or attorneys from the Justice Department to participate in the search or to see any documents.

Consequently, the police investigators and the Justice Department lawyers suspected that the White House was hiding something.

Foster's suicide was the most important White House death since the 1963 assassination of President John Kennedy. Immediately, the media went into a frenzy. They detailed the close friendship that Foster had enjoyed with the president and the first lady—with whom Foster, her one-time law partner, was rumored to have had an affair.

Although there was little initial speculation that any foul play had occurred, journalists quickly discovered that Foster had been involved in several recent controversies, including a scandal involving the White House Travel Office. As a result of this and other problems, the *Wall Street Journal* had written several editorials critical of Foster.

During the week after Foster's suicide, the White House continued to maintain that he had not been depressed. But, after an attorney in the Counsel's Office discovered a torn-up note in Foster's briefcase—a note that bitterly derided enemies of the president—the White House's position changed.

Suddenly, Foster's family and colleagues began to reveal details of the growing depression that had led to his suicide. His sister had given him the list of three psychiatrists found in his wallet, urging him to make an appointment with one of them; her husband had given Foster a list of attorneys in case he faced a legal battle over the Travel Office matter. Later, Foster's wife told police investigators that her husband—the day before his death—had contacted their family doctor, who had prescribed a mild antidepressant.

The torn-up note was concealed from police investigators for nearly thirty hours. It had been found in Foster's briefcase, which had been supposedly emptied by Nussbaum during the search of Foster's office several days earlier. The U.S. Capitol Police eventually confirmed that the note was in Foster's handwriting.

Although the note contained no fingerprints, the Park Police, in concert with the Department of Justice and the FBI, concluded that Foster had committed suicide.

Then, on the basis of erroneous information from a Park Police official, reporters alleged that documents had been removed from Foster's office on the night of his death by three White House staffers who had entered the office. Other articles, supposedly based on information from the Park Police, charged that the documents removed referred to the Whitewater Development Corporation. These stories led to more articles about Foster's connection with the Whitewater real-estate venture and the Clintons' business partner, James McDougal, who owned Madison Guaranty, a failed savings and loan, which had been represented by Mrs. Clinton.

Even though many of these stories were based on false information, Whitewater became a major issue. Soon after, reporters learned that, on the final day of his life, Foster had received a telephone call from the attorney who had handled questions about Whitewater during the 1992 presidential campaign. Also on Foster's last day, a search warrant had been authorized for the offices of Arkansas businessman David Hale, who had been linked to Whitewater and Madison Guaranty.

Even though Foster's role in Whitewater appeared minor, at best, the implications from the news stories led to editorials, essays, and opinion pieces—particularly in the *Wall Street Journal* and, now, the *New York Times*—that openly suggested a White House cover-up. Speculation ran rampant that a truly depressed Foster might have killed himself in order to avoid prosecution or to protect some dark secret about the Clintons.

Consequently, even though no wrongdoing had been shown, the media demanded that the White House release the documents that had been in Foster's office, especially those concerning Whitewater. At first, the White House agreed to cooperate; then it balked, provoking further charges of a ever-widening cover-up.

Pressed by news reports and editorials that continued to suggest the White House was covering up facts about what happened in the wake of Foster's death, Attorney General Janet Reno agreed to the appointment of an independent counsel, Robert Fiske, to investigate the Foster case, as well as the Clintons' involvement in Whitewater and Madison Guaranty.

Meantime, on the basis of a series of erroneous—but quickly

cleared up—statements made by the same Park Police official about the evidence in the case, a right-wing media-watchdog group, Accuracy in Media, and an aggressive reporter, Christopher Ruddy of the *New York Post*, began their own separate investigations.

Ruddy discovered what he claimed were more problems with the Foster case, which might indicate that Foster didn't commit suicide:

- Two rescue workers at the Foster crime scene had seen little or no blood and no exit wound in Foster's head.

- Skull fragments and brain matter were not recovered at the crime scene.

- The ambulance driver who had picked up Foster's body had coded the death as a homicide.

- The Park Police did not have Foster's gun tested by firearms examiners until *after* the case had been publicly closed.

- The former director of the FBI, who had been fired by the president the day before Foster's death, claimed that the investigation had been politicized.

- The Park Police and the coroner who conducted Foster's autopsy had, in previous cases, wrongly determined that murders had been suicides.

These charges caused a sensation, forcing Fiske to investigate them.

But, after a six-month investigation, Fiske, in cooperation with the FBI, was able to explain away most of the controversies in the Foster case—including those surrounding the mystery man in the white van—and corroborated the conclusion by the Park Police that Foster had committed suicide. Fiske declared that Foster had been depressed over his role in the Travel Office scandal, as well as the bad press he had received from the *Wall Street Journal*. Fiske found no evidence that Foster was depressed over anything related to Whitewater.

But his final report and the results of a subsequent oversight probe by the U.S. Senate Banking Committee raised even more problems:

- The mystery man in the white van did not see a gun in Foster's hand.

- No coherent soil had been found on Foster's shoes, even though he had walked more than 250 yards to the site of his death.

- There were no grass or soil stains on Foster's clothing.

- Semen was found in his underwear.

- Blond hair and carpet fibers were found on his clothing.

- Gunpowder was found on Foster's clothing that did not come from the gun in his hand.

- A paramedic present at the crime scene claimed to have seen a bullet wound in Foster's neck; another paramedic saw a wound on his forehead.

- The medical examiner who pronounced Foster dead at the crime scene reported seeing little blood, seemingly corroborating what two rescue workers had earlier claimed.

- Although the coroner had claimed in his official report that X rays of Foster's head had been taken during the autopsy, no X rays existed. The coroner explained that he had noted that X rays had been taken before realizing that the X ray machine was broken, and insisted that this was a simple error.

- The statements of the visitors in the parking lot, who had seen men behaving suspiciously, were ignored.

- Still, no one from Foster's family could identify the gun. His wife reported that a photograph the FBI had shown her was not the "silver-colored gun" she had earlier seen at their home. The gun in Foster's hand was black.

- Foster's widow had concealed her knowledge of guns in their Washington home from the Park Police.

Instead of putting the case to rest, Fiske had unintentionally opened new avenues of official and unofficial investigation.

Indeed, the political controversy became so intense that Fiske was ousted as independent counsel before he completed his investigation into the circumstances of the search of Foster's office. The new independent counsel, Kenneth Starr, was given, among other responsibilities, the authority to reinvestigate Foster's death.

But Starr had his problems, too. Miquel Rodriguez, one of Starr's staff attorneys, suspected that Foster had been murdered. After allegedly suggesting before a federal grand jury that the police officer who had found Foster's body was involved in the killing or a cover-up, Rodriguez was reined in by Starr's deputies. Complaining that his investigation was being sabotaged, Rodriguez resigned from the independent counsel's staff and became a key source for the critics of the Foster investigation.

At the time of Starr's appointment, the Democrats controlled both houses of Congress. But, in November 1994, the Democrats were annihilated during the midterm elections.

With the Republicans now in control of both the House and the Senate, investigations were aggressively renewed into Whitewater and the Travel Office controversy, along with a proposed probe of the alleged White House cover-up stemming from the search of Foster's office.

Soon after, a Special Committee of the Senate was empaneled to investigate Whitewater and its possible connection with the documents allegedly removed from Foster's office.

As part of this investigation, the longest in U.S. history, Senate Republicans alleged, among other things, that:

■ the Clintons were legally vulnerable because of their relationship with Whitewater and Madison Guaranty;

■ Foster had been deeply involved with Whitewater prior to his death;

■ telephone logs showed that the first lady had been in constant communication with Maggie Williams, her chief of staff, who was in Foster's office on the night of his death, and Susan Thomases, a New York attorney and an old friend of Mrs. Clinton;

- Thomases had asked Nussbaum to keep law-enforcement officials from "unfettered access" to Foster's office;

- Nussbaum reneged on his agreements with the Department of Justice and the Park Police in order to protect the Clintons' secret files; and

- Williams removed a box of documents from Foster's office and placed them in the Clintons' private quarters at the White House.

On the basis of supposed evidence supporting these allegations, the committee concluded that a conspiracy existed to sanitize Foster's office, directly involving the first lady.

Meantime, a coalition of right-wing special-interest groups, as well as a handful of politically conservative journalists, continued to pursue the Foster case, trying to prove that he had been murdered and that the federal government had covered up the real facts of the case. Nearly all of these groups and individuals had a common connection: They received money, directly or indirectly, from the same wealthy benefactor, Richard Scaife, the heir to the Mellon banking fortune.

Adding to their growing list of charges, the critics now alleged that, among other things:

- Foster had booked no fewer than three trips to Switzerland, including one shortly before his death.

- A paramedic, not the Park Police officer, had actually found Foster's body.

■ An official report by the medical examiner who pronounced Foster dead at the scene indicated that Foster's fatal wound traveled "mouth to neck," and that a crime-scene photograph allegedly showed the neck wound.

■ Although the police didn't find Foster's car keys in his right pocket at the crime scene, they later recovered them from the same pocket at the morgue.

■ White House staffers had given conflicting accounts about when they were notified of Foster's death.

■ The X ray machine used during the Foster autopsy was in good working condition, despite the claims by the coroner.

■ A former prosecutor who had seen Foster's body at the mortuary told one of the critics that he, too, had seen a wound on Foster's neck.

■ Foster's briefcase—the same briefcase in which the torn-up note was found in his office—had been seen by eyewitnesses in his gray Honda at Fort Marcy Park.

■ The handwriting expert who was used by the Park Police had unwittingly repudiated his opinion that the torn-up note had been written by Foster.

■ Foster's torn-up note had been forged and planted, according to three experts hired by the critics.

■ None of five witnesses in the parking lot appeared

to have seen Foster's *gray* Honda in the parking lot
prior to the arrival of the rescue workers and the
police. Three of these witnesses remembered seeing
several never-identified men behaving in an unusual
manner in and around a *brown* Honda. In fact,
one of these witnesses, claiming that the FBI had
lied in its report about what he had and had not
seen, filed suit against the federal government.

Nevertheless, the second independent counsel's analysis, the *Starr
Report*, corroborated the basic findings of the Park Police investigation and the final conclusion of Robert Fiske. In response, the
critics claimed that this latest report, issued in October 1997, was
nothing more than part of the continuing cover-up.

I know the critics are wrong. And as a professional crime
reporter with nearly twenty-five years' experience, I intend to
prove just that in the pages that follow.

Investigating the suicide of Vincent Foster is a nightmare of sourcing for any investigator, official or unofficial. Considering all the
conflicts among the witness statements and official reports, the
loose and contradictory estimates of the times of important events,
and the continuing controversies over physical evidence—as well as
the supercharged political atmosphere that further complicated the
investigation of Foster's death—it is no wonder the case remains
unresolved in most people's minds. But by following the track of
the investigations we will discover how a simple suicide of a troubled White House official developed—and was manipulated—into
a long-running soap opera with historical significance.

In other words, this is a story about how Washington works.

PART TWO
Examining the Crime Scene

66 **T**ake time out for yourself. Have some fun, go fishing; every once in a while take a walk in the woods by yourself. Learn to relax, watch more sunsets."

—VINCENT W. FOSTER
TO LAW-SCHOOL GRADUATES
MAY 8, 1993

1.

TUESDAY, JULY 20, 1993
Northern Virginia

The Washington metropolitan area, notorious for its horrific summers, is in the midst of another long and miserable drought. The temperature has routinely been in the high 90s, and the oppressive humidity during these dog days makes walking just to the corner nearly unbearable.

Today is just another day in which everyone seems to be seeking relief.

Officer Marianne White's telephone rings at the Fairfax County Public Safety Communications Center (PSCC) just one second before 6 PM. She answers, "Fairfax County 911. Do you have an emergency?"

The caller, who doesn't identify himself, replies, "Yes, ma'am. There's a guy that came up to Turkey Run Park and reported that there was a dead body at Fort Marcy," a federal park just off the George Washington Memorial Parkway.[1]

"You saw this person?" White asks.

"Yes, ma'am," the caller replies. "He left in a contractor's van, a white van…. This guy told me [that there] was a body laying up there by the last cannon."

"Last what?… There's a body laying near what?"

"There's a man laying up there by the last cannon gun…."

"Cannon?"

"Yes, they have cannons up there. Those big guns…."

"Okay, you're sure he's dead?…"

"That's what this guy said. I'm taking his word, you know?"

"Okay, I'll get ahold of [the U.S. Park Police], and I'll send the ambulance, okay?"

"All right."

White ends the conversation without getting the caller's name.

At 6:03 PM, the unidentified man talks to dispatcher James Myers of the United States Park Police (USPP).[2] "You've got a dead body," he says to the officer.

"We do?" Myers asks.

"Yeah."

The caller repeats what he had earlier told White, saying that a man in a white contractor van had driven into Turkey Run, the location of the maintenance yard for the National Park Service just off the parkway. There, the mystery man in the white van told him about the dead body he'd found at Fort Marcy.

Myers asks, "Did you get the guy's name that told you?"

"No," the caller responds, "that sucker told us [what happened], then took off."

The caller describes the mystery man as a white, heavy-set man, driving a 1978 or 1979 model van with Virginia tags.

"Are you a [National] Park Service employee?" Myers inquires.

"Yes, sir," the caller answers.

"Okay, [who] are you? What's your name?"

"Do I have to do that?"

"Well, yeah. Really. What if this guy that stopped and told you is the guy that killed him? The detectives just want to talk to you a little bit." Getting no answer, Officer Myers continues, "Okay, this guy came up the road, pulled into the parking lot... and told you what?"

"He said, 'You got a dead body down there at the Fort Marcy.'"

"Okay, did he say it was in the parking lot or back in the woods or... ?"

"He said it was back up there by the cannon...."

"The dead body is back by the cannon?"

"Yeah."

"Okay, and what else did he say?"

"That was it."

Myers presses again, "Okay. What's your name?" When he gets no answer, he pleads, "Come on, man. You work for us. You've got to help us. You might be headlines. You might be on *Unsolved Mysteries*.... Hello?"

But the anonymous caller has already hung up.

The crime scene.

2.

AT 6:05 PM, IN THE MIDST OF rush-hour traffic, the USPP
Communications Center radios Officer Franz J. Ferstl in Car 211,
asking that he investigate the report of a dead body at Fort Marcy
Park. Ferstl is at the USPP's Glen Echo station in Maryland,
across the Potomac River, and a considerable distance from Fort
Marcy Park. Ferstl races to his marked police car and immediately heads for the location, followed by Officer Julie Lynn Spetz
in her own squad car.

Another uniformed patrol officer, Kevin Fornshill in Car 261,
also hears the report and radios his supervisor, Sergeant Robert
Edwards, asking for and receiving permission to respond.
Fornshill, also based at Glen Echo, has been working overtime,

sitting in his unmarked white Ford Crown Victoria at the parkway entrance of the CIA—less than two and a half miles northwest of the reported location of the dead body.[3]

At 6:11 PM, Fornshill, a six-year veteran of the USPP, arrives at Fort Marcy Park and pulls into the parking lot, which already contains two fire and rescue vehicles from the Fairfax County Fire and Rescue Department (FCFRD), whose personnel are preparing to search for someone who might still need medical attention.

Among the FCFRD personnel, the senior officer is twenty-nine-year-old Sergeant George O. Gonzalez, a twelve-year veteran of emergency-response work, including his service as a volunteer in high school. Although he normally works in Reston, Gonzalez is currently on temporary detail in McLean, serving as the officer-in-charge of a unit in the county's Fire Station One.

At 6:03 PM, Gonzalez and his unit, Medic One, had been dispatched to respond to Fort Marcy Park. They had arrived about seven minutes later—at 6:10, just before Fornshill.

Gonzalez's driver in his unit is Todd S. Hall; his Advanced Life Support assistant is twenty-six-year-old technician Richard Arthur, a trained Emergency Medical Service paramedic.

A second group of fire and rescue personnel arrived in Fairfax County Station's Engine One. Now accompanied by paramedic Arthur, they are already en route to one of the southern trails of the park. Both search groups are carrying emergency, life-saving equipment.[4]

As Gonzalez entered Fort Marcy with his unit, he saw an abandoned, light-blue, four-door Mercedes 300E with Virginia license plates with its flashers blinking near the entrance to the park. Driving into the parking lot, which has space for more than twenty cars, he noticed two cars in parking slots. One was a white, four-door Nissan Stanza with Maryland tags, which had been backed into the fifth parking space from the rear of the lot;

the other was a four-door Honda Accord with Arkansas plates, RCN-504, parked head first and in the fourth space from the front of the lot.[5]

Fornshill joins Gonzalez and Hall, who have split off from the second team, for their search of the northern portion of the park, running up a small hill that crests into a large grove. As they sprint into the area, Fornshill sees a cannon to his left. Gonzalez does a quick visual search around this cannon but sees nothing.

Fornshill, Gonzalez, and Hall, who are now looking for a possible second cannon, continue onto a small plateau at the west end of the grove. As the two paramedics peel off to the south toward a picnic table, Fornshill runs north and finds a path partially covered with heavy foliage that leads to a hidden second grove. There, Fornshill spots another cannon and begins running toward it.

About thirty feet from the cannon, he sees what appears to be the back of a head, resting near the top of a slope just in front of the cannon's barrel. Fornshill's first thought is that it's a mannequin; that, as a hoax, someone has placed a dummy in the park.

Then, as he stops to the left of the object, Fornshill quickly realizes that he has found the body of a middle-aged man, lying on his back and at nearly a forty-five-degree angle on a steep embankment in the middle of a dirt footpath—later measured as 735 feet, or about 245 yards, from the parking lot.

The time is 6:14 PM, about three minutes after Fornshill's arrival in the park.

A thick patch of leaves and branches extends across the right side of the body, impeding Fornshill's view.

The officer moves in a 180-degree arc from the victim's left to right for a cursory look. The man's legs are straight, pointing west down the hill; his arms seem relaxed and fully extended at his sides. The officer cannot see the man's hands through the foliage but does not disturb the crime scene by moving anything.

The victim's head appears to be resting on his right shoulder to the north; a stream of dried, dark blood runs from the right corner of his mouth and down his chin toward his shoulder.

Although flies are buzzing about the victim's partially open mouth, his well-coiffed hair seems in place. His starched white shirt, open at the collar, as well as his dark, pin-striped trousers, neatly creased and not rumpled, appear clean and have not been soiled. The victim is not wearing a suit coat or tie.

Immediately, Fornshill, who never touches the body and gets no closer than five feet from it, calls out for the paramedics, breaking an eerie silence in the park. Then, he radios to USPP Communications, reporting that he has found the dead man by the second cannon in the hidden grove.

Rushing to the scene, thirty-year-old Todd Hall, a member of the fire department since May 1986, is the first rescue worker to arrive. Fornshill backs away several feet, giving Hall room to work in the tight area where the body lies. Hall kneels down at the crest of the hill, to the right of victim's head and, reaching across his body, checks his carotid pulse on the left side of his neck. Hall finds the victim cool to the touch.

Then, in the midst of the thick foliage, Hall, still kneeling and looking downhill, notices a gun on the ground but still in the man's right hand, partially concealed under his right thigh.

"We've got a gun here!" Hall exclaims to Fornshill, whose view of the body is still blocked by Hall, who has jumped to his feet. "Do you see the gun?"

Fornshill replies, "No, I didn't see it."

"There's a gun in his right hand!" Hall declares.

Although Fornshill never sees the gun—but never really looks for it, even after it's pointed out by Hall—he radios to USPP Communications, reporting that a gun has been found and adding

The gun in Foster's right hand. (USPP)

that the death is "an apparent suicide."[6]

Seconds later, Sergeant Gonzalez arrives. Hall immediately shows him the gun in the victim's right hand. Among all of the fire and rescue workers at Fort Marcy Park at that moment, Gonzalez clearly has the most experience. He has worked at the scenes of fifty previous suicides, including ten who had shot themselves in the mouth.

Gonzalez observes the man's pale-gray skin color, his slightly open eyes, the lividity that has started to fix in the lower portions of his hands and fingers, and more blood inside his mouth and on his dark pants and shoes.

Without using any of his equipment or touching the body after examining it from arm's distance, Gonzalez unofficially pronounces the man dead. Gonzalez reports the news to his dispatcher at the Public Safety Communications Center, describing the situation as an "obvious... suicide with gun."

Gonzalez also radios the other fire unit in the park. After receiving directions to the second cannon in the hidden grove, Arthur and the second group of rescue workers race to that location.

When they arrive, this second team reports seeing a middle-aged couple, a man and a woman, having a picnic in the woods.[7]

As nothing can be done for the victim, both fire and rescue teams return to the parking lot with their unused lifesaving equipment, leaving Fornshill alone with the body.

3.

USPP OFFICER CHRISTINE A. HODAKIEVIC is driving north on the George Washington Parkway toward Fort Marcy Park when she hears the radio call about the dead body. Even though she has just come off duty and is in her own car, she goes to the park and arrives at about 6:30 PM.[8] She is followed by Sergeant Robert Edwards.

At the same time, USPP Officers Franz J. Ferstl and Julie Spetz arrive in their separate squad cars. Ferstl joins Fornshill at the crime scene, leaving Spetz behind in the parking lot with Hodakievic, who is collecting information. Ferstl, working in Car 211, had originally received the call to report to Fort Marcy Park, which is part of his regular beat on the parkway.

Ferstl, who is briefed by Fornshill, takes charge of protecting the crime scene until the USPP investigators arrive. As the beat officer for the area, Ferstl, not Fornshill, will be responsible for filing the official USPP incident report.

Just after Hodakievic, Ferstl, and Spetz arrive, Lieutenant Patrick

S. Gavin, the USPP shift commander who was driving southbound
on the Fourteenth Street Bridge when he received the radio call, also
rolls into Fort Marcy Park. After parking his car, he notices the
Arkansas plates on the gray Honda and wonders out loud whether
the victim might have worked somewhere in the government for
President Bill Clinton, the former governor of Arkansas.

As Gavin looks through a window of the car, he sees a tie and
a neatly folded blue pin-striped suit coat on the front passenger
seat, which, according to the paramedics, appears to match the
pants worn by the dead man. Neither Gavin nor anyone else as
yet tries to enter the car.

After a quick briefing from those present, Gavin and
Hodakievic walk up to the crime scene together. Although the
senior officer in the park, Gavin does not assume any active role
in the investigation. He is principally concerned with getting the
necessary personnel to the park to help with the probe.

Seeing Edwards, Ferstl, and Fornshill all present, Gavin tells
Fornshill to clear out, telling him that this is not his beat; Sergeant
Edwards, Fornshill's immediate supervisor, tells his officer to
return to his overtime duty at the CIA. Soon after, Gavin leaves
the crime scene.

Ferstl—who, along with the others, sees the dead man's face
now pointing straight up toward the sky—asks for and receives
permission from Edwards to return to his cruiser to get his
Polaroid camera and a roll of yellow police tape.

When Ferstl returns to the crime scene, he secures the area,
placing the tape around the perimeter. Ferstl then takes five pictures of the body with his camera.[9]

Ferstl gives Sergeant Edwards the Polaroid photographs he has
just taken. Edwards marks the pictures he receives from Ferstl as
"from C202 Sgt. Edwards 7-20-93 on scene."[10]

Meantime, as Fornshill is leaving the parking lot, USPP Officer

Julie Lynn Spetz, who had arrived at the same time as Officer Ferstl in her own patrol car, is stretching yellow tape near the entrance to Fort Marcy Park. However, no crime-scene log, chronicling the arrival and departure of official personnel, is being kept.[11]

Officers Hodakievic and Spetz, before checking the ownership of the two private cars in the parking lot, continue talking to the fire and rescue personnel who are still loading their equipment in their two vehicles, Medic One and Engine One. The only person involved in the search for the dead body who had already left the scene is Fornshill.

While Hodakievic and Spetz are obtaining the names of the fire and rescue personnel, FCFRD Sergeant James Iacone, the leader of the second rescue unit, starts talking about the gray Honda with the Arkansas tags. Adding up this circumstantial evidence, just as Lieutenant Gavin had, Iacone jokes that the dead man might be someone who couldn't get a job in the government and, as a result, killed himself.[12]

During the officers' conversations with the rescue workers, paramedic Richard Arthur remarks to Spetz that he doesn't believe that the dead man had committed suicide, insisting that he had seen a number of suicides and that the body in this case was "too clean." Arthur also informs her about the couple in the park and points her to their location, just south of the parking lot.

Then, just before the fire and rescue workers leave, they call an ambulance unit to transport the dead body.

Meantime, Spetz finds the path that leads to the park's southern route. After walking only about seventy-five yards, she sees the man and woman sitting and talking on a blanket in a partial clearing in the forest.

The officer approaches them; they are pleasant and cooperative, barely curious about all the activity in the parking lot. The woman, Judith Doody, explains that she had picked up her friend, Mark Feist, at 4:30 PM for a late-afternoon picnic. They have been at Fort Marcy Park since about 5 PM.

Spetz asks the couple to accompany her back to the parking lot, so that they can identify their car and provide some background information. Complying, the couple—whose peculiar situation seems like the basis for a Neil Simon comedy—returns with Spetz to the lot.

At 6:35 PM, plainclothes investigators Cheryl Braun, John Rolla, and Renee Abt of the USPP's Criminal Investigations Branch— who had received the initial radio call at the USPP's Anacostia Park Station in southeast Washington—arrive at Fort Marcy Park in the same car.

Among the three, Braun, an eight-year veteran with the USPP, is the senior investigator. As Braun drove to the scene, both Abt and Rolla were having their dinner. Rolla, riding shotgun, chowed down on a container of macaroni, mixed with hamburger, cheese, and tomato sauce; Abt, sitting in the back seat, ate a petite garden salad and drank her diet ginger ale.

After parking their car, Braun and the other investigators wait for USPP Identification Technician Peter Simonello, the criminalist who is en route from the Anacostia station, before going to the crime scene. Braun and Rolla have been to Fort Marcy Park before on job-related field-training assignments and know that the park has a reputation as a meeting place for homosexuals.

Meantime, Spetz introduces Doody and Feist to Investigators Braun and Abt, who also begin asking them questions; Ferstl, who has returned to the parking lot and gives the investigators their initial briefing, is also present for part of the interview.

The couple identifies their car as the white Nissan with the Maryland tags. Just moments earlier, the owner of the disabled blue Mercedes, parked near the entrance to Fort Marcy Park, had been identified by Officer Hodakievic.[13]

Now, the only unidentified car is the gray Honda. Investigator Rolla uses his cellular phone to call USPP Communications, asking for a check on the ownership of the Honda. After a short wait, Rolla receives the name of the owner: *Vincent W. Foster—Little Rock, Arkansas*; his address is unknown.

The name means nothing to Rolla.

Simultaneously, Braun, Abt, and Spetz ask Doody and Feist if they have seen any other cars or people in the park. The couple replies that there was only one car in the lot when they arrived. From her own observations and Spetz's notes, Braun has already begun to compose her report, stating:

> [W]hen [Doody and Feist] arrived, there had been a small car with a man without a shirt sitting in it, who left shortly after their arrival…. [Another] vehicle that they observed was a light-colored old model car that pulled in next to [the Honda]. [Feist] said that the driver put the hood up and then walked up into the woods for a while and then returned to his vehicle and left. [Feist and Doody] described the driver as a white male with scrungy hair, but could not provide anything further.

Doody and Feist also describe a white van with blue lettering, adding that they observed the driver get out and empty some trash. None of those present—neither the couple nor the police—are aware that the mystery man in the white van is the person who first found the dead body.

After talking to the couple—and receiving their names,

addresses, and telephone numbers for her report—Braun walks to
the crime scene. She is accompanied by Investigators Rolla and
Abt, as well as USPP criminalist Peter Simonello, who has just
arrived. Simonello will be taking his direction from the investigators at the crime scene, which is still manned by Sergeant Edwards
and Hodakievic.

John Rolla—who has nine and a half years' experience with the
USPP, most of it in the narcotics branch—is designated by Braun
as the principal investigator at the crime scene. Although he had
played back-up roles at other crime scenes, this is the first time he
has been in charge of an actual death investigation.

Rolla, Simonello, and the other two investigators receive a
briefing from Sergeant Edwards, who gives Rolla the five Polaroid
pictures of the crime scene taken by Ferstl. The victim has
remained untouched since Todd Hall checked the carotid pulse on
the left side of his neck.

Immediately, Rolla is agitated that Fornshill, the officer who
found the body, is not at the scene and requests that Edwards ask
him to return. Edwards, however, decides that Fornshill is not
needed and decides to keep him in place at the CIA.

While viewing the dead body, Abt, who has been with the USPP
since 1988, takes notes, giving the first detailed official description of what can be seen without moving the victim's body. Rolla,
who bases his report, in part, on Abt's notes, states:

> I observed the decedent to be a white male, approxi-
> mately 45 to 50 years of age with dark hair, graying, and
> slightly receding. The decedent was laying face up on an
> embankment in front of the second cannon. The decedent's
> head was facing east and his feet facing west. I observed
> blood on his nose and mouth area, on his right shoulder
> area and underneath his head. The blood on the ground and
> on his shirt appeared to still be wet. There was no blood
> spatter on the plants or trees surrounding the decedent's

head. I observed a dark colored revolver in his right hand. The decedent's right thumb was still in the trigger guard....

The decedent was dressed in a white long sleeve button down dress shirt, white undershirt, dark blue dress pants with blue pin-stripes, black dress shoes, black socks and a black belt. The decedent was wearing a Seiko watch with a gold colored face and brown leather band on his left wrist; a silver colored metal ring with a white stone on his right ring finger; a gold colored metal ring, band type, on his left ring finger.... The decedent also had a Motorola Bravo style pager on his right side. The pager was turned off.

Seeing that the dead man had switched off his pager, Rolla believes that this simple act symbolized the victim's final decision to end all contact with the outside world.

About fifteen feet to the right of the second cannon, both Abt and Rolla see an empty and muddied bottle, with a faded and dried label, which they believe might have contained some sort of wine cooler. But because of its apparent age, the investigators do not mention it in their notes, believing it has no connection to the crime scene.

Taking his own notes and measurements, the forty-five–year-old Simonello, who has handled evidence at over a hundred previous death scenes, including fifteen gunshot suicides, adds:

> Approximately 20 feet west of the [cannon's] axle*, the body... was laying face up with the head upslope in an east-west alignment. There was blood staining around the chin area and from the nose down the right cheek. Blood stains also were found on the right shoulder and neck area as well as the right ribcage area of the shirt. The victim's arms were at his sides and the victim had his right hand on a black

---

* Confused by the position of the cannon's moveable axle and the immoveable cement anchor that held the cannon in place, Simonello made an error of five feet, nine inches in his measurement, which he later corrected. The actual distance from the center axle to Foster's head was fourteen feet, three inches.

> revolver.... A cursory examination of the victim's hands for
> blood spatter evidence revealed one droplet on the right
> index finger, above the second joint. No discernible forward
> or back spatter blood evidence on the victim's shirtsleeves. I
> observed dark residue along the edge of the right index finger
> facing the thumb between the thumb's joint and finger tip.

All of the investigators, along with Sergeant Edwards, agree that there is no indication that a struggle had occurred at or that the body had been dragged to the location. However, Simonello, who draws a rough sketch of the crime scene, does notice "some disturbance of the brush," attributing it to the number of police and rescue personnel who have been standing and walking around the area.

While the investigators view the body as Edwards returns to the parking lot, Braun searches the area, specifically looking for a suicide note—but doesn't find one. But Rolla finds a pair of brownish-colored plastic-framed glasses, partially covered by foliage at the bottom of the slope, thirteen feet below the dead man's feet.

Before taking his own pictures, Rolla, who is wearing latex gloves, lifts the victim's left hand about six inches off the ground to check for flexibility and then drops it. With this brief physical check, Rolla believes that the body is still fairly warm with little indication of rigor mortis—although the warmth of the body might be due to the oppressively hot weather. (Earlier, Todd Hall, the only other person to touch the body, believed it to be cool to the touch.)

Simonello begins his crime-scene photography with his 35 mm camera, which contains a twenty-four–picture roll of color film. He asks Rolla to take back-up pictures with a Polaroid of the same scenes that the criminalist is shooting; Rolla's camera is capable of taking ten photographs without reloading.

Following Simonello, Rolla takes several Polaroid shots of the crime scene, initialing and dating each; Simonello's 35 mm film will be developed later.

When Rolla and Simonello complete their picture-taking, Rolla reaches into the front pockets of the dead man, rolling the body slightly to gain access, hoping to find some identification or the keys to the gray Honda. He doesn't find anything. Without the car keys, Braun and Simonello leave the crime scene and return to the parking lot. Moments later, they are joined by Rolla, leaving Investigator Abt alone with the body.

Using the Polaroid camera from her black nylon briefcase, which she places on the pavement next to the gray Honda Accord, Braun takes five photographs of the car, initialing and dating each on the back, as Simonello continues shooting with the same roll of film he had used at the crime scene.[14]

Simonello writes in his report:

> I photographed the exterior of the vehicle, opened all of the doors, which had been [closed] but not locked, and photographed the interior. Inv. Braun searched the interior of the car for identification.

Since they now believe that the victim had likely taken his own life, Braun and Simonello, both of whom are wearing gloves, see no reason to dust the car and its door handles for fingerprints immediately. They plan to have the car impounded and will later arrange for a USPP identification technician to process the car for prints.

Then, finding a wallet inside the car, Braun confirms the dead man's identity, the same name that Rolla had earlier received, writing in her report:

> I obtained identification for the deceased from his wallet.
> The wallet was located in the interior pocket of the suit
> jacket lying on the front passenger seat.... The Arkansas
> [driver's] license identified the deceased as:

> Vincent W. Foster
> W/M, DOB: 01/15/45
> Address: 5414 Stonewall Rd.
> Little Rock, Arkansas

> Also, present on the front passenger seat was a White
> House Identification in the name of Vincent W. Foster.... I
> performed a thorough search of the vehicle and was unable
> to locate a suicide note.

Still, none of the officers present has ever heard of Foster; they
have no idea who he is.

Braun asks Officer William Watson of the USPP SWAT team—
who has just arrived at the park with a police intern, a young college student—to inform Lieutenant Gavin, who has already left
the park, that the dead man is a White House employee. Braun
knows that Gavin, as the shift commander, will notify the Secret
Service and the White House.

4.

AFTER LEARNING OF FOSTER'S WHITE HOUSE CONNECTION, Rolla and
Simonello return to Foster's body with his driver's license while
Braun continues to go through Foster's car. Abt, who has been
alone with the body while the others searched the Honda, receives
Foster's driver's license and compares the picture with the dead
man lying in front of her.

Because she is looking at Foster backward, she holds the license
upside down, matching her view of Foster's face. Although the
man in the picture appears a little heavier, she is sure that this is
Vincent Foster.[15]

With Rolla watching, Simonello, who is wearing cotton
gloves[16], lifts Foster's right arm to remove the weapon in his
hand: a .38-caliber, six-shot revolver with a four-inch barrel. In
his report, Simonello states:

> The victim's hand was flexible with little or no rigor. The
> thumb was wedged between the trigger and front inside
> edge of the trigger guard, indicating that the hammer was
> in the cocked position prior to the thumb being inserted.

In order to remove the gun, which is trapped at the knuckle of Foster's right thumb, Simonello must recock the revolver, which causes the trigger to ease back and free the thumb. While removing the weapon, Simonello notices a deep impression on Foster's right thumb where it had been jammed. Simonello can now also see powder burns along the edge of Foster's right index finger to the joint of his right thumb, which, he believes, resulted from the cylinder blast from the gun.

Simonello secures the gun as evidence and logs it at 7:30 PM, along with the eyeglasses that Rolla has found. Simonello also notices that the revolver's cylinder contains one spent cartridge and one live round; the other chambers are empty. The spent shell and the live round are also recorded as evidence.

Rolla and Simonello speculate that Foster, using a tree root that runs across the berm as a seat, appears to have placed the revolver in his mouth with his right hand, which was wrapped around the cylinder of the gun, the butt of the handle curving toward him. Presumably, Foster steadied the weapon with his left hand. After cocking the revolver's hammer, causing the trigger to draw back, he must have inserted his right thumb in the trigger guard and then, at some point, squeezed the trigger, firing the single shot that ended his life.

After the blast, Foster seems to have fallen back on the hill with each arm dropping to their sides, his right thumb jammed in the trigger guard.

As Braun is winding down her search of Foster's Honda at 7:40 PM, a medical examiner from Fairfax County, Dr. Donald Haut, who had just finished his dinner at home when he received the call, arrives at Fort Marcy Park.

Upon his arrival, three of the officers at the scene who spoke with Dr. Haut—Hodakievic, Braun, and Rolla—smell alcohol on his breath; two others, Abt and Simonello, do not.[17]

On call but not actually on duty that evening, Dr. Haut is a private physician, who has been paid on a case-by-case basis by the county for the past eleven years. This crime scene is the twelfth suicide he has seen since going to work, part-time, for the county; half of those suicides had resulted from gunshot wounds to the head, including at least one in which the victim had placed the gun in his mouth.

After Dr. Haut is escorted to the crime scene by Officer Hodakievic, Rolla and Simonello lift Foster's head. While probing the top of his skull, they find a mushy spot that appears to be an exit wound. Aside from the pool of blood on the ground, which Dr. Haut views as "matted and clotted under the head," very little, if any, obvious brain matter is present. Rolla points out the suspected exit wound in his notes, saying:

> I observed trauma to the center portion of the back of the decedent's head. The skull appeared to be fractured from the inside out.

Then, after Dr. Haut officially pronounces Foster dead, Rolla and the doctor roll the body onto its stomach, lifting the right shoulder and pushing the body right to left.

This maneuver causes a sudden stream of blood to flow freely from Foster's mouth and nose. Also, as it is turned over, the body slips a short distance down the steep slope. Investigator Abt assists Rolla and Dr. Haut, to stop Foster's body from sliding further down the embankment.

In the midst of this tragic scene, there is a comic moment. As Foster is being stabilized, the position of his arms and hands make him appear to be crawling back up the hill. Abt wisecracks that this looks like a scene out of the 1979 low-budget horror film, *Dawn of the Dead,* in which the dead come back to life.

After the body is secured but before it is turned on its back, Rolla takes two pictures with his Polaroid.[18]

Simonello reports what he sees:

> When the body was turned onto its stomach, I observed a large area of blood pooled where the head had been resting. The area was photographed and probed for the expended round with negative results. I also observed a larger area of blood where the victim's back had been, coinciding with blood stains on the back of [his] shirt. The pooled blood was beginning to show signs of coagulation.

Dr. Haut, who leaves about thirty minutes after he arrived, notes Foster's time of death in his official report as 6:15 PM—the approximate time that the body was found, which is an appropriate estimate for a medical examiner to use when the actual time of death is unknown.

Clearly, Foster had died hours earlier.

Dr. Haut also disagrees with Rolla and Simonello's theory that Foster had shot himself while sitting; the medical examiner believes that he shot himself while lying down.

At about 8 PM, as darkness descends in the woods around the crime scene, Fairfax County Emergency Medical Technician Corey Ashford and ambulance driver Roger F. Harrison arrive to take Foster's body to the morgue at Fairfax County Hospital in Ambulance One. Wearing gloves, Ashford grabs the body by the armpits while Harrison hoists the legs. In one sweeping move-ment, they place him face up in the body bag, which is immedi-ately zipped up.

By the time the Truck One crew arrives at the crime scene to aid with the recovery, Foster's body is already in the sealed plastic bag.[19]

The rescue workers pick up the body bag and place it onto a gurney, which they roll back to the parking lot. After reaching the ambulance, one of the medics unzips the bag and places a toe-tag on Foster's right foot. He then reseals the bag and helps load it into the ambulance, which heads for Fairfax County Hospital.

Because no one at the scene had told him that Foster's death is a suspected suicide, because the body had been found in the woods, and because he didn't notice any blood on the body, no exit wound, and no gun, Ashford leaves the park assuming that the dead man is a murder victim.[20]

Braun, Rolla, and Simonello complete their searches of Foster's car and the crime scene. Later, numbers will be assigned to the items of evidence on their USPP property report:

1.   Colt, Army Special, .38-caliber revolver, four-inch
     barrel, six shot, serial numbers 356555 and
     355055 (the gun has two serial numbers: one is
     on the frame but another appears on the yoke
     that holds the cylinder)

2.   One round/.38 caliber

3.   One casing/.38 caliber

4.   One pair of eyeglasses

5. Brown leather wallet containing $292.00 (U.S.); an Arkansas driver's permit (with Foster's name and photo); credit cards for American Express Gold, a Schwab One Visa, Exxon, and Shell; a White House Federal Credit Union card; a Blue Cross/Blue Shield card; a Delta Frequent Flyer card; an AT&T calling card; "and other miscellaneous cards, papers and photos"[21]

6. One Seiko quartz watch with brown leather band

7. One Motorola Bravo pager, cap code 052943, inscribed WHCA

8. One silver-colored ring with a large white stone

9. One gold-colored band ring with inscription, "E.B.B. to V.W.F. 4/20/68"

10. Black suit jacket—Norman Hilton/Mr. Wicks (actually, the jacket was blue pin-stripe)

11. Blue silk tie with swan designs

12. White House photo identification for Vincent W. Foster

13. Six "miscellaneous papers" (found in the glove box and the storage area in the door and trunk)

16. One white-colored, long-sleeved, buttoned-down shirt with blood stain

17. One white-colored, short-sleeve T-shirt with blood stain

18. One pair of white-colored boxer shorts

19. One pair of blue-colored pants with gray pin-stripes and a black-colored belt

20. One pair of black-colored socks

21. One pair of black-colored dress shoes, size 11M

22. One lock-seal envelope, containing pulled head hairs

23. A folded Rand McNally map of Washington, D.C. (found on the right-front floor area)[22]

24. Two pairs of sunglasses

25. Birthday card for "Tom" (found on the right-front floor area)

26. A piece of white paper with red writing, containing a list of abbreviations and numbers (found on the right-front seat)

27. One box of Deluxe checks, containing four check books, numbered 251-350, in the name of Laura B. Foster

28. An insurance identification card in a clear plastic envelope, listed to "Vincent or Elizabeth Foster" (according to the USPP property report, the policy expired on August 6, 1990)

29. A twelve-ounce Sierra Nevada Pale Bock Malt Liquor (found in a white and green canvas bag on the left-rear seat)

30. A twelve-ounce Miller Lite beer (found under the right-front seat)

31. An empty box of Marlboro Lights (found under the right-front seat)

32. An eight-ounce bottle of Kaopectate (found under the right-front seat)

33. A cork screw—Clos Du Bois (found on the right-rear seat)

34. The contents of the car's ashtray in the front: thirty-five pennies, two quarters, one nickel, a Mexican coin, a Compton's Foodland disk, a Chevron USA National Travel Card (containing Foster's name), a Texaco gas card (containing Foster's name), and one Fender guitar pick

Braun also notices a kitchen oven mitt in the glove compartment of Foster's car; but she and Simonello do not include it on the property report.

The officers do not collect any of the evidence at the scene; instead, they leave everything in the car and order it impounded. Simonello seals each of the doors, the trunk, and the hood with strips of thin red tape, and writes his name on each strip with a black marker. If anyone tries to enter the car while it is in the USPP impound area, the fragile seal will break.

Braun arranges for a flat-bed tow truck from Raley's Towing, an independent contractor in Capitol Heights, Maryland, which does work for the USPP. The tow-truck driver picks up the car and later delivers it to the locked impound area at the USPP's Criminal Investigations Branch (CIB) at the Anacostia station.

While the tow truck is en route, Simonello and Investigator Abt return to Anacostia together, leaving Ferstl behind at the park with Braun and Rolla. Ferstl will clear the crime scene and follow the tow truck back to CIB.

Upon her arrival in Anacostia, Abt photocopies her crime-scene notes and places a set on Rolla's desk.[23]

After Simonello arrives at the USPP laboratory, he photographs the .38 Colt revolver found in Foster's right hand and notes that the gun contains two serial numbers. Then, according to his report:

> I unloaded it and documented its information and condition onto a USPP Firearms Examination Report.... I then wrapped the barrel in brown paper secured with rubber bands to preserve any blood spatter, blowback, gunpowder residue, hairs, fiber, or tissue evidence. Weapon placed in sealed evidence bag in the [evidence] locker to await submission to the FBI labs.

Also, before locking up the gun, Simonello, for identification purposes, removes one of the grips of the revolver and, on the handle underneath the grip, engraves his initials—"P.J.S." He then places a handwritten note on top of it inside the evidence bag, warning: "Not processed. *Do not* handle."

Completing that task, Simonello sits down at his desk and writes up five questions about Foster's suicide that are still puzzling him:

1. How did gunpowder residue pattern get on index finger of right hand?

2. Was Foster right handed?

3. Blood stain on chin appears to be transfer stain. If so, who moved body?

4. Does not appear to be any blowback[24] or blood spatter on sleeves or any other area of white shirt. Why not?

5. Coroner at scene believed victim was lying on back when shot. Why?[25]

Meantime, Braun and Rolla—realizing that they still have not located Foster's car keys during the search of his pockets or his car—decide to go to Fairfax County Hospital for another search of Foster's clothing, which is the sole purpose of this trip.

Also, while earlier searching Foster's car and discovering that he was a member of the White House staff, Investigator Braun knew that notifications had to be made. She had told USPP Officer Watson to call Lieutenant Gavin—the USPP shift commander, who had been at Fort Marcy Park—and to inform him of the victim's identity.

But, unknown to Braun, Watson didn't hear her request; consequently, Gavin didn't receive Braun's message.[26] Now, reporting to Gavin while heading for the hospital, Braun quickly realizes that Watson hadn't given Gavin the news. Braun immediately provides him with Foster's identity and notification of his White House status.

5.

AS THE SUN SETS AT ABOUT 8:30 PM, Lieutenant Gavin officially notifies the U.S. Secret Service of Foster's death.[27] Shortly after that, Gavin receives a call from William Burton, the White House assistant chief of staff.

"Do you know whose gun it was?" Burton asks.

Surprised by the question, Gavin simply replies that the Park Police has yet to make any determination about the ownership of the revolver.

As soon as Gavin hangs up with Burton, he receives a call from David Watkins, the White House director of personnel. Watkins, who had been at a local movie theater on Wisconsin Avenue with his family when he received the page from the Secret Service, tells Gavin that he had known Vincent Foster for years and asks to accompany the USPP on their official, in-person notification to Foster's family at their home.

Lieutenant Gavin passes this request to Braun on her car phone while she and Rolla are still en route to Fairfax County Hospital. Braun places the call on the speaker in her squad car so that Rolla can participate. The three of them discuss the advantages of having Watkins accompany the investigators to Foster's home.

Braun and Rolla decide that they will pick up Watkins at his home as soon as they leave the hospital. Actually, Braun is relieved that Watkins is coming, because a family friend can help ease the inherently harsh delivery of such terrible news.

Soon after, Braun and Rolla receive calls from White House Associate Counsel William Kennedy and Craig Livingstone, the chief of White House Security. The grieving men are in disbelief and want to confirm the report of Foster's death on behalf of the White House. Kennedy and Deputy White House Counsel Foster had worked together for years at the prestigious Rose Law Firm in Little Rock; First Lady Hillary Clinton had been another partner in the firm.[28]

Although Rolla feels that the police have already confirmed Foster's identity through photographs, he agrees to make the arrangements with hospital security so that they can identify the body.[29]

Soon after, Braun and Rolla arrive at the hospital. They go to a private room in the hospital morgue where Braun unzips Foster's body bag. A fly buzzes out of the bag as soon as it is opened.

Braun puts on a pair of latex gloves and reaches into Foster's right pocket—and only his right pocket—pulling it inside out. She finds two sets of keys—as Rolla, who is still new to death investigations, stands by, somewhat embarrassed for not having turned Foster's pockets inside out at the crime scene.

Braun logs her discoveries on the property report; the keys, which are placed in an evidence bag, become item numbers 14 and 15.[30] Braun and Rolla return to their car and drive back to Washington.

While Foster's body lies in the morgue after Braun and Rolla leave, Dr. Julian Orenstein, who is on the Department of Emergency Medicine staff, conducts a cursory examination, assisted by Fairfax County police officer David Tipton, who is on his regular assignment at the hospital. Dr. Orenstein sees nothing to indicate that Foster's death had resulted from anything but a suicide.

Rescue worker Corey Ashford, who officially codes Foster's death a murder when he returns to his station, never said anything to the doctor about his conclusion when he delivered Foster's body to the hospital.

Meantime, Lieutenant Gavin fields several calls, including additional inquiries from the Secret Service and the Department of Justice, expressing concern for any sensitive materials that might have been discovered in Foster's car. Gavin gives his personal assurance that the Honda and everything found in it will be safe and kept under lock and key. He adds that if any sensitive materials are found, they will be turned over to the Secret Service immediately.[31]

Lieutenant Gavin also makes a call to Major Robert H. Hines, the media liaison for Robert Langston, the chief of the USPP since 1991, whom Gavin has also called.[32] Hines, in turn, calls Bill Burton at the White House to determine the timing and contents of a jointly coordinated press release. Both men agree that family notifications have to be made before they release Foster's name. Consequently, they decide to place a notation on the press release: "Do not release name until next of kin notified."

Without any trouble, Braun and Rolla locate David Watkins's residence. After picking him up, the USPP investigators drive to the Fosters' rented townhouse at 3027 Cambridge Place in Georgetown.[33] Watkins's wife, who had played tennis with Foster's wife earlier in the day, follows in the Watkins's family car.

Braun has done death notifications before, although this is her first for a suicide; this is Rolla's first death notification of any kind.

During the brief drive, Braun asks Watkins if he knows of anything that had been bothering Foster, something that could have triggered the suspected suicide. Explaining that he had seen no indication of depression, Watkins adds that Foster had been troubled over the well-publicized investigations of the White House Travel Office but provides no details.[34]

6.

ARRIVING AT THE FOSTERS' HOME at about 10 PM and parking at the far end of the Fosters' block, Braun, Rolla, and Watkins see several people approaching the Fosters' home. The group includes Vincent Foster's sisters, Sheila Anthony, a top attorney at the Department of Justice[35], and Sharon Bowman of Little Rock, who had arrived earlier that day to visit her family in Washington. Bowman had expected her brother to give her a tour of the White House during her stay.

Also in the group is Associate Attorney General Webster Hubbell—number three in command at the Department of Justice and the former managing partner at the Rose Law Firm—who had received the news while having dinner at the Lebanese Taverna on Connecticut Avenue with his family and Marsha Scott, a presidential aide and another longtime friend of the Clintons and Hubbells from their days in Arkansas.[36]

Asking the others to stay back, Braun, Rolla, and Watkins go to the door and knock. Laura Foster, the Fosters' nineteen-year-old daughter and a student at Vanderbilt University, opens the door. After the USPP investigators identify themselves, they watch as Laura looks past them and sees her family's friends in tears.

"Can we speak to your mother?" Rolla asks, stepping inside the house with Braun and Watkins as Laura, who is already alarmed, calls out to her mother.

The Fosters' two sons—twenty-one-year-old Vincent III, an aide to Arkansas Senator Dale Bumpers, and seventeen-year-old John, also known as Brugh, who had just finished his junior year in high school in Arkansas—are not at home.

Seconds later, Lisa Foster, Vincent Foster's wife of twenty-five years, comes down the steps wearing her bathrobe.

"What's wrong?" she asks quietly. She still doesn't know.

Rolla goes up the steps and asks her to sit down. When she sits on a step, he continues, "Mrs. Foster, I am very sorry to tell you that your husband, Vincent, is dead."

Lisa Foster and her daughter fall apart. Everyone outside moves silently into the house, and Watkins's wife runs through the open door and up the steps to comfort Lisa, her close friend.

After their brief embrace, Lisa turns and runs back upstairs alone, disappearing for a few minutes. Braun and Rolla assume that she has gone to collect herself and to put on some other clothes.

While waiting for Lisa to return, Braun and Rolla try to interview the family and friends who are present. Webb Hubbell, who is on his cellular phone, appears reluctant to make a statement or answer any questions.

Rolla asks those who will talk to him, "Did you see this coming?" "Were there any signs that this was going to happen?" "Was he depressed?"

Without exception, everyone seems stunned by the news, saying that Foster had been fine, and that his death, particularly by suicide, was totally unexpected. No one even suggests that Foster had been depressed or, in any way, suicidal.

During the confusion and the grief at the Fosters' home, Braun speaks again with David Watkins, asking him to order that Foster's office at the White House be sealed. She says that she wants to search through Foster's desk, files, and appointment book, hoping to find a suicide note or some clue as to why he had taken his own life—and in whom he might have confided. According to Braun, Watkins agreed to comply with her request.[37]

When Lisa returns fully dressed, she speaks briefly to Rolla but, inexplicably, refuses to talk to Braun.

Trying to compose herself, Lisa asks Rolla, "What happened?"

"Ma'am," Rolla replies, "he shot himself."

"Did he put it in his mouth?" she asks tearfully, even somewhat bitterly while looking directly at Rolla.[38]

Laura Foster, who is standing nearby with Braun and hears the conversation between her mother and Rolla, screams and runs upstairs. Rolla is so stunned by Lisa Foster's question that he is momentarily speechless.

Then, trying to move ahead with his fact-finding, Rolla asks Lisa whether she had noticed any change in her husband's demeanor.

Lisa insists, "No, he was so happy."

Rolla then asks Lisa, who has put her arm around his shoulder for support, whether her husband owned a gun.

She replies, "I don't know. What kind of gun? What did it look like?"

As Rolla begins to describe the gun—"a black-colored .38-caliber revolver"—she angrily responds, "How would I know? I don't know what guns look like!"

Then, Lisa turns away from Rolla and storms into the kitchen.

Knowing how overwrought she must be, Rolla decides not to press her further.

At about 10:50 PM, Bill Clinton, the president of the United States—red-eyed, grief-stricken, and accompanied by White House Chief of Staff Thomas "Mack" McLarty and two Secret Service agents who had driven the president in an unmarked vehicle—walks into the house. The president, after giving the hard eyes to strangers Braun and Rolla, goes up to Lisa and Laura Foster and seats them on the couch in the living room. Sitting between them, Clinton, a lifelong friend of Vincent Foster, gently and softly consoles Foster's wife and daughter.

Following a trip to California, First Lady Hillary Clinton and her daughter, Chelsea—along with Lisa Caputo, the first lady's press secretary—had flown to Little Rock and were staying with Mrs. Clinton's mother. They arrived at about 8:30 PM, eastern time.

Mrs. Clinton, another close friend of Vincent Foster and a former law partner in the Foster-Hubbell-Kennedy Rose Law Firm in Arkansas, had been notified of Foster's death by McLarty, a childhood friend of both Foster and the president, who called her at her mother's home at or about 9:30 PM. Mrs. Clinton took the news extremely hard.[39]

McLarty heard of Foster's death from Bill Burton, another Rose Law Firm alumnus, who told him that William Kennedy was on his way to identify the body at Fairfax County Hospital and that David Watkins went with the police to notify Foster's wife. McLarty told George Stephanopoulos and other presidential aides right away, but decided *not* to tell the president—who was in the midst of a live interview from the Presidential Library in the White House with CNN's Larry King—until the conclusion of the show.

Shortly before 10 PM, while still on the air, King asked the president, who had already been on for nearly an hour, to remain on the program beyond its usually allotted time. Clinton, who was enjoying the interview, happily agreed.

During the commercial break that followed, McLarty asked the president not to stay for the additional time. When both the president and King scoffed at that suggestion, McLarty insisted. Seeing that McLarty was deadly serious, the president relented and went with McLarty to the Clintons' upstairs residence where he received the terrible news.

Immediately, the president called the first lady in Little Rock for a private conversation while McLarty made the arrangements for Clinton's trip to Georgetown to pay respects to Foster's family.

About ten minutes after the president arrives at the Fosters' home, Braun and Rolla, seeing they will learn nothing more, return to their office in southeast Washington. Rolla briefly notes in his formal report:

> [Neither] Mrs. Foster nor other relatives or friends were able to provide any insight as to why Vincent Foster would take his life.[40]

Both Braun and Rolla are obviously disappointed. They want to know, among other things, whether anyone might have wanted to hurt Vincent Foster. What were his personal, physical, and professional problems? Was he on medication? Was he an alcoholic? Was he having an affair?

They have no idea when these questions might be asked and answered.

Back at the USPP office, while completing her paperwork, Braun calls Lieutenant Phil Cholak, the new USPP shift commander, and Major Benjamin Holmes, the commander of the USPP's Criminal Investigations Branch, to give them her report.

Meantime, Rolla pays particular attention to a piece of paper he discovers in Foster's wallet, writing in his own report:

> While going through the decedent's personal effects for possible motives for suicide, I observed a piece of White House stationery in the decedent's wallet, upon which was written, among other things, the names of three doctors and their phone numbers. The names and numbers were listed as follows: (1) Dr. [Robert] Hedaya, [two telephone numbers], (2) Dr. [Stefan] Pasternack, [telephone number], & (3) Dr. [Martin] Allen, [telephone number].

That same night, a Secret Service agent comes to CIB headquarters to pick up Foster's White House identification and pager—which Rolla had found switched off at the crime scene. Rolla never turns on the pager to check for messages. However, he has recorded the pager's serial number and other relevant information, knowing that he can trace any calls received by the pager through its service company.[41]

In addition, Rolla photocopies everything he finds in Foster's wallet, which he places in a locked evidence locker.

In a White House press release sent off the wire that night, President Clinton, speaking of Vincent Foster, states: "His family has lost a loving husband and father. America has lost a gifted and loyal public servant, and Hillary and I have lost a true and trusted friend....

"My deepest hope is that whatever drew Vince away from us this evening, his soul will receive the grace and salvation that his good life and good works earned."

7.

Both the *New York Times* and the *Washington Post* publish front-page stories about the White House deputy counsel's death. *Times* reporter Gwen Ifill writes in her lead that Foster had been "recruited for the job by Hillary Rodham Clinton," adding that Foster was "a senior partner at the Rose law firm in Little Rock, Ark.," until he accepted his appointment at the White House, joining several top Clinton aides whom the president had brought from Arkansas, including Webster Hubbell, William Kennedy, Mack McLarty, and presidential assistant Bruce Lindsey.[42]

"Mr. Foster was a close associate of Mrs. Clinton," Ifill continues, "and had acted as her representative on many legal matters at the White House, including the search for a Supreme Court justice and arguments over [Mrs. Clinton's] status as a de facto federal official, which validated the secret hearings of her task force on health care."

Ruth Marcus of the *Washington Post* adds: "Foster was involved in the decision in May to fire seven employees of the White House travel office, helping to bring in the auditors to review procedures and overseeing the work of associate counsel Kennedy, whose telephone call to the FBI created part of the controversy in the incident. He also discussed the issue with Hillary Clinton and made certain she was informed about the progress of the inquiry...."

"Sources who knew Foster said he had been upset by negative publicity about the administration and his role in it."

In the aftermath of what had become known as "Travelgate" and in the midst of problems with Hillary Clinton's federal task force on health care, the *Wall Street Journal* had published four editorials—on June 17 ("Who Is Vincent Foster?"), on June 24

("Vincent Foster's Victory"), on July 14 ("FBI Director Rose?"), and on July 19 ("What's the Rush?")—in which Foster, who was involved in both issues, was criticized.[43] In the cruelest cut of all, the *Journal*, complaining about the task force's secret meetings, had written in one of these editorials, "[We] suspect that Vincent Foster and Ollie North might hit it off."

Friends and colleagues claim that Foster was unaccustomed to such public criticism and deeply resented it.

Dressed in plainclothes, Captain Charles W. Hume, the assistant commander of the Criminal Investigations Branch and a twenty-three–year veteran of the USPP, arrives at his office at Anacostia station, carrying an unopened newspaper, at about 6:15 AM. He immediately goes to the detectives' section of the CIB, where everyone seems to meet over coffee to discuss events that have just happened and others that are coming up. Hume sees Cheryl Braun and John Rolla, who have been working through the night.

Pete Simonello had left just after midnight on a scheduled four-day leave and isn't expected to return until Sunday, July 25.[44]

Hume hears Rolla and Braun—who had briefed Major Holmes, Hume's boss, the night before—talking about Foster's death, about the death notification at the Fosters' home, and about their aborted attempt to have detailed interviews with Foster's widow and friends. All of this is news to Hume.

While briefing Hume, Braun and Rolla tell him about the list of doctors in Foster's wallet, as well as a handwritten list, which seems to have four columns of abbreviations and dates. The investigators cannot decipher Foster's code.

Talking to Hume about the family notification—which included the appearance of the president—Braun tells the captain that she had asked David Watkins to seal Foster's office.

In response to Hume's question about the autopsy, Rolla assures him that he has already talked to county coroner Dr. James Beyer and arranged for the autopsy to be performed the following day, Thursday, July 22.

After the briefing, Hume visits with Sergeant Robert A. Rule, who is responsible for handing out the daily assignments. Rule, who has already been briefed by the crime-scene investigators, mentions that he plans to send Braun and Rolla to the White House for further investigation—and to search Foster's office. Rule also wants them to interview those White House personnel who had personal and working relationships with Foster and might have seen him before he went to Fort Marcy Park.

Using his "supervisory prerogative," Hume changes the assignment and chooses Sergeant Pete Markland—a USPP detective and a former uniformed Secret Service officer who had been assigned to the White House for twenty-two months between 1976 and 1978—as the new lead investigator on the Foster case, and himself as the second man to accompany Markland to the White House.

In effect, Hume has bumped Rolla into a subordinate role in the case because of his inexperience. Braun is cut out entirely, primarily because she will be promoted to sergeant in two weeks and is slated to be transferred to the USPP office in Greenbelt, Maryland.

After receiving word that Detective Markland will be taking over the investigation, Rolla leaves the USPP office at 6:30 AM and goes home; Braun departs a half hour later.

Before turning in, Braun switches on the television to watch the morning news, which is already in full cry reporting on Foster's death.

After Markland, who is in the office, receives his assignment, he calls the White House and makes arrangements for Secret Service officials to meet him and Hume at the southwest gate of the White House at 10 AM.

Major Robert Hines, the USPP media liaison, also arrives early at police headquarters at Hains Point on the Potomac River. After hearing of Foster's suicide at 9:45 the previous night from Lieutenant Gavin, Hines began collecting information about Foster, including from Bill Burton at the White House. Hines has already been besieged with calls from the media, so he asks to see all of the existing USPP/CIB reports about Foster's death.

After getting up to speed by reading the officers' reports, which are faxed by Hume, Hines briefs his boss, Chief Robert Langston, adding that Foster is from Hope, Arkansas, and a childhood friend of President Clinton, who is a year younger. Soon after, Hines receives another call from Bill Burton, who asks for a USPP briefing to key White House staffers concerning what is known about Foster's death.

Major Hines talks to Captain Hume after receiving Burton's call from the White House, but he doesn't mention the upcoming briefing to him. However, during his conversation with Hume, Hines asks him to call the coroner's office and arrange Foster's autopsy for later that day—as opposed to the next day, July 22, as scheduled by Rolla.[45]

Following orders, Hume calls Dr. James Beyer at the county coroner's office and asks him to move up the Foster posting. Reluctant, because he is busy, Dr. Beyer finally agrees to do the autopsy at 10 AM.

Sergeant Rule calls Rolla at home, asking if he wants to attend the autopsy. Rolla, who is dog tired after being up all night, takes a pass.

That means that no one who was at the crime scene will be at the autopsy.

8.

AT 10 AM, HUME AND MARKLAND ARE MET, as planned, at the White House by Dennis Martin, a uniformed inspector for the Secret Service. As they are being escorted through the White House parking lot, Hume and Markland run into USPP Chief Langston, also in uniform, and Major Hines, in his civilian clothes. Surprised, neither Hume nor Markland have any idea why their supervisors are there, but they don't ask any questions.

Hume and Markland are escorted by Martin through security into the lobby of the West Wing of the White House. The two USPP officials are invited to have a seat until a White House representative arrives to escort them upstairs.

Markland specifically asks Martin—if not already done—to seal Foster's office and post a guard at the door until they can conduct their search. Martin leaves and, minutes later, returns, saying that a Secret Service agent is standing at Foster's door, guarding his office.

While Hume and Markland wait downstairs, Chief Langston and Major Hines are in the West Wing office of David Watkins, who hosts the USPP's briefing with the White House staff. Also present is fifty-six–year-old White House Counsel Bernard Nussbaum—a product of New York's Lower East Side, Columbia University, Harvard Law School, and the U.S. House Judiciary Committee, where he served as a senior attorney during the 1974 impeachment hearings against President Richard Nixon. During his tenure with the committee, Nussbaum supervised the work of a bright young graduate of Yale Law School, Hillary Rodham, and became acquainted with her future husband, Bill Clinton.

Others in attendance at the USPP briefing are Nussbaum's associate in the Counsel's Office, William Kennedy, and about a dozen others, including George Stephanopoulos and Bill Burton, as well as James Hamilton, a prominent Washington attorney who represents the Foster family and formerly served as assistant chief counsel on the Senate Watergate Committee from 1973 to 1974. Hamilton had graduated from Foster's alma mater, Davidson College in North Carolina.

Along with Chief Langston, Hines, who speaks for most of the half-hour briefing, gives a "just the facts" tour of the Fort Marcy Park crime scene, noting that, even though all of the evidence points to a suicide, they are still handling the case as if there had been a homicide—at least until the results of the autopsy are received later that morning.

Langston is immediately struck that while most people in the room are grieving and even in tears, Nussbaum appears to be impatient with it all. He seems overly eager to get it all done and have everyone go back to work.

Hines mentions during his talk that USPP investigators are expecting the full cooperation of the White House, especially during the search of Foster's office and several anticipated sit-down interviews. There is no reaction from the White House lawyers, except for Nussbaum, who says that the Justice Department or the FBI will be present and will set out the format and restrictions for the search.

When Langston and Hines leave the briefing, they aren't exactly clear which law-enforcement agency will ultimately be in charge of the investigation. But they do know that they will be coordinating their probe in concert with the Justice Department and the FBI.

With the question of security outside Foster's office supposedly resolved, Hume and Markland are still waiting in the West Wing lobby where they are momentarily joined by Langston and

Hines, who mention that they have just briefed several White House officials.

When Hume complains about the delay, Hines tells him that he and Markland will have access to Foster's office as soon as the FBI arrives.

After Langston and Hines leave the White House, Officer Bruce Abbott of the Uniformed Secret Service Division, standing guard in the West Wing reception area, approaches Markland, who doesn't remember him from his previous tour of duty at the White House. Abbott tells Markland that, earlier that morning, he had seen White House security chief Craig Livingstone come from the second floor, carrying a cardboard box that Abbott believes might have contained some documents.

9.

AT THE COUNTY MORGUE ON BRADDOCK ROAD in Fairfax, Dr. James C. Beyer, a seventy-five-year-old forensic pathologist who has performed over twenty thousand autopsies, begins the one on Vincent Foster. Present are Beyer's assistant and four representatives of the USPP, including Investigator James C. Morrissette and Sergeant Rule, as well as Shelly Hill of ID Tech and trainee Wayne Johnson.[46] All of these police officers are fairly new to seeing an autopsy. This is only the third for Morrissette, who had to prepare Johnson—assigned to fingerprint Foster—for his first. The sights, the sounds, and the smells at an autopsy take some getting use to.

As Morrissette walks into the room, he sees the black-powder-stained soft palate of Foster's mouth on a dish, next to Foster's tongue, which does not visibly contain the same black residue. The palate and the tongue were removed before the officers arrived; Foster has already been weighed and measured.

Even in death, Vincent Foster, whose clothes have been removed and body washed down, is a big, well-groomed man: just over six-foot-four and 197 pounds. Although clearly not a body-builder, he didn't appear to have any excess fat. He has hazel eyes, which have been closed, and graying black hair. His fingernails and toenails seem manicured. And, although he appears to have shot himself in the mouth, he has no broken teeth.

Dr. Beyer—who has his own photographs of the autopsy taken, along with those of Officer Hill—sees that Foster's rigor mortis is complete. His coloring is pale red; lividity is apparent, fixed on his backside and indicative of the position in which he was found—which is observed in several crime-scene Polaroid pictures Morrissette has brought along.

Almost immediately, Dr. Beyer points to the webbing of Foster's right hand, between the index finger and thumb, which also has gunpowder residue. The lesser burns on Foster's left hand seem to confirm Rolla and Simonello's earlier belief that Foster had used his right hand to fire the gun, which was steadied with his left hand.

Early in the autopsy, a stiff metal rod is inserted and pushed through the entrance wound in the back of Foster's mouth and through his brain; it emerges from the exit wound in the back of Foster's head, confirming the path which the bullet traveled. It is a perforating wound: the bullet did not lodge inside the skull; it crashed through it.

The exit wound is clearly visible after the skin on Foster's lower neck is cut from ear to ear and pulled over his head toward his face, exposing the skull. This wound is an inch and a quarter long and an inch wide, not including the nearby fracture lines.

As photographs of all these maneuvers are taken, Dr. Beyer comments to the USPP officers that Foster couldn't have killed himself any quicker than he had with that single shot.

Morrissette adds in his report:

During the autopsy, Dr. [Beyer] noted that the bullet trajectory was "upward and backward" exiting in the center
line of the back of the head. *Dr. [Beyer] stated that X-rays
indicated that there was no evidence of bullet fragments in
the head.* [Emphasis added]
   Dr. [Beyer] stated that it appeared that the victim had
eaten a "large" meal which he believed to have occurred
within 2-3 hours prior to death. He was unable to state positively what type of food was consumed but stated [that] it
might have been meat and potatoes.

This estimate places Foster's death between 3 and 4 PM, but Dr.
Beyer cannot calculate an exact time of death.

From what everyone in the room can see, there is no indication
of any trauma on Foster's body, apart from that caused by the single gunshot wound.[47] There are no defensive wounds that would
indicate that Foster had tried to ward off an attacker.

Officer Johnson, who fingerprints Foster after the autopsy, takes
custody of Foster's clothing—his pants and boxer shorts, his dress
shirt and T-shirt, and his belt, socks, and shoes. Someone from the
coroner's office has placed them in an unsegregated pile on an
adjoining table. Later, the clothing will be separated and laid out on
brown paper on the floor of the USPP crime lab's drying room.

Also, Dr. Beyer has taken a sample of Foster's blood, which will
become item number 36 on the property report. Although he
takes no semen sample, Dr. Beyer retains a section of Foster's
liver, a vial of vitreous humor (the clear gel-like substance
between the retina and the lens of the eyeball), and a urine sample for serological and toxicological analysis.

Dr. Beyer orders no test at the autopsy to determine whether
Foster had the HIV virus. (Later, however, at the request of the
USPP, an AIDS test would be conducted at the state crime lab
from a sample of Foster's blood taken at the autopsy. The results
were negative: Foster did *not* have the virus.[48])

In his professional opinion, Dr. Beyer concludes that Vincent Foster, as suspected, had committed suicide.

Meantime, the USPP places a special lookout and patrol near Fort Marcy Park, in an attempt to find the mystery man in the white van, who had initially found Foster's body but chose to have someone else call 911.

10.

BACK AT THE WHITE HOUSE, at the exact same time as the autopsy concludes at 11:05 AM in northern Virginia, the official Secret Service log notes:

> Officer Michelle Macon relieved ATSAIC Flynn and was
> instructed to maintain a log of any persons entering
> [Vincent Foster's] office, to observe their actions, and not to
> permit the removal of items.

A few minutes later, White House Counsel Nussbaum appears in the West Wing lobby where Hume and Markland are now fuming.

"Are you still here?" Nussbaum abruptly snaps at the police investigators.

Initially taken aback by Nussbaum's antagonism, Markland asks politely but firmly when he and Hume are going to be allowed to search Foster's office.

Nussbaum says that they will have access as soon as representatives from the Justice Department arrive.[49]

Unsatisfied, Markland wants to know exactly when they are coming. Nussbaum replies that he hasn't called them, adding that he thought the USPP had made the arrangements. Completely frustrated, Hume and Markland now believe they are being given the runaround. As Nussbaum leaves, they joke bitterly that they are waiting for permission to do their jobs.

Hume then calls the FBI's Washington field office. A supervisor agrees to dispatch two FBI special agents that afternoon to aid the police in their quest.

Before Hume and Markland leave, Secret Service guard Bruce Abbott returns to Markland and points out Craig Livingstone, who is crossing the lobby.

As Abbott calls out to Livingstone, Markland walks over and stops the security chief. Markland introduces himself and says that he has been told that Livingstone was spotted earlier that morning carrying a box of documents from the second floor. Before Livingstone—who appears to have been crying—has a chance to reply, Markland asks him two questions: "Did the documents come from Foster's office?" "Have you been in Foster's office since his death?"

Livingstone replies that although he was carrying a box of documents that morning, they had not come from Foster's office, and he had not been in Foster's office. When Markland presses him on where he had received the documents, Livingstone responds, without being defensive, that they were from "a different location."

Hume and Markland return to their offices in Anacostia and eat their brown-bag lunches at their desks.

At around midday, a sad and grieving Mack McLarty tells the White House staff, gathered in room 450 of the Old Executive Office Building, "Those of you who knew Vince only for a short time, and those of you that had the rare pleasure, as the president and I have had for some forty years, to know Vince Foster since childhood, you saw those same qualities, regardless of that forty-year relationship, of wisdom, genuineness, substance, a deep commitment to family and to work, and an absolute commitment to friends."

After being introduced by McLarty, Bernard Nussbaum, apparently speaking extemporaneously, says that he had last seen Foster between noon and 12:15 PM the previous day, just before Foster returned to his office to eat his final lunch. Nussbaum continues, "He walked into my office. The TV set was on.... I was watching Judge [Ruth Bader] Ginsburg's opening statement [during her U.S. Senate confirmation hearings as an associate Supreme Court justice]. And I had just come from the Rose Garden, which he did, with Judge [Louis] Freeh, who had been nominated by the president to be the head of the FBI. And I was flipping from one channel to another, watching the replays of the Freeh thing, the Ginsburg thing.

"And I said to my partner, 'Vince,' I said, 'Hey, Vince, not a bad day.' I said, 'We hit two home runs. Not home runs for you, Vince, or even for the president; really home runs for the country. So I think we're doing our job, and I think we're doing it well.'[50] And he just sort of smiled. And I said, 'I'll see you later.' And that's the last time I saw Vince."

After his own remarks, Nussbaum introduces "our client," President Clinton, who still seems to be dismayed and in shock. In a moving address, the president states:

> Forty-two years ago, when I met Mr. McLarty in kindergarten, I lived with my grandparents in a modest little house around the corner from Vince Foster's nice, big, white brick house....
> Yesterday, last night, when I finished the "Larry King Show," and I was told what happened, I just kept thinking in my mind of when we were so young, sitting on the ground in the back yard, throwing knives into the ground and seeing if we were adroit enough to make them stick.
> When I started my career in Arkansas politics, he was

there to help me. When I decided to run for attorney general, he was the first lawyer in Little Rock I talked to about supporting me. When the Rose Law Firm hired Hillary after I moved to Little Rock, Vince Foster and Webb Hubbell became her closest friends....

No one can ever know why this happened. Even if you had a whole set of objective reasons, that wouldn't be why it happened, because you could get a different, bigger, more burdensome set of objective reasons that are on someone else even in this room. So what happened was a mystery about something inside of him. And I hope all of you will always understand that.

The next thing I want to say is, this should teach us all, again, a little humility. We come here and labor and work like crazy as if the idea of progress were a given, if only we worked hard enough, pushed enough rocks up a hill and, yet, every time you'd look around, there is some reminder that we are not really fully in control of our own destiny, even though we are morally obliged to try to be....

And the last thing I want to say is that Vince Foster spent a lifetime knowing when not to put himself first. And maybe he did that too much. But he had an extraordinary sense of propriety and loyalty....

Those of us who knew him a long time, we're having a real hard time dealing with this. Because everybody who had known him any length of time could remember sometime when we were weak and he was strong, and, virtually, never an occasion where he was weak and we were strong. And so, think about that. We ought to leave here with humility.

On top of all the personal accolades he receives in death, Foster, the son of a wealthy real-estate broker and developer, appeared to have been at the top of his professional game at the time he had supposedly ended his life. A former student-body president at Hope High School who studied psychology at and graduated from Davidson College in 1967, Foster began law school at Vanderbilt but, facing the military draft, left school and joined the National Guard in order to avoid the draft and Vietnam. Later, he enrolled at the University of Arkansas School of Law in Fayetteville.

Graduating first in his class in 1971 and earning the highest score on the state's bar examination, he immediately joined the Rose Law Firm and was made partner two years later. He quickly became known as a "can-do" lawyer who worked best when under pressure. He handled stress throughout his career by swimming, jogging, and reading.

Nicknamed "Pencil" because of his tall and lanky frame, Foster was making nearly $300,000 a year as a top corporate attorney and lived in a big home in the exclusive Heights area of Little Rock. He had already announced his candidacy for president of the Arkansas Bar Association[51] when he decided to move to Washington in January 1993 to accept the job as White House deputy counsel in "Nussbaum & Foster"—which didn't pay half as much as the Rose Law Firm—and to live in a cramped rented townhouse in Georgetown with his wife and three grown children.

On May 8, 1993, about ten weeks before his death, Foster, who had skipped his own commencement ceremony, gave a moving speech to the law-school graduates of his alma mater. He told the class of 1993:

> The reputation you develop for intellectual and ethical integrity will be your strongest asset or your worst enemy.... I cannot make this point to you too strongly: There is no victory, no advantage, no fee, no favor which is worth even a blemish on your reputation for intellect and integrity. Nothing travels faster than an accusation that another lawyer's word is no good.... Dents to the reputation in the legal profession are irreparable....
>
> [T]here will also be failures, and criticisms and bad press and lies, stormy days and cloudy days, and you will not survive them without the support of [your] spouses, law partners and friends.

Then, throwing a verbal bouquet to his wife, Foster continued:

> Three weeks ago, my wife, Lisa, and I celebrated our
> twenty-fifth anniversary, and it was here in Fayetteville, in
> law school, where we celebrated our first. Like many in this
> audience, she began by putting me through law school. For
> twenty-two years, she has always encouraged me to perse-
> vere and aim higher. She has been my editor, my jury con-
> sultant, and my best friend. I wish for all of you, a Lisa.

Toward the end of his commencement address, Foster para-
phrased his close friend, Hillary Clinton, whom he had recruited
for the Rose Law Firm in 1977, saying:

> The First Lady said it best recently. She said service
> means you get as well as you give. Your life is changed as
> you change the life of others. It is the way we find meaning
> in our lives.

In the midst of the 1992 presidential campaign, amid
allegations of Governor Clinton's womanizing, Foster had been
romantically linked to Mrs. Clinton, with whom he shared a
trusting professional friendship. Hearing this rumor, Foster had
gone so far as to meet with John Phillip Carroll, the senior partner in the Rose Law Firm, just to deny it.

Now, with no obvious explanation for why Foster had died,
many in the White House braced for the media's resurrection of
this gossip, which had never been proved—but, unfortunately,
couldn't be disproved, even if the affair had never occurred.

11.

AT 1:10 PM, ACCORDING to the official Secret Service log:

Inspector Dennis Martin UD/WHB met the following persons at the southwest gate, and escorted them to his office awaiting approval from the Justice Department to proceed to Mr. Foster's office to conduct interviews and a search.

Captain Charles Hume (USPP)
Det. Pete Markland (USPP)
SA Scott Salter (FBI)
SA John Danna (FBI)

The earlier wait, however, simply shifts from the lobby of the West Wing to Inspector Martin's office in the Old Executive Office Building. Although Martin is in and out of the office, two other Secret Service agents, Paul Imbordino and Don Flynn, remain with the two USPP investigators and the two FBI special agents during their seemingly endless stay, still waiting to enter Foster's office to do their jobs.

Both Hume and Markland have been permitted to keep their guns, although the Secret Service officers forced the FBI special agents to check theirs before entering the grounds of the White House.

Meantime, at 2:15 PM, over at the USPP's Criminal Investigations Branch in Anacostia, USPP criminalist Eugene J. Smith, Peter Simonello's partner since 1986 and an eighteen-year veteran of the USPP, begins to photograph and fingerprint Foster's 1989 gray Honda Accord, which is in the USPP's fenced-in impound lot and still sealed with the thin red tape signed by Simonello.

After photographing all of the seals on the car with his 35 mm camera—confirming that they have not been broken—Smith breaks the seals and removes the items in the car.

He finds nothing out of the ordinary—except, possibly, an oven mitt, which he sees in the glove compartment, just as Braun had the previous day. "What is an oven mitt doing in this guy's car?" Smith thinks to himself.

Meanwhile, USPP firearms-identification experts—with the help of the Bureau of Alcohol, Tobacco and Firearms in the Treasury Department—learn that the .38-caliber Colt Army revolver found in Foster's right hand is a collector's item that had been manufactured as part of a two-gun set in 1913. But, because of the age of the gun, tracing its ownership will probably be impossible.

Back at the Old Executive Office Building, Hume, now steaming with anger, calls Chief Langston in late afternoon, saying, "Chief, here's where we are at this point: no interviews have been conducted; we haven't gotten into the office. None of that's been done."

Perhaps as furious as Hume and Markland, Chief Langston calls Attorney General Janet Reno, whom he knows to be a pro-cop prosecutor, and she takes his call, personally.

Langston tells her that his men are languishing at the Old Executive Office Building, unable to perform their duties because of a White House-imposed stall. Langston says he fears a potential conflict is about to erupt between the White House and the Park Police and asks that Reno intervene and "send some of your prosecutors to help us."

Reno sounds accommodating, even apologetic.

A few minutes later, at 4:26 PM, while still in the Secret Service office, Hume receives a call from Philip Heymann, the deputy attorney general. Pleasant and cooperative, Heymann, Reno's second-in-command at Justice, promises Hume that he is sending two representatives from the Justice Department to meet them. Heymann adds that they are "career employees," an obvious code to Hume that they are not Schedule-C, political appointees.

Unknown to Hume and Markland, earlier in the day, Mark Gearan, the White House director of communications, had told reporters that "the investigation will be coordinated by the Department of Justice and the office of the attorney general and her deputy, Phil Heymann."

The message is that the Justice Department will play an active role in the probe of Foster's death, which will probably include a full-field FBI investigation in concert with or parallel to that of the USPP. But, under U.S. law, the Park Police clearly has jurisdiction in this case.

Soon after, Heymann calls Hume again, saying that the two "career employees" he is sending over are senior attorneys David Margolis and Roger Adams. Hume knows Margolis as the former chief of the legendary Organized Crime and Racketeering Section.

Heymann goes on to give Hume some idea of what to expect when they enter Foster's office later in the day. Heymann says that, after White House examination, Margolis and Adams will review documents for potential attorney-client and executive-privilege conflicts and then hand the "unprotected files" to Hume and Markland for their own examination.

At or about 5 PM, Hume, Markland, and the two FBI special agents are escorted by the two Secret Service agents to Bernard Nussbaum's suite of offices on the second floor of the West Wing. There, they meet Margolis and Adams, who had arrived at 4:40 PM.

Because there are so many people in Nussbaum's office, Hume decides to stay in the outer suite of the White House Counsel's Office with FBI Special Agent Danna while Nussbaum meets with the others in his office. Hume believes the meeting to be nothing more than a prelude to entering Foster's office.

While waiting near the secretaries' desks, Hume sees a Secret

Service guard standing by a closed door next to Nussbaum's office. Hume asks the guard if he is protecting Foster's office. The Secret Service man confirms that he is.

But when Hume asks the guard if anyone has entered the room during the day, he replies that anyone who wanted to has simply walked in. Hume's impression is that the guard is powerless to stop anyone, indicating that the promised sealing of Foster's office has been a sham. However, a log kept by the guard shows that only Nussbaum had entered Foster's office at 11:10 AM.

Meantime, Nussbaum is giving Detective Markland, Department of Justice attorneys Margolis and Adams, and FBI Special Agent Salter a briefing about what he knows and has done since hearing about Foster's death.[52]

According to Markland's report:

> —Mr. Nussbaum had determined that Mr. Foster had left his office after lunch at 1310 hours on 7/20/93. Mr. Foster had not exhibited any unusual behavior on that day. Mr. Nussbaum tried to page Mr. Foster at approximately 1830 hours. After waiting a brief period of time without receiving a response, Mr. Nussbaum left and proceeded to his domicile, arriving at approximately 1900 hours.

> —On 7/20/93 after Vincent Foster's death became known to him, Mr. Nussbaum [returned] to the White House where he went through Mr. Foster's office with Patsy [Thomasson, an aide to David Watkins] and [Hillary Clinton's Chief of Staff] Maggie Williams. Mr. [Nussbaum] stated that they conducted a brief, quick search to see if Mr. Foster may have left a suicide note on his desk. This search lasted from 2200 hours to 2400 hours.* Mr. Nussbaum stated that no documents were removed from the office.

---

*During my interview with Markland, he stood by his notes, indicating that Nussbaum said that he had been present in Foster's office that night for two hours.

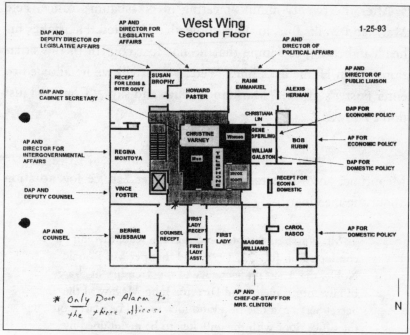

Diagram of the second floor of the West Wing. (USPP)

—Mr. Nussbaum stated that... [at] about 0700-0715 hours [on July 21] one of the secretaries [Betsy Pond] had entered Mr. Foster's office and "piled papers" on his desk top "to make it neat."

—At approximately 0900 hours Mr. Nussbaum again entered the office to look around.[53]

—It was determined that the cleaning lady had emptied Mr. Foster's trash. The trash was retrieved and returned to the office.

—Mr. Nussbaum requested that the [Secret Service] secure the office and the room was posted at approximately 1015 hours.

However, later, under oath, Nussbaum insisted, "*We were there no more than ten minutes*" (emphasis added).

Both Patsy Thomasson and Maggie Williams agreed with Nussbaum in their sworn statements.

After the twenty-minute meeting in Nussbaum's office, Pete
Markland walks out, looking somewhat dejected. He shakes his
head, indicating to Hume that he has lost control of the situation. When Hume asks him, "Pete, when will we be allowed to
enter Foster's office?" Markland shrugs and says, "Charlie, I just
don't know."

Meantime, according to the official Secret Service log notation
about the meeting:

> Mr. Nussbaum announced that the search would be
> conducted on July 22, 1993, and that per Mr. Ronald
> Noble, the Assistant Secretary of the Treasury in charge
> of law enforcement, and Director John Magaw of the
> Secret Service, a one-of-a kind lock would be placed on
> the office door with the only key to be maintained by
> ATSAIC Flynn.

Behind the scenes, however, an undated memorandum from
Noble to Secretary of the Treasury Lloyd Bentsen reveals:

> An agreement was reached concerning the
> disposition of items housed in Mr. Foster's office by
> and between members of the White House Legal
> Counsel, Department of Justice (DOJ), and a Foster
> family attorney.

Significantly, the U.S. Park Police is not mentioned as a party
to this agreement, indicating that—unknown to the USPP—this
agreement among the White House, the Department of Justice,
and James Hamilton, the Foster family's attorney, had been cut
prior to the meeting.

However, even without being aware of this arrangement,
Hume and Markland already have full confidence particularly in

Dave Margolis, knowing that he is working quietly to bring them into the process—so that they can finally do their jobs.

Outside, under a green-and-white–striped canopy that stretches several yards from the entrance of the West Wing to the parking lot, another brief meeting takes place. Because Margolis and Markland are smoking, Hume, an ex-smoker who is now allergic to cigarette smoke, steps away from the others. When Markland joins him moments later, he tells Hume that, according to Margolis, "Nussbaum has invited everyone back tomorrow morning to conduct interviews of the White House staff and to search Foster's office."

During the ride back to their office, Markland adds that the White House has requested that the USPP return some of Foster's personal effects, such as his rings, watch, and wallet. He explains that the president wants, personally, to return Foster's property to his widow before she and her children leave for the funeral in Little Rock.

After returning to Anacostia, Hume and Markland call John Rolla, who has kept Foster's belongings in his locker. Rolla, still at home, tells them where they can find the locker key.

After retrieving the wallet and the jewelry, Markland, repeating what Rolla had done the previous night, removes the items from Foster's wallet and photocopies everything.[54]

Meantime, Clifford Sloan of the White House Counsel's Office calls Hume, asking him to get to the White House as quickly as possible, because the president is ready to leave.

After completing their photocopying, Hume and Markland return to the White House with the wallet and all of its contents, as well as Foster's rings and watch. At 7:35 PM, while Hume, who is behind the wheel, remains in the car, Markland steps out and asks Sloan to sign a receipt, preserving the chain of custody of the items.

Both Hume and Markland cannot help but notice the presidential motorcade lining up nearby. They know that, within seconds, the president will be in possession of Foster's personal property.

This quick action will upset Rolla, who had wanted to return Foster's personal effects himself, hoping for another opportunity to question Foster's wife and, perhaps, her children.

At 8:02 PM, according to the official Secret Service log:

> ATSAIC Flynn relieved the uniformed officer controlling [Foster's] office door. SS Kevin Robbins and Mr. Kenneth Blair commenced to install the aforementioned lock at that time.

Two and a half hours later, at 10:32 PM:

> The lock installation was completed and the door secured by ATSAIC Flynn.

12.

THURSDAY, JULY 22, 1993

For a man in Washington, it has been said, the two most unforgivable sins are getting caught with a live boy or a dead girl. But as rare as those acts are, suicide is an even rarer occurrence. Despite all of the contemporary scandals the nation's Capitol has endured—ranging from bribery, racketeering, and influence peddling to Watergate, ABSCAM, and Iran-Contra—*none* of the disgraced participants at Foster's level or above had ever ended his or her own life.

To find a suicide by such a top government official, researchers have to go back to the post–World War II era. On May 22, 1949, the first Secretary of Defense, James V. Forrestal, in the wake of his dismissal from office and an emotional breakdown two months earlier, jumped out a window on the sixteenth floor of the Bethesda Naval Hospital and fell to his death. In his suicide note, written on hospital stationery, Forrestal simply quoted Sophocles, saying:

> **Worn by the waste of time**
> **Comfortless, nameless, hopeless save**
> **In the dark prospect of the yawning grave.**[55]

Before that, the last suicides were those of Charles F. Cramer, the general counsel of the Veterans Bureau, and Jesse W. Smith, a close friend of Attorney General Harry M. Daugherty. Cramer and Smith committed suicide in 1923 in the midst of the Harding Administration's Teapot Dome scandal. Both men had shot themselves in the head.[56]

With such an unusual event at hand, Washington gears up to make the most of this sad occasion for its usual purpose: leveraging and exploiting political vulnerability.

In the morning newspapers on Thursday, reporters have begun to stitch together some of Foster's movements on the day of his death. They tell how Foster had worked at his desk during the morning of July 20, leaving to attend President Clinton's announcement of the appointment of Judge Louis Freeh as the new FBI director.*

---

* Freeh replaced William Sessions, who had been fired by President Clinton on July 19, 1993, after he was accused of allegedly misusing FBI resources and staff. The White House had been trying to force Session's resignation since the president's inauguration.

After the ceremony in the Rose Garden for Judge Freeh, Foster, who had waved goodbye to reporters, returned to his office, spoke to Nussbaum, and ate lunch at his desk.

Ruth Marcus and Ann Devroy of the *Washington Post* report that Foster's friends and associates painted a picture of a man overwhelmed with work, adding that Vincent and Lisa Foster had accompanied Webster and Suzy Hubbell "to the Eastern Shore last weekend for a break from the pressures."

Marcus and Devroy add: "A search of Foster's White House office is scheduled for today.... Two senior Justice Department lawyers, David Margolis and Roger Adams, are participating because 'there is apparently a great deal in the office on paper and in the computer concerning Foster's privileged communications with the president,' [Justice Department spokesman Dean] St. Dennis said."

But the coverage of Foster's death already begins to darken.

Ominously, Pulitzer Prize-winning reporter Thomas L. Friedman of the *New York Times* writes: "So much was left unanswered that in their uncomprehending grief, some of Mr. Foster's friends and associates raised the possibility of foul play."

Friedman also notes a rumor that the "*Washington Times* was preparing a story about Mr. Foster, and a reporter there, Michael Hedges, acknowledged that he had made preliminary inquiries about him. He would not describe the nature of the inquiry.

"But Mr. Hedges said he had not interviewed Mr. Foster about the story. He added, 'We were not at a point where anything was imminent that we were going to break on the guy.'"[57]

In his own report on Foster's death in today's *Washington Times*, Hedges publishes an article, "Hillary loses longtime friend, investment partner, in suicide." The centerpiece of Hedges's story is the 1983 creation of Midlife Investments, a partnership established by Hillary Clinton, Webster Hubbell, and Vincent Foster—all members of Little Rock's Rose Law Firm, the official address for the partnership. Each of the three attorneys had contributed $15,000 in the investment, which appears to be a joint stock-buying concern, working in concert with E.F. Hutton in Little Rock. According to Hedges, the partnership "still existed at the time of Mr. Foster's death."

Also that morning, the *Wall Street Journal,* frequently critical of President Clinton for placing his "attorney friends" from Little Rock in top government positions, publishes another editorial, recommending the appointment of a "special counsel" within the Justice Department to conduct a "serious investigation" of Foster's death. The *Journal* also states: "As readers of this page are aware, we have devoted considerable space to inquiring after the precise nature of the activities of the four Rose Law Firm partners from Little Rock working in the Clinton Administration.... If anything, Mr. Foster's tragic death adds to the curiosity. Those who knew him consider him an unlikely suicide. We're told he had no history of depression. His legal specialty was litigation, which is to say he was scarcely a stranger to stress....

"We had our disagreements with Mr. Foster during his short term in Washington, but we do not think that in death he deserves to disappear into a cloud of mystery that we are somehow ordained never to understand."

In other words, Foster's death presents a golden opportunity to scrutinize the Clinton White House.

At 9 AM, Captain Hume and Sergeant Markland of the USPP and FBI Special Agent Scott Salter and another agent, Dennis Condon, return to the White House for a series of official interviews with four aides to Vincent Foster: Betsy Pond, Deborah Gorham, Tom Castleton, and Linda Tripp. Hume and Condon interview Pond while Clifford Sloan takes notes for the Counsel's Office; Markland and Salter speak with the other three staffers.

Betsy Pond says that she came to work on July 20 just aftter 9 AM.
Nussbaum and Foster's regular staff meeting was already under
way, so she didn't see Foster until later in the Rose Garden, when
President Clinton introduced Judge Freeh as his nominee to head
the FBI.

Hume continues in his notes:

> [Pond] doesn't recall Vincent Foster having any visitors
> on Tuesday. The first conversation she had with him was
> about lunch around 1200-1230 hours. He said he would
> eat at his desk. He ordered a medium-rare cheeseburger,
> french fries, and Coke. She and Linda Tripp went to the
> cafeteria and ordered his lunch. She recalled there were M
> & Ms on the tray with the food, because Linda wanted
> them. He sat on his sofa and ate lunch in his office.
>
> At around 1300 hours, he came out of the office and
> stated, "I'll be back. There are M & Ms left in my office."
> Ms. Pond recalled that she and Linda were in the office
> when he left....
>
> There was nothing unusual about his emotional state. In
> fact, over the last several weeks, she did not notice any
> changes, either physically or emotionally. She noticed no
> weight loss. She was unaware of him taking any medication
> or seeing any doctors.... She was not aware of any depres-
> sion problems. She had no information whether he owned
> any weapons.
>
> Ms. Pond said she left work at approximately 1845-
> 1850 hours on Tuesday; but, before she left at around 1820
> or so, Maggie Williams (Mrs. Clinton's Chief of Staff)
> called for Vincent. [Pond] paged Vincent and left the White
> House number for him to call. She recalled no other phone
> messages for Vincent.[58]

In the midst of Hume's interview with Pond, Nussbaum, for no
apparent reason, suddenly bursts into the office where they are
talking, simply to ask, "Is everything all right?" As an indication

of a growing animosity between the Park Police and the White House Counsel's Office, Hume believes that Nussbaum has intentionally disrupted the interview.

When Nussbaum leaves, Pond admits to Hume that she had entered Foster's office on the morning after his death "and 'squashed' the papers together that were on his desk." Hume adds, "She realized that she shouldn't have touched the papers as soon as she did it but probably did it out of habit."

Hume concludes in his notes:

> When I questioned her if she had been told how to respond to our questions, she stated that Clifford Sloan (who was present during our interview) and Steve Neuwirth, both associate counselors, had called them all together on Wednesday evening and told them they would be questioned by the police and for them to tell the truth.

Deborah Gorham, whose desk is in the outer area between the doors to Nussbaum and Foster's offices, had worked as Foster's executive assistant since March 8, 1993, and had been recommended for the job by Foster's sister, Sheila Anthony.

In his report of the interview, Markland writes:

> On 7/20/93, [Gorham] left the office at approximately 1130 hours, which is the last time she saw Mr. Foster alive. She stated that she did not note any unusual behavior by Mr. Foster on that day.
> Ms. Gorham recalled a conversation with Mr. Foster on Thursday, 7/15/93, when he discussed the differences in working for a law firm and working for the government. She placed no significance on the conversation at the time and, in retrospect, it still seemed to be a normal comparison.

As the interview winds down, Steve Neuwirth—an assistant

White House counsel whom Nussbaum had brought from his law firm in New York and who is sitting in on the interview—asks to speak privately with Gorham in another room. When they return, Gorham adds, according to Markland:

> On Thursday, 7/15/93, Mrs. Foster had called [Gorham] and asked for Mr. Foster's pay schedule, explaining that she believed their checking account was overdrawn. The Credit Union was contacted, and they stated that they would work with Mrs. Foster on a weekly, instead of biweekly, basis. After that conversation, Ms. Gorham was authorized by Mr. Foster to pick up a statement every Friday for Mrs. Foster. Ms. Gorham did not see this as a real problem or place any significance on it....
> Within the last two weeks, Ms. Gorham had received calls from Mr. Foster's eldest son and Mrs. Foster, inquiring about Vincent Foster's mood. They specifically asked how "he" was doing, not how the work was going, and seemed genuinely concerned.

At 10 AM, Markland and Salter interview Tom Castleton, a staff assistant in the White House Counsel's Office. Markland writes:

> Mr. Castleton... remembers that Mr. Foster ate lunch at the office, although he could not place the time. Mr. Castleton was present when Mr. Foster left the office after eating lunch and said, "So long." Mr. Foster did not respond and seemed to Mr. Castleton to be "in his own world," focused, disturbed.

Simultaneous to the interview with Castleton, USPP identification technician Shelly Hill and ID trainee Wayne Johnson arrive at Fort Marcy Park, along with Sergeant Rule and Detective Morrissette, to conduct a two-hour search of the crime scene. None of the four officers had been at the park on the day of the shooting, so they base their work on the notes, reports, and photographs of other officers.

According to Hill's report:

> We were led to the area of the death and proceeded to
> conduct a search of the vicinity with a metal detector. After
> a lengthy search for a bullet, the results were negative.

The officers agree with those at the original crime scene that
the bullet had gone upward and, thus, could be anywhere in or
out of the park. Surrounding the open area of the second grove is
a heavily wooded area, leaving them with little chance of finding
the bullet within a reasonable amount of time. For all they know,
the bullet could be up in a tree somewhere.

Nor while at Fort Marcy Park, does the USPP conduct a search
for any bone fragments from Foster's head. Although they can
still see Foster's blood, they do no digging in that area.

After this search, however, they go to the nearby Saudi Arabian
compound across Chain Bridge Road, just a few hundred feet
from where Foster's body was found. Morrissette asks the Saudi
security people whether they had seen anything suspicious or
heard a shot on Tuesday afternoon. No one had. The detective
also talks to some construction workers who are doing road
repairs nearby, but they didn't see or hear anything either.

At 11:50 AM, Markland and Salter conduct their final interview
of the day with Linda Tripp, Nussbaum's executive assistant.

Although she had no personal contact with Foster on the morning of his death, Tripp had seen him as he left his office at a little
after 1 PM, adding that his "demeanor seemed normal" and essentially confirming Betsy Pond's account of the lunch they delivered
to Foster from the White House cafeteria. Markland continues in
his report:

> Ms. Tripp makes it a habit to notice what the staff
> members are taking with them when they leave the office in
> order to determine for herself how long she may expect
> them to be away from the office. Ms. Tripp was absolutely
> certain that Mr. Foster did not carry anything in the way of
> a briefcase, bag, umbrella, etc., out of the office.

Foster left quickly after lunch, saying, "I'll be back." Tripp didn't
think it was appropriate for her to ask him where he was going.

In short, the interviews with four of the last known people to have
seen Foster alive yield little. Markland and Salter have received
statements that the deputy counsel appeared normal—although
his wife and son had expressed some concern for him during the
past two weeks, amidst signs that he might have been experienc-
ing some money problems.

The investigators hope that their search of Foster's office will
produce something more.

13.

THE SEARCH FOR INFORMATION IS ALSO CONTINUING away from the
White House. USPP personnel arrive at the National Park Service's
maintenance yard at Turkey Run. There, they play the 911 tape,
recorded on July 20, for two NPS supervisors, in an effort to find
someone who can identify the voice on the recording.

According to Investigator Morrissette's report:

> During the course of the [911] conversation, this uniden-
> tified person stated that he worked for the Park Service and
> that he was making the call from Turkey Run Park. With

this information, Sgt. Rule and myself responded to the
park office at Turkey Run Park. There we met with two
people who we believed might be able to recognize the
voice on the tape. Subsequent to this conversation, we
searched and located the following person: Francis Swann...
[who] works at the National Airport work yard for the
National Park Service [NPS].

Rule and Morrissette immediately drive to the NPS maintenance area, near National Airport, and find Swann.

Morrissette doesn't give Swann any opportunity to deny making the call, pretending that he has already been positively identified. Without any hesitation, Swann spills.

According to Morrissette's report:

During the interview with Mr. Swann, he stated that [a
co-worker] and himself were sitting outside the Turkey Run
Headquarters at approximately 1750 hrs. At this time, a
large white van, thought to possibly be a General Motors
make, drove into the parking area. The van was best
described as follows:

1987-1990, Chevy, white in color
construction writing on the side, Va. tags—unknown, no
windows, described as "well used."

The operator of this van was described as follows:

W/M, 47-50 yrs., chunky/heavyset, 220-225 lbs.
mostly graying hair, light sun tan, clean shaven with
whiskers, possibly gay

This operator advised Mr. Swann that there was a body
in the area of the [second] cannon in Ft. Marcy Park. Based
on this notification, Mr. Swann called the Fairfax County
Police and reported the incident. Subsequent to this call, he
called the U.S. Park Police and made the same report. Mr.

> Swann stated that there was no other conversation with
> regards to the body.

Swann, who vehemently denies that *he* had originally found the
body, tells Rule and Morrissette that he and his co-worker, Charles
Stough, had gone to Turkey Run to split a six-pack of beer. Knowing
that they shouldn't have been there—and drinking—he became worried when he heard details of Foster's suicide on the news. He didn't
step forward because he didn't want to get involved or into trouble.

Meantime, back at the USPP/CIB office, Investigator Rolla, still
playing a back-up role in the investigation, receives an assignment
to contact the three doctors whose names appear in Foster's handwriting on a piece of White House stationery. The paper had been
found by Rolla in Foster's wallet.

Rolla starts calling the doctors, whom Investigator Abt learns
were members of the Department of Psychiatry of Georgetown
University. Rolla writes a report of his findings, saying:

> On 07/22/93, myself and Inv. [Abt] spoke via telephone
> to all three of the... doctors. I spoke with Dr. Hedaya and
> Dr. Pasternack and Inv. [Abt] spoke with Dr. Allen. All
> three doctors are psychiatrists. All three doctors also stated
> that they did not know Vincent Foster, Jr., and that he was
> not a patient of theirs.

Shortly after 1 PM, White House spokeswoman Dee Dee Myers
begins a press conference in the White House briefing room. After
she fields only three questions about President Clinton's morning
meeting with President Jean-Bertrand Aristide of Haiti, all attention focuses on Foster's death on Tuesday.

In perhaps the most interesting exchange of the briefing, a reporter asks, "Let's assume that the [Park Police] determines to its satisfaction that, in fact, this was, as everyone thinks, a suicide. From the White House perspective, does this simply end there in terms of further examining what the circumstances might have been, or whether this was related to work or whatever?"

"It is a mystery," Myers replies, "and I think the president made that very clear yesterday...."

The reporter persists, "I don't mean mushy little reasons—"

"But how can you know?" Myers asks. "How can you know? Even if you come up with—"

The reporter continues, "All I was trying to ask was whether or not, beyond establishing whether it was a suicide, whether an effort would be made to go further than that to see if there was any evidence to indicate why—not trying to get back into somebody's mind to know how they were feeling, but—"

"That's what you have to do," Myers says somewhat sarcastically.

"Yes, but, Dee Dee, suicide is always, to some extent, kind of an inexplicable act."

"Right."

"Nonetheless, in many, many cases, one can understand at least the chain of events that could have driven someone to that level of despair. In this particular instance, no one can offer any reason why this man, at the prime of his life, the seeming pinnacle of his career, would do this. This is, I think everyone would agree, a particularly mysterious set of circumstances that raises potentially troubling questions...."

"Right," Myers responds, seemingly trying to move on.

But the reporter presses, "It does leave that question open, and all I can say to you is: This is a question that is going to be asked again and again. And from what you are saying, I take it, no one is trying to answer it."

Myers responds, "All I've said and what I'll say again is, at this point, there are no other investigations."

Soon after, in a different setting and in response to a reporter's question about whether he can add anything to the mystery of Foster's motive for suicide, President Clinton replies sharply, "No, and I don't think there is anything more to know."

14.

AT 1:15 PM, BERNARD NUSSBAUM authorizes Don Flynn of the Secret Service to unlock the door to Vincent Foster's office. Accompanying Nussbaum and Flynn are Captain Hume and Detective Markland, as well as Dave Margolis and Roger Adams of the Justice Department, Special Agents Scott Salter and Dennis Condon of the FBI, and Paul Imbordino of the Secret Service.

Also present are Clifford Sloan and Stephen Neuwirth of the White House Counsel's Office, Assistant Chief of Staff Bill Burton, and Michael Spafford, who is from Jim Hamilton's law firm and representing the Foster family in his absence.

According to Captain Hume's notes, they are all present "to determine if [Foster] left a suicide note or if there [was] any other information that might have led him to take his own life."

Earlier that morning, while Hume and Markland were conducting interviews with the four White House staffers, Margolis and Adams had met privately with Nussbaum. During this meeting, Nussbaum told the two Justice Department officials that there had been a change of plans, explaining that all privileges would be reserved on behalf of the White House. This meant that the

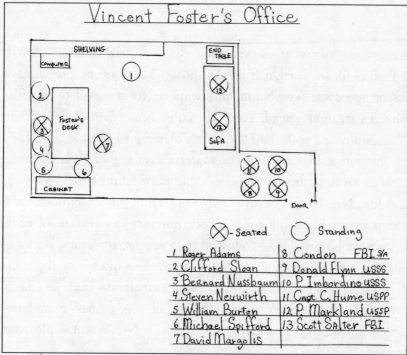

The seating arrangement during the search of Foster's office. (USPP)

White House, specifically Nussbaum, would maintain complete control over the documents in Foster's office that the Park Police, the FBI, and the Department of Justice might and might not see.

Upset with this new format, Margolis asked Nussbaum if he had spoken to Philip Heymann about this. When Nussbaum replied that he had not, Margolis suggested that they get him on the phone.

Nussbaum explained the new arrangement to Heymann, who replied, "Bernie, you are messing this up very badly. I think you are making a terrible mistake." Playing his trump card, Heymann threatened to pull both Margolis and Adams from the White House if Nussbaum insisted on his new plan of action.

Seeing how angry Heymann was, Nussbaum told Heymann not to do anything with Margolis and Adams, adding that he would call him back. But he didn't.

Regardless of what is assumed or expected, this is clearly
Nussbaum's show right from the outset. There are no preliminar-
ies or speeches; Nussbaum, just wanting to get it all over with,
plunges straight ahead. And Margolis and Adams believe that
Nussbaum had received Heymann's blessing to do so.

Nussbaum first reviews the materials on top of Foster's desk,
then in his desk drawers, and in other parts of the office. Moving
quickly, Nussbaum, occasionally conferring with Neuwirth and
Sloan in a whispering tone, gives a cursory description of each
document he picks up—followed by a simple, unilateral declaration of whether or not it is relevant to the police investigation.
From time to time, either Margolis or Markland—both of whom
are visibly upset by the way this process is going—complains
about the speed and carelessness in which Nussbaum is plowing
through the files.

Exhibiting their frustration, Hume's report states:

> Bernard Nussbaum did the actual review of the docu-
> ments in a very hurried and casual fashion.... Nussbaum
> carried his interpretation of what was considered privileged
> to the extreme; one example was when he picked up a
> xeroxed copy of a newspaper article and declared that it
> was privileged communication.

After unilaterally reviewing a document, Nussbaum places
each in one of three piles. The first pile contains records of ongoing White House business. Another stack contains Foster's personal and family matters. The third consists of the private papers
of president and Mrs. Clinton.

Hume writes in his report:

Occasionally, Detective Markland or Margolis would ask [Nussbaum] to place a certain note or document in a pile for possible police examination.

In the process of his review, Nussbaum turns in Foster's desk chair and sees a worn black-leather briefcase—with no snaps or zippers and only two compartments—on the floor on the right side of the desk.

Hume continues in his report:

> Nussbaum pulled some papers out of a leather valise/brief-case…. He put them on the desk and went through them. He then looked in the valise/briefcase again, but did not take any-thing out of it. A little later he moved the valise/briefcase away from the desk and placed it on the floor adjacent to the exterior wall directly behind him and the desk.

Markland has a clear view of Foster's briefcase through the opening in the late deputy counsel's desk and observes Nussbaum each time he handles it. At one point, Markland watches Nussbaum as he tilts the briefcase back and forth while it's still on the floor, apparently making sure that it's empty.[59]

Hume also complains in his notes that during the ninety-minute search, Nussbaum does not show a single document or file to the two Park Police investigators, the two Justice Department attorneys, or the two FBI special agents.

In fact, adding to the growing tension in the room, according to Hume's report:

> At one point Special Agent Scott Salter got up to stretch and Clifford Sloan challenged him and asked him if he was standing up in an attempt to get a look at the documents.

The tall and lean Salter, who has been sitting patiently on the small couch next to Markland, simply needs to stretch his legs. Salter turns visibly red after Sloan accuses him of trying to "peek" at the files. Salter protests at being scolded by Sloan, saying, "I'm not trying to do anything!"

At that point, Nussbaum says, "Everyone just calm down!"

A few minutes later, as Sloan is looking over Nussbaum's shoulder at a document on the desk, Margolis says, "Hey, Cliff, you're not looking over Bernie's shoulder so you can read the documents that he's looking at, are you?"

Refusing to lighten up and see the humor in what Margolis has just said, Sloan carps, "Hey, wait a minute! I'm authorized to do that! What are you talking about?"

At 2:49 PM, with all six of the law-enforcement personnel seething with anger, Nussbaum concludes the search, leaving all of the documents in Foster's office—with the exception of the stack of Foster's personal papers, which he gives to Foster-family attorney Spafford.

Before the meeting, Nussbaum and Margolis had agreed to allow these documents to be returned to Foster's family, adding that, with the approval of Lisa Foster, the USPP could examine them.

But, Nussbaum, who announces that Foster's office will no longer be sealed, denies the police investigators immediate access to Foster's telephone logs. In other words, the investigators from the Park Police, the FBI, and the Department of Justice leave Foster's office with absolutely nothing.

Later that night, Heymann calls Nussbaum and chastises him for failing to call back, as promised, before the search was conducted. Having no real explanation, Nussbaum remains silent, provoking Heymann to say, "Bernie, are you hiding something? Is there some terrible secret here that you are hiding?"

"Phil, I promise you," Nussbaum replies, "we're not hiding anything."

Back at the USPP's Criminal Investigations Branch, Investigator Morrissette receives a telephone call from a man named Patrick Knowlton of Etlan, Virginia, who claims to have been at Fort Marcy Park on the afternoon of Foster's death.

Morrissette, who spells the name "Nolton," reports:

> During this conversation, [Knowlton] stated that he was travelling N/B on GWMP at approximately 4:30 p.m. at which time he pulled into the Fort Marcy parking lot for the purpose of relieving himself. He stated that he recalled that as he was parking, he noted a "brown foreign car with Arkansas plates" that was pulled into one of the first parking spaces available. Approximately 2-3 spaces away was what was described as a 1990 light metallic blue Honda with Va. tags. This vehicle was backed into the parking spot. It was occupied by a W/M described as follows:
>
> W/M, 25-30 yrs, 5'10"-5'11", 170 lbs, thin, mixed Mexican/American, short hair, tan complexion
>
> Mr. [Knowlton] stated that as he got out of his vehicle, this male subject was staring at [him] which made [Knowlton] feel uncomfortable. Mr. [Knowlton] relieved himself and immediately left the area. He stated that as he was pulling out from the Ft. Marcy area, he noted an older Chevy or Ford van, 1980s, dark brown, possibly a conversion type, to be driving into the parking area.

Morrissette shrugs off this report, believing that Knowlton, who is straight, had simply encountered a gay guy looking for some action.

15.

FRIDAY–SUNDAY, JULY 23–25, 1993

On Friday, July 23, Stephen Labaton of the *New York Times* reports his sources' view of the previous day's events: "With Justice Department lawyers looking over his shoulder, the White House counsel, Bernard W. Nussbaum, went through Mr. Foster's papers in his West Wing office,... looking for anything that could shed light on the death.

"'Nothing was found that was even remotely connected to his death,' said Dean St. Dennis, a spokesman for the Justice Department. 'Nothing was found to indicate foul play or murder.'

"Officials said the procedure for searching Mr. Foster's office was set up so it would protect the attorney-client privilege between Mr. Foster and the Clintons."

Meantime, the *Washington Times* publishes a quote from former congressman Beryl Anthony, Foster's brother-in-law, who was asked about a rumor that Foster had been depressed for the past two weeks and had taken Anthony into his confidence about this. According to the *Times's* article: "'There's not a damn thing to it. That's a bunch of crap,' Mr. Anthony said yesterday, slamming down the telephone at his El Dorado, Ark., home."

Also that morning, USPP criminalist Eugene J. Smith receives a request from Sergeant Rule to process Foster's gun for fingerprints. Because his partner is Peter Simonello, who is still on his scheduled four-day leave, Smith doesn't immediately respond to Rule's directive. After all, Simonello recovered, wrapped, and booked the gun. For identification purposes, Simonello had even scratched his initials underneath the grip of the revolver and placed a "Not processed. *Do not* handle." handwritten note on the gun.

Thus, Smith waits to talk to Captain Hume, who had given the initial request to Rule, before tampering with Simonello's evidence.

During that conversation, which is witnessed by Investigator Renee Abt, Hume confirms that he wants Smith to check the gun for latent prints, saying he wants to expedite the Foster case.

However, Smith warns Hume that the process of dusting for prints might destroy any other trace evidence—blood, fibers, hair, tissue, and other materials not clearly visible. Hume nevertheless tells Smith to proceed, even though Hume is not in Smith's normal chain of command. Smith and Simonello usually receive their work assignments from their immediate supervisor in ID Tech, Sergeant Danny Lawston. This is the first time that Smith has ever received a direct order from Hume of CIB.

But Hume is also under extreme pressure. His bosses, particularly Major Hines—and even Foster-family attorney Jim Hamilton, who has been calling him regularly on the telephone—are pushing him to get things done.

After recovering Foster's .38-caliber revolver from the evidence room and unwrapping it, Smith, still reluctant, dusts the gun with black powder and a fingerprint brush, ready to use lifting tape to pick up any latent prints. But when he examines the freshly powdered gun, he finds no prints at all, just possible smudges.

Smith isn't really greatly surprised, realizing that a number of factors might have contributed to this, including the slick surface of the gun and the coarseness of its handle, as well as the ambient temperature when the gun was used. And if Foster was sweating when he clutched the gun in the 90-degree-plus heat, his perspiration could have contributed, to some extent, to the destruction of his own and any other latent prints.

Soon after completing his assignment, Smith, during a conversation with Sergeants Lawston and Rule, says that he regrets conducting the test; that other tests on the barrel should have been conducted first, as Simonello had wanted.

Smith leaves a copy of his report for Simonello, whom he had decided not to call after receiving the direct order from Hume.

At Foster's 11 AM funeral service on Friday in a packed St. Andrew's Roman Catholic Cathedral in 103-degree Little Rock, a stoic President Clinton—accompanied by his wife and daughter, Chelsea—eulogizes his old friend, saying, "We owe it to him to make sure that he will never be evaluated by how his life ended, but by how it was lived."

Foster's body—which had been flown to Arkansas the day before on a Department of Defense plane, accompanied by Webb Hubbell—lay in a flag-draped coffin.

Foster is buried in Memory Garden Cemetery, 105 miles southwest of Little Rock off U.S. 67 in Hope, where he and the president had grown up together and Foster's mother, Alice Fae, still lives. The passengers in the forty-car motorcade to the cemetery include everyone who had been to the Fosters' home on the night of his death, as well as Janet Reno, Bernard Nussbaum, and U.S. Senators Dale Bumpers and David Pryor, both Arkansas Democrats, among many others.

On Sunday, July 25, USPP criminalist Peter Simonello returns to his office after his scheduled four-day leave. Over the next two days, he confirms that the five Polaroid pictures taken by Ferstl and the eight by Rolla have fully memorialized the crime scene.[60] They include pictures of the gun in Foster's right hand, as well as Foster's face with two streams of blood—one from his right nostril toward his right temple; the other from the right corner of his mouth that ran below his right ear—as well as blood stains on the right shoulder of his dress shirt and an apparent "transfer stain" on his right cheek and jaw.

But the twenty-four–shot roll of film Simonello had taken at the crime scene with his 35 mm camera is underexposed, with the negatives showing only faint images of Foster's body and the surrounding crime scene with virtually no detail. These pictures, which will become item number 39 on the property report, appear to be completely worthless—even though Simonello had used a flash for several of them. This is only the second time in Simonello's long career that anything like this has happened.[61]

Even though 35 mm film would have provided better pictures and clearer blow-ups, Simonello is relieved that, at least, he has the Polaroid shots taken by Ferstl and Rolla.

But, then, Simonello receives more bad news when he is told by Shelly Hill that his partner, E.J. Smith, had been ordered by Captain Hume to remove Foster's gun from the evidence locker, unwrap it, and dust it for fingerprints.

Simonello is furious that he had not been notified. After all, he had carefully wrapped the barrel of the gun, intending to test the weapon for trace evidence when he returned from his leave—and had punctuated his intention with his handwritten note on the gun. He can't blame his partner, because Smith had acted under orders of both Sergeant Rule and Captain Hume.

In his report, Simonello writes:

> On Sunday, July 25, 1993, I was advised by Tech. S. Hill that item #1 [the gun] had been processed for latent prints by Tech E.J. Smith and that the results were negative. The paper which I had placed around the barrel to preserve trace evidence had been removed and placed in a separate bag. Item #1 will be secured in the evidence locker to await any other testing deemed necessary.

Simonello then angrily confronts Hume, insisting that Foster's gun should not have been examined without his approval. Hume—who is still feeling the pressure from his own bosses, as well as Jim

Hamilton, to complete the investigation—defends his decision, criticizing Simonello for locking up all the evidence and then taking his leave without completing his work on such an important case. Simonello, a USPP shop steward, replies that he would have been willing to come in if Hume had simply called him.

Simonello then returns to his lab and checks Foster's glasses for fingerprints. However, he finds nothing more than an indistinct smudge and no clear prints.

Later, Simonello collects Foster's clothes that have been on a sheet of brown paper on the floor of the USPP crime lab's drying room. He takes each article of clothing, individually wrapping and storing them. As per standard operating procedure, he places the brown paper in a large evidence bag and books it as item number 38 on the property report.

Then, he receives even more bad news: Foster's articles of clothing had not been separated from each other at the coroner's office. In other words, they had been placed in an unsegregated pile and brought to the crime lab for drying.

Immediately, Simonello fears that Foster's clothing—with the exception of his suit coat and tie, which were found in the gray Honda—has probably been cross-contaminated.

16.

MONDAY, JULY 26, 1993

On Monday morning, July 26, Dr. Anh N. Huynh, a toxicologist for Virginia's Division of Forensic Science, submits the findings of his analysis of Foster's blood, urine, and tissue samples, provided by Dr. James Beyer, who had conducted the Foster autopsy. Dr. Huynh concludes that there is no evidence that Foster had been drinking alcohol or taking any legal or illegal drugs.

Meantime, Justice Department spokesman Carl Stern, a former television news reporter for NBC, announces that the department will not be conducting its own investigation of Foster's death. Instead, he says, Justice officials are cooperating fully with the U.S. Park Police, which has jurisdiction in the case. "There is no suspicion that a crime occurred," Stern states.

Major Hines, in his own statement on behalf of the USPP, describes their investigation as "routine," adding that the probe is concentrating more on Foster's motive than whether he committed suicide.

Back at the USPP/CIB office in Anacostia, Captain Hume is told that a CIA employee, Jim Ferris, who works at the Washington Navy Yard in southeast D.C., might have some information for investigators. Hume calls Ferris and writes in his report:

> On July 20, Ferris was on his way home to Sterling Park, Virginia, from Washington, D.C. where he works for the CIA. He always takes the George Washington Parkway home from work and drives past Fort Marcy Park. He passed Fort Marcy between 2:45 p.m.-3:05 p.m. on July 20, 1993. He was driving north on the Parkway in the right lane when he noticed a dark metallic gray, Japanese sedan, cut from the left northbound lane into the right lane and turn abruptly into Fort Marcy. The vehicle was occupied by a single white [male] who was the driver. He remembered an out-of-state license tag with blue letters, Midwestern, State of Ohio or Arkansas.[62] He recalled the state lettering in the lower right corner.... He thought [it] was unusual to see an out-of-state vehicle go into Fort Marcy. He was unable to offer any further description of the vehicle or driver.

Had Ferris really seen Foster enter the park?

That same day, July 26, the August 2 issue of *Newsweek* is released. In the lead story, staff writers Howard Fineman and Bob Cohn report that at about the same time as Foster was leaving the White House on July 20, his wife, Lisa, and her close friend, Donna McLarty, Mack McLarty's wife, were having lunch at the Garden Terrace Restaurant in the Four Seasons Hotel on M Street in Georgetown. The reporters then say that Lisa Foster had confided in Donna McLarty that her husband had been under extreme pressure, that he was not sleeping well and losing weight.[63]

Fineman and Cohn add: "[O]n Sunday night, the president himself called and tried to buck up his friend with 20 minutes of chatter. On Monday night, Bruce Lindsey, the White House personnel director and another close friend and lawyer from Little Rock, dropped by and asked Foster if he wanted to catch a movie. Too busy, replied Foster. At a staff meeting earlier that day, Foster seemed preoccupied. His mind was elsewhere. It was too late."

17.

TUESDAY, JULY 27, 1993

At the beginning of Dee Dee Myers's afternoon briefing to the White House press corps, the session is dominated by a proposed budget summit between the White House and Congress, recent violence in the Middle East, the Iranian government's support for the Hezbollah, the president's proposed legislation for National Service and the threatened Republican filibuster opposing it, and the American economy.

Finally, one week after Foster's death at Fort Marcy Park, things seem to be getting back to normal at the White House.

But, whatever illusions the White House has that the Foster case is going to go away are quickly dashed. The article in

Newsweek has set the Washington press corps off on a frantic search for Foster's motive.

The cracks in the White House's cool facade begin to appear when ABC White House correspondent Brit Hume asks, "Could you comment on the *Newsweek* report that President Clinton spoke to Vince Foster on Sunday? A, is it true? B, do you know what he said to him, [and] why the president didn't mention it when he was asked about it?"

"I think it's something that we've said before," Myers replies.

"No," Hume fires back. "Trust me."

"No? [The president] did speak to him on Sunday. He called him, as he often did. Vince Foster was somebody that the president spoke to frequently."

"Did he call him to 'buck him up,' as *Newsweek* suggested?"

"He called to talk to him, I think—[about] a number of things. I think that he knew, as a number of people did, that Vince was having a rough time."

"Wait a minute," Hume interrupts. "That's the first time you've said that from this platform."

Defensively, Myers answers, "No, it's not. I think what we have said in the past was that people have their ups and downs and that—"

"Your tone has completely changed."

"Okay," Myers relents, "I apologize. I'm sorry. It is not. Okay. Let me just try to say what I think. What I said certainly on Thursday [was that] there was absolutely no reason to believe that Vince was despondent, that he was in any way considering doing what happened. Nobody believed that. At the same time, I think that the Counsel's Office had its trials and tribulations.... "

The correspondents continue to insist that during the July 22 press briefing, as well as in all other authorized statements from the White House, no one had even suggested that Foster was suffering from depression.

Another reporter asks, "Could you ask the president why he called?"

"I've talked to him about this and he—"

"And he said?"

"He called him for a number of reasons. Because he called him frequently, and he wanted to see how he was, among other things. Because, as was well known and documented, the Counsel's Office had a rough go of it."

Another reporter asks, "A rough go in what respect?"

"There have been a number of editorials [in the *Wall Street Journal*] and other things quite recently. The president obviously was close to Vince.... He checks in on people regularly. That's not to say that the president was oblivious to what might have been going on, but nobody, including the president, expected that to happen."

"We understand that," the correspondent continues. "No one is saying that."

"So, all I'm trying to do is stay away from this notion that somehow—"

"You knew," the reporter says, trying to finish Myers's sentence for her.

"...that things were different than what we've thought they were last week," Myers says, finishing her own sentence.

Later in the press briefing, after a reporter tries to change the subject, another journalist asks, "Can I go back to Foster, please?... The way that you, the president, and McLarty spoke last Wednesday about this was it was an unexplained mystery. There was no reason to go beyond the evidence that it was a suicide. And there seemed to be, given the characterization you're providing today, that he was obviously troubled. You were widely aware that he was having difficulty. There seems to be a sense at the time that the president didn't say, 'I was trying to help my friend, and it failed.' Instead of that, he said, 'I accept this as an unexplained mystery, and there's no need to go into it.' Why did he portray it that way when, obviously, he was trying—and his friends were trying—to bring this fellow some hope?"

"That is way too dramatic a reading," Myers insists. "There was no reason to believe that it was anything other than the kinds of ups and downs that people have gone through in this White House...."

"But why [do] you believe otherwise? Today, some of your answers indicate that you all have basically come to a conclusion that the job got him down and could have led to it."

"I don't mean... to suggest that I have any answers to it."

"But," the reporter continues, "this is the overriding theme: That he was depressed and despondent."

"No," Myers replies, beginning to stumble badly. "That he was suffering. I don't even want to say 'suffering.' You guys are reading too much into it...."

Finally, a reporter comes to Myers's rescue and tries to sum up what she is attempting but failing to articulate, asking, "Would it be fair to say that everyone who knew him well here thought he was discouraged, but no one thought he was suicidal?"

"Absolutely," Myers concludes with considerable relief.

Soon after Myers's briefing, the White House corrects the report published in *Newsweek*, saying that the president had not talked to Foster for twenty minutes on Sunday night—but, rather, on Monday, July 19, the night *before* Foster died. The White House adds that the president had called Foster, because he knew that Foster was "having a rough time" with his job. The president had called Foster at home, asking if he wanted to see a movie, Clint Eastwood's *In the Line of Fire*, at the White House, along with Webster Hubbell and Bruce Lindsey.

As *Newsweek* had accurately reported, Foster declined the invitation.

But why is the White House now suddenly conceding that Foster was depressed?

Unknown to just about everyone at this time, including the Park Police and the Department of Justice, a torn-up note has been found among his possessions.

18.

ALSO ON TUESDAY, JULY 27, Captain Hume and Investigator John Rolla meet with and interview Vincent Foster's brother-in-law, Washington attorney Beryl F. Anthony, Jr., a former seven-term U.S. representative from Arkansas, who had been defeated in 1992. It was Anthony who, four days earlier, in response to a *Washington Times* question about Foster's depression, allegedly replied, "There's not a damn thing to it. That's a bunch of crap."

Changing his tone considerably, Anthony tells the police investigators that when Foster first arrived in Washington as part of Clinton's team from Arkansas in January 1993, he stayed with him and his wife, Sheila Anthony. But Foster really did little more than sleep at their home. As the USPP had already learned, Foster spent most of his time working—and even ate most of his meals—at the White House.

Foster stayed with the Anthonys for nearly three months and was finally reunited with his family in early June when his youngest child, Brugh, finished his junior year of high school in Little Rock. With the school year completed, Lisa Foster came to Washington, and the Fosters moved into their rented townhouse in Georgetown. The Fosters kept their own home in Little Rock but rented it out, providing a steady cash flow. They wanted their son to finish high school in Washington.

According to Rolla's report of the interview with Anthony:

> Mr. Anthony stated that he and his wife had noticed a gradual decline in Mr. Foster's general disposition to the point of depression. Mr. Anthony stated that Mr. Foster was not handling the politics in Washington, D.C., very well and blamed himself personally for the failed nominations for Attorney General and some of the sub-Cabinet posts. Mr. Foster also was very upset over some unfavorable articles printed by the Wall Street Journal in the last several weeks and seemed to take them personally. Mr. Anthony stated [that] Mr. Foster was also concerned about his legal advice and his role in the firing of seven White House travel office aides, aka (Travelgate)....
>
> Mr. Anthony stated that he believed his wife had given Mr. Foster a list of three counselors, psychiatrists or other doctors who do counseling. Mr. Anthony stated that during a conversation approximately three weeks prior to Mr. Foster's death, Mr. Foster made a comment to the effect, "I have spent a lifetime building my reputation, and now I am in the process of having it tarnished."

When Anthony mentions the three doctors recommended by his wife, Hume and Rolla assume that this explains the names of the three doctors Rolla had found in Foster's wallet on July 20. Yet, during Rolla and Abt's earlier follow-up calls, none of the doctors said that they had ever seen or met Foster.

Anthony also says that Foster had possession of "an old gun" that had been owned by his father. But, when shown photographs of the .38-caliber revolver found in Foster's hand at Fort Marcy Park, Anthony can't positively identify it as the one he had previously seen in his father-in-law's gun collection.

Anthony recalls that he had last spoken to Foster on July 12 at which time the deputy counsel expressed his concern about an official investigation into the Travel Office matter. Foster had asked Anthony "to refer him to an attorney," according to Rolla's report. Anthony says that he responded to Foster's request on July 15 at 6:53 PM; a messenger delivered a package from Anthony to Foster's home, containing background information about six Washington attorneys.[64]

Captain Hume and Rolla leave the interview extremely impressed with Anthony and believe that they are finally starting to get some cooperation, which over the past week has been sorely lacking.

Just before 8 PM on Tuesday night, Captain Hume receives a call at home on his beeper from David Margolis of the Justice Department. Hume immediately calls back, and Margolis tells him that a note, written by Vincent Foster, has been discovered. Margolis invites Hume to come to the White House and pick up the note.

Because Hume lives in Charles County, Maryland, and has settled in for the evening, he calls his office where Detective Joseph Megby is on duty. Hume instructs Megby to drive to the White House and pick up the note, adding that he will be cleared for entry.

Megby arrives at the West Wing to meet with Nussbaum at about 9 PM, but waits fifteen minutes before Philip Heymann comes to escort him upstairs. Along with Heymann, Jim Hamilton, Mack McLarty, and Bill Burton are also present for the transfer of this mysterious note.

Megby writes in his report:

> Mr. Nussbaum had before him on the table small pieces of
> yellow lined note paper which he was assembling into a
> whole page. The assembled pieces revealed a note, identified
> to be in the handwriting of the deceased Vincent Foster. Mr.
> Nussbaum read the contents of the [note] to [me] of which I
> took notes. He then placed the pieces back into a white legal
> White House envelope and handed [it] over to me.

After writing out the contents of the note on his detective's pad, Megby learns that Steve Neuwirth, Nussbaum's associate in the Counsel's Office, had found the note the day before while conducting an inventory of the "files and material" in Foster's office. Neuwirth discovered the torn-up note in a briefcase, which had been "thought to be empty," according to Megby's report.[65]

Megby places the envelope containing the torn-up note in his pocket and leaves the meeting. Just before Megby leaves, Nussbaum asks him, "Are you going to fingerprint the note?"

As Megby is walking out, Foster-family attorney Jim Hamilton, who was present for only part of the meeting, stops him and expresses his concern "about the confidential nature of the note and other news leaks attributed to the U.S. Park Police," according to Megby's report.

On returning to the USPP/CIB office after 10 PM, Megby, who had dropped off Heymann at the Justice Department, slides the envelope under Hume's locked office door—as Hume had earlier instructed.

19.

WEDNESDAY, JULY 28, 1993

Not yet aware of the discovery of the torn-up note, the *Wall Street Journal*, which had already called for the appointment of a "spe-

cial counsel" to investigate Foster's death, publishes another editorial, "Self-Fulfilling Prophecy," on Wednesday, complaining
that the Justice Department, instead of making the appointment,
has backed away from any independent scrutiny of the case.

The *Journal* adds: "The vigorous investigation has not taken
place, and apparently will not. White House counsel Bernard
Nussbaum sorted through Mr. Foster's papers, removing any that
fell under attorney-client privilege with the President, and gave us
his word that nothing shed light on the suicide. So nothing will be
done to tell the public why so sensitive an official took his own
life, or for that matter, reassure us that he indeed did. The mystery, we suspect, will haunt the White House as further scandals
pop up, as they do in most administrations."

When Captain Hume arrives in his office early that morning, he
finds the envelope that Detective Megby has placed under his door.
Without touching the contents, Hume gives it to Pete Simonello.

Hume then walks over to Detective Markland and tells him
that a torn-up note from Foster has been found. When Markland
asks where the note was discovered, Hume replies, "In Foster's
briefcase—the one Nussbaum searched on the floor."

"Bullshit!" Markland exclaims in total disbelief. "Either it didn't
come out of the briefcase, or Nussbaum was lying that he didn't see
the note!"

After slipping on a pair of cotton gloves, Simonello carefully opens
the envelope and finds a twenty-seven–piece jigsaw puzzle. The
note, which has seemingly been torn up with a vengeance, is written in black ink on a piece of lined paper from a yellow legal pad.

Working slowly and deliberately, Simonello pieces together the
note, which states:

*I made mistakes from ignorance, inexperience and
overwork*

*I did not knowingly violate any law or standard of
conduct*

*No one in the White House, to my knowledge, violated
any law or standard of conduct, including any action in
the travel office. There was no intent to benefit any individual or specific group*

The FBI lied in their report to the AG

*The press is covering up the illegal benefits they received
from the travel staff*

*The GOP has lied and misrepresented its knowledge
and role and covered up a prior investigation*

*The Ushers Office[66] plotted to have excessive costs
incurred, taking advantage of Kaki and HRC[67]*

*The public will never believe the innocence of the
Clintons and their loyal[68] staff*

The WSJ editors lie without consequence

*I was not meant for the job or the spotlight of public life
in Washington. Here ruining people is considered sport.*

After assembling the note, Simonello discovers that one piece of
the puzzle—the twenty-eighth piece, triangular in shape, in the
lower-right portion of the page—is missing. Simonello thinks this
strange, even though the text of the note is above the missing piece.
He believes that the author of the note might have possibly signed,
initialed, or dated the page where the missing piece should be.

Simonello places the document in a clear plastic folder—to prevent anyone's fingerprints from appearing on the note inside.
With the pieces of the note clinging to the plastic, Simonello photographs and photocopies the note; he identifies this new evidence
as item number 35 on the property report.

But after reading the note repeatedly, Simonello personally concludes that it is *not* Foster's suicide note, because there is no mention of his family or why he had decided to take his own life.

After discussing the matter with his supervisor, Sergeant Lawston, Simonello decides to obtain another confirmed sample of Foster's handwriting and then call in a handwriting expert to compare the two documents.

News of the existence of the note—but not its contents—leaks quickly. CBS Radio is first to break the story, followed by an avalanche of follow-up reports by other news organizations.

Trying to get ahead of the media frenzy before the evening television news, the White House decides to confirm the discovery of the torn-up note. White House communications director Mark Gearan tells reporters that an attorney in Nussbaum's office had stumbled across the note—which Gearan also refuses to classify as a suicide note—while packing up Foster's personal effects in his office. Gearan insists that the note "goes to [Foster's] state of mind" and is consistent with the USPP's preliminary conclusion that Foster had committed suicide.

Gearan adds, "There was no discussion about not turning the note over [to the Park Police]. It was being examined for any protected material. And basic decency required that Mrs. Foster and the president be told of its contents first."

The general response to that statement is: How long did all of that take?

At 2:35 PM on Wednesday, the Park Police releases Foster's 1989 gray Honda Accord to Craig Livingstone, the director of White House security, who then parks it on West Executive Avenue near the White House.[69]

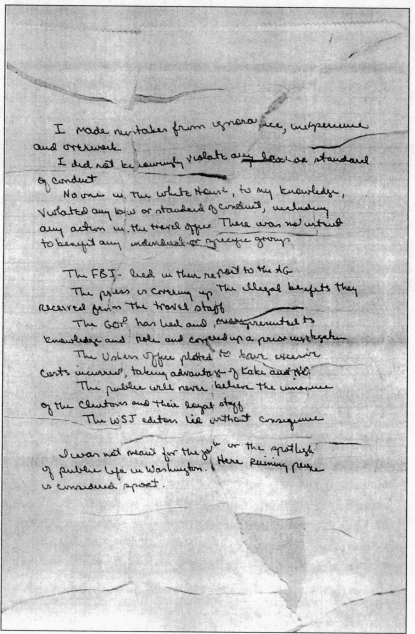

The torn-up note found in Foster's briefcase. (USPP)

Meantime, USPP/CIB Lieutenant Robert Kass and Investigator Rolla go to the office of Foster-family attorney Jim Hamilton, who has gained possession of Foster's personal documents that had been found in his office during the July 22 search. (These files are from one of the three stacks of documents that Nussbaum had created during the search. The other two were the Clintons' personal files and general White House records.)

Under Hamilton's watchful supervision, Kass and Rolla—finally—are permitted to view these records, which are contained in three boxes. Also present during the meeting is John Sloan, an architect from Arkansas and the executor of Foster's estate.

In the midst of their review, Rolla comes across a hardbound-journal book with approximately a hundred lined pages, about nine inches long and six inches wide. Seeing what Rolla is holding, Hamilton protests, claiming that the contents of the journal are personal and confidential.

Rolla replies, "We don't want to embarrass anybody, but this is potential evidence. And, if there's something here we need, we're going to take it."

Reluctantly, Hamilton permits Rolla to read the journal.

As Rolla opens the book, he sees that the first several pages are blank. However, they are followed by ten to fifteen pages of Foster's handwriting. The pages that come after that are also blank.

Realizing that he has what appears to be some sort of diary, Rolla bends back the binding of the book at each page of written copy in order to examine whether any pages have been torn or cut out. He concludes that none of the pages is missing.

But, as he reads what Foster has written, Rolla quickly determines that the time frame of this short diary is between the Clinton's election on November 3, 1992, and his inauguration on January 20, 1993.

As Rolla, who takes no notes, continues to read, he finds nothing particularly revealing. Although Foster makes much of his close friendship with Hillary Clinton, Rolla sees that there is nothing unwholesome in what has been written. To the contrary, Foster is very respectful of Mrs. Clinton, proudly predicting that she will be an activist first lady, especially with regard to health-care issues.

In fact, when Rolla finishes going through the diary, he asks rhetorically why Hamilton made such a fuss about it in the first place.

After their meeting with Hamilton, Kass and Rolla, at the request of Pete Simonello, are permitted to take a photocopied, not original, sample of Foster's handwriting, which can be compared to the handwriting on the torn-up note.[70]

20.

THURSDAY, JULY 29, 1993

The mad rush to delve into Vincent Foster's private life in the hope of finding something sensational continues.

In the morning newspapers, reporter Douglas Jehl of the *New York Times*, quoting federal officials and sources close to Foster, writes that Foster "had displayed signs of depression in the final month of his life," revealing that Foster "had been so depressed about his job that before his death he had spent several reclusive weekends working at home in bed with the shades drawn."[71] Jehl, who also knows about the names of the Washington psychiatrists found in Foster's wallet, adds that Foster's family doctor in Little Rock had "sent anti-depressant medication to Mr. Foster.

"The medication arrived in the final days of Mr. Foster's life, but he apparently had only just begun to take it, said a person close to the family."

Ann Devroy of the *Washington Post*, who also reports about the list of psychiatrists, sums up the White House's self-inflicted predicament, writing: "After originally describing Foster's death as a shock that mystified the White House and President Clinton, the White House over the past several days has—in the face of revelations from friends and law enforcement officials—acknowledged a far more depressed and unhappy official than it first described."

A little more than merely curious about the circumstances under which the torn-up note had been found, Captain Hume and Detective Markland return to the White House at 11:30 PM to interview Nussbaum and Associate Counsel Steve Neuwirth.

Although there is, once again, tension in the room, Nussbaum doesn't appear to be at all defensive. In fact, the White House counsel is almost matter-of-fact about the whole situation and gives the Park Police investigators "take-it-or-leave-it" answers to their pointed questions.

Jotting down notes during the meeting, Markland reports that the document was discovered by Neuwirth, saying:

> [Neuwirth] stated that he was in the process of gathering and packaging Mr. Foster's personal [effects] for delivery to the family when he turned the briefcase sideways in order to fit it into a box without causing damage to a photograph of the president with Mr. Foster's daughter, Laura. When he did this, some torn yellow paper scraps fell out of the briefcase, and he noticed handwriting on them. He then retrieved a number of other similar scraps from the bottom of the case and took them to the table in Mr. Nussbaum's office where he assembled the document which was, ultimately, turned over to Detective Megby.

Neuwirth even brings Foster's briefcase into Nussbaum's office and re-creates for Hume and Markland how he stumbled across the note. After Neuwirth finishes, Markland takes the briefcase and looks inside, hoping to find the missing twenty-eighth piece of the torn-up note. But he discovers only a paper clip.

Clearly upset with this recent development, Markland asks both Nussbaum and Neuwirth two questions:

> "How could this note have avoided detection during the search of Mr. Foster's office by Mr. Nussbaum and other members of the White House Counsel's office in our presence on 7/22/93?" and

> "If the note was found on 7/26/93, why were the police not notified of [its] existence until approximately 8 p.m. on 7/27/93?"

Reporting Nussbaum's response to the first question, Markland writes:

> Mr. Nussbaum stated it was his recollection that he removed materials from the briefcase, which remained on the floor, and placed them on the desk in front of him. He then went through the materials. He [implied] that because of this he had missed the small scraps of yellow paper that obviously remained in the bottom of the briefcase.

Refusing to believe Nussbaum's story, Markland challenges him, writing in his report:

> I informed Mr. Nussbaum that I was seated on the small couch directly across from and facing him and that I had a clear view of the briefcase when he removed [its] contents.... [A]fter the contents were removed, I could see that he spread open the briefcase and visually inspected it as if to confirm that it was, indeed, empty. Mr. Nussbaum did not recall doing what I described. Captain Hume stated that he observed that Mr. Nussbaum handled the briefcase a third time when he slid it back towards the wall behind him in order to access the desk's file drawer. Mr. Nussbaum agreed with Captain Hume's recollection of sliding the case to the rear.

In response to the second question, Nussbaum states that after he realized that Foster had written the note, he contacted Mack McLarty and Bill Burton in the White House Chief of Staff's Office and Lisa Foster (via James Hamilton),[72] as well as Philip Heymann and Janet Reno, who instructed Nussbaum to give the note to the Park Police immediately.

Nussbaum also mentions to Hume and Markland that President Clinton had been told of the note—although he has not seen it—adding that only Nussbaum and Neuwirth have actually handled the note.

At 3:22 PM on Thursday, in another briefing for the White House press corps, Dee Dee Myers is bombarded with questions about the Foster case, especially regarding the torn-up note, whose contents have still not been either released or leaked.

One reporter asks, "How many hours did the White House have the note before they turned it over to the Park Police?"

Myers replies, "The note was discovered Monday afternoon and turned over Tuesday evening, so a little over twenty-four—"

"So somewhere between twenty-four and thirty hours before you gave that evidence to the Park Police?"

"Yes. It was our judgment that the best thing to do was to make sure that the family had a chance to see it. Lisa Foster was coming to Washington on Tuesday for business unrelated to this letter and was informed about it when she got here. And the president, who was out of town on Monday, was also informed on Tuesday."

"Did the president see the note?"

"He didn't see the note, but he was briefed as to its contents."

"So your position on this was rather than turn over the evidence in an investigation,... you would wait however many hours or days it took to show the family first?"

"And then we promptly called the Justice Department," Myers says, defending the White House.

During this press briefing, Myers also notes that President Clinton and Foster, during their telephone conversation on July 19, had agreed to meet on Wednesday, July 21—even though it did not appear on Foster's calendar.

That scheduled meeting never occurred, of course.

21.

SHORTLY AFTER THE PRESS BRIEFING at the White House, Captain Hume and Detective Pete Markland begin their first and only interview with Lisa Foster, Vincent Foster's widow—nine days after his death. They meet at the law offices of Swidler & Berlin; Washington attorney James Hamilton, who had done legal work for the Clinton transition team, represents Mrs. Foster and insists from the outset that there will be no waiver of his attorney-client privilege with her or her late husband.[73]

Also in attendance, at the request of Mrs. Foster, are Beryl Anthony and family friend John Sloan, Vincent Foster's executor.

The atmosphere in the room is relaxed and comfortable, but Hamilton is clearly in control and totally protective of his client. Lisa Foster appears composed, dignified, and cooperative.

In her verbal statement to the investigators, she confirms published reports that she and her husband lived apart while their youngest child finished the school year. She explains that, finally, on June 5, 1993, the family reunited in Washington.

Almost immediately, she began to notice that her husband wasn't sleeping well, attributing it to the pressure he was under at the White House. He had even told his sister, Sheila Anthony, that he had developed high blood pressure. Mrs. Anthony, Lisa Foster confirms, had provided Vincent Foster with the names of the three psychiatrists. But Mrs. Foster does not know whether he had ever contacted any of them.

Lisa Foster adds that—the day before his death—her husband had called their family physician, Dr. Larry Watkins in Little Rock, saying that he wasn't feeling well. Dr. Watkins prescribed Trazodone, a mild antidepressant medication, for her husband. At her suggestion, he took one 50 mg tablet on the night before his death. Curiously, neither Dr. Beyer, who performed the autopsy, nor his lab technicians found any trace of any kind of drug in Foster's system.

Providing some background information, Mrs. Foster says that her husband, once a top attorney in Little Rock, had always felt in control while living in Arkansas. In Washington, however, he had begun to fret that he was losing that control.

In the past, when her husband felt stress, he relieved it through activities with his family. But now with their children grown, Vincent and Lisa Foster had decided, after she moved to Washington, to spend more time with each other.

To the police investigators, this explains such ventures as the couple's trip to Maryland's Eastern Shore where they socialized with Webb and Suzy Hubbell[74] at the sprawling estate of Washington attorney Michael Cardozo, who had the same position as Foster in the Carter White House, and his wife, Harolyn, on Saturday and Sunday, July 17 and 18, the weekend before Foster's death on the 20th.

Although Mrs. Foster confesses that this final getaway "had not gone particularly well," the couple had made a decision to be patient, knowing that "things would take time and not change overnight."

Markland continues in his report of the interview with Mrs. Foster:

> The criticism of the president in the news media, the Travel Office investigation, the scrutiny by the press of the people from Arkansas, and even the stress of the family

> move to Washington in June all seemed to Lisa Foster to
> have a cumulative effect on Vincent Foster. He "took it all
> personally" and once stated to her, "How did I get myself
> into this?"...
>
> Vincent Foster had an extreme loyalty to the Clinton
> administration and was trying to protect it. He felt he had
> personally failed and talked to Lisa about quitting.
> [H]owever, [he] would not return to Arkansas (because of
> the personal humiliation he felt). Lisa Foster felt that
> something physical came over Vincent quickly.

Regarding the torn-up note found in Vincent Foster's battered black-leather briefcase, Mrs. Foster tells Hume and Markland that she had advised him "to write down his concerns, and he probably did so in preparation for any upcoming investigation into his activities and decision-making processes."

She estimates that Foster had written the note a week to a week and a half before his death.

Although she says she is aware of guns in their home in Arkansas, Mrs. Foster cannot identify a photograph of the black .38-caliber revolver found in her husband's right hand. However, she suggests to Hume and Markland that they show the photograph to her sister-in-law, Sharon Bowman, who has a "better knowledge of firearms owned by and passed down through the Foster family."

Hume and Markland provide a copy of the photograph to John Sloan, asking him to show it to Mrs. Bowman, who lives in Hope, Arkansas.

Speaking of the day of his death, Mrs. Foster remembers that her husband's "mood seemed better than it had been 'in a while.'" She volunteers that she has never been to Fort Marcy Park and doesn't even know where it is. The investigators state in their report:

> The last time Lisa Foster saw her husband was on the
> morning of July 20th at approximately 8:30 a.m. when he left

for work driving the Honda.[75] She left the house shortly
thereafter for an appointment and does not know whether or
not he returned to the residence that afternoon. Her son
[Brugh] may have been in the basement during the early afternoon, but it would be possible for Vincent Foster to enter and
exit the residence without the son realizing his presence.[76]

Soon after the three-hour interview concludes, Hume already
regrets not asking Lisa Foster several lingering questions. Were
there any problems between her and her husband at home? Was
the family in the midst of a financial crisis? Was her husband
involved with another woman?

Nevertheless, the interview with Mrs. Foster, to all intents and
purposes, ends any official suspicion that Foster's death is anything but a suicide.

Back at the USPP/CIB office, Captain Hume gives the photo-
copied page of Vincent Foster's handwriting, which Lieutenant
Kass and John Rolla had received from Jim Hamilton, to Pete
Simonello to compare with the handwriting on the torn-up note
found in Foster's briefcase. Because the Park Police do not have a
handwriting expert on staff, Sergeant Larry G. Lockhart of the
U.S. Capitol Police receives the call from Simonello to come to
Anacostia to make the comparison.

Upon Lockhart's arrival, Simonello gives him Foster's confirmed photocopied writing sample and Foster's torn-up note that
Simonello had pieced together. Lockhart, who considers the photocopied page of "excellent quality," performs his examination
there at the USPP/ID Division office.

In his written statement, Lockhart, who inspects the materials
for about an hour, reports:

> The examination consisted of studying the Standard Writings [Known] and locating writing characteristics that appear throughout the written words and letter characters which are unique to the writer. Then, the Signature Document [Questioned] [was] studied to locate those characteristics that are unique to a particular writer in the way alphabetical characters, groups of alphabetical characters, numerical digits and written words are completed.... Both the Known and Questioned Documents were completed by the same writer/author and that writer/author is known as Vincent W. Foster.

After receiving Lockhart's report and the two documents written by Foster, Simonello gives the original of the torn-up note to Captain Hume.

22.

FRIDAY, JULY 30, 1993

The story of the day appears in the *Washington Post*, co-written by reporters Ann Devroy and Michael Isikoff, who have uncovered several key events in the wake of the discovery of the torn-up note.

Devroy and Isikoff report that after White House Associate Counsel Stephen Neuwirth found the note in Foster's office and realized its significance on Monday, he called Nussbaum, who then telephoned McLarty, who was with President Clinton and presidential advisor David Gergen in Chicago. Told that the note wasn't an actual suicide note, McLarty discussed the matter with Gergen.

According to Devroy and Isikoff, McLarty and Gergen decided that in view of potential issues involving executive privilege and "basic decency" toward the Foster family, they wanted a legal review and to "discuss it with the president."[77]

"On Tuesday,..." the *Post* story continues, "[McLarty and Gergen] had a series of meetings as they awaited the arrival in Washington of Lisa Foster and her attorney [James Hamilton]. [Janet] Reno and Deputy Attorney General Philip B. Heymann were asked to go to the White House for a discussion late in the day, as soon as Clinton's tight schedule allowed him to fully discuss the matter.

"Reno said the note should not be given to the Justice Department but to the Park Police as the lead investigators. By 8 p.m. Tuesday, more than 30 hours after its discovery, police investigators were called to the White House and given the note."

The *Post* also quotes USPP Chief Robert Langston, saying, "It's been hard getting some material out of [the White House]... [A] lot of political sensitivity has been brought into it."

For the first time, the nonparticipation of the Park Police and the Department of Justice during the search of Foster's office by Nussbaum is reported.

But, unknown to the *Post*, Heymann had already ordered the FBI to conduct an investigation into the circumstances surrounding the White House's handling of Foster's note. The bureau's interviews with White House personnel had begun the previous afternoon.[78]

Also on Friday, still frustrated with their inability to obtain Foster's telephone logs from the White House, Captain Hume and his superiors appeal to Tom Collier, Secretary Bruce Babbitt's chief of staff at the Department of the Interior, which oversees the USPP. Collier had already read the article in the *Post*, which appears to stimulate more aggressive official action.

Hume and USPP Assistant Chief Andre Jordan, accompanied by USPP Detective David Rayfield, visit Collier. Hume complains that the White House Counsel's Office has not provided them with, among other items, Foster's telephone log. Collier tells them that he will see what he can do.[79] Soon after, Hume and Rayfield go to the Old Executive Office Building—this time to meet with Associate Counsel Clifford Sloan. According to Hume's report:

> The purpose of the meeting was to examine the
> telephone message log of Vincent Foster during the month
> of July and, in particular, to attempt to determine if he had
> gotten a call just prior to his departure on July 20.

In a somewhat surprising turnabout, Sloan is totally cooperative and provides the police investigators with Foster's telephone log without the usual White House hassle.

However, Hume and Rayfield quickly discover that the log is only messages. Whoever answered the calls recorded the callers' name, phone number, and message, as well as the time of the call. But any call that Foster actually accepted is *not* listed on the log.

Regardless, Hume and Rayfield learn that at 10:47 AM on July 19, the day before his death, Foster had received a call from Dr. Larry Watkins, who left no message other than that he had called.

Then, on the day of Foster's death, the log lists the following:

- At 10:55 AM, a man named C. Brantley Buck called. He left his telephone number in Little Rock but no message.

- At 11:01 AM, William Kennedy called; he left no message.

- At 11:11 AM, Maggie Williams, Hillary Clinton's chief of staff, called; no message.

- Then, Cheryl Mills of the White House staff called; she left no message.

- Soon after, a man named Jim Lyons called. He left his telephone number in Denver, Colorado, but no message.

- Brant Buck called again. He left the same number but still no message.

Foster had walked out of his office between 1:00 and 1:10 PM. After he left, he received the following calls:

- At 1:40 PM, Kennedy called again; again, no message.

- Also at 1:40 PM, Stephen Neuwirth called; no message.

- At 2:14 PM, Mills called again. This time she left a message: "[She] needs to call Justice on a new matter; if she cannot reach you, she will go ahead and call."

- Soon after, a man named Gordon Rather called. He left his telephone number in Little Rock and the following message: "personal matter."

- At 3:35 PM, Williams called again; again, no message.

- At 5:10 PM, Lisa Foster called; she left no message.

Hume concludes his report, stating:

> Clifford Sloan requested if any information about the phone logs is contemplated being released, he would like to have the Counsel's Office notified at the White House prior to any release. I told him that I would put his request in my report. This caused him some concern, because he didn't want special or unusual attention drawn to his request.[80]

At 1:47 PM, Dee Dee Myers faces the White House press corps again, this time to respond to many of the questions raised by Devroy and Isikoff in the *Post*.

"Dee Dee," the first reporter asks, "in connection with the Vince Foster case, the police are described in this morning's paper—the *Washington Post*—as saying that the White House hindered their case by slowing down the examination of the evidence, especially the note. Do you have a reaction to that? And, also in the search of Foster's office, was it actually Bernie Nussbaum who physically went through all of that evidence?..."

Myers replies, "Bernie did actually do the physical going through, because many of those documents are protected by either executive privilege or attorney-client privilege. And so Bernie went through and sort of described the contents of each of [Foster's] files and what was in his drawers while representatives of the Justice Department, the Secret Service, the FBI, and other members of the Counsel's Office were present."

"Was that the only time any White House official had gone through those documents?"

"That was the first time. And I believe, then, an associate counsel catalogued the files in Vince's office.... I think that Mr. Nussbaum conducted a very thorough investigation, particularly in terms of what they were looking for. I mean, he went through the files and described what the issues were, and what the contents of the files were without having them read the specific documents."

"So the investigators had to rely on his characterization of everything?"

"That's correct."

"And, Dee Dee, he missed the note. Didn't Nussbaum miss the note?"

"Well, it was at the bottom of Vince's briefcase, torn up. So, yes, they didn't discover it until Monday."

"Well, how can you characterize it as a thorough investigation when he didn't find the most salient piece of evidence that's been found so far?"

"Your characterization," Myers snaps back, "not ours or anybody else's...."

A reporter asks, "Was it a thorough search?"

"Yes," Myers replies, "I think we feel it was a thorough investigation."

23.

SATURDAY–MONDAY, JULY 31–AUGUST 2, 1993

Saturday, July 31, is the first day of rest in the Vincent Foster case. No major developments occur; no major revelations about the probe appear in the newspapers or on television.

Sunday is a slow day, as well. The *Washington Post* publishes an editorial, criticizing the White House for its repeated missteps, saying: "We don't think Mr. Gearan or Ms. Myers were trying to cover up anything. But it is not helpful—to the administration or to Mr. Foster's family—to send top aides out to give briefings when they have not been given much in the way of information.... But too much has been leaked, and the White House has shifted its ground too often to let matters sit where they are now."

At 2 that afternoon, Captain Hume and Detective Markland inform Officer Simonello that Foster's torn-up note has been given to the FBI; once again, the pressure has come from above. Simonello had been planning to process the note for latent prints that day. Instead, the FBI will perform the task—even though Foster's note is critical of the FBI, which, Simonello fears, will lead to more controversy. But Simonello does not know that Deputy Attorney General Heymann had already ordered the FBI to investigate the events before and after the discovery of Foster's note.

On Monday, August 2, the August 9 issue of *The New Yorker* features a detailed article by Sidney Blumenthal in his "Letter from Washington" column in which he quotes Hillary Clinton saying, "Of a thousand people, of those who *might* commit suicide, I would never pick Vince."

Among other aspects of the case, Blumenthal lists the theories being discussed about the presumed suicide of Vincent Foster, writing: "Perhaps Foster had even known of [a] terrible exposé that was coming and had sought to preempt it by killing himself. Was he a closet homosexual? Had he attempted a gay liaison at Fort Marcy Park and been spurned? Or would the *Washington Times* publish a story about his having had a secret affair with his former law partner Hillary Rodham Clinton?"

Seeming to believe that Foster had killed himself at least in part because of what he considered the intense and allegedly unfair press coverage of his activities, Blumenthal continues: "The concept of service has little political currency in Washington. Everyone is fair game, simply for being on the other side. Humiliating one's prey, not merely defeating one's foes, is central to the process. The press is hardly an impartial referee; rather, it is often caught up in a blindered game of chase."

Blumenthal notes that Foster had several discussions about the press with distinguished journalist Walter Pincus of the *Washington Post*, who is married to a woman from Little Rock. "[Foster] couldn't understand why the press was the way it was," Pincus told Blumenthal. "It was a sense that people would print something that was wrong, and that other people would repeat it. I'd say, 'You can't let the press run you, get your goat; you have to go on. This is how the game is played.' He'd say, 'Fine.'"[81]

At this time, Pulitzer Prize-winning columnist William Safire of the *New York Times*—a former speechwriter for President Nixon who had supported President Clinton in 1992, largely because of his distaste for President Bush—weighs in with his own view of the Foster case. Criticizing the White House for its obviously misdirected actions during the probe, Safire also describes the USPP as "keep-off-the-grass cops… adept at catching parkway speeders and removing cats from trees but ill-equipped for White House confrontation."

Commenting on the *Wall Street Journal's* coverage of Foster before his death, Safire concludes: "Journalists have a job to do, and cannot pull their punches at wrongdoing on the assumption that high officials may be mentally ill.

"Presidents and their appointees have a job to do, too; it includes the swift protection of the public interest when a person entrusted with the nation's secrets is found with a bullet in the head."

Back at the USPP/CIB office in Anacostia, Captain Hume, still pursuing more than "parkway speeders," calls Dr. Larry Watkins in Little Rock, who, according to the White House telephone log, had called Foster at 10:47 AM on the day before his death. Hume writes in his report:

> [Dr. Watkins] confirmed that he did, in fact, call. He was returning Foster's earlier call to him. Foster told him he was under a lot of stress; that he had a loss of appetite and was losing weight.
> Dr. Watkins asked him if he was depressed, and he said he was. [Dr. Watkins] prescribed an antidepressant, Desyrel, generic name, Trazodone. [The doctor] called the prescription into a Washington, D.C., pharmacy....[82]
> Dr. Watkins said that was the first time he had prescribed medication to Foster for depression. He gave Foster a complete physical December 31, 1992, and, at that time,

Foster was not taking any medication.[83] Lisa Foster called him at approximately 10:20 p.m., central time, on July 20th to discuss [Foster's] death.

But when Hume tries to discover details about Foster's general state of health, Watkins invokes his doctor-patient privilege and will only say that Foster was in generally good shape.

Hume then tries to reach the three men who had called Foster and left their names and telephone numbers on the day of his death: C. Brantley Buck, Jim Lyons, and Gordon Rather.

Regarding his interview with Buck, a partner in the Rose Law Firm in Little Rock, Hume writes:

> I called Buck's office and spoke to his secretary, Linda Johnson. Buck was on vacation. She said Buck did get a return call from Foster,... but Buck had stepped away from his desk. Foster returned the call to Buck at 11:17 a.m., central time (12:17 [p.m.], eastern time). Linda had a brief conversation with Foster that was characterized as normal, nothing unusual.

Hume then calls Jim Lyons, an attorney in Denver, and reports:

> [Lyons] had known Foster since the late 1980s. He met him through Hillary Rodham Clinton and the Rose Law Firm. They had worked together on the campaign. Lyons was going to be in Washington on Wednesday, July 21st. He had called and spoken with Foster [on] Sunday, July 18th, between 8:00-9:00 p.m., eastern time, and they had agreed to meet for dinner Wednesday.
>
> Lyons had told Foster he would call him and let him know when he would leave Denver and arrive in Washington. This is the reason for the phone message on the morning of July 20, 1993.

Finally, Hume telephones Gordon Rather, an attorney with Wright, Lindsey & Jennings in Little Rock—in which presidential advisor Bruce Lindsey is a partner.[84] Rather had left a message that he wanted to discuss a "personal matter" with Foster. Hume states:

> [Rather] had known Foster for about 22 years, ever since Foster was a member of Rose Law Firm. He did not speak with Foster on 7/20/93. However, Foster's office called back and wanted to know if it was alright if Foster returned his call the next day.
>
> The purpose of the call was to discuss items of interest to the American Board of Trial Advocacy (ABOTA), even though Foster was no longer a member. The items for discussion were [the] selection of federal judges, health reform; and to let Foster know that the Arkansas Chapter of ABOTA had a meeting in July in Memphis, and it went well.

Captain Hume and the USPP conclude that there is no reason to believe that any of these calls had any impact on Foster's state of mind or his apparent decision to take his own life.

24.

TUESDAY–MONDAY, AUGUST 3–9, 1993

In response to Vincent Foster's claim in his torn-up note that *"The FBI lied in their report to the AG,"* Deputy Attorney General Philip Heymann, who had ordered the FBI's current investigation, writes an August 3 memorandum to the acting chief of the Criminal Division, John C. Kenney, and Michael E. Shaheen, counsel for the Office of Professional Responsibility (OPR), the watchdog unit within the Department of Justice. Heymann also sends them photocopies of Foster's torn-up note and handwriting samples, stating in his cover letter:

Attached is an unsigned, undated reproduction of notes the originals of which the Laboratory has determined were written by Vince Foster. I would like OPR to review the assertion in the notes dealing with the FBI and to give me its recommendation as to what, if any, further inquiry is necessary and appropriate. I would like the Criminal Division to review the other assertions in the notes and to give me its recommendation as to what, if any, further inquiry is necessary and appropriate. Please contact me or David Margolis if you have any questions.

In an August 3 letter faxed to Captain Hume, John Sloan, who had been present in Jim Hamilton's law office when Lisa Foster was interviewed on July 29, responds to the USPP's query about Sharon Bowman's knowledge of the 1913 .38-caliber Colt revolver found in Foster's hand, which some have assumed came from their father's gun collection.

In fact, Sloan confirms, prior to the elder Foster's June 1991 death, he had given guns to several members of his family from his personal gun collection.

In his handwritten note, Sloan states that he had shown Mrs. Bowman the photograph of the pistol, adding:

Mrs. Bowman said it looked like a gun she had seen in her father's collection. She particularly pointed out the "wavelike" detailing at the base of the grip. I asked if she remembered any other features. She did not.

Two days later, on August 5, the Metropolitan Police Department, in response to a request from the USPP, submits a report, stating that Foster had never obtained a permit for this or any other gun, a clear violation of D.C. law.

The gun found in Foster's hand continues to cause controversy within the Park Police. Still under pressure to wrap up the case, Captain Hume pushes Simonello, but Simonello reminds Hume that the revolver has not been tested by firearms experts. They still don't know for sure whether it will fire.

 Simonello balks at sending the gun to the FBI for the same reason he didn't want to send Foster's torn-up note—because Foster had attacked the FBI in his note, causing, at the very least, the appearance of a possible conflict of interest.

 Considering the circumstances, Simonello suggests sending the gun to the Department of Alcohol, Tobacco and Firearms.

On Thursday, August 5, Detective Markland, without the firearms analysis, completes his "Synopsis/Conclusion" of the Foster case. His two-page report, which concludes that Foster had committed suicide, implicitly addresses the issues of motive, means, and opportunity.

Regarding motive, Markland declares:

> The investigation has revealed that Mr. Foster was, within the past two weeks, experiencing a great deal of difficulty handling the stress associated with his office. He had considered seeking psychiatric help and was provided with several doctors' names by a family member. He had confided in his wife his difficulties and had recently tried to set aside family time to relieve some stress. The Foster family doctor was contacted in his home state of Arkansas. The doctor prescribed an antidepressant drug and one tablet was consumed by Mr. Foster on the evening before his death....
>
> A handwritten note that the White House Counsel's Office reported they found on 7/26/93 and was turned over

to this department on 7/27/93 documents the observations of a very disturbed and overworked individual who sees himself as having failed the Clinton administration.

Regarding the issue of means, Markland states:

> The autopsy and resulting toxicology revealed no signs of pre-existing health problems, alcohol or drug usage by the decedent. The cause of death was a "perforating gun-shot wound to the mouth-head."...
>
> The revolver recovered at the scene of Mr. Foster's death (from his hand) had probably been passed down to Mr. Foster after his father's death.

Regarding the issue of opportunity, Markland writes:

> Interviews conducted at the White House revealed that Mr. Foster had left his office on 7/20/93 at approximately 1310 hours. Mr. Foster, who was always instantly accessible in the past, did not answer an electronic page initiated by Mr. Bernard Nussbaum, chief counsel to the president, at 1830 hours. The White House-issued pager had been recovered by investigators at the death scene. The pager had been turned off.
>
> Further investigation and calls from citizens support a finding that Mr. Foster drove into Fort Marcy at approximately 1445-1500 hours by himself in the vehicle found at the scene....
>
> [A]t approximately 1800 hours, this department was notified by an anonymous caller that a dead body was discovered by a citizen at Fort Marcy, Virginia.

In his final paragraph, Markland concludes:

> Based on the aforementioned synopsis of the facts and

circumstances presented, the writer requests that the investigation be "Closed" and that the Manner of Death [be] ruled as "Suicide."

After Major Hines approves Markland's report, Captain Hume sends a copy to Dave Margolis at the Justice Department for his review. The USPP then makes an agreement with the Department of Justice that they will announce their findings together at a press conference on Tuesday, August 10.

On Friday morning, the *New York Times* reports that the FBI investigation, probing the White House's handling of the Foster note, "had concluded that White House officials did nothing improper when they waited for 30 hours last week before giving police investigators the scraps of a torn-up note found in Mr. Foster's briefcase."

And the *Wall Street Journal* publishes its third editorial since Foster's death, "Re Vincent Foster."

Defiant but clearly bruised over the criticism it has been receiving for its earlier editorials while Foster was alive, the *Journal*, echoing William Safire's earlier column, states: "[T]here is no way to cover national government on the assumption that a high official and steeled litigator secretly suffers from depression, and may commit suicide if criticized. What we said about Mr. Foster was nothing compared to the abuse heaped on the likes of Ed Meese, Robert Bork, and Clarence Thomas."

25.

TUESDAY, AUGUST 10, 1993

As agreed upon, the U.S. Department of Justice, represented by Deputy Attorney General Philip Heymann, and the U.S. Park Police, represented by Chief Robert Langston, conduct a joint press conference at 1:30 PM at the Justice Department on Constitution Avenue—midway between the White House and the Capitol—to announce its official findings on the death of Vincent Foster and to release the text of the torn-up note found in Foster's briefcase.

In his brief opening statement, Heymann reveals that the Office of Professional Responsibility is continuing to investigate whether the sentence in Foster's note—"*The FBI lied in their report to the AG*"—has any basis in fact. He adds that the department is continuing to probe those matters involving the White House Travel Office.

Discussing the Foster case, Heymann explains, "The FBI joined the Park Police in the initial stages of the inquiry... because of [Foster's] status as a federal official and [because of] assassination statutes. As it became apparent that this was a suicide, the FBI gradually assumed a secondary role to the Park Police. The bureau reentered the inquiry at our request to examine the handling of the note."

Heymann then yields to Chief Langston who quickly summarizes the evidence of Foster's suicide, concluding, "Our investigation has found no evidence of foul play."

After throwing open the session to questions, the first reporter asks, "Chief, have you ever found the person who reported [Foster's body] to the park maintenance man?..."

Langston replies, "We can only identify that a white male in a white van may have been the person that notified a park maintenance employee at the Turkey Run maintenance center, and that white van was also placed in the parking lot near the time of the incident."

Heymann then introduces Robert Bryant, the FBI special-agent-in-charge of the Washington field office, who says in his statement, "We followed this case from the time we were notified until we were basically of the opinion, along with Chief Langston's staff, that this was a suicide. Subsequently, there was an issue raised about a note and the handling of the note and the processing of the note and its turnover to the United States Park Police or law enforcement. We were ordered then by the Department of Justice to look into the handling of this note and to bring that investigation to the forefront.... I would just like to say that during this time, the cooperation between our two agencies [the FBI and the USPP] has been outstanding."

When another reporter asks about Nussbaum's search of Foster's office—while FBI agents and investigators from the USPP sat by without participating—Chief Langston, as if he has been waiting for that question, replies, "Let me comment on that. We certainly weren't pleased at the way that was conducted. Our investigators would like to have seen that briefcase and would like to have examined the contents of the files. Executive privilege was invoked. And we raised those concerns with the Justice Department, and those concerns from the Justice Department were raised with the White House. And the White House staff became very compliant. And everything that we had asked for, they provided to us fully...."

"Gentlemen," another reporter asks, "the note refers to both the president and Mrs. Clinton. Did anybody interview the president or Mrs. Clinton as part of this investigation?"

"Not from the Park Police, no."

Bryant adds, "We did not."

"Why not?" the reporter continues. "The president was one of the last to talk to him? [He] had a [scheduled] meeting with him the day following his suicide."

Bryant answers, "I think what we were trying to do here, first, was trying to find out if there was a violation—if he had been harmed, you know, assaulted or assassinated or whatever. We concluded, 'No.' The second part of our inquiry was the note. And we didn't consider the president or Mrs. Clinton to be relevant witnesses to that."

"Why?"

"Because, in our investigative view, they were not...."

"Where does the investigation go from here?"

Firmly, Langston replies, "The Park Police has concluded its investigation into the death inquiry of Mr. Foster."

"What about the FBI?" a reporter asks.

Bryant responds, "And we've concluded our investigation as to the handling of the note."

But, even though the text of the torn-up note has now been released, the Park Police's final summary of the case and Dr. Beyer's autopsy report have not.

More questions are sure to be asked.

26.

R.W. APPLE, JR., OF THE NEW YORK TIMES publishes the most talked-about article on Wednesday, August 11, the day after the joint USPP-FBI-Department of Justice press conference. Apple reports that Bernard Nussbaum might have been present when a box was taken out of Foster's office during the evening of his death.

Nussbaum reacts angrily, saying, "I removed nothing from Foster's office on July 20. This is totally made up. The Park Police have interviewed me several times, and they never talked about any box."

Regardless, Major Robert Hines, who spoke on the record, insists that "either Nussbaum or one of his assistants had removed the materials," Apple writes. Hines also told the reporter, "I don't have any idea whether they were all brought back or not. I could only trust that they were, but I would never bet money on it or say for sure."

Apple, however, leaves open the possibility of a simple misunderstanding after a spokesman for the Department of Justice concedes that a bag of trash had been removed from Foster's office on July 20 but that it was later brought back, adding that a box of Foster's personal property had also been removed and given to the Foster family's attorney—but not until July 22, the day of the official search.

In other words, other than statements from the Park Police, there is no evidence that Nussbaum had removed anything from Foster's office on the night of his death. Nevertheless, this article tees up the ball for more reporting and speculation.

In its Thursday edition, *New York Times* reporter Gwen Ifill reveals that Foster's files had been "removed from his office in recent days and dispersed to the offices of other presidential legal advisors."

Quoted in the story, Carl Stern, the Justice Department spokesman, appears to scoff at the suggestion that the department should examine the files, "since no indication of wrongdoing had been uncovered."

Ifill continues: "It is not clear exactly when Mr. Foster's superiors began removing papers from his office, but the task of reassigning his work to others in the White House is continuing, [a] senior official said."

The *Times* reporter surmises that, with the Justice Department refusing to review Foster's files, "there is now little chance that anyone outside of Mr. Foster's immediate colleagues will ever know whether White House officials have accurately accounted for his papers."

Also on Thursday, William Safire publishes a column in the *Times*'s op-ed page, "The 28th Piece," which concentrates on all of the unanswered questions in the wake of the release of the text of the Foster note, as well as the lingering doubts about the overall investigation.

Safire concludes: "What's the point of this questioning, when 8 out of 10 suicides are driven by depressive illnesses, not external pressures? It may not lead to revelations, but will surely show us how this White House malfunctions in an emergency and its aftermath. That's worth pursuing."

On the page before Safire's column, the *Times* also publishes an editorial that trumps the July 22 editorial in the *Wall Street Journal* that called for a "special counsel within Justice." Getting even tougher, the *Times* insists that "an independent counsel wholly free from executive branch control needs to be appointed" to investigate the White House Travel Office matter. The newspaper, which calls for Nussbaum's removal from office, further contends that a "special prosecutor-style inquiry is also needed into how the White House handled Mr. Foster's death."

On August 12—a week to the day after Detective Markland's final report that closed the Foster case, and two days after the press conference with the Department of Justice and the FBI—the U.S. Park Police formally asks the Bureau of Alcohol, Tobacco and Firearms to help with the analysis of the .38-caliber revolver found in Foster's right hand.

The request comes from USPP Major Benjamin J. Holmes, the commander to the CIB, who asks the Department of Alcohol,

Tobacco and Firearms to answer five questions that obviously should have been resolved before the case was closed:[85]

- Could Item #1 [the gun] be tested to determine whether or not it operates properly?

- Could it be determined if the residue on the victim's right hand could have been the result of discharging Item #1 in a manner consistent with other available evidence?

- Could it be determined if Item #3 [the spent casing found in the gun's cylinder] and Item #2 [the live round found in the gun's cylinder] are similar in manufacture?

- Could it be determined if the primer on Item #3 was struck by the firing pin of Item #1?

- Could Item #16 and Item #18 [Foster's white, long-sleeve shirt and blue, gray trousers, respectively] be examined for gun powder residue and if found could any information concerning position of weapon at time of discharge be determined?

No harm, no foul, the Department of Alcohol, Tobacco and Firearms will later confirm the gun found in Foster's right hand is in good working order and that the gunshot-residue patterns found on his body are consistent with the conclusion that he committed suicide.[86]

The *New York Times* reveals on Saturday, August 14, that an earlier report that a "smudged, unreadable palm print had been found on an anguished note left by Vincent Foster," is wrong, and that the palm print, although partial, was "identifiable." However, reporter David Johnston writes, the palm print "had never been investigated," adding that even though law-enforcement agencies have a set of Foster's fingerprints, they never obtained his palm prints. Also, they have no prints of the White House officials known to have handled the note.

"No one was suspected of wrongdoing," Johnston quotes Justice Department spokesman Carl Stern, "so what would the purpose have been running around the White House taking everybody's palm prints?"

On August 15, staff writer David Von Drehle of the *Washington Post* publishes a lengthy and remarkably detailed article about Foster's life and career while Michael Isikoff writes an accompanying story, explaining some of the facts behind the Park Police investigation.

In one portion of his article, Von Drehle quotes one of Foster's friends, who had tried to tease him about the June 17 "Who is Vincent Foster?" editorial in the *Wall Street Journal*. But Foster had no sense of humor about it, the friend said, adding, "He spent his whole career building the Rose firm, and now [the *Journal*]—which his former clients and fellow lawyers were reading back home—was saying that not only are these guys from Little Rock a bunch of clowns, but there's some conspiracy going on to subvert the law."

Further, Isikoff has uncovered that Foster had been shopping for an attorney to represent him in the event of a congressional probe into the Travel Office. The reporter is also the first to publish what the Park Police had learned during its investigation: that Nussbaum, Maggie Williams, and Patsy Thomasson had entered Foster's office on the night of Foster's death.

Isikoff continues: "Nussbaum confirmed that he and Thomasson conducted what he described as a brief, 10-minute search of Foster's office the night of his death, examining the top of his desk and shelves, but removing or disturbing no documents.[87] He said Williams was too distraught to participate. 'Maggie was sitting on a sofa,' he said. 'She wasn't looking at any documents. She was crying.'

"But Nussbaum vigorously disputed that he had hindered the efforts of investigators, saying he was at all times seeking to 'balance the interests' of Foster's privileged communications with the president with the 'legitimate' needs of the police. 'I could have said no one is going into Vince's office, unless you have a subpoena, except me,' he said. 'We're not dealing with a crime.'"

On the same day as the publication of these revealing articles by Von Drehle and Isikoff, the *Post* runs an equally remarkable op-ed piece by Jody Powell, the former press secretary to President Carter, which is nothing short of an all-out assault on the media's reporting on the Foster case.

Powell writes: "When Vincent Foster wrote about ruining people as 'sport' and about journalists being free to do it without fear of consequences, he spoke the truth. Were there any doubt, the conduct of Washington journalism since his death has surely removed it....

"Now, after weeks of frenzied investigative activity, there is still no evidence of anything other than a personal tragedy. But that hasn't been a problem in the no-consequence crowd. On Thursday, the *New York Times* ignored or dismissed Vincent Foster's criticisms of journalism and decided that everything else he said should be taken seriously and warrants appointment of a special counsel."

As if to illustrate Powell's critique, on August 22, the *New York Times* returns with its own in-depth investigative report about Foster's suicide by Jason DeParle, as well as a chart of twelve known "key events" in Foster's life between May 19 and July 20. Four of the citations are the June 17, June 24, July 14, and July 19 *Wall Street Journal* editorials that were critical of Foster, indicating, as DeParle writes, "[T]he wounds went deeper than anyone knew."

But, the following day, the *Times* runs an unusual "Editors' Note," declaring: "An article yesterday about Vincent W. Foster Jr.... was accompanied by a chart headed 'Key Events in Mr. Foster's Last Months.' The chart listed, as separate events, four editorials in the *Wall Street Journal* that were critical of Mr. Foster.

"As the article noted, these editorials disturbed Mr. Foster, but there is no way to specify what moved him to suicide. The editorials should not, therefore, have had such prominence in the chart."

27.

THROUGHOUT THE FOSTER INVESTIGATION by the Park Police, the word "Whitewater" was mentioned by investigators and in the media—but only in passing, little realizing that it would suddenly come to prominence and open a whole new area of speculation and suspicion deriving from Foster's death.

During the 1992 presidential campaign, allegations had surfaced against the president and the first lady that resulted from their August 1978 partnership with businessman James McDougal and his wife, Susan, in a 230-acre parcel of land that stretched along the White River in Arkansas.

At the time, Bill Clinton had been the state's attorney general for nearly two years; Hillary Clinton had been an associate with the Rose Law Firm in Little Rock for about a year. Although the McDougals ran the corporation and put up $92,000, the Clintons invested nearly $69,000.

Three months after the purchase, Bill Clinton was elected to his first two-year term as Arkansas governor. And in June 1979—the same year that Mrs. Clinton became a partner in the Rose Law Firm—Clinton, McDougal, and their wives created the Whitewater Development Corporation, hoping to develop the property. But, from the outset, the business didn't do very well.

In 1981, the year after Clinton was defeated for reelection and had gone to work for the Wright, Lindsey & Jennings law firm in Little Rock, McDougal bought Madison Bank & Trust in Kingston, Arkansas, which loaned Mrs. Clinton $30,000 for her Whitewater investment. The following year, McDougal purchased a thrift in Woodruff County with about $3 million in assets, Madison Guaranty Savings & Loan.

Meantime, after Clinton returned to the governor's mansion in 1982, federal and state banking authorities began investigating McDougal's savings & loan, which opened an office in Little Rock in 1983, for a series of allegedly questionable practices.

By March 1985—after Bill Clinton had won his third term as governor the previous November—Madison Guaranty was on the verge of total collapse and, that spring, retained Hillary Clinton and the Rose Law Firm to help prepare a recapitalization plan.

After more investigations and charges by federal banking authorities, McDougal was removed from the board of Madison Guaranty in August 1986 and indicted in 1989 by a federal grand jury for defrauding depositors out of nearly $60 million. At the same time, the federal regulators ordered Madison Guaranty shut down. However, at his 1990 trial, McDougal was acquitted.

Meantime, Governor Clinton had been reelected to his fourth term, and, after McDougal's acquittal, he won a fifth term in November 1990. This was followed by his announced bid for the presidency eleven months later on October 3, 1991.

On March 8, 1992, in the midst of the presidential campaign, *New York Times* reporter Jeff Gerth published an article about the

Whitewater Development Corporation and candidate Clinton's relationship with McDougal. Clinton, also plagued by charges of womanizing, had only managed to win the Georgia primary on March 3,
but failed to win the other six party caucuses and primaries in Iowa,
New Hampshire, Maine, South Dakota, Maryland, and Colorado.
But, on March 10, two days after the *Times*'s Whitewater story,
Clinton won eight of eleven primaries and caucuses on Super
Tuesday, which gave him a wide lead. Clearly, a vast majority of vot-
ing Democrats couldn't have cared less about Whitewater. And, by
the time of Vincent Foster's death, few Americans, Republicans
included, knew anything about this real-estate venture.

This point was made again on November 3, 1992, when
Governor Clinton defeated President George Bush.

Stemming from the alleged "sanitizing" of Foster's office on the
night of his death and two days later during the official search,
the word, "Whitewater," after a long hiatus, once again becomes
part of the American political lexicon.

The serious mainstream press begins publishing and broadcasting investigative reports about the Clintons' real-estate deals with
the McDougals while the tabloid and some of the right-wing media,
notably *The American Spectator*, revisit President Clinton's sex life,
as well as Foster's alleged affair with Mrs. Clinton.

Meanwhile, even among the establishment press, speculation is
rampant that Vincent Foster had somehow managed to learn—on
the day of his death—that a federal judge had signed a search
warrant for the Little Rock offices of David Hale. A former
municipal judge, Hale is the owner of Capital Management
Services, an Arkansas finance company, subsidized by the Small

Business Administration (SBA) as part of a program designed to help disadvantaged companies.

Back in April 1986, Hale's company had loaned $300,000 to Master Marketing, an advertising company owned by Susan McDougal. Allegedly, a portion of this sum wound up in the bank account of the Whitewater Development Corporation to help finance the purchase of a parcel of land near Little Rock from the International Paper Company.

Now indicted by a federal grand jury on September 23, 1993, Hale claims that Bill Clinton and Jim McDougal had "pressured" him to make the loan.[88]

Clinton immediately insists that he has "no recollection" of any such conversation with Hale—although he admits receiving large sums of money from the McDougals, who had raised funds to pay off much of Clinton's 1984 campaign debt. Meantime, Jim McDougal, despite his 1990 acquittal for fraud, is still under investigation by the U.S. Department of Justice for the money he raised for then-Governor Clinton—and for what, if any, favors he had received in return on behalf of his troubled Madison Guaranty.

28.

BUILDING ON AN EARLIER ARTICLE by Michael Tackett and William Gaines, which was buried in the *Chicago Tribune* on November 21, investigative reporter Jerry Seper of the *Washington Times* publishes a front-page story on December 6 with the headline, "S & L scandal shadows Foster's last days."

Seper reports that on the final day of Foster's life he had received a call from Denver attorney James M. Lyons, who had prepared the official statement on behalf of the Clinton campaign in response to the revelations about Whitewater during the summer of 1992. Lyons reported that the Clintons had lost

$68,900 on the Whitewater deal. By the time Bill Clinton had received the Democratic nomination for president on July 16, the issue, for the most part, ceased to exist.

Combining the timing of Lyons's call with that from another unnamed attorney from the Rose Law Firm, also on the day of Foster's death, Seper links them to recent reports of the search warrant issued that same afternoon on David Hale's Capital Management Services.

At the time that USPP Captain Charles Hume interviewed James Lyons—as well as the secretary to Brantley Buck, Seper's unnamed Rose Law Firm attorney—on August 2, the Park Police knew of no Foster connection to Whitewater.

Seper's story continues that on December 24, 1992, "Mr. Foster handled the sale of [the Clintons'] half-ownership of Whitewater and filed the necessary tax forms when it was discovered that Whitewater had failed to file corporate tax returns for a three-year period when the Clintons were still half-owners....[89] The omission was discovered after Mr. Foster met with Mr. McDougal [in December 1992] to execute the sale of the Clintons' interest in Whitewater."

In June 1993, the month before he died, Foster had sent three years of Whitewater tax returns to McDougal's lawyer.

The reporter suggests that copies of some of these documents might have been in Foster's office when Bernard Nussbaum conducted his unilateral search while the Park Police, FBI, and attorneys from the Department of Justice merely watched.

Meantime, Reed Irvine, the chairman of Accuracy in Media (AIM), and Joseph Goulden, AIM's director of media analysis, have begun their own investigation of the Foster case.[90]

Irvine's organization—whose specific purpose is combating what it perceives as inherent biases in the liberal mainstream press—has long been known in Washington as a media gadfly.[91]

Since the late 1980s, AIM has been receiving, on average, over $100,000 a year from foundations controlled by financier Richard Scaife, the great-grandson of Thomas Mellon, who was the founder of Mellon banking empire.[92] Scaife, an heir to the $750 million family fortune, is a long-time contributor to a wide range of right-wing causes.

On Saturday, December 11, Irvine and Goulden publish an op-ed piece in the *Washington Times*, which questions the conclusion that Foster's depression had led to his suicide. In their article, Irvine and Goulden give the back of their hand to the Park Police, saying that its "specialty is policing parks, not detective work."

After publication, Major Hines calls Irvine and complains about the story. Irvine invites Hines to lunch to talk about the Foster case. They are joined by Goulden.

During their lunch, Hines tells the AIM officials that Foster did not place his revolver inside his mouth but had fired it from several inches away—which is inconsistent with the conclusions from the autopsy. He also insists that there was no exit wound in the back of Foster's head.

Both of Hines's claims are wrong. But Irvine has no reason to doubt what Hines is saying, especially considering Hines's position with the U.S. Park Police.

After lunch, Irvine, who is now even more intrigued, calls Christopher Ruddy, a reporter at the *New York Post*, and encourages him to write about the Foster case.

Ruddy, who has already taken an interest in the Foster case, once claimed in an article that a public-television documentary he had debunked was "a prime example how the media can manipulate facts and narratives to create a revised history both believable and untrue."⁹³

On December 19, thirteen days after Seper's article, staff writer David Johnston of the *New York Times* reports that Foster had kept a separate file in his White House office about Jim McDougal. The reporter's "law-enforcement" sources speculate that the file might be part of the cache of documents given to attorney Jim Hamilton; and, thus, they have asked Hamilton for access. But, Johnston notes, Hamilton, to date, "has refused to comply."⁹⁴

In reality, Hamilton has no such file, and never did.

Johnston quotes an unnamed senior White House official as insisting: "We are not aware that any law-enforcement official is looking into the fact that a file relating to Whitewater or McDougal disappeared or in any way was improperly handled. All the files in Vince Foster's office were properly handled."

On December 20, Jerry Seper strikes again in the *Washington Times* in a story titled "Clinton papers lifted after aide's suicide." Although, in part of his story, Seper merely repackages Isikoff's report on August 15 that Nussbaum, along with Maggie Williams and Patsy Thomasson, had entered Foster's office on the night of his death, there is much more.

While the *New York Times* and the *Washington Post* had merely speculated about the disappearance of Foster's files on McDougal during the July 20 and July 22 "searches" by Nussbaum, Seper, citing "two U.S. Park Police investigators," flat-out declares: "White House officials removed records of business deals between President Clinton, his wife and an Arkansas partnership known as Whitewater Development Corp. from the office of Vincent W.

Foster Jr. during two searches after the deputy presidential counsel's suicide." Then Seper makes the same mistake the *New York Times* had made the day before, saying, "The Park Police investigators familiar with the Foster inquiry say the Whitewater documents were among those taken from the office by White House officials and later turned over to Mr. Foster's attorney, James Hamilton."*

Consequently, even though this claim in Seper's story is inaccurate, White House Communications Director Mark Gearan is forced to issue a statement, saying:

> Following the death of Vincent Foster and following the examination of the files in his office on July 22, 1993, by White House counsel [Nussbaum] in the presence of representatives of various law enforcement agencies, Mr. Foster's files were distributed as follows: (1) those files pertaining to his White House duties remained in the counsel's offices; (2) those files that were personal to Mr. Foster and his family were sent to his family's personal attorney [Jim Hamilton]; and (3) those files that pertained to the personal legal affairs of the president and Mrs. Clinton (including documents relating to their personal tax returns, the filing of Whitewater Development Corp. tax returns, and the disposition of their interest in Whitewater)—all of which were preserved—were sent to the Clintons' personal attorney [Robert Barnett and, later, David E. Kendall, both of Williams & Connolly].

Gearan adds that the decision to remove Foster's personal files had been made by Nussbaum.

Soon after Gearan's statement, Hillary Clinton tells a reporter

---

* During my separate interviews with Captain Hume and Detective Markland, who were the only two Park Police officials present for Nussbaum's search of Foster's office, they each told me that, at the time of the search, they had no idea what Whitewater was. Also, both Lieutenant Robert Kass and Investigator Rolla, who went through Foster's personal files in Jim Hamilton's office on July 28, told me that they, too, neither saw Whitewater documents, nor had any knowledge of what Whitewater was at that time.

for the Associated Press, "I am bewildered that a losing investment which for us was significant—$69,000, which is provable by the accountants—is still a topic of inquiry."

Nevertheless, on December 22—faced with having his own attorney general subpoena documents as part of her own investigation—President Clinton vows to cooperate with law-enforcement officials probing his ties to Whitewater, Madison, and the McDougals.

In an editorial summed up by its headline, "Release the Whitewater Files," on Thursday, December 23, the *New York Times*—which had first trumpeted the Whitewater story to deaf ears in March 1992—appears skeptical of the president's pledge of cooperation but now smells vindication, saying that Clinton "and his people have said things like this before." Clearly upset by what appears to be a series of conflicting statements from the White House, the *Times* specifically describes Nussbaum as "a threat to the president's political health."

Soon after, President Clinton announces through a spokesman that those papers dealing with the Whitewater corporation, found in and removed from Foster's office on July 22, will be turned over to federal agents by his new attorney at Williams & Connolly, David Kendall, next week.

The president's spokesman adds that the files will show no wrongdoing but that, because of their complexity, they will probably raise as many questions as they answer.

But the following week, this matter, at least for the moment, is moot: The White House simply doesn't turn over the files to investigators, as promised.

Washington is immediately electrified.

Highlighting this now-supercharged political atmosphere, Representative James A. Leach of Iowa, the ranking Republican on the U.S. House Banking Committee, publishes an op-ed article in the *Washington Post* on December 31.

Leach, who demands that Attorney General Janet Reno appoint a special counsel to investigate Whitewater and the White House search of Vincent Foster's office, writes: "[T]he public has the obligation in the next election to give particular attention to the role of character in public life. For the sake of the American political system the Bush administration was right not to proceed or make public allegations against candidate Clinton. For the sake of the presidency—i.e., American national interest—criminal proceedings should not be instituted against President Clinton.

"The jury for abuse of the public trust should be the people at the ballot box."

Official Washington doesn't need a crystal ball to understand that Leach appears to be foreshadowing the forthcoming political battle—over the White House's handling of the Foster case.

29.

ON SUNDAY, JANUARY 2, 1994, Attorney General Reno is being besieged with demands for the appointment of an independent counsel. Most prominent among these are Senate Minority Leader Robert J. Dole and House Minority Whip Newt Gingrich.

During an appearance on NBC's *Meet the Press*, Senator Dole charges that Reno has been "dragging her feet," insisting, "It's high time that she did what she knows she should do…. The Democrats aren't going to touch this. If it were a Republican, on the other hand, we'd have five or six hearings going on right now."

On ABC's *This Week With David Brinkley*, Representative Gingrich asks, "If [the Clintons] are innocent, why don't they go ahead and agree to an independent counsel to clear their name?"

Speaking on behalf of the White House during the ABC program, presidential advisor George Stephanopoulos replies, "[The Republicans] have been fighting the independent-counsel law for many years. Now that they sense that there might be some perceived political advantage to going after this, they're all for it all of a sudden."

Even among those who believe in President Clinton and what he stands for, the actions and inactions by his staff make him appear Nixonian—arrogant, defiant, and paranoid. And now, the bizarre behavior of the Clinton White House over the Foster case gives plenty of fodder to the president's detractors.

By now, too, the president's critics have come to view Whitewater as the Democrats' Watergate.

Reenter William Safire, Nixon's former speechwriter, whose January 6 column, "Foster's Ghost," spells out the conspiracy theory embraced by many Republicans. Safire writes that the problem for the Clinton White House—which, to its chagrin, has been inviting such speculation—is that there might be plenty of circumstantial evidence to support the conspiracy theory.

In short, Safire appears to promote the theory that the Clintons and the McDougals had gone into the real-estate business and failed. In their desperate attempt to save their real-estate business and then McDougal's bank, Safire speculates, corners were cut, laws were broken, and a paper trail was left behind.

When the entire mess became an issue during the presidential campaign, Vincent Foster, Mrs. Clinton's law partner, tried to work out the problems, leading to a special report, written by Denver attorney James Lyons, whitewashing the entire Whitewater matter.

Safire's theory continues: The pressure to keep the lid on everything fell upon Foster, who had kept key records that proved the Clintons' alleged complicity in his White House office.

Dreading another embarrassing scandal after Travelgate and further disgrace or even prosecution, Foster left his office on July 20, drove to Fort Marcy Park, and killed himself.

After hearing of Foster's death, White House aides entered his office and sanitized it, allowing the U.S. Park Police—whom Safire calls "the Keystone Kop Park Police"—to control the investigation and be manipulated by Bernard Nussbaum. The police weren't allowed to see the damaging documents, which were quickly given to the Clintons' personal attorney, completing the cover-up.

Putting on its own spin, the White House then blamed the media, particularly the *Wall Street Journal*, for driving Foster to suicide.

In response to demands for the records, the Clinton White House promised to release them on a specific date, and then began the big stall.

To Safire, the promised documents would probably be in the same condition as the note found in Foster's briefcase—torn apart with a key piece missing.

Safire concludes: "If I were Louis Freeh, the new F.B.I. Director chosen by Mr. Nussbaum and known as 'Bernie's Good Deed,' I would... demand that Justice seek subpoenas to force the Clintons and their former law partners and accountants to produce all other relevant papers."

On the same day as the Safire column, Attorney General Reno, fearing that a *special* counsel's independence will be challenged if *she* makes the selection, announces that she is considering the court appointment of an *independent* counsel by a three-judge federal panel, which will require congressional action.

The Independent Counsel Act, which was created in 1978, permitted the attorney general to ask a federal court to appoint an independent counsel when a conflict of interest potentially impeded an investigation by the Department of Justice. The law had expired on December 15, 1992, when Senate Republican leaders threatened a filibuster to block its renewal. Back then, as Stephanopoulos had charged, the Republicans had come to view independent counsels as potentially abusive; they singled out for specific criticism the investigation of the Iran-Contra scandal by Independent Counsel Lawrence Walsh, who is now in the seventh year of his probe.

"In the current state of the law with respect to the Whitewater case," Reno says during a press conference, "I'm going to be damned if I do and damned if I don't."

Regardless, the pressure is on Reno to make a decision.

On Friday, January 7, the day after Safire publishes his neat and clean conspiracy theory, conservative columnist Paul A. Gigot of the *Wall Street Journal* writes his own, essentially paralleling Safire's—but adding the David Hale subpoena and James Lyons's telephone call to Foster on the day of Foster's death to the mix. Gigot writes: "Whitewater may not be Watergate, but the Clinton White House's skill in handling the real estate-S&L suspicions has certainly earned it the right to be called Nixonian."

Also on Friday, the *New York Times* continues its no-nonsense editorials with its latest installment, "Janet Reno's Shameful Delay." The *Times* states: "[Reno] holds out the possibility that she will seek a court-appointed independent prosecutor as soon as the House passes legislation authorizing such positions. But Ms. Reno does not have to wait. She already has the authority to appoint a special prosecutor from outside her department, and congressional Republicans are right to insist that she do so. When the Independent Counsel Act is revived—as it ought to be—then this special prosecutor can give way to a court-appointed prosecutor operating with even more independence."

Two days later, New York Senator Daniel Moynihan becomes the first Democrat in the U.S. Senate to appeal to the attorney general to appoint a special prosecutor. "Presidents can't be seen to have any hesitation about any matter that concerns their propriety," Moynihan says on NBC's *Meet the Press*. "And this is an honorable man. We have a fine president. He has nothing to hide."

Finally, on January 12, Janet Reno relents, announcing that she will appoint a "special counsel"—someone who will be "ruggedly independent." Reno adds, "Sometimes we have to go beyond what is generally appropriate simply to assure people that we have gone the extra mile."

As for the president, during an interview with CBS News the previous day, he rejected all charges that he had done anything illegal in the Whitewater matter, insisting, "The most important thing to me and the most important thing to the American people is I'm completely relaxed about this—because I didn't do anything wrong, except I made a bad business deal."

Officially, the request for the "special counsel" came from President Clinton, who appeared boxed in a corner. He had authorized a letter, written by Bernard Nussbaum, to Attorney General Reno, stating:

> The president has directed me to request you to appoint as special counsel a respected, impartial and qualified attorney, who is not a member of the Justice Department or an employee of the federal government, to conduct an

appropriate independent investigation of the Whitewater
matter and report to the American people.

Meantime, in the *Washington Post*, reporter Michael Isikoff
reveals on January 13 that the Park Police had found a list of
handwritten abbreviations, and that the Justice Department's
Office of Professional Responsibility had decided to include it in
its investigation of the FBI's role in Travelgate.

Speaking of this odd list, Isikoff reports on his interview with
Betsey Wright, a former top confidante to Clinton when he was
governor of Arkansas, who says that she believes that the letter
"C," which is repeated throughout the list, is an abbreviation for
Chelsea Clinton. She also opines that the document is "a worksheet on Chelsea Clinton's assets," which is part of the Clinton
family's blind trust that Foster had been working on during his
final days—but had not completed. One of the dates mentioned,
"2/80," is the month and year of Chelsea Clinton's birth.[95]

On January 14, Howard Kurtz, who analyzes media issues for the
Washington Post, writes an article about the sudden interest in
the president's Whitewater problems by the television networks.
Kurtz observes: "In the last three weeks,... ABC, CBS, and NBC
have jumped on Whitewater night after night. On Wednesday,
when President Clinton agreed to the appointment of a special
counsel to investigate the matter, the network anchors traveling
with Clinton in Ukraine and Russia dealt with Whitewater before
the news of the trip itself....

"Media analysts say no national scandal can reach critical mass
until it becomes a television story."

Clearly, the Vincent Foster case is not going to go away in the near future. Already coalitions are forming to exploit and to politicize the upcoming investigation of his death.

PART THREE
Reviewing the Evidence

"The White House must let Justice do its investigation without interference. Any hint of attempts at interdiction or manipulation would raise the spectre of Watergate."

—JAMES HAMILTON TO PRESIDENT CLINTON, JANUARY 5, 1994

1.

ON THURSDAY, JANUARY 20—one year after President Clinton's inauguration and the six-month anniversary of Foster's death—U.S. Attorney General Janet Reno names Wall Street attorney Robert B. Fiske, Jr., as the Department of Justice's special counsel; eleven days later he officially becomes known as "independent counsel."[1]

Fiske is known as an aggressive prosecutor with high integrity who had served as the U.S. attorney in the Southern District of New York from 1976 to 1980. President Ford had originally appointed him to the position, and President Carter retained him.[2]

Attorney General Reno charters Fiske with the responsibility to probe the relationship between the Clintons and the Whitewater Development Corporation, as well as their association with the Madison Guaranty Savings & Loan and Capital Management Services.

The attorney general also empowers Fiske to reinvestigate the death of Vincent Foster. Consequently, all documents relating to the Foster case—police and FBI reports, crime-lab summaries, and even the autopsy report—will continue to remain publicly unavailable while Fiske conducts his probe.

Upon his appointment, Fiske, who says he will establish an office in Little Rock immediately, tells reporters, "I think the charter is written so that I can do anything I feel I have to do to do this job right. I have been told time and time again by the top officials of the Justice Department, including the attorney general, that there are no limits on what I can do."

Questioned that night on CNN's *Larry King Live* about the appointment of a special counsel to reinvestigate the death of Vincent Foster, President Clinton insists, "I don't think we know any more than we did in the beginning, because I really don't believe there is any more to know. You know, he left a note. He was profoundly depressed."

Editorials in the *New York Times* and the *Washington Post* laud Fiske's appointment. In a January 21 profile about Fiske in the *Times*, reporter Stephen Labaton writes: "Robert B. Fiske Jr.'s reputation for integrity and thoroughness is so entrenched that if he finds no wrongdoing during his investigation of the Whitewater affair, his findings could put rumors about Bill and Hillary Clinton's business dealings to rest."

But the *Wall Street Journal* is less enthusiastic, entitling its editorial, "Too Much Baggage," and challenging the selection of Fiske because of, among other reasons, his legal representation of Democratic powerbroker Clark Clifford, the owner of a Washington bank linked to the Bank of Credit and Commerce International, during the recent BCCI banking scandal.

2.

ON JANUARY 27, 1994, a week after Robert Fiske's appointment and the same day that Philip Heymann resigns as deputy attorney general, Christopher Ruddy publishes his first story about the Foster case in the *New York Post* titled "Doubts Raised Over Foster's 'Suicide.'" Ruddy reports on his interviews with Fairfax County Fire and Rescue personnel about the crime scene at Fort Marcy Park, claiming that they have "raised new questions about the 'suicide' of the White House deputy counsel."

Two of the rescue people Ruddy had talked to are George Gonzales of Medic One and Corey Ashford of Ambulance One. Ruddy also had a telephone conversation with Kevin Fornshill, the first Park Police officer at the scene who found Foster's body.[3]

Both Gonzalez and Ashford told Ruddy that they had seen very little blood on or around Foster's body. Ruddy writes that Gonzalez stated that Foster's arms and legs were suspiciously straight alongside his body—"as if it was ready for the coffin"—with the gun in his right hand, "perfectly perpendicular to Foster's leg"; Foster's fingers, Gonzalez said, were wrapped around the gun's grip, and the gun appeared to be clean and free of any blood stains.

Ruddy adds that Ashford, who says he saw no blood at all, claimed that, even though he had helped to place Foster in a body bag, he did not see an exit wound.[4]

According to Ruddy, a variety of homicide experts he had contacted propose that: "The apparent contradiction—a scarcity of blood in a death involving a gunshot wound to the head—[raises] the possibility that Foster may have been killed elsewhere and that his body was dumped in the park."

In a sidebar to his article, Ruddy also asserts:

■ Foster's family cannot identify the gun found in his hand.

- The official investigation does not account for Foster's time from 1 PM until his body was found.

- No one had heard any gunfire in the park.

These three assertions are true.

The following day, Ruddy publishes a second story about Foster's death, "Cops: Foster Gun Was Never Tested," reporting that USPP Major Robert Hines had told him that the USPP might not have conducted a "ballistics" test of the gun found in Foster's right hand. Hines also claimed that the District of Columbia's Metropolitan Police Department (MPD) had conducted the firearms testing on the gun—for which Ruddy received an official MPD denial.

In fact, Hines was wrong: the ATF *had* conducted the firearms testing on the gun found in Foster's right hand *after* the USPP had closed its investigation; the MPD had only checked its records to see whether Foster had registered any gun—which he had not, in violation of D.C. law.[5]

Later that day, as the furor over the Foster case continues to mount, a scheduled press conference featuring Ashford and Gonzalez is canceled at the request of the Fairfax County Fire and Rescue Department. Of course, this raises even more suspicions.

Also, on January 28, reporter Michael Hedges of the *Washington Times* highlights Ruddy's interviews with the Fairfax County rescue workers. And he questions the decision by official investigators not to release Foster's autopsy report, adding: "Speculation has in fact grown stronger—not only in Washington, but in Mr. Foster's native Arkansas and elsewhere, as columnists, editorialists and radio and television talk show hosts continue to raise questions about the circumstances of the death and the thoroughness of the investigation that followed."

In New York, Robert L. Bartley, the editor of the *Wall Street Journal*, and Dow Jones, the newspaper's parent company, file suit in federal court, asking for the reports prepared by the U.S. Park Police and the FBI in the Foster death investigation. Bartley opts for litigation after his August 10 request under the Freedom of Information Act was delayed because of the chronic "backlog" of initial requests to the Department of Justice.

Park Police and FBI officials have continued to resist releasing their reports, including the autopsy report, because Robert Fiske and the Office of the Independent Counsel (OIC) insist on reviewing them without interference.

In his lawsuit, Bartley claims: "The public has a keen interest in several of the matters on which Mr. Foster was working at the time of his death, particularly a relationship between the president and Mrs. Clinton and the Whitewater Development Co.... The reports of the Park Police and the FBI on Foster's death are therefore agency records of substantial public interest and should be available to the press and public for review and discussion."

To emphasize Bartley's litigation, the *Wall Street Journal* publishes an editorial, "Release the Foster Report," featuring Ruddy's "enterprised" reporting in the *New York Post*, stating: "The *Post* reports of last Thursday and Friday... are either wrong or right. If they are wrong, it's a great pity the complete Park Service Police report has not been released to still such speculation. If they are right, the Justice Department and the Park Service Police have had a great deal to hide. Either alternative suggests that the report should be released forthwith."[6]

After the *Journal's* Freedom of Information Act suit, Ruddy's two articles in the *New York Post*, and Hedges's story in the *Washington Times*, the *Washington Post*, in a January 29 article by staff writer Robert O'Harrow, Jr., also cites Ruddy's work, reporting that rescue workers Ashford and Gonzalez had been asked by their supervisors "not to discuss their suspicions publicly." And O'Harrow allows Major Hines to correct his previous statement about the firearms testing.

The following day, giving the Foster case an atmosphere of international interest, Washington correspondent Ambrose Evans-Pritchard of the *Sunday Telegraph* in London, mentioning Ruddy's reporting, writes in his column: "The death was investigated last summer by the Park Police. The poor fellows were so brow-beaten, so far out of their depth, that they stood sheepishly outside Mr. Foster's office as White House aides ransacked the place. According to the *New York Post*, the Park Police even forgot to do a ballistics check on the revolver. No wonder they don't want to release the report."

Of course, the USPP's Hume and Markland were *inside* Foster's office at the time of the search, but who is going to complain? No one expects to hear from Evans-Pritchard again.

3.

ON WEDNESDAY, FEBRUARY 2, former FBI Director William Sessions— who was fired the day before Foster's death—sends a stunning, handwritten letter to Christopher Ruddy, in response to the reporter's inquiry as to why the FBI was not the lead investigative agency in the Foster case.

Sessions states that Foster had taken part in a "power struggle within the FBI and the Department of Justice, of long duration, [which] was ongoing at the time of President Clinton's inauguration." Sessions adds that because of the FBI's Travel Office investigation, which involved Foster, "[t]he decision about the investigative role of the FBI in the Foster death was therefore compromised from the beginning."

The following day, February 3, Ruddy features Sessions's letter in an article, headlined "Ex-Chief: Politics Kept FBI Off Foster Case."

Later that day, Attorney General Janet Reno is asked by reporters about Sessions's letter to Ruddy. She replies, "I got the FBI as involved as they thought was necessary.... I don't know what [Sessions is] talking about."

Ruddy continues his blasts against the Park Police, quoting law-enforcement experts who criticize the way the police handled the crime scene. Calling the police investigation "sloppy," Ruddy's specifies:

- The police did not conduct a "hand and knee" search of the area around Foster's body.

- The police did not "canvass the neighborhood around the park."[7]

- The police did not "interview regular park visitors."

Ruddy also claims that the police were unaware of a "rear park entrance—closer to the death scene than the main entrance."[8]

These statements are correct. But Ruddy cites two other criticisms that are based on false information: that the police didn't use a metal detector to search for the bullet, and that the police didn't dust Foster's car for fingerprints.

The Park Police performed both of these tests.

On February 4, a senior economic advisor to former President Ronald Reagan, Martin Anderson, now a senior fellow with the conservative Hoover Institution at Stanford University, writes an op-ed piece for the *Washington Times*, suggesting that Foster may have been murdered. Anderson's evidence is based entirely on Ruddy's work in the *New York Post*.

Anderson states dramatically: "But the murder of a White House senior advisor is monstrous to even contemplate. As the horror of that possibility began to sink in, most people, quite understandably, shied away from it. Facts and clues that did not point toward suicide were shunted aside. Questions that should have been asked were not asked."

On the same day as Anderson's column, Pierre Thomas of the *Washington Post* reveals that the Park Police had delayed asking the ATF to conduct firearms testing on Foster's gun until two days after publicly declaring Foster's death a suicide. Thomas reports: "Park Police spokesman Maj. Robert Hines said yesterday the agency did not need [ATF] 'forensics to make our conclusion.' He said the autopsy, interviews, and site examination by investigators pointed to a suicide.

"Asked why the ATF tests were requested at all, Hines said: 'I don't know why there was a difference in time.... It was one of those things to back up our conclusion.'"

Also on February 4, the *New York Times* scores big with the publication of an article by David Johnston and Neil A. Lewis: "Report Suggests Clinton Counsel Hampered Suicide Investigation." The two reporters have managed to get a first look at the Park Police's still-confidential report on the Foster case, which claims that Bernard Nussbaum had "impeded" its investigation while presenting a "dubious account" of the events leading to the discovery of Foster's torn-up note.

But, in fairness to Nussbaum, Johnston and Lewis add: "Though the report in several instances indicates the investigators' frustration over Mr. Nussbaum's efforts, it offers no evidence that they challenged him and were rebuffed. Instead, the report indicates that the investigators acceded to the restrictions placed on them, acting in deference to the authority of the White House and because the case seemed to be a straightforward suicide."

The following day, February 5, the *Washington Times* continues its attack on Nussbaum after reporter Michael Hedges receives his own look at the Park Police report on the Foster case. Hedges highlights a particular report by "a Park Police detective," presumably by USPP Detective Markland, saying that he had a "clear view" of Foster's briefcase as Nussbaum searched it, and that "it was empty."

That same day, the *New York Times*, which had earlier called for Nussbaum's dismissal, publishes a profile of the White House counsel, "Litigator on a Tightrope," written by Neil Lewis. Now under siege for months, Nussbaum appears to share Vincent Foster's views about Washington, particularly with regard to Republicans and the media.

Lewis writes: "Like others who have been assailed before him, he contends that Washington is imbued with a 'culture of attack.' In Washington, he said, it is normal 'to look very critically at what people are doing—not only not to give them the benefit of the doubt but to read every doubt against them.'"

As Nussbaum continues to receive a pounding in the press, *Los Angeles Times* reporters John M. Broder and Ronald J. Ostrow interview him on February 9.

Regarding the home-run question of whether he "impeded" the Park Police's case, Nussbaum replies defiantly, "We did not interfere with the investigation one whit. To accuse me of interference is not to understand the role of the lawyer, the obligations of the lawyer."

That same day, the *Washington Times* alleges that the Rose

Law Firm had authorized the shredding of Whitewater documents just six days before.[9]

4.

THE BRITISH NEWSPAPERS ARE COVERING the Foster investigation like an incestuous relationship gone bad within the Royal Family. On February 10, reporter Stephen Robinson of the *Daily Telegraph* presents his view of Washington: "Dinner party talk concerns the unproven suggestions that Foster and Hillary Clinton had an affair; some are convinced he took his life because she jilted him after having achieved her ambition of becoming First Lady."

Robinson also credits the American press for politicizing the Foster case and inciting the rebirth of Whitewater, writing: "In the months ahead, two factors will be crucial. One is the behaviour of the media. Whitewater may be looking more and more like a Watergate, but then, a largely liberal media, led by the *Washington Post,* pulled no punches against a Republican president. Whether or not the American media have the stomach to press investigations which could destroy a Democrat in the White House is questionable.

"So far the *Post*'s rival, the right-wing *Washington Times*, has led the pack from the beginning on the Whitewater saga, and only now are the other heavyweight papers beginning to catch up. The second factor is the official inquiry by a liberal Republican lawyer from New York named Robert Fiske."

That same day, Christopher Ruddy publishes his latest installation on the Foster case, claiming that the Park Police has "quietly revised" its conclusion that Foster had placed the gun in his mouth. According to Ruddy, the Park Police are now claiming that "Foster held the gun a few inches away from his mouth and fired." Based on the outside experts contacted by the reporter, neither theory was consistent with the wounds and evidence on Foster's body.

Ruddy does not say who at the Park Police had told him the official position has changed—but most insiders surmise that this erroneous information has come, once again, from Major Hines—because he had made the same claim to Reed Irvine and Joe Goulden at AIM.[10]

Ruddy adds in his story that his outside experts suspect that the gun found in Foster's right hand—"because of its age and the fact that its history is unknown"—is nothing more than a "drop gun."[11] Ruddy also questions whether Foster could have fired the gun with his thumb, as described by the police.

On Friday, February 11, the *New York Daily News*—in what appears to be its opening volley against Ruddy and its rival, the *New York Post*—publishes an article by reporter Karen Ball, "Foster's Wife Tells Why."

Through her sources in the Park Police, Ball, too, has obtained access to the USPP's final report, which includes the interview that Captain Hume and Detective Markland had with Lisa Foster. In an apparent effort to debunk Ruddy's work and the conspiracy theories concocted by conservative opinion writers, Ball repeats the tales about Foster's depression and the bad press he received in the *Wall Street Journal*, and adds, "Nowhere in the 100-page police report still being kept secret did the controversy over the Clintons' land dealings with Whitewater Development Corp. ever surface."

The widening confusion over the facts of the Foster case now reaches Congress.

On February 14, William F. Clinger, Jr., the ranking Republican

on the U.S. House Committee on Government Operations, sends
a letter to Secretary of Treasury Lloyd M. Bentsen, indicating:

> Recent press stories have raised concerns regarding the
> procedures observed by the U.S. Park Police and other law
> enforcement agencies following the tragic death of White
> House aide Vincent Foster. These stories have suggested,
> among other things, that investigators were "impeded" in
> their investigation of Mr. Foster's death.
>
> As a result, I have asked the staff of the Committee on
> Government Operations to conduct a review of the opera-
> tions of the law enforcement organizations responsible for
> conducting the investigation of this event. I would appreci-
> ate your assistance in this congressional review by provid-
> ing me copies of all documents filed within the Department
> of Treasury regarding the death of Mr. Foster and make
> available relevant personnel. This should include, but not
> be limited to, the ATF ballistics and Secret Service reports.

Representative Clinger sends similar letters to President
Clinton, Attorney General Reno, and Secretary of Interior Bruce
Babbitt, who has jurisdiction over the National Park Service and
the U.S. Park Police.

Soon after, Clinger announces on the House floor that he has initiated his own probe of Foster's death within the Government
Operations Committee.[12] Clinger says that he wants to know
"exactly what role the White House played and to what degree, if
any, White House officials hindered or impeded the investigation."

On February 23, 1994, Fiske selects fifty-six-year-old Roderick C.
Lankler, a thirteen-year veteran of the respected Manhattan
District Attorney's Office, to direct the Foster probe. Lankler
chooses Mark J. Stein, an assistant U.S. attorney for the Southern
District of New York, as his chief lieutenant.[13]

In addition, the FBI details two veteran special agents to the Fiske team, William Colombell and Larry Monroe, each of whom has been with the bureau for nearly thirty years. With the FBI's participation, the Fiske investigation will also have full access to the FBI's crime lab.

The OIC and the FBI are determined to answer three basic questions about the Foster case:

- Did Foster commit suicide, or was he murdered?

- If he committed suicide, did the incident occur at Fort Marcy Park, or was his body moved there from another location?

- If Foster committed suicide, what were his motives for doing so—and were they, in any way, related to the legal issues concerning the Clintons' relationship with Whitewater Development and Madison Guaranty?

Even though this investigation is supposed to be about Foster, the targets are clearly the president and Mrs. Clinton.

5.

IMMEDIATELY, RODERICK LANKLER AND Mark Stein of the OIC, along with the FBI, conduct their first two interviews—with the two rescue workers who had talked to Christopher Ruddy.[14]

Sergeant George Gonzalez of the Fairfax County Fire and Rescue Department confirms what he had already told the reporter: that Foster was lying straight with his hands at his sides and the gun in his right hand, and that there wasn't much blood at the scene.

However, during his statement, Gonzalez says something startling about his first look at Foster's body that either he didn't tell Ruddy or Ruddy had failed to catch:

> From visual inspection it was obvious that Foster had suffered a gunshot wound to the head. *The wound was recalled to be located in the upper, right front portion of the skull.* (Emphasis added)

Gonzalez's report completely contradicts the autopsy report—which documents the bullet entering in Foster's mouth and exiting out the *back* of his head—as well as the recollections of nearly everyone else at the crime scene. Gonzalez, in fact, is the only known person to have noticed such a wound.

Gonzalez also claims that he had seen a briefcase in Foster's car, although none was ever reported by those who searched it. According to the USPP, Foster's briefcase had been left in his office at the White House; his torn-up note was later found in that same briefcase.

Also interviewed on February 23 by Lankler, Stein, and the FBI is Corey Ashford, who had helped place Foster's body in the body bag, drove the ambulance that carried Foster's body to Fairfax County Hospital, and coded Foster's death as a homicide. Ashford confirms that he had spoken over the telephone to Ruddy with the permission of the rescue unit's public affairs office.

The FBI report states:

> [Ruddy] asked [Ashford] if he had seen any blood on Foster's body. Ashford informed the reporter that he had not seen any blood. When asked for his opinion regarding whether the death was a suicide or not, Ashford declined further comment....

> It was initially believed by Ashford that Foster was the
> victim of a murder. This belief was based upon Foster's
> body having been located in a wooded area. Ashford was
> not told by anyone at the incident scene that Foster com-
> mitted suicide.

Meantime, that same day, yet another scandal brews for the
Clinton White House, stemming from the newly revived interest
in Whitewater.

Earlier in the month, on February 2, Deputy Treasury Secretary
Roger Altman, who was also the acting head of the Resolution Trust
Corporation (RTC), had met with top-ranking members of the
White House staff—including Bernard Nussbaum and the first lady's
chief of staff Maggie Williams—and had given them a "heads up"
about an RTC investigation of Madison Guaranty and the Clintons,
in which criminal referrals had been filed with the Department of
Justice in the fall of 1992. The case had bounced back and forth
between Washington and Little Rock during early 1993.

Before the February 2, 1994, meeting, two previous "heads-
up" meetings had taken place on September 29 and October 14,
1993. At the first meeting, Jean Hanson, the general counsel of
the Department of Treasury, had spoken to Nussbaum about the
criminal referrals. Nussbaum gave the information to presidential
assistant Bruce Lindsey, who then talked with the president.

On November 4, 1993—just four days after *Washington Post*
reporter Susan Schmidt broke the RTC story—Webb Hubbell, the
number-three person at the Department of Justice, recused himself from all Whitewater and RTC matters. Later, in the midst of
the Senate Banking Committee's investigation of the "heads-up"
meetings, Hubbell—who is also having other legal problems,
stemming from charges that he had earlier overbilled his clients at
the Rose Law Firm—will resign as associate attorney general.[15]

What is either suspicious or remarkably coincidental about this chain of events is that the president had called Foster on the night before his death to meet—or to watch a movie—with him, Webb Hubbell, and Bruce Lindsey.

What, if anything, did Vincent Foster know about the RTC matter, as well as Hubbell's problems at the Rose firm?

On February 28, Robert Fiske signs and faxes a letter to Steven I. Froot, an assistant U.S. attorney in the Southern District of New York. Froot had asked Fiske in a February 22 letter for his position on releasing the investigative reports of the U.S. Park Police and the FBI. In his letter, Fiske replies:

> The public disclosure of all or any part of the Park Police or FBI report at this time would substantially prejudice the ability of the Office of the Independent Counsel to conduct its investigation. For example, if a witness has access to what another person has said about a particular fact or to conclusions reached in a report, that witness' testimony or statements in an interview could be tainted by that knowledge. As a result, the requirements of the Freedom of Information Act do not apply to these reports at this time, because the reports were "compiled for law enforcement purposes" and their release "could reasonably be expected to interfere with enforcement proceedings."

Fiske's arguments appear sensible but seem somewhat hollow, because much, if not all, of the final report of the Park Police, the lead investigative agency in the Foster case, has already been leaked to the media.

6.

ON FRIDAY, MARCH 4, reporter Douglas Jehl of the *New York Times* quotes both President Clinton and Secretary of Treasury Lloyd Bentsen as distancing themselves from Bernard Nussbaum and others who have participated in the series of early-warning meetings about pending RTC investigations of Whitewater and Madison Guaranty.

The following day, Bernard Nussbaum, who had been subpoenaed by the Fiske investigative team the night before in connection with the RTC probe, resigns as White House general counsel, effective April 5. In his letter to the president, Nussbaum insists that his departure has been prompted by "those who do not understand, nor wish to understand the role and obligations of a lawyer."[16]

On Monday, March 7, Robert Fiske sends a letter to Senator D'Amato, as well as Donald W. Riegle, Jr., of Michigan, the chairman of the Senate Banking Committee. Fiske wants to express his concern over the proposed hearings by the committee, saying:

> Inquiry into the underlying events surrounding
> [Madison Guaranty], Whitewater and [Capital
> Management Services] by a congressional committee would
> pose a severe risk to the integrity of our investigation.
> Inevitably, any such inquiry would overlap substantially
> with the grand jury's activities....
> For these reasons, we request that your committee not
> conduct any hearings in the areas covered by the grand jury's
> ongoing investigation, both in order to avoid compromising
> that investigation and in order to further the public interest
> in preserving the fairness, thoroughness, and confidentiality
> of the grand jury process.

In his written response to Fiske that same day, Riegle, a Democrat, states: "It is my view that the Banking Committee should defer to your investigation."

In his own reply, D'Amato, predictably, takes a different tact, saying:

> I continue to be sensitive to the concerns you have expressed about the potential for congressional action to complicate your investigation. At the same time, Congress, and particularly our committee, has a duty to the American people to examine the facts and take appropriate oversight action involving government agencies within the Banking Committee's jurisdiction. Therefore, your "request that [the Banking] Committee not conduct any hearings..." may be a premature and overly broad remedy.

After lengthy negotiations among party leaders, the U.S. Senate votes, 98 to 0, to hold off on any proposed hearings that might compromise Fiske's investigation.[17]

The *Wall Street Journal*'s editorial page still appears tormented by the line in Foster's torn-up note: *"The WJS editors lie without consequence,"* along with the continuing claim that Foster had killed himself because of the newspaper's harsh editorials about his work in the White House Counsel's Office.

In a March 9, 1994, editorial, "The Fiske Coverup," the *Journal*, in its critical discussion of Fiske's investigation of the Foster case, appears remarkably high-handed: (*"[W]e were the only people suggesting there might be an issue concerning ethics among former members of the Rose Law Firm"*), yet defensive (*"Mr. Foster's death was widely blamed on us"*), finger-pointing (*"'Reporters got unsolicited calls from the White House saying that they were at fault, that the press was vultures picking over*

[Foster's] bones'") but paranoid and thin-skinned *("Mr.
Nussbaum... [and] Maggie Williams? These people or those who
work for or with them, we feel entitled to suspect, are also behind
the spin... intended to blacken our name").* (Emphasis added)

Apparently, the *Wall Street Journal* is no longer viewing its
problems with the Clinton White House as merely political business; it is now personal.

7.

CHRISTOPHER RUDDY CONTINUES HIS series of articles: "Cops Made
Photo Blunder at Foster Death Site."

But, in this March 7 installment, Ruddy makes his first truly bad
mistake, wrongly claiming that, based on his "FBI sources": "[T]he
worst police omission of all in the mishandled investigation, experts
say, was the failure to take a crime scene photograph of the body."

Ruddy uses this erroneous information to incite his growing list
of law-enforcement experts to denounce the entire investigation
by the Park Police. For instance, retired FBI official Robert
Ressler tells Ruddy, "It's unspeakable. I can't imagine [why] any
competent investigator would not take crime scene photographs."

But the Park Police *did* take pictures. Even though USPP criminalist Pete Simonello's 35 mm photographs were underexposed,
thirteen Polaroid pictures of the crime scene, taken by Officer
Franz Ferstl and Investigator John Rolla, do exist.[18]

On Friday, March 11, in a story titled "Foster's Secret Apartment
Hideaway Revealed," Ruddy strikes again, alleging that, based
upon information supplied by a confidential White House source,
Foster had "shared a secret apartment with several senior administration officials at the time of his death." In his story, Ruddy

adds: "The source said the apartment was 'not far from the White House. Maybe just across the [Potomac] River [in suburban Virginia].' Other sources said they believed the apartment was in the Crystal City development in suburban Virginia."

Ruddy insists that a White House employee had told the Park Police about the apartment, but that the police had not revealed it in their final report on the Foster case.[19]

Ruddy also reports that the initial story about Foster's alleged hideaway had appeared in a financial newsletter published by Manuel Johnson of Johnson Smick International.[20] White House spokeswoman Dee Dee Myers describes this claim as "a complete fabrication."

Also on Friday—four days after Ruddy claimed that no crime-scene photographs had been taken by the Park Police—ABC's *World News Tonight* broadcasts one of the existing crime-scene photographs, picturing only the .38 revolver in Foster's right hand. Foster's thumb can be clearly seen in the gun's trigger guard.

Using this photo, correspondent James Wooten states: "The White House may have fueled some of the rumors with its own incompetence in the hours after Foster's death. But there is little reason now to doubt that, for whatever reasons he may have had, the president's boyhood friend drove himself across the Potomac one afternoon last July and tragically took his own life."

But, cooler heads notwithstanding, the conspiracy theories are proliferating.

On Sunday, March 13, Michael Isikoff of the *Washington Post* continues his reporting on the Foster case, detailing some of the conspiracy theories circulating inside and outside the Capital Beltway.

Along with the theory that Foster was either murdered or had killed himself in a Virginia apartment and was moved to Fort Marcy Park, other speculation had Foster being "murdered by a three-man hit squad from Germany... [linked] to an aborted coup against Iraqi President Saddam Hussein and the firing of FBI Director William S. Sessions."[21]

Yet another theory connected Foster's death to the "execution-style murder of a former Clinton campaign security official in Little Rock last September."[22]

Isikoff also spotlights Floyd Brown, the chairman of Citizens United, a nonprofit conservative group, which has hired two "full-time investigators" to investigate Foster's death.[23] One of the investigators is David Bossie, known by some as a young "attack dog" who has been brought on, specifically, to investigate President Clinton in a practice known as "opposition research."

Surprisingly, Isikoff doesn't address one of the biggest pieces of gossip spreading throughout the nation. But Walter Scott, the popular Sunday *Parade* newspaper columnist, does. Asked by a reader whether Foster and Hillary Clinton ever had an affair, Scott replies: "No one has produced a shred of evidence to suggest that they were ever more than friendly colleagues or that Foster's death was not a suicide. Any rumor you've heard is sheer speculation."

The following day, Monday, March 14, the *Wall Street Journal*'s schizophrenia between its news and editorial pages becomes obvious when news reporter Ellen Joan Pollock writes an article, "Fiske Gets Off to Fast Start in Whitewater Probe by Moving Forward Aggressively on All Fronts."

Concerning Fiske's investigation of Foster's death, the reporter says: "The goal is to solve the mystery of why Mr. Foster killed himself and whether the Whitewater controversy contributed to his despondent mood. Even if a definitive answer can't be found, investigators hope to quash some of the zanier conspiracy theories."

But the *Journal*'s Robert Bartley and his editorial board publish an editorial on the same day and in the same edition, titled "The Fiske Coverup II." In the first paragraph of this remarkable contrast to Pollock's news story, the *Journal*'s editorial staff declares: "Subpoenas notwithstanding, Independent Counsel Robert Fiske's investigation into Whitewater/Madison is beginning to look less like an effort to get the facts and more like a sophisticated exercise in political damage control. In a word, like a cover-up."

Meantime, in the latest battle in the continuing war between the *New York Daily News* and the *New York Post*, the *Daily News* runs a photograph of Vincent Foster on the front page of its March 14 edition with the words, "Case Closed," stenciled across his face.

Supposedly closing the case is *Daily News* columnist Mike McAlary, a former reporter for the *Post*, who applauds the investigation by the USPP, claiming that the "FBI was with them every step of the way. There are no loose ends."

But the columnist, among other mistakes, cites the wrong date of Foster's death (July 21 instead of July 20) and identifies Foster's car as a Toyota, not a Honda.

In the biggest mistake of all, McAlary further claims: "The body was discovered by a park maintenance worker who had slipped into the area for a quiet midday drink. He reported finding the body, but then made up a story about having seen a white van. He has since recanted the white van story, admitting it was created to cover up his own behavior."

This has to come as a surprise to Francis Swann, the park maintenance worker, who neither found Foster's body nor made up a story about who did.

Christopher Ruddy, who is already way out on a limb on the Foster case and under attack for it, doesn't write the *New York Post*'s rebuttal; it is written by another *Post* reporter, Thomas Ferraro, on March 16.

Exploiting and even having some fun with the mistakes in McAlary's column, Ferraro declares that "the matter is still open."

Even though embarrassed, Martin Dunn, the *Daily News*'s editor-in-chief, stubbornly insists that he "stands by McAlary's story."[24]

In the meantime, the March 21 edition of *Newsweek*, which hit the newsstands on March 14, features reporter Russell Watson reviewing the widespread speculation about Foster's death ranging from the usually responsible sources—such as the *Wall Street Journal* editorial page and William Safire's column in the *New York Times*—to the less responsible claims by Manuel Johnson and right-wing heartthrob Rush Limbaugh, who had claimed that Hillary Clinton owned the "hideaway" apartment, and that Foster had been murdered there.

Watson notes: "Partisan, if not downright malicious, speculation that the death might not have been suicide spread like a bad odor. Roger Ailes, the former Republican campaign consultant who is now president of the CNBC cable TV network, suggested in a radio interview with Don Imus that Foster's death could have been murder. Right-wing televangelist Pat Robertson devoted a segment of his *700 Club* show to the subject, 'Suicide or murder? That's the ominous question surfacing in the Whitewater swell of controversy concerning Vincent Foster's mysterious death,' [Robertson] intoned."

8.

ON WEDNESDAY, MARCH 16, the FBI interviews paramedic Richard M. Arthur, who had arrived at Fort Marcy Park in Medic One with George Gonzalez and Todd Hall but had gone to search for the reported dead body in another direction with the crew from Engine One. A four-year veteran of FCFRD at the time of Foster's death, Arthur questions whether Foster had really committed suicide.

According to the FBI report on the interview with Arthur, who had learned of the discovery of the body from Gonzalez and then went to the crime scene:

> In Arthur's judgment, Foster was obviously dead, and so he did not check for a pulse. He noted that the body was lying perfectly straight—like it was "ready for a coffin." A gun was lying on the ground under [Foster's] right hand, with the barrel partially under Foster's thigh.

On these points, Arthur appears to be in agreement with others at the crime scene. However, according to the FBI report:

> [Arthur] remembers the gun being an automatic weapon of approximately .45 caliber. *He noted what appeared to be a small caliber bullet hole in Foster's neck on the right side just under the jaw line about half way between the ear and the tip of the chin.* He did not note anything else he thought might be a bullet hole. [Emphasis added]

Arthur, who believes that Foster was murdered, didn't mention this supposed entrance wound in Foster's neck to any of the police officers at the scene. Also, the gun in Foster's hand has been clearly identified as a .38 revolver.

Because Arthur's observations are contrary to what everyone

else at the crime scene and the autopsy had reportedly witnessed, his statement is, ultimately, not taken very seriously.[25]

Arthur, however, has not yet spoken with Christopher Ruddy.

On Friday, March 18, FBI agents speak with Todd Hall, who was the first paramedic to reach Foster after USPP Officer Fornshill had located his body. Blocking Fornshill's view of the victim, Hall had kneeled down on the small hill to Foster's right to check the carotid pulse on the left side of his neck. While doing so, Hall—who, like Ashford and Gonzalez, had not seen very much blood—noticed the gun in Foster's right hand.

The FBI report adds:

> During a cursory search of the area surrounding Foster's body, Hall thought he heard someone else in the woods. He subsequently saw something red moving in the woods. He was unable to determine if it was a person. Hall never saw anyone else in the vicinity of the death scene other than EMS personnel and Park Police officers.

At a later interview with Hall, the FBI points out that the red object that appeared to be in the woods had come from Chain Bridge Road, which is just to the north of the crime scene. Hall acknowledges that he might have simply seen the flash of a red car speeding by.

On the same day as the Hall interview, Michael Shaheen, counsel for the Department of Justice's Office of Professional Responsibility, completes his summary about the claim by Foster in his torn-up note that the FBI had lied in its report about the Travel Office matter.

After reviewing the relevant documents and interviewing more than fifty people from the White House, Department of Justice, FBI, Park Police, "as well as private citizens," Shaheen states:

> OPR tentatively found... that the statement in Mr. Foster's note reflected his belief, based on no independent evidence, that his friend and colleague, William Kennedy, did not threaten the FBI agents with the prospect of alternative IRS involvement or inform them that the "highest levels" of the White House were interested in the Travel Office matter. Accordingly, it was our view that since the FBI's report on the Travel Office matter was to the contrary, Mr. Foster concluded that the FBI lied in its report.[26]

On Thursday, March 31, Roderick Lankler of the OIC, along with several FBI special agents and doctors, including James L. Luke and Charles J. Stahl III, interview Dr. James C. Beyer, who conducted the July 21, 1993, autopsy on Vincent Foster, which has still not been publicly released. Dr. Beyer and the others review the results, which are not disputed.

However, they do learn that, even though Dr. Beyer had claimed on his official report that X rays had been taken of Foster's head, there are no existing X rays. According to Dr. Beyer, the X ray machine didn't function properly that day.

9.

ON MONDAY, APRIL 4, reporter Ellen Joan Pollock of the *Wall Street Journal* publishes an article, "Fiske Is Seen Verifying Foster Killed Himself." According to Pollock's sources, Fiske's OIC team is "expected to release a report this month, declaring the death of White House aide Vincent Foster a suicide." She adds that the *Fiske Report* will "largely confirm earlier findings by the U.S.

Park Police," continuing: "Mr. Fiske's staff have been eager to put a stop to speculation that Mr. Foster was murdered or that his body was moved after his death, according to people familiar with the Fiske investigation."

That same day, the FBI Laboratory's Evidence Response Team and representatives from the National Park Service, at the direction of the Independent Counsel's Office, meet at a prearranged staging area in Roosevelt Park on the George Washington Memorial Parkway. After assembling, the large group drives, en masse, to Fort Marcy Park for what becomes almost a bizarre re-creation of the crime scene.

Upon their arrival at Fort Marcy, the group receives a briefing and splits up into teams. The official search begins at 8:10 AM. The FBI report states:

> The major objectives of the search were concentrated on the location and recovery of physical evidence that could be associated with the victim, such as the lead projectile which passed through the victim's head, bone fragments from the victim's skull and the presence of body fluids (blood) in the soil beneath or in the area where the victim was located.

Using the Polaroid photographs taken at the original crime scene by the USPP, FBI lab technicians place a focal point, representing Foster's head, fourteen feet, three inches "in a westerly direction from the center axle of the stationary cannon on site."

The area around where Foster's body had been found is already surveyed; grid stakes, two and a half meters apart, have been placed close to the body. In those areas where the bullet might have possibly landed, the grid stakes are five meters apart.

Using metal detectors, the FBI personnel, who photograph and videotape nearly every activity and maneuver, sweep the entire vicinity. Then, on hands and knees, they target the individual grid areas, using their fingers to dig into the soil, placing the dirt and debris into sifters.

At the location of Foster's body, the crime-scene specialists dig as much as eighteen inches into the ground—"the soil and roots removed and then meticulously hand searched by various screening methods. No bone fragments or bullets of any kind were found in this area."

In the end—after the nine-and-a-half-hour search, ending at 5:30 PM—the FBI reports:

> Fourteen specimens considered to be of probative value on site were collected, photographed, documented and preserved for further Laboratory analyses. These items included various bullets, cartridge cases and shotshell casings....
>
> Numerous items were found that were not considered to be of any evidentiary value. These items included but were not limited to bottles, cans, pop tops, nails, foil, bottle caps, wire and other "trash" materials. Additionally, numerous Civil War artifacts/relics were found during the search. These artifacts were turned over directly to... [the] National Park Service for inventorying and cataloging.[27]

But after the analysis of all the spent bullets, most of which were from the Civil War, the bullet that crashed through Vincent Foster's head has still not been found.

The OIC and the FBI believe that without a firearms examination of that bullet and the gun it supposedly came from, legitimate and not-so-legitimate questions and conspiracy theories will continue to haunt them.

In the meantime, the list of scandals for the Clinton White House, real and imagined, is growing: the Foster case and Travelgate, as well as the continuing fallout from the Whitewater Development Corporation and Madison Guaranty (which includes the indictment of David Hale of Capital Management Services and the "heads-up" warnings about Resolution Trust Corporation criminal referrals that had led, in part, to the resignation of Bernard Nussbaum) are among other alleged acts of wrongdoing.

Plagued by all of this, the president and Mrs. Clinton begin fighting a public-relations battle, trying to salvage the administration's public agenda, especially its revolutionary health-care reform proposals, which are being spearheaded by the first lady. However, the seemingly endless barrage is clearly taking its toll; both the president and Mrs. Clinton appear perpetually on the defensive.

10.

AFTER INTERVIEWING THOSE WHO SAW Foster's body at the crime scene, the OIC and the FBI head for the White House to interview the last known people to see Foster alive.

On Tuesday, April 12, Roderick Lankler and attorney Carl Stich of the OIC, accompanied by the FBI, interview Linda Tripp, Bernard Nussbaum's former executive assistant. Tripp gives the group the same basic story she had earlier given to the USPP about Foster's final day: She hadn't talked to Foster during the morning of his death, but she and Betsy Pond had brought Foster his lunch, which he ate in his office while reading a newspaper. Foster left the office shortly after 1 PM, without his briefcase, saying, "I'll be back."

For the OIC-FBI, Tripp adds details about events that had occurred at the White House prior to the afternoon Foster entered Fort Marcy Park. According to the FBI report:

Tripp advised that she never saw an incident where
[Foster] did not handle stress well. She heard that he lost
his temper on one occasion over the Travelgate matter. As
Tripp understood the matter, Foster wanted to take the
"fall" instead of Nussbaum, and was overheard to say,
"This is *my* blame. Let *me* take it."

A second story Tripp tells, also secondhand, is even more interesting. The FBI report continues:

[Tripp] advised that sometime soon after the death,
[Foster's personal assistant Deborah] Gorham told Tripp
that the morning of his death, much earlier than his leaving,
Foster had placed three pieces of personal correspondence
in the outgoing mail. The pieces were definitely personal,
Foster having addressed them by hand and used stamps
instead of officially franked envelopes. This was sufficiently
unusual that Gorham noted it, and told Tripp who two of
the items were addressed to. Tripp was unable to recall one
of the items, but said the other was to Foster's mother.
Tripp does not know if Gorham knows who the third piece
was addressed to. Pieces of mail are not logged.

Tripp adds that the day before Foster's death, Marsha Scott,
deputy assistant to the president, had spent one to two hours in
"a closed-door session" with Foster. Tripp says that "this was
highly unusual—both her coming to see him and anybody taking
up that much time with Foster."

Foster's executive assistant, Deborah Gorham, who had earlier been
interviewed by USPP Detective Markland and FBI Special Agent
Scott Salter, is reinterviewed by OIC attorneys Roderick Lankler,
Carl Stich, and Mark Stein at the headquarters of the OIC.[28]
Gorham had previously told Markland and Salter that she had

last seen Foster at about 11:30 AM on July 20, 1993, and had noticed nothing unusual about his behavior.

Regarding her general observations about Foster, the FBI report states:

> Even with hindsight, Gorham did not see anything in Foster's behavior which would indicate a distressed state of mind.... Gorham never saw him lose his temper. She saw him angry once, in response to the *Wall Street Journal* article, "Who Is Vincent Foster?" ...An attack on his character was the most hurtful thing to him, because his reputation was the most important thing to him, next to his family.

Although Gorham admits that she didn't know Foster very well personally, they did have a "spiritual" conversation on Thursday, July 15, just five days before his death. The FBI report explains:

> Foster and Gorham were alone in his office. He asked her, "How are you doing?" in a casual way, and she answered, "Some days [are] fine. How are *you* doing?" He answered using the illusion of trying to build a building that people keep knocking down. You rebuild it, and they keep trying to knock it down. Gorham asked him during this conversation, "Do you ever feel like you're in 'spiritual deficit'?" Foster responded, "Yes, I know what you mean."

Speaking of the day before Foster's death, Gorham tells Lankler and his OIC-FBI colleagues that her boss appeared to be in an "uncharacteristic 'lull' in his work pace."

> [Foster] spent it going through his papers and drawers and taking care of a lot of unfinished business he had not been able to get to. He was doing a lot of straightening and cleaning.
> The previous Tuesday, Wednesday, and Thursday he had generated a lot of personal "thank you" letters and several

memos. Monday [July 19], however, he started looking
through the stuff in his drawers, looking calm and staying
quieter than usual and spending more time than usual alone
with the door to his office closed.

She explains that while the rest of the office was busy with the
Freeh FBI nomination, Foster was not involved.

Also on July 19, she says, Foster left the office twice. The first
time he went to his credit union; the second "was without explanation, which was very uncommon." However, Gorham can't
remember what time he left or how long he was away. Gorham
only remembers that Foster left work for the day before she did.

Gorham also confirms what Linda Tripp had told the FBI ear-
lier: that Foster had a long, closed-door meeting with Marsha
Scott on July 19, which was equally uncommon. Gorham, like
Tripp, has no idea what they discussed.

Confirming something else Tripp had said, Gorham tells the
OIC lawyers and the FBI about the three pieces of personal mail
that Foster had sent out—although Tripp thought they went out
on the day of his death. Gorham says they were mailed on
Monday, the day before. The FBI report states:

> Foster placed three items of personal mail in the out-going
> mail tray in the Counsel's Office. Gorham checked to make
> sure they were sealed and had postage on them. It was com-
> mon for Foster to mail bills this way, but unusual for him to
> mail personal letters. Gorham recalled that all were in plain
> white envelopes which Foster had hand addressed. One was
> in a plain white large business (4" x 9 1/2") envelope, was
> rather thick and had two stamps on it and was addressed to
> Foster's mother in Arkansas. The second was in a plain white
> small business... envelope, and Gorham recalls nothing about
> the addressee except the words "Insurance Company."

Gorham can't remember anything about the third envelope, except that it was also hand-addressed and in a small white envelope. However, she doesn't believe that it was either to his wife or another member of his family. And, as Tripp had said, the White House does not log out-going mail.

Gorham, who says she was unaware of the rumors that Foster and Hillary Clinton "were romantically involved," tells the OIC-FBI group that Mrs. Clinton had only come to his office about four times since she began working for Foster in early March 1993. She remembers Foster being called to the first lady's office about three times.

Gorham adds that Lisa had called her husband three times during the week and a half before his death. "Each time," the FBI report notes of Gorham's remarks, "[Lisa] asked how he was doing." Gorham recalls that their son, Vincent III, had also called once during that time, asking, "How's he doing today?"

On the day of Foster's death, Gorham couldn't help but notice that he had arrived at work later than usual—at about 8:50 AM. He usually was at his desk by 8:00. Upon his arrival, he drank a cup of coffee and ate a muffin, then attended the regular 9 AM meeting with Nussbaum and the staff of the Counsel's Office.

According to Gorham, Foster returned to his office after the meeting but left at 10:30 AM with his suit coat over his shoulder—without saying where he was going. He came back an hour later.

Gorham left the office soon after Foster returned, asking whether she could do anything for him before she went to lunch. "No," Foster answered, seemingly relaxed and normal, "I believe I have everything." That was the last thing Foster ever said to her.

By the time she returned to the Counsel's Office between 1:20 and 1:30 PM, Foster had already gone, without leaving a message about where he was going or when he might return.

However, he did leave Gorham "a couple letters and a memo

for her to type." She spent the rest of the afternoon performing this task for Foster—who was never coming back.

Gorham left for the day at 5:45 PM; Linda Tripp called her at 11:30 PM to give her the news of Foster's death.

According to the FBI report, Gorham asked Tripp, who was equally baffled, "What could have been so bad that he would have done such a thing?"

A nineteen-year veteran of the Uniform Division of the U.S. Secret Service, John S. Skyles has spent the past six years on detail at the White House, usually stationed at the ground floor entrance to the West Wing, called guard post "E-4," where he was positioned on the afternoon of July 20, 1993.[29]

This is the first time that any official investigator has interviewed Skyles, the last known person to see Foster alive—probably between 1:00 and 1:30 PM of that day. The FBI report states:

> [Skyles] said that while he cannot recall exactly when he saw Foster, he does distinctly recall that it was "about lunchtime." He said that as Foster walked [past] the guard desk at entrance E-4, [Skyles] asked Foster, "How are you doing, sir?" He said that Foster replied, "Hello, fine," and nodded his head to Skyles with what Skyles remembers as a "half smile."

Skyles adds that he did not recall Foster carrying a briefcase.

11.

AFTER SKYLES, THE FBI INTERVIEWS several people seemingly peripheral to the case: Jim Ferris, Patrick Knowlton, Judith Doody, and Mark Feist.

CIA employee Jim Ferris had told Captain Hume during the USPP investigation that while he was driving home on the parkway between 2:45 and 3:05 PM on July 20, 1993, he saw a gray Japanese-made sedan suddenly cut from the left lane in front of him and make a quick right-hand turn into Fort Marcy Park. At the time of his interview with Hume, Ferris, who worked in the CIA's Office of Security, said that the license plate on the Honda had blue lettering—with "the state lettering in the lower right corner." At the time of the USPP interview, Ferris had reportedly said that the tag was from a midwestern state, possibly Ohio or even Arkansas.

However, during his interview with the FBI, Ferris, who identifies photographs of Foster's car as "similar" to the car he had seen on July 20, isn't as sure about the license plates.[30] According to the FBI report:

> [Ferris] stated that while this vehicle depicted in the photographs was similar to the vehicle he observed... the license plate was different. He once again reiterated the fact that the license plate he observed had the name of the state located in the lower right hand corner of the plate, further stating that since the Arkansas plate has, in bold letters, the name of the state at the top of the plate, he would have clearly remembered the identification of the state.

Refusing to let this contradiction go by, the FBI allows Ferris to resolve it. The FBI report explains:

> In response to questions regarding his initial interview with U.S. Park Police officials regarding the possibility of this car having an Arkansas plate, [Ferris] stated that he probably informed officials of this fact but after viewing an actual photograph of the Arkansas plate on Mr. Foster's vehicle, was positive that the plate he observed on this particular vehicle contained the identification of the state in the lower right hand corner of the license plate.

The obvious problem is that the USPP—in its August 5, 1993, report—had used Ferris's statement as its source for stating that Foster had arrived at Fort Marcy Park at or about 3 PM. Now, the FBI isn't so sure.[31]

Patrick Knowlton, who was driving a Thrifty Rental truck on the afternoon of July 20, 1993, had called the USPP two days later.[32] Investigator Jim Morrissette had taken his statement.

Knowlton repeats his story to FBI Special Agent Larry Monroe, who reports:

> [Knowlton] stated that at approximately 4:15 p.m. while approaching Fort Marcy Park, he had to urinate and entered Fort Marcy Park in order to relieve himself. He indicated that he was somewhat familiar with Fort Marcy Park since, in 1991, he had toured this particular park in the company of his girlfriend. He stated that upon entering the parking area, he immediately noticed an unoccupied vehicle parked front end in facing the park in one of the first parking slots on the left-hand side. He identified this particular vehicle as a 1988–1990 brown or rusty brown in color Honda with Arkansas plates....

Seemingly identifying the position of Foster's gray Honda, Knowlton then moves into an area that can potentially launch a thousand conspiracy theories.

> [Knowlton] further indicated that a second vehicle, located approximately three spaces past the above mentioned Honda, was observed backed into a parking space in the immediate area of a path leading to the northern section of the park. This vehicle was described by [Knowlton] as a Japanese make vehicle, metallic blue in color, with Virginia license plates and in his opinion was [considerably] newer that the previously described Honda. [Knowlton] described the

occupant of this vehicle as a male in his late twenties, probably Mexican or Cuban, with dark complexion, dark brown
or black curly hair worn short, 5'10" to 5'11" in height.
[Knowlton] stated that he specifically remembers this individual since when [Knowlton] departed his vehicle, this male
exited his vehicle and was closely watching him as he proceeded into the park to urinate. He further mentioned that
this male was staring at him, [making Knowlton] feel
extremely nervous and uneasy. [Knowlton] could not further
identify this particular individual nor his attire and stated
that he would be unable to recognize him in the future.

[Knowlton] continued by stating that he proceeded into
the park for approximately 200 feet where he relieved himself to the right of a trail. He then returned to his vehicle...
and once again observed the occupant of the second vehicle
now inside the vehicle with the driver's window slightly
down continuing to stare at him. [Knowlton] stated, however, that upon returning to the parking lot, he walked
behind the brown Honda and peered inside the vehicle where
he observed a dark-blue jacket draped over the driver's seat.
He further stated that he observed in this Honda a leather
briefcase or leather folder on the passenger side seat.[33]

Once again: the U.S. Park Police had found no briefcase or
leather folder in Foster's car. Linda Tripp at the White House told
both the USPP and the FBI that Foster had left his briefcase in his
office; Officer Skyles of the Secret Service didn't see Foster carrying a briefcase as he left the White House.

According to the FBI report, Knowlton says that he had been
in the park for "no more than five minutes and remembers exiting Fort Marcy Park at approximately 4:30 PM and proceeding
north on the George Washington Memorial Parkway."[34]

In other words, Knowlton appears never to have seen Foster's
gray Honda—even though Foster, according to Dr. Beyer's general
estimate of his time of death, had been dead in the woods for at
least a half hour before Knowlton arrived.

Subsequently, the OIC-FBI investigators receive more ammunition for the critics of the USPP investigation of Foster's death, perhaps corroborating a portion of Knowlton's story.

The previously identified male and female in the woods, who were having a late-afternoon picnic on July 20, 1993, are Judith Doody and Mark Feist. According to their original statements to the Park Police, they had arrived in the park at about 5 PM in Doody's white four-door Nissan with Maryland tags, carrying beer and wine coolers.

After Foster's body was found, they were located and interviewed together by Officer Julie Spetz and Investigator Cheryl Braun. In her report, Braun noted that the couple had seen:

- "a small car with a man without a shirt sitting in it, who left shortly after their arrival";

- "a white van with blue lettering, and advised that they observed the driver get out and empty trash"; *this is the mystery man in the white van;*

- "a light-colored old model car"; Feist said that "the driver put the hood up and then walked up into the woods for a while and then returned to his vehicle and left. [Doody and Feist] described the driver as a white male with scrungy hair, but could not provide anything further."

Now, as part of the Fiske investigation, FBI special agents interview Doody and Feist. But this time, they are interviewed separately.

Feist, who says he had a briefcase on the rear seat of Doody's car, confirms to the FBI agents that they arrived at about 5 PM.[35] According to the FBI report of Feist's recollections:

As they drove into the parking lot, he observed a vehicle, possibly a small station wagon or "hatchback" model, brownish in color, parked to his left. The vehicle was parked close to the path leading up to Fort Marcy, with the front of the car pulled into the parking space. The hood of the vehicle was up and a white male was standing in the vicinity of the vehicle. He described the white male as in his mid-to-late 40s, approximately six feet in height, medium built, long blonde hair and beard, appeared unclean and unkept.[36]

Apparently, Feist is describing the position in which Foster's Honda is parked; but who is this man with "long blonde hair and beard?" Did Feist actually see someone tampering with Foster's car?

During her interview with FBI special agents, Doody corrects their time of arrival, saying that they had entered Fort Marcy Park between 5:15 and 5:30 PM.[37]

According to the FBI report of her interview:

To the best of [Doody's] recollection, she maintained that upon entering the parking lot at Fort Marcy Park, she noted that the only vehicle in the parking area was a relatively old (mid-1980s) Honda, possibly a Honda Accord, either tan or dark in color, parked close to the entry of the parking lot, adjacent to a path leading to the northern section of the park. [Doody] believed that... a white male was seated in the driver's seat of this particular vehicle.

Although she was extremely vague on the description of this individual, she believed the occupant had dark hair and could have been bare-chested. After passing this particular vehicle, she drove approximately mid-way into the parking area, backing her Nissan... into a parking space.

During her interview with USPP Investigator Cheryl Braun, Doody had supposedly mentioned seeing a "light-colored old model car" parked next to the Honda. However, according to the FBI report:

> Doody stated that she is positive that her initial comments that a vehicle that she observed as a light-colored older model pulling in next to the Honda [were] untrue. She maintained that the only vehicle she recalls that was positioned between her vehicle and the Honda... was the white van.

In other words, Doody is apparently now saying that she didn't see Foster's "light-colored Honda" until *after* the police arrived; instead she saw a "bare-chested man" in "a relatively old Honda... either tan or dark in color."

According to Braun's report, the couple had stated that the man in the car, who was not wearing his shirt, left soon after they arrived. But, in the FBI report, Doody doesn't indicate whether the man left, stayed, or took a walk in the woods.

Nevertheless, Doody tells the FBI that when the mystery man in the white van pulled into the lot, he backed in between her car and the dark-colored Honda, and that he left about ten minutes later. At about 6 PM, the couple went ahead with their picnic.[38]

While they picnicked in the woods, Doody, like Feist, did not hear any sounds resembling a gunshot. And when the emergency vehicles pulled into the lot, the couple just went on with their picnic.

The FBI appears completely baffled by Doody and Feist's story, because, if they are correct, they, like Patrick Knowlton, appear to have never seen Vincent Foster's gray Honda.

Forced to some conclusion about all of this, the FBI simply allows Doody to self-destruct as a potential witness, saying:

> [Doody] continually advised interviewing agents that her
> recollections of the activities on July 20, 1993, at Fort Marcy
> Park were extremely weak, based on the fact that she was
> engaged in an intensive and personal conversation with
> [Feist]. In this regard, she advised that she would be unable
> to identify either the vehicles in question or, for that matter,
> any individuals she observed.

12.

SUDDENLY, NEWS OF THE MYSTERY MAN in the white van turns up.

A package arrives for Roderick Lankler at the OIC office in
Suite 490 North at 1001 Pennsylvania Avenue, N.W.; it has been
sent by G. Gordon Liddy, the former FBI special agent who was
convicted and imprisoned during the Watergate scandal. The
cover letter, attached to a six-page memorandum, is nothing less
than sensational.[39]

Liddy, whose radio talk show originates from WJFK-FM in
Fairfax, Virginia, writes:

> I enclose my report of interview, dated 27 March 1994,
> of a man who claims to have found the corpse of the late
> Vincent Foster. The report of interview is self-explanatory...
> I am available to you or any of your special agents for
> interview. I will tell you anything other than the identity of
> the individual, unless and until he should release me from
> my promise not to identify him.

Liddy had interviewed the man, whom he refers to as
"Anonymous Witness," on March 22 after receiving a telephone
call from him at WJFK. The phantom witness identified himself
as the mystery man in the white van and invited Liddy to his
home, which was not far from the radio station. The interview
was conducted at the kitchen table in the mystery man's home. He

even gave Liddy a spiral-ring pad on which to take notes. As stated in his cover letter, Liddy typed his formal memorandum of the interview.

On Tuesday, April 12, FBI special agents interview Liddy at his WJFK-FM office about his interview with the mystery man. Liddy, widely known for his stubborn silence during Watergate, cooperates with the agents but refuses to name the man who found Foster's body.

Now, the OIC-FBI team must get Liddy to convince his Anonymous Witness to speak to them.

On Thursday, April 14, FBI special agents go to the home of the mystery man in the white van, "who made himself available to investigators for the Office of Independent Counsel on condition that his identity remain confidential," according to the FBI report.

Actually, the man's name is Dale Kyle; Liddy had persuaded him to speak to the OIC. The FBI report notes, as does Liddy in his own report, that "[Kyle] did express a concern for his safety and welfare because of what he perceived as the high profile government personalities involved in this investigation."

The Anonymous Witness, as Liddy still calls him, tells the special agents that he had been to Fort Marcy Park—which is on his way home from work—about fifty times over the past twenty years.

On July 20, 1993, the day of Foster's death, Dale Kyle was driving home in his white van. Heavy traffic on the George Washington Memorial Parkway had slowed him down considerably. On that day, as on any other day, Kyle, a coffee buff, had drunk enough so that he decided to stop and urinate, driving into Fort Marcy Park between 5:30 and 5:45 PM.[40]

The FBI report continues:

> [Kyle] stated that upon pulling into the Fort Marcy parking lot, he noticed two vehicles, both of which were unoccupied in the parking lot. He stated that the first of the two vehicles was parked to his left, at the beginning of the parking lot; and [he] estimates that this vehicle was in the second or third parking place. He described this vehicle as a compact Japanese made sedan, color possibly light blue or tan, adding that to the best of his recollection, it was a 2-door model.

Judging by the accounts of the Park Police, the car Kyle is really describing is Foster's gray, four-door Honda Accord, which was parked, head first, in the fourth space in the lot. The FBI report goes on:

> [T]he second vehicle was located towards the rear of the parking lot, adding that he's positive that this vehicle was backed into the parking space. He described this vehicle as a white colored Honda, 2-door sedan, with blue interior.

Clearly, this is Judith Doody's white-colored, four-door Nissan, which *was* backed into the parking space and had a blue interior.

> [Kyle] stated that he parked his van between these two vehicles, in closer proximity to the white [Nissan] located toward the rear of the lot. As best he recalls, he backed in. He stated it was very hot and humid and before walking up into the park, he took his shirt off and hung it on the side mirror to dry, as it was wet with perspiration.

In fact, Doody had described a "bare-chested" man in the parking lot to the USPP and the FBI. But during both interviews, she had placed him in the Honda, not the white van, which, she said, had pulled into the lot minutes later.

Doody's companion, Mark Feist, never mentioned anything about anyone having his shirt off while in the parking lot.

As the FBI interview moves forward, Kyle says that he had taken the path that led toward the end of the parking lot, then bent left into a large first-grove area. The FBI notes that Kyle had accurately described the area and the locations of the landmarks in the main grove, which includes a cannon.

> [Kyle] explained that the reason why he went to the highest level of the park, in close proximity to the second cannon, was because that was the area that afforded the most privacy. He stated that because of the two vehicles in the parking lot, he felt that there were people in the park; and the lower levels of the park were more open, and he didn't want someone walking up on him unexpectedly while he was urinating.
>
> [Kyle] stated that once he assured himself that there was no one up at the upper level by the second cannon, he walked up over the berm, at a point approximately fifteen to twenty feet to the right of the cannon. He walked down the berm several feet to a point where his waist was level with the top of the berm and proceeded to urinate.

While relieving himself, Kyle, who was facing north and looking down toward Chain Bridge Road, turned his head and thought he saw some trash on the ground, partially concealed under heavy foliage.

> [Kyle] stated that he walked over to investigate [what he thought to be the trash] and when he got within ten feet, he recognized the object as a body. He stated that at that point, he stopped because he thought it was someone who had fallen asleep. [Kyle] stated that he then decided to take a closer look and moved to within approximately three feet of the body. [Kyle] stated that he is positive that at this point, he was standing directly behind and above the head,

with his right foot extended forward to within thirty to
thirty-six inches of the top of the head. Since he had
approached the body from its right (his left side), it is possible that he was positioned at a slight angle to the right of
the body (his left side). [Kyle] stated that he bent directly
over the head, looking directly into the face of the individual. He was able to observe that the eyes were partially
opened and appeared glazed; that traces of dried, black
blood were on the lips and around the nostrils and that a
number of flies were in the vicinity of the mouth and nostrils. He does not recall blood or traces of dried blood running down the right or left side of the face.

The FBI report continues with Kyle's general description of the
dead man:

> [Kyle] stated that there were what appeared to be light
> purple wine stains and what appeared to be traces of vomit
> on his shirt on the right upper shoulder and chest. He stated
> that he did not observe blood or dried blood on the shirt. He
> stated that there was also a wine bottle that he described as
> approximately ten inches in height, tapered top, with the
> remains of some wine, purplish in color, still contained in the
> bottle. He stated that the bottle was located on the side of
> the berm, approximately two and a half feet to the right of
> the body.

Although the Park Police had seen blood on Foster's right
shoulder, no one else had noticed vomit or "purple wine stains"
on Foster's shirt. Also, Investigators Rolla and Abt had both seen
an old and weather-beaten bottle of wine cooler near the body.

> [Kyle] stated that he stood directly over the body, look-
> ing down, for several seconds, specifically recalling that he
> looked at both hands. He stated that the arms were down
> by the body's sides and that the hands were palms up. He
> stated that while he was not looking for a gun, he has no

recollection of there being a gun present in either hand.
[Kyle] pointed out that upon observing the blood in the
vicinity of the mouth and nostrils, the thought entered his
mind that someone had hit the person in the head and that
was possibly how he had been killed.

[Kyle] advised that there was [extremely] dense and
heavy foliage in the area and in close proximity to the body
and the possibility does exist that there was a gun in or
near his hand that he might not have seen. [Kyle] stated
that he did not, in any way, touch or disturb the body. He
stated that he did not attempt to walk down the bank or
approach the body from either side, nor did he go to the
lower part of the bank and observe the body from the point
looking upward. He stated that as best he recalls from his
vantage point on the top of the berm, the foliage and brush
at the bottom of the berm or slope (approximately fifteen
feet below the body) was trampled down as if the individual might have been walking or pacing in that area.

Kyle then returned to the parking lot. As he passed the car he
described as the "white Honda," which appears to have been in
the position of Judith Doody's white Nissan, he recalls that he
saw a "four-pack wine cooler in the front passenger floor of the
car;... to the best of his recollection, there was a suit coat or
jacket and possibly a brown briefcase in the car."

Significantly, both Doody and Feist had already told the FBI
that they had a bottle of wine cooler on the floor in Doody's car.
Also, Feist had told the FBI that his briefcase was on the rear seat.

Obviously, Kyle is describing Doody's car, not Foster's.

Kyle tells the FBI that he was only in the park for "approximately ten minutes," which is consistent with Doody's estimate.

Kyle says that he left Fort Marcy Park and drove about two
miles north to Turkey Run where he saw the two Park Service
employees. Kyle motioned in their direction and one of them
came over to his white van. Kyle told the park employee that "he

had just come from Fort Marcy Park, and that there was a body located up by the second cannon; and that it appeared to be dead." He asked the man to call the police.

Kyle then left Turkey Run, hoping "that the two park employees did not get his license tag number."

After the formal interview with the FBI, Kyle agrees to accompany special agents to Fort Marcy Park where he retraces his movements and discoveries. After that, Kyle and the FBI go to the Turkey Run Maintenance Yard, just north of the park, where Kyle gives the agents a walkthrough of the location where he had talked to the employees from the National Park Service who eventually called the police.

At the end of the day, the FBI has no doubt: Dale Kyle is the mystery man in the white van who had found Vincent Foster's body.

The following day, April 15, the FBI interviews Kyle again. But this time, Kyle remembers that he *did* see blood on Foster's shirt. Specifically, the FBI report, without noting the contradiction from the previous day, states:

> [Kyle] further advised that there were traces of blood
> stains on the shirt, to include the upper right shoulder area,
> along with traces of what he considered to be either vomit
> or spilled wine possibly purplish in color.

During the first interview, Kyle had also said he didn't see a gun at the crime scene. But during this second interview, according to the FBI report:

> [Kyle] further maintained that he was fixated on the face
> of the body and did not pay specific attention to body
> extremities including the hand. In this regard, [Kyle]

advised he could not remember the exact position of the
thumbs, stating that while he didn't observe a gun, there
could have been a gun in the hand.

Kyle is still confused about the "white Honda" that he had clearly
mistaken as Foster's car when, from his own description of its position and contents, it appears to be Judith Doody's white Nissan.
This time, however, the FBI report gives him an out, stating:

> When further questioned relative to these particular vehi-
> cles, [Kyle] advised that he was not very observant of the cars
> in the parking lot that day and therefore his description of
> these vehicles was in his opinion very sketchy.

With the interviews of the known people at Fort Marcy Park
completed, the OIC-FBI team turns to those closest to Foster in an
effort to determine why he had apparently decided to kill himself.

13.

TO DETERMINE FOSTER'S ACTIONS and attitudes during his final days,
the OIC-FBI team approaches his Arkansas circle of friends and
relatives.

Both Linda Tripp and Deborah Gorham had described Foster's
long, closed-door July 19 meeting in his office with Marsha Scott,
deputy assistant to the president, as highly unusual. Now, the FBI
wants to know what that meeting was all about as they interview
Scott in the office of her attorney.[41]

Scott, a member of President Clinton's most-trusted inner circle
from Arkansas, had known Foster since 1967, the year before he
married his wife. Although they ran among the same group of
friends, she describes her relationship with Foster during these early

days as "merely acquaintances… never romantically involved with one another."

As the years passed, they became personal friends and, when they came to the White House, she made a point of stopping in to see Foster "every day or every other day" just to say hello.[42]

Scott, who had briefly dated a younger and unmarried Bill Clinton in Arkansas, tells the FBI that she can't understand why Foster had taken his own life, saying that depression is nothing unique at the White House. The FBI report explains:

> Scott advised that everyone was depressed. Their whole circle of friends from Arkansas who had come to the White House were overworked and under constant pressure and constant scrutiny by the press and others in the Washington environment. They were "down."

She adds that the regular dinners among the Arkansas group, which used to be held "several times a week," had been reduced to only once a week, on Tuesday nights, because of their overwhelming workload. Foster, in particular, had missed several of these dinners, even the ones on Tuesdays.

On Monday, July 19, the day before Foster's death, Scott recalls that she went to Foster's office to ask about his weekend on the Eastern Shore. Usually, Foster would give her a friendly hug. But this day he didn't. To Scott, "he seemed preoccupied and a little quieter," but not alarmingly so.

Although Tripp and Gorham believed that Scott had stayed with Foster for "an hour or two," Scott believes that their meeting was only twenty to thirty minutes—although "it could have been longer." But she insists that this visit was no different from any other.

The FBI report adds:

> [Scott] advised that she was uncomfortable talking about

some of the private thoughts Foster shared with her. She
said she believed Foster had painted himself into a box with
no windows. But she got the sense during the July 19th
meeting that he had come to some sort of decision and was,
if anything, somehow relaxed as a result....

Scott is of the opinion that Foster committed suicide for
personal reasons but commented that he didn't separate
work from personal matters. He had talked about "wanting
out." He talked about "wanting to rest."

But, she then goes on to say that she "was not aware of any personal matters which were disturbing him." Foster, she reveals for the first time, had been extremely upset over anticipated cuts at the White House, including in the Counsel's Office. The FBI reports:

In fact, the very last words that [Foster] spoke to her were,
"The staff cuts are killing us."... Scott advised that the reac-
tive mode that everybody was in all the time at the White
House prevented the kind of care and thoughtfulness that
Foster liked to bring to his work product.

All in all, the Scott interview, from which the OIC-FBI expected so much more, is a complete anticlimax.

Deciding to take a second crack at Scott, the OIC and the FBI return to interview her.[43] During her first interview, she seemed to have little recollection about the specific topics of their conversation. Mark Stein of the OIC insists on attempting to learn more.

Once again, they are disappointed. But Scott does tell the OIC-FBI that Foster, in the midst of the barrage from the *Wall Street Journal*, had become extremely wary of the media. According to the FBI report:

[Scott] felt that Foster thought that the press was being absolutely ruthless. It seemed to him a personal, mean and vicious attack at a time when he was working extremely hard. Foster (and others in the Arkansas group) felt that [the press, specifically the *Wall Street Journal*] would stay at it until they "took somebody out"—until they drove a wedge to separate the President from his Arkansas friends.

14.

THE OIC THEN TURNS TO Associate White House Counsel William Kennedy, widely described as the "fall guy" in the Travel Office scandal.[44]

During the interview, he describes Foster as his personal mentor. Kennedy is still troubled over the death of his "best friend."

Kennedy explains that, when President Clinton officially moved to Washington in January 1993, Foster, who had accepted his job in the Counsel's Office, convinced Kennedy to join the staff as an assistant counsel. Kennedy explains to the OIC-FBI that he came to Washington on February 10 and again began working with Foster "on a daily basis." The FBI report states:

Kennedy was asked if Foster's departure from RLF [Rose Law Firm] created any problems. Kennedy answered yes. RLF was a partnership of 55-60 partners and Foster, Webb Hubbell and Hillary Clinton were thought of as the senior litigators of the firm. Kennedy said the Litigation Section of RLF "took a hit" with the departure of these three individuals. There was a perception among clients that RLF was not as strong and lacked experience after these three left for Washington, D.C. Kennedy believed that Phillip Carroll, another RLF partner and mentor of Foster, was disappointed when Foster left RLF, but would not describe it as a "falling out."[45] ... Kennedy did not believe the circumstances under which Foster left the firm would have

made it difficult for Foster to come back.... Kennedy noted,
however, that he did not recall in conversations with Foster
that he (Foster) wanted to go back.... Kennedy did recall
Foster making one comment to him in the second week of
June, saying "[Foster] was thinking about finding a job
with less pressure," another job in the administration with
not as much strain.

Kennedy tells the OIC that he had noticed "behavioral [and]
emotional changes" in Foster's demeanor, adding that, as early as
February, he saw that Foster had been losing weight and "seemed
exhausted." The FBI report continues:

Kennedy said the pace and demands of the White House
are astounding. He said the pressures weighed on everyone.
They were constantly being asked questions they hadn't
seen before, with no rule book available. Foster was not
able to operate as he had at RLF. Kennedy believed the
increase in stress for Foster was a cumulative thing....
Kennedy said he "had no indication" of extra-marital relationships of Foster. Kennedy said the rumors regarding Foster
and Mrs. Clinton had kicked around in Arkansas for years.
Their origin was probably political enemies. It was no secret
that Vince Foster, Webb Hubbell and Hillary Clinton were
good friends. Foster "hated" the rumors regarding himself
and Mrs. Clinton. Kennedy remembered a 1992 campaign
comment Foster made that he (Foster) was considering not
talking to the press because of these rumors. Kennedy said
Mrs. Foster had to have heard these rumors.

Kennedy says that he had never talked to Foster about either
Whitewater or Madison Guaranty and was completely unaware
that Foster had anything to do with these issues until he read
about them in the newspapers after Foster's death. He explains,
as others had previously stated, that Foster was extremely upset
with the "Who Is Vince Foster?" article in the Wall Street Journal,

adding that "Foster realized that Arkansas people read the *Wall Street Journal* and being trashed in the *Wall Street Journal* meant being trashed in Arkansas. Foster lived his life to maintain his reputation." The FBI reports:

> Kennedy was asked about Foster's view of Kennedy's involvement in the Travel Office matter. Kennedy said that Foster was very upset that Kennedy got reprimanded. Foster had been heavily involved and felt strongly regarding the FBI leaks in this case. Foster came to the conclusion that he couldn't trust anyone in Washington, D.C. [Foster] was worried about Kennedy's emotional health.

Kennedy recalls that he had last seen Foster at the morning staff meeting on July 20, 1993. At the time, Foster had been working on health-care issues and the lingering fallout from Travelgate. The two men talked briefly after the meeting, about jogging and Foster's family, but they kept missing each other's telephone calls for the rest of the morning. Foster had called Kennedy, who never found out what he wanted to discuss.

That night, Kennedy says, an hour or so after getting home from the White House at 7:20 PM, he received a call from Craig Livingstone, who said he had taken a call from an inspector from the Secret Service, informing him that Vincent Foster was dead. Kennedy refused to believe the news and asked Livingstone to get confirmation. Minutes later, Livingstone called Kennedy back—after confirming Foster's death, which was being investigated by the U.S. Park Police. Kennedy and Livingstone then made arrangements, through the USPP, to view Foster's body and make the identification. They met at the hospital after driving there in their separate cars.

15.

NEARLY NINE MONTHS AFTER FOSTER'S DEATH, Webster Hubbell, who had resigned from the Department of Justice just a month earlier, appears for his interview with the OIC-FBI team, still troubled over his close friend's death.[46]

Hubbell had known Foster for nearly twenty years, since their earliest days at the Rose Law Firm. After coming to Washington in January 1993, Hubbell, who also describes Foster as his "best friend," explains that he "spoke with Foster on a daily basis, at least concerning business matters."

Hubbell had last seen Foster in the deputy counsel's office on July 19, the day before his death but tells the FBI that he "can't remember the business matter discussed." The FBI report continues:

> When asked if there may be any stress associated with working on Whitewater tax returns, Hubbell answered that he was not sure—Vince never mentioned this as a point of stress. He said Foster felt responsible for the Travel Office matter and didn't like the criticism being received on this issue....
>
> Hubbell believed that Foster thought that the option of going back to Little Rock or the Rose Law Firm would have been an acknowledgement of failure.

Upon further questioning, Hubbell adds that he was unaware that Foster had any interest in guns or that he ever owned one—until the night of his death. Hubbell then tells the FBI something else they don't know when he recounts the night of Foster's death while at his home, comforting his widow, Lisa. According to the FBI report:

> [Hubbell] said Lisa Foster believed that Vince had two guns and maybe more. Foster had been given these guns when his father died. On the night of Foster's death, they

found only one gun at the Foster residence and no ammunition.[47]

Mrs. Foster had never mentioned this to Investigators Braun and Rolla on the night of their death notification; nor did she tell Captain Hume and Detective Markland when they interviewed her on July 29, 1993.

The FBI also asks Hubbell about the time he and his wife, as well as Michael Cardozo and his wife, spent with the Fosters on the Eastern Shore the weekend before Vincent Foster's death.

Actually, the Hubbells and the Fosters had made plans to have dinner in Washington on Friday night, July 16. But Foster had called him and said that he and his wife had suddenly decided to go to the Eastern Shore and were staying at the Tidewater Inn in Easton, Maryland.

The following morning, the Hubbells left Washington and went to the Cardozos' estate near Easton. When they arrived, Hubbell mentioned to Michael Cardozo that Foster and his wife were in the area, so Cardozo called the Fosters and invited them to his home. The FBI report continues:

> During their association on both Saturday and Sunday,
> Foster spent his time reading the paper, boating, hitting some
> golf balls and being introduced to eating fresh crab. They
> talked about how their lifestyles had changed and how they
> needed to have a life outside work.

Still concentrating on the rippling effect of Travelgate as a possible motive for Foster to take his own life, the OIC-FBI later conducts a second interview with Hubbell.[48] The FBI report states:

> Hubbell was asked if he had noticed any change in
> Foster concerning the Travel Office matter. Hubbell replied

that Foster continued to be upset, focused on the matter
and concerned that Congress was talking about holding
hearings on the issue. Foster expressed concern that people
should be hired to represent the White House....
    Hubbell said he thought that Foster was overreacting to
this. Hubbell advised Foster to get outside counsel if that
was what was needed.

Hubbell adds that, as part of his general overreaction, Foster had
even appealed to Bernard Nussbaum to retain an outside attorney.

16.

THE FBI SPECIAL AGENTS HAVE a lengthy exchange with the assistant
attorney general for legislative affairs, Sheila Foster Anthony,
Vincent Foster's sister.[49] In attendance for this session are Mark
Stein and Carl Stich of the OIC, as well as Jim Hamilton, the
Foster family's attorney. During the 1993 investigation by the
Park Police, Mrs. Anthony was not formally interviewed—
although her husband, Beryl Anthony, had been.

Mrs. Anthony confirms earlier reports about Foster's concern
over Travelgate and the *Wall Street Journal*.

In early July, she tells the OIC-FBI, the Fosters threw a dinner
party to celebrate Anthony's appointment as an assistant U.S.
attorney general and had surprised the Anthonys by flying their
daughter to Washington from her home in Texas. This was one of
the last times Sheila Anthony saw her brother.

The FBI further reports:

At the last dinner which Foster shared with Anthony,
Foster confided to her that he was considering resigning
from his post at the White House. Foster indicated that the
job in the White House Counsel's office was not right for
him. Foster was not specific about what was causing him to

consider resignation. Among the reasons that became
apparent to Anthony were the Travel Office investigation,
the stress of his job, and the constant overwork. Anthony
hoped that Foster would choose to resign the position.

On Friday, July 16, Anthony and Foster talked on the telephone,
just before Foster and his wife left for the Eastern Shore. Saying that
her brother had "*gained* a significant amount of weight while
working at the White House," Anthony tells the OIC-FBI team that
"Foster's voice was different in its tenor." The FBI report adds:

> Anthony recalls noticing the strain in Foster's voice,
> because it sounded so much like the strain she had heard in
> her father's voice when he had been distraught during his
> [cancer] illness. Anthony believes that the phone call that
> Friday was the first time that she had heard the change in
> tenor in Foster's voice. Foster exhibited many characteristics
> of a depressed person, most noticeable of which was the
> fact that he had no sense of humor left.

Further discussing this telephone call with Foster later in the
interview, Anthony detected more evidence of her brother's deteriorating state. The FBI report indicates:

> Foster told her that he was battling depression for the first
> time in his life. Anthony responded by asking Foster to allow
> her to help him. She offered to contact a doctor for Foster.
> Foster then expressed concern that if he were to be seen by a
> doctor, his security clearance could be jeopardized. Anthony
> attempted to reassure Foster by saying that she would deter-
> mine the parameters for a visit with a doctor prior to actually
> scheduling an appointment for Foster.... Anthony called a
> friend who had received treatment from a psychiatrist in the
> past. The friend provided Anthony with the name of one psy-
> chiatrist. The friend later called Anthony back approximately
> thirty minutes later and furnished Anthony with the names of
> two additional psychiatrists....

Anthony called one of the psychiatrists [Dr. Robert Hedaya] and asked how she could structure a visit to him so that the visit would be unrecorded until Foster could decide whether to start a course of treatment.[50] Anthony then called Foster back that same day and furnished him with the names of the three psychiatrists. She encouraged Foster to make an appointment with one of the psychiatrists, but he said that he wanted to think about that course of action over the weekend.

Anthony called Foster on Monday morning, July 19, the day before his death. The FBI report continues:

Foster said that he was not yet ready to see a psychiatrist in Washington, D.C., but he told Anthony that he had called his physician in Little Rock and had gotten a prescription.

Anthony also tells the OIC-FBI group that her brother, to her knowledge, wasn't having financial troubles or extramarital affairs. She adds that the Fosters' marriage was "warm and real."

Although she cannot clear up the confusion over how her brother obtained the gun found in his right hand, she does give her opinion—as Foster's other sister, Sharon Bowman, via John Sloan, had said earlier to the USPP—that the gun came from their father's gun collection.

Regarding the personal correspondence that Foster sent their mother on the day before his death, Anthony says that she was with their mother when she opened it. The FBI report explains:

The letter from Foster concerned oil leases which had been passed on to Foster's mother from her late husband's estate. In attempting to recall what was in the envelope, Anthony now believes that there was an extremely brief cover letter which had been typewritten, and which contained one or two sentences asking Foster's mother to sign the enclosed form and return it to the oil company. The cover letter bore the handwritten signature of Foster.... Anthony is not aware of any other letters which may have been sent by Foster shortly before his death. Anthony has no knowledge of whatever insurance policies were maintained by Foster, but she assumes that there were such policies.

Anthony concludes by saying that she "does not believe that there was a single cause for Foster taking his own life." She thought that the Travel Office matter, pressure from the media, and his incredible workload—as well as his general realization that coming to Washington had been a mistake—might have contributed to his decision.

17.

ON THURSDAY MORNING, MAY 5, Robert Fiske issues a broad subpoena on the White House, demanding "any and all" communications, computer records, documents, indexes, lists, and notes referring to Vincent Foster, including everything that was found in his office in the aftermath of his death, as well as his beeper and anything found about Foster in any White House safe. Fiske requests full compliance by May 10.

The previous December, the Department of Justice had subpoenaed and, on January 5, received a box of documents from Foster's office relating to Whitewater.

President Clinton's new White House counsel, Lloyd Cutler, promises that the White House will comply with this latest subpoena, as well.

During her July 1993 interview with Captain Hume and Detective
Pete Markland, Lisa Foster told the Park Police that her husband
had appeared down and unable to sleep, that his sister had given
him the name of three psychiatrists whom he had never seen, that
he had taken one tablet of a mild antidepressant drug the night
before his death, and that he had fretted over and took personally
all of the criticism the Clinton administration had been absorbing.
As a result, she said, Foster had talked "about quitting."

The tenor of Mrs. Foster's interview with Roderick Lankler
and the FBI on May 9 is much the same—but much more
detailed. Once again, she is accompanied by Washington attorney
James Hamilton.

According to Lisa Foster, her husband was a physically fit man
who jogged three to four times a week and frequently played tennis
while they were in Little Rock—where they had a swimming pool.
Although he continued to run after he came to Washington, he had
cut back considerably on his exercise because of his workload.

She explains to the OIC that when she came to Washington on
June 5, 1993, she was stunned by her husband's appearance,
telling the OIC-FBI team that "he appeared awful,... worried and
stressed." She also says he was losing weight.[51]

She adds that he complained that "nothing at White House was
going right, and he mentioned the example of Zoe Baird," the
aborted nominee for attorney general. She recalls that the night
Baird withdrew her candidacy, Vincent Foster came to bed at 2:30
AM, "sweating profusely and just sick."

Mrs. Foster also recalls that her husband had "sounded choked
up and intense" during the final confrontation with the Branch
Davidians in Waco, Texas. In particular, Mrs. Foster remembers
that her husband "was horrified when the Branch Davidian com-
plex burned. Foster believed that everything was his fault,"
including the mess in the Travel Office.

The FBI report says:

> On Tuesday night, July 13, 1993, Foster spoke with Lisa
> Foster about resigning. Lisa Foster encouraged him to stay in
> his position in the White House Counsel's office. She advised
> him that Congress would take a recess in August 1993. Lisa
> Foster then suggested that he should stay in his current post
> until Christmas of 1993. Lisa Foster understood clearly that
> Foster was speaking about the Travel Office when he was
> speaking of his depression and his concerns.

Mrs. Foster knew that her husband "was compiling a list of
attorneys to represent him, regarding the White House Travel
Office matter. Foster wanted to have an attorney represent him,
because he did not have time to do his work at the White House
and to prepare a defense for himself."[52]

The FBI report continues:

> Lisa Foster is not aware of any indication, nor does she
> suspect, that her husband had become aware of anything
> illegal or highly damaging to either the Clintons or the
> White House which would have presented him with irrec-
> oncilable pressures. Lisa Foster notes that Foster never told
> her anything about his clients.
>
> Foster never mentioned any concern to Lisa Foster about
> either Whitewater or Madison Guaranty Savings & Loan.
> Lisa Foster had never even heard of either of these entities
> at that point in her life.

Regarding the Fosters' marriage, the FBI report simply declares:

> There were no domestic problems between Lisa Foster
> and Foster during the entirety of their twenty-five–year
> relationship.

She adds that on or about Friday, July 16, four days before his

death and just before they left for their weekend on the Eastern
Shore, Vincent Foster had his blood pressure checked twice at the
White House infirmary—after complaining that he felt his heart
pounding too hard. The first reading, she says, was "160/100";
ten minutes later, it had gone down to "140/90."[53]

When her husband told her about the two readings, she said that
she wanted to call his doctor in Little Rock, Dr. Larry Watkins.[54]
She noted that, at one time, her husband had a heart monitor
hooked up to his chest "but no abnormalities were found."

On the same day as his trip to the infirmary, Foster and his wife
drove to the Tidewater Inn in Easton, Maryland, leaving late in
the afternoon and catching the usual heavy traffic. Although her
husband became stressed out because of all the traffic, he refused
to let her take the wheel.

Regarding the Fosters' Honda Accord, which Mrs. Foster
describes as "taupe or grayish," the FBI report states:

> Lisa Foster's daughter, Laura Foster, was the primary
> driver of the Honda automobile which was found at Fort
> Marcy Park, Virginia, on July 20, 1993. The Honda auto-
> mobile belonged to Laura Foster and also to one of Lisa
> Foster's sons. The son and daughter shared the automo-
> bile.... The Honda automobile was the only car which
> Foster and Laura Foster had with them in Washington until
> Lisa Foster arrived with the other family members and with
> the Lexus automobile....
> It was not only typical for Foster to drive the Honda to
> work at the White House, it was imperative.
> The contents found in the Honda on July 20, 1993, e.g.,
> the cigarette pack, beer cans, and corkscrew, belonged to Lisa
> Foster's son. Foster himself did not smoke. Foster's sons had
> gone to the beach the weekend preceding July 20, 1993, and
> the refuse from the weekend was still in the passenger

compartment of the Honda when it was searched by police at Fort Marcy Park.

When the Park Police had asked about the day of her husband's death, Mrs. Foster told Captain Hume and Detective Markland that his "mood seemed better than it had been 'in a while,'" according to the official USPP report.

However, according to the FBI report:

> Lisa Foster still remembers her last contact with Foster on the morning of July 20, 1993, in their kitchen. She recalls that Foster was standing very stiffly in the kitchen prior to departing for work.[55] Lisa Foster now believes that he may have had the gun with him in his briefcase at that time....[56] It is difficult for Lisa Foster to believe that Foster may have come home on July 20, 1993, to get a gun.[57]

Mrs. Foster tells the OIC-FBI that she had no further contact with her husband, and had since "checked both gas receipts and credit card receipts," looking unsuccessfully, for clues as to where he might have gone after he left the White House. Foster made no credit-card charges on the day of his death.

After her husband left for work, Mrs. Foster had played tennis with David Watkins's wife at 8:30 AM. When Lisa returned home, she asked her youngest son, Brugh, to drive her to a meeting of the Multiple Sclerosis Society.

After that, as *Newsweek* had reported in its August 2, 1993, edition, Lisa Foster met Donna McLarty for lunch at the Four Seasons Hotel on M Street in Georgetown. Afterward, they took a cab back to the Fosters' home. Then, along with Brugh Foster, they went to the McLarty's home where Brugh met the McLartys' son.

When she and her son returned home at 5 PM, Lisa Foster called

her husband at work, little realizing he was already lying dead in
Fort Marcy Park with a .38-caliber revolver in his right hand.

During the interview, the FBI shows her the eyeglasses that
Investigator Rolla had found near her husband's body. She says
that they appeared to be his, noting "that the tips of the stems of
the eyeglasses had bite marks on them.... Foster had frequently
chewed on the tops of his eyeglasses as a nervous habit."

Regarding her husband's possession of guns, Mrs. Foster said that
he had received several from his father's estate. The FBI report states:

> [Lisa Foster] is aware of a handwritten note from the
> elder Mr. Foster regarding the disposition of his property
> after he passed away. According to this note, all of the elder
> Mr. Foster's guns were left to Foster and a diamond was left
> to Lisa Foster. After the funeral for [his] father, Foster went
> down to his father's house and retrieved the guns. Lisa
> Foster believes that there were approximately three to five
> handguns included in the guns retrieved by her husband.
> She believes that her husband obtained all of the guns
> which were left by Foster's father.[58]

Mrs. Foster tells the FBI that her husband had packed a "silver-
colored gun" in a travel trunk, which Mrs. Foster brought to
Washington when she left Little Rock in June 1993.

As a further indication of Mrs. Foster's knowledge of her husband's guns, the FBI report states:

> Lisa Foster also knows that Foster kept a gun in a closet
> in their home in Washington, D.C. Lisa Foster was aware of
> the location of one gun inside her residence in Washington,
> and she found that gun still in its usual location on the
> night of July 20, 1993. The gun which she found on that
> date was not the silver gun which she had earlier found in

the trunk in Little Rock. Lisa Foster believes that the gun found at Fort Marcy Park may be the silver gun which she brought up with her other belongings when she permanently moved to Washington.

The obvious problem here is that the gun found in Foster's right hand—according to all reports, except this one—is black, not silver.

According to her statement to the OIC, Mrs. Foster had made at least two, perhaps three, complaints to her husband about the guns in their house. The first was in early June when she moved to Washington and the silver gun was unpacked. And the second and, perhaps, the third came within two weeks before his death. Specifically, the FBI report states:

> Sometime within the last two weeks prior to July 20, 1993, Lisa Foster told Foster to remove the guns from their house in Washington. Foster told Lisa Foster not to remark about the guns in front of the boys. Lisa Foster believes that she may have told her husband twice during that time to remove the guns, but she never checked to see if the guns had actually been removed.

Remarkably, Lisa Foster had denied any knowledge of a gun in the house at the time she was notified of her husband's death by Investigators Cheryl Braun and John Rolla. Nor, during her interview with Captain Hume and Detective Markland, did she make mention of this gun or her arguments about guns in the house with her husband.[59]

Regarding Foster's torn-up note—which was written on or about July 11, 1993—Mrs. Foster tells the OIC-FBI team the same basic story that she told the Park Police, with some additional details. The FBI report states:

Lisa Foster invited Foster to go with her to the store, but he declined to accompany her. Foster was upstairs in bed, alternately trying to sleep and work. Lisa Foster suggested to [him] that he write down everything that "they" did wrong. She suggested to Foster that he go on the offensive and not continue to take responsibility for every mistake which was made in the White House. Foster agreed with Lisa Foster's suggestion, and he sat up in bed and appeared energized. Foster told Lisa Foster that he had not resigned yet, and he said that he had already written his opening statement in his defense. Lisa Foster believes that the torn note which was found was actually Foster's opening argument in the event he had to testify before Congress.

Finally, as she had told the Park Police, Lisa Foster tells the OIC-FBI team that she has no doubts that her husband had taken his own life.

18.

AS QUESTIONS ABOUT THE EXECUTION TIME of the search warrant for David Hale's office linger—and whether Foster had found out about it, triggering a decision to kill himself—the FBI, moving further afield in the search for information on Foster, contacts Fletcher Jackson, the assistant U.S. attorney in Little Rock on May 16, who was involved in the Hale investigation. The FBI report indicates:

[Jackson] advised that the only people who knew of [the approval of the search warrant] were Judge David Young, who signed it; Judge Young's secretary (name unknown); Sandra Garrett, who is Jackson's secretary and who typed some of the applications for the search warrant; and Richard Pence, who was Acting U.S. Attorney;[60] and Jackson, himself. The only other individuals to know of it

would have been FBI [personnel], some of whom knew that
it had been planned for over a month.

Another contact, Denver attorney James M. Lyons, had telephoned Foster at 11:11 on the morning of his death but didn't
reach him, leaving a message instead.

On August 2, 1993, Lyons had been interviewed by Captain
Hume over the telephone. Lyons told the captain that he had met
Foster through Hillary Clinton during the late 1980s and worked
with him during the presidential campaign. Lyons added that he had
last talked to Foster during the evening of Sunday, July 18, at which
time Lyons told him that he planned to be in Washington on July 21.
They agreed to meet for dinner, and Lyons had called on July 20 to
make the specific arrangements. Foster neither returned his call, nor
did he note their anticipated meeting on July 21 on his calendar.

Since Foster's death and his interview with the Park Police,
Lyons had become a reluctant player in numerous conspiracy theories about Foster—because of Lyons's role in preparing the
Clinton campaign's official report about Whitewater in 1992,
revealing that the Clintons had lost nearly $70,000 in the venture.
Many in the media had tried to link Lyons's Whitewater connection and his July 20 call to Foster to the search warrant issued for
Capital Management Services, which was owned by David Hale,
on the afternoon Foster died.

Lyons reveals to the OIC-FBI that on either Wednesday, July 14,
or Thursday, July 15, the week before Foster's death, the deputy
counsel called Lyons and asked him whether he could come to
Washington "on short notice."

Lyons continues that "Foster was... anticipating a legal attack
in connection with the Travelgate scandal." Foster considered
retaining Lyons as his personal attorney and had asked him to

read the White House's report on the Travelgate matter. Foster had been particularly upset that his old friend and Rose Law Firm alumnus, William Kennedy, who also worked in the White House Counsel's Office, had taken the fall during Travelgate.

Lyons knows that Foster had also contacted two other attorneys: Susan P. Thomases of New York and Jim Hamilton.

Later, realizing that they hadn't discussed Whitewater with Lyons, the FBI calls him on the telephone.[61] The FBI report states:

> Asked whether he had ever discussed Whitewater or Madison Guaranty Savings and Loan with Vincent Foster, Jr., Lyons said that he was sure that they had discussed Whitewater at some time…. He advised that the last time they spoke about it was in the context of Foster's preparing corporate tax returns which included statements on the Whitewater properties. Nothing was ever discussed about Madison Guaranty Savings and Loan.
>
> Foster wanted to wrap and conclude the Clintons' interest in Whitewater Development Corporation. And there were loose ends to attend to with regard to James McDougal, because he had the physical records pertaining to the company. It was not, however, a burning issue or one that presented the possibility of a scandal as evidenced by the fact that Foster took approximately six months to get around to tying up these administrative matters and getting to McDougal for his signature on the tax return.

Lyons added that, after March 1993, he had no further conversations with Foster about Whitewater.[62]

Another attorney who called Foster on the day of his death was C. Brantley Buck, another partner in the Rose Law Firm. Buck had called Foster at 10:55 and 11:11 AM. However, when Captain Hume called Buck on August 2 to discuss these calls, the captain was told by Buck's secretary that her boss was on vacation. Thus, the Park Police never interviewed Buck about his two calls to Foster on July 20, 1993.

When the FBI interviews Buck on May 18, the attorney says that he had known Foster for nearly twenty years but hadn't seen him since President Clinton's inauguration on January 20, 1993. They were both, however, working on the Clintons' blind trust, which was the reason for his call. The FBI report continues:

> Buck [already] had in his possession documents for Hillary Clinton to sign, and it was expected that Hillary Clinton would be coming through Little Rock and would be available to sign remaining documents on or about July 21. She had been gone for two or three weeks on a trip to Japan.... Vince Foster was supposed to make sure that the president signed the documents and [that they were mailed back] to Buck in Little Rock....
> There were no difficulties with the blind trust.... As it turned out, Buck did not receive the documents from President Clinton. [B]ut there was no permanent damage, because he evidently did get all the documents executed within the 30-day period.

During one of their final telephone conversations, Buck, teasing Foster about the spate of bad press he had been receiving, asked him if he had read the *Wall Street Journal* that day. Foster replied curtly, "No, and I hope I never do again."

During Denver attorney James Lyons's May 12 interview with the OIC team, he mentioned that Vincent Foster had been in the process of interviewing lawyers, fearing a congressional investigation of the

Travel Office matter; one of the attorneys Foster had been considering was Susan P. Thomases.

The FBI telephones Thomases at her law office in New York.[63]
Agreeing to cooperate, Thomases explains that she met Foster in
1976 via Bill and Hillary Clinton, whom she had known for
nearly twenty years. Thomases had served with Mrs. Clinton on
the board of the Children's Defense Fund—where Maggie
Williams, the first lady's chief of staff, had worked as the director
of communications. In 1991, Thomases began working full-time
in Arkansas for the Clinton presidential campaign, scheduling
events for the candidate. After Clinton's election, she continued
working, part-time, during the transition period. By the end of
1992, she returned to New York and rejoined her law firm.

Thomases tells the FBI that the last time she saw Foster was on
either Wednesday, July 14, or Thursday, July 15, 1993, just days
before Foster's death. They had lunch together; other people were
present, she says. She adds that she could "offer no reason or
speculation as to why he may have taken his life."

19.

ON SUNDAY, JUNE 12, at 2 PM, Independent Counsel Robert Fiske and
his associate Roderick Lankler go to the White House, first to
depose the president of the United States—who is represented by
his White House counsel, Lloyd Cutler, and President Clinton's personal attorney, David Kendall—and then to depose the first lady.

After placing the president under oath, Fiske explains that his
sworn statement will relate "to the death of Vincent Foster, events
in the White House following his death, and questions relating to
the contacts between people in the White House and Treasury."

After several questions about President Clinton's lifelong

PART THREE ■ REVIEWING THE EVIDENCE

friendship with Foster, as well as the professional relationship between Foster and Hillary Clinton, Fiske asks the president how he came to select Foster as his deputy counsel.

Clinton replies that he was, unilaterally, responsible for offering him the job. In fact, he didn't even consult Mrs. Clinton before making the selection—although Mrs. Clinton didn't object. The president adds that he didn't name Foster as his chief counsel, because Clinton wanted someone with more experience in Washington, and who was not his personal friend. Clinton didn't want to invite criticism from the media by appointing one of his cronies from Arkansas to the top position in the Counsel's Office.

Once settled in, Foster, according to the president, worked hard and performed well. But the president explains that he would only see him one to three times a month, either at work or social occasions.

Acknowledging that Foster worked on his family's blind trust, Clinton denies knowing that Foster had worked on the Whitewater Corporation's income tax returns for 1990–1992.

Fiske continues, "Well, let me ask you, right up to let's say July 19, the day before his death, right up to then, had he ever expressed any concern to you personally about anything that was bothering him about his job or anything in his personal life?"

"The answer to your specific question is no," the president replies. "I wouldn't characterize it that way."

"Well, is there some way that I could have put that that would... have produced a better answer?"

"No. Well, yes," Clinton replies.

"A more complete answer, I mean?"

"I knew that he felt badly that he had been personally criticized in the *Wall Street Journal*, and I knew that he—even though he thought it was unfair and inaccurate. And I knew that he was a perfectionist who was concerned at the bad publicity the administration had gotten over two or three issues relating to the organization of the White House."

"What were those issues?"

"Well, specifically, I know the Travel Office issue. And that he was concerned that these problems were not serving me well and were undermining my—or at least not undermining, but interfering with my ability to do my job as well as possible. But I have to tell you, sir, that didn't surprise me. I mean, he was a serious man and a perfectionist. So, he didn't like to see things go wrong in the office on the one hand. And, on the other, he had, as far as I know, never been subject to any sort of criticism about his professional work or his judgment before the *Journal* editorial-page issues."

Fiske continues, "Other than the *Wall Street Journal* and the concern about the Travel Office, was there anything else specific that you heard was concerning him?"

"No...."

"Had you heard from him or anyone else that he was depressed?"

"No. Not depressed. Now, again, leading up to the day... when I talked to him, I knew that he had been concerned about these things that I mentioned earlier. But I wouldn't use the word 'depressed.'"

"Okay. Let me ask you now about the telephone conversation on the nineteenth. I understand, at least from press reports, that you initiated that call?"

"Yes, I called him," Clinton answers. "I called him because I hadn't seen him in a while and I had talked that day to Mr. Hubbell who told me that the Hubbells and the Fosters and another couple had spent the weekend in Maryland and had a very good time. It was a time of high stress for the Counsel's Office because of the White House Travel Office matter and other things. And he said he thought Vince had had a great time and that it had been good for them to get away from the grind of the office and had been a very good weekend. And, so, I hadn't seen Vince in a while, and I hadn't had a chance to talk to him in a few weeks. So, I decided I would call and invite him to the movie that night. So, that's what prompted the call. I called him and asked him if he wanted to come and watch the movie."

"That was *In the Line of Fire*?"

"Uh-huh."

"And you were watching that in the White House?"

"Uh-huh, in the theater here."

"Who else was there?"

"I think there was just a couple of us. I think Mr. Hubbell was there. I think Mr. Lindsey was there. I'm not sure if anybody else was there."

"Where did you reach Mr. Foster?"

"I got him at home."

"How long did you talk?"

"Ten, fifteen minutes."

"Can you give us the conversation, to the best of your memory?"

"Yes," Clinton responds. "When I called him, I thought he might still be at work, but it was in the evening. I don't remember exactly what time it was, but it was already night. First I asked him if he wanted to come to the movie. And he said that he would like to, but that he was already at home with Lisa, and he didn't think he should leave and come back to the White House. I understood that. And then I asked him, you know, if he had a good time over the weekend, and he said they had a great time. Then I told him that I wanted to talk to him about some matters relating to the White House, and I wanted to ask his advice on some organizational issues. But I could not see him the next day, because we had the announcement of Mr. Freeh, the FBI director, and several other things on my schedule, and 'Could we please meet on Wednesday?' And he said, 'Yes, I've got some time on Wednesday, and I'll see you then.' And that was it. That's basically what we talked about."

"And how did he seem to you?"

"Well, he didn't seem unduly distressed. I mean, Vince Foster was a very low-key guy. And when you talk to him on the phone, I mean it was not that different from any other conversation I ever had with him."

"When you hung up the phone, did you have any cause for concern about...?"

"None. None. As a matter of fact, I was just pleased that I was going to be seeing him Wednesday, because I hadn't seen him in a while. I mean, whole weeks would go by, and I wouldn't see him. And I missed that. So, I wanted to see him."

"Was that the last time you talked to him?" Fiske asks.

"Yes, it was," Clinton replies.

A few moments later, Fiske says, "Just one last question about this phone call. Did you place this phone call to him because you had heard from other people that he was sort of down and you thought he might need a little cheering up?"

"No, because I knew he had been under a lot of stress, as all the members of the Counsel's Office were, trying to deal with this Travel Office issue and other things that were going on, just general burden of work. But, in fact, I had heard from Mr. Hubbell that they had had a very good weekend and that he seemed much more relaxed. And that it was a good thing for him to have a chance to get away with his wife and with two other couples who were friends of his. So, I called him just because I genuinely missed him, and I wanted to talk with him. I wanted to see how he was doing, but I also wanted to ask his advice on some things."

"Did you talk to him on the twentieth?"

"Yes. I believe I saw him in the Rose Garden. I think when we named Mr. Freeh, he was in the back of the Rose Garden, watching the ceremony. And that's the last time I ever saw him."

20.

AT 3:55 PM, AFTER FISKE COMPLETES his questioning of President Clinton, Hillary Clinton sits down for her sworn deposition with Fiske and Lankler. She is also represented by Cutler and Kendall.

After explaining the same parameters of the OIC's inquiry to Mrs. Clinton, Fiske begins, "We would like to start by talking about Mr. Foster. I take it you knew him for a long time?"

"Yes, I have," the first lady replies.

"You worked together with him at the Rose Law Firm?"

"Yes."

"In terms of the lawyers that you worked with at the Rose Law Firm, how would you place Mr. Foster in terms of the frequency with which you were associated with him, as opposed to other lawyers?"

"Oh, I was probably associated with him among the three or four frequent associations with respect to work that I did with other lawyers during my time at the Rose Law Firm."

"Okay. And you were personal friends as well?"

"Yes, we were."

"Did you have the kind of personal relationship where he would from time to time discuss confidential matters with you?"

"Very rarely. That was not something that he did with me at least, and I don't believe very often with anyone...."

"Would it be fair to say that you and your husband included the Fosters in your close circle of friends?"

"Yes, I would."

"Did you have any role in his selection as deputy White House counsel?"

"Well, I certainly thought it was a good idea."

"Other than expressing that opinion?"

"I don't know that it really was much of an opinion needed. My husband thought very highly of Vince and wanted him to come to Washington, and I think decided that would be the appropriate role, which I certainly thought was a good idea."

"Did you have any conversations with Mr. Foster yourself about that prospective appointment?"

"I'm sure I did. But I don't recall anything specifically, other than urging him to do it if he thought it was a good idea for him...."

"From the period of time that you all came up to Washington and your husband became president in January of '93, right through the time of Mr. Foster's death, how frequently did you see him?"

"Well, when I went over to the West Wing office, I would sometimes see him several times a day or sometimes not at all. There [were] no [regularly] planned meetings. So, it was a very random kind of series of contacts. Socially, we tried to have all of the people from Arkansas over for movies or for dinners. And we would always invite Vince, because he was up here for the first five or six months without his family. Toward the end of that time, his daughter came and then Lisa came. But we always tried to invite him, as we did with the Hubbells and the others. So, you know, I couldn't tell you exactly how many times, but, you know, a number of times, but particularly in the sort of Friday night gathering of friends and people, and we would try to mix it up with some of the new people we were meeting. But we always invited him...."

"Was he doing any personal work for you or the president other than the blind trust?"

"Not that I'm aware of, no. Oh, wait. The only thing I would add to this is I think he also did some personal advising, or at least in some way involved in the tax returns when they were being finalized for '93, but that was part of the blind trust work, as I recall."

"Your own tax returns?"

"Yes."

"Was he doing work, to your knowledge, with respect to the filing of the Whitewater tax returns?"

"Not that I know of, no."

White House Counsel Cutler interrupts, "This is while in the White House?"

"Pardon me?" Fiske asks.

Cutler repeats, "While in the White House?"

"Yes," Fiske confirms.

"Not that I know of," Mrs. Clinton again responds.

Continuing his questioning, Fiske asks, "When was the last time that you talked to Mr. Foster?"

"You know," she answers, "I've thought about that a lot, because I don't recall it. I don't think I talked with him for a week before we left for Asia. And I did not talk to him all the time I was gone, and I left July 5 or 6, as I remember. And then I got back to Arkansas on July 20. And I just don't have any memory of—I never thought it would be the last time I ever saw him or talked to him. And I don't have any memory of when that was. But I don't think it was for about a month before his death."

"So, as you sit there, you can't sort of bring back the last conversation you had with him?"

"No. I know that I had a conversation with him in mid-June, because there were a bunch of people up here from Arkansas, and my husband was out of town. And he and Lisa called to see if I would go to dinner with them. And I talked to both of them, as I remember. But I couldn't do it. And I'm sure I saw him in and around the office after that, after that mid-June phone call.... But

I just don't have any specific memory of when [I last] saw him or talked to him after that, and I've tried to remember it. Because I would like to remember it, but I can't."

"Again, talking about the time from January '93 right up through July, did he ever express to you during that period of time any concern about anything that was troubling him, either in his job here at the White House or in his personal life?"

"No, I mean, he, like everybody, would say things about, you know, how tough this was, and how different it was, and how stressful it was. And I would, you know, express the same feelings. I think we were all amazed at some of what we found when we got here. But he never confided in me. He never told me—I didn't know until after he died that he took the *Wall Street Journal* editorial seriously. If I had known that, I would have, you know, said something funny or dismissive in some way. But he never said that to me. So I don't have any specific memory of any conversation that went beyond the, you know, general blowing off steam about, 'I can't believe this place' or 'Can you get over this?' or stuff like that...."

"Did he ever express any concern to you about anything relating to any potential legal problems that you or the president might have relating to Whitewater?" Fiske asks.

"No," she answers. "We never talked about that. That was— that was something that I can't ever recall having any conversation with him about after we got here. He had handled the sale [of our interest in the Whitewater Development Company] right before we left, because, as I recall, somebody else was going to do it and couldn't. And [Foster] did it. But that's the only conversation—and that was before we moved here—that I can remember with him about Whitewater."

On Tuesday, June 21, in the wake of extreme pressure from the Republicans, the U.S. Senate adopts S.R. 229, proposed by Senate Majority Leader George J. Mitchell (D-Maine), authorizing oversight hearings by the Committee on Banking, Housing, and Urban Affairs into Whitewater-related activities. According to the resolution, the Senate investigation will also include "the Park Service Police investigation into the death of White House Deputy Counsel Vincent Foster; and the way in which White House officials handled documents in the office of White House Deputy Counsel Vincent Foster at the time of his death."

Immediately, the committee chairman, Senator Riegle, and the ranking minority member, Senator D'Amato, begin writing letters to top officials at the Justice Department, including Attorney General Reno and former Deputy Attorney General Philip Heymann, who is now teaching law at Harvard University, requesting any and all documents in their possession about the subjects of their investigation.

21.

ON THURSDAY, JUNE 30, after interviewing nearly 125 people and having the key evidence reexamined, or examined for the first time, Robert Fiske releases the Office of Independent Counsel's fifty-eight–page report on the death of Vincent Foster.[64]

In the "Summary of Conclusions" at the beginning of the report, Fiske and the OIC state:

> On the afternoon of July 20, 1993, in Fort Marcy Park, Fairfax County, Virginia, Vincent W. Foster, Jr., committed suicide by firing a bullet from a .38 caliber revolver into his mouth. As discussed below, the evidence overwhelmingly supports this conclusion, and there is no evidence to the contrary. This conclusion is endorsed by all

participants in the investigation, including each member of
the Pathologist Panel.

We found no evidence that issues involving Whitewater,
Madison Guaranty, [Capital Management Services,] or
other personal legal matters of the president or Mrs.
Clinton were a factor in Foster's suicide. While Foster did
confide to family and friends in the weeks prior to his death
that certain matters were troubling him, we have learned of
no instance in which Whitewater, Madison Guaranty, CMS,
or other possible legal matters of the Clintons were mentioned.[65] Moreover, in the spring and summer of 1993,
Whitewater and Madison Guaranty related matters were
not issues of concern either within the White House or in
the press.

Fiske also concludes that his simultaneous investigation of the
"heads up" meetings between RTC and White House officials
yielded "insufficient" evidence that anyone had "acted with the
intent to corruptly influence an RTC investigation."

Although much more detailed, the *Fiske Report*, which contains
138 pages of attachments,[66] essentially agrees with the basic conclusions in the two-page report written by USPP Detective Pete
Markland on August 5, 1993, regarding motive, means, and
opportunity.

Fiske, however, comes up with some important new details in
these areas.

Motive

Although he believes that Whitewater-related activities played
no role in Foster's death, Fiske does conclude that the Travel
Office situation had been "the single greatest source of his

distress" in the final weeks of Foster's life. In fact, on or about July 13, he had mentioned to his wife that he was considering resigning from the White House Counsel's Office.

Moreover, according to the *Fiske Report*, the series of editorials in the *Wall Street Journal*, criticizing Foster for this and other matters, further exacerbated Foster's deteriorating state of mind. The report explains:

> Foster was unaccustomed to such criticism. He was distraught over these editorials, and told others that they were mean-spirited and factually baseless. He believed the *Journal* would continue attacking him and others within the administration until someone from Arkansas was forced out of the White House.

Fiske reveals that, as a consequence of these troubles, Foster's work had suffered. In his report, Fiske states:

> Bernard Nussbaum noted a marked decrease in Foster's productivity in the weeks prior to his death. During his first few months in Washington, Foster actively involved himself in most of the important matters within the Counsel's Office. Nussbaum came to rely on him to accomplish matters quickly and with sound judgment. During the particularly busy period of late June and July, however, Foster was virtually uninvolved. For example, Nussbaum noted that Foster uncharacteristically provided little assistance in the selection of a new FBI director, a task that Nussbaum considered one of the most important he faced during his time in Washington. Nussbaum repeatedly suggested to Foster during this period that he should take some time off, but Foster was reluctant....
>
> Nussbaum felt that Foster was overreacting [to Travelgate] and tried unsuccessfully to allay his concerns.

Foster had admitted his depression to his sister, Sheila Anthony, who gave him a list of three psychiatrists in Washington, D.C. Although Foster did not talk to any of these three psychiatrists, Fiske discovered that Foster had tried to reach one of them. The *Fiske Report* indicates:

> Telephone records reflect that in the early afternoon of July 16, Foster made two calls to [Dr. Hedaya]. At 12:41 p.m. and again at 1:24 p.m., Foster called the psychiatrist from the telephone in his office, and charged the calls to his home telephone. Each call lasted one minute or less.[67] The psychiatrist called by Foster often uses an answering machine during the lunch hour when no one is in the office. It is possible that Foster reached the answering machine and did not leave a message.

However, as the Markland/USPP report had noted, on July 19 Foster called his own doctor in Little Rock, Dr. Larry Watkins, who prescribed a mild antidepressant.

Earlier that day in his White House office, Foster spent much of his time with his door closed, "taking care of unfinished business," which included the three personal letters that Foster had sent. Although Foster's assistant, Deborah Gorham, didn't remember to whom one of the three letters was addressed, she did recall that one was to his mother and the other to an insurance company.

The *Fiske Report* continues:

> During the evening [of July 19] Foster received a call from President Clinton. The president had heard that Foster was feeling down about the Travel Office matter and called to invite Foster to watch a movie with him and others at the White House. Foster declined the invitation.... They agreed to meet on Wednesday, July 21. The President did not perceive during this conversation that Foster was downcast or depressed.

Then, on the morning of July 20, Lisa Foster saw her husband standing "stiffly" before he left for work.

Regarding the only known written statement Foster left that could possibly explain his action, the *Fiske Report* observes:

> There are ten separate entries in the torn-up note found in Foster's briefcase. Five of them appear to relate to the Travel Office matter.

Means

The *Fiske Report* identifies Dale Kyle, who admitted finding Foster's body months after the USPP closed its case, only as "a confidential witness" or "CW" in the report. Fiske confirms that he is the mystery man in the white van and details the events that led to his discovery of Foster's body, as well as the arrival of the rescue workers and the Park Police.

The *Fiske Report* declares that Officer Kevin Fornshill had first located Foster's body, followed by rescue workers Todd Hall and George Gonzalez.

To the credit of Fiske and the OIC, they also note that Gonzalez and paramedic Richard Arthur believed that they saw separate bullet wounds on Foster's forehead and neck, respectively. But the *Fiske Report*, which mentions that both men had doubts about whether Foster committed suicide, concludes: "These wounds did not exist."[68]

The report explains how USPP criminalist Peter Simonello carefully removed the .38-caliber revolver from Foster's right hand, adding that "the knuckle of Foster's right thumb was trapped between the front surface of the trigger and the inside of the trigger guard of the gun." The OIC also confirms Simonello's discoveries of a wedge mark on Foster's right thumb where it had been trapped in the trigger guard, as well as powder burns on Foster's right index finger and thumb.

With the arrival of the Fairfax County medical examiner, Dr. Donald Haut, the *Fiske Report* states:

> At that point Foster's body was rolled over and those present observed a large pool of blood located on the ground where Foster's head had been. Haut observed a large exit wound in the back of the skull.

The FBI crime lab also confirms the large amount of blood at the scene, noting the "extensive bloodstaining on Foster's shirt and undershirt, covering a vastly greater amount of his shirt than that depicted in the photographs taken at the scene. This staining is attributable to the movement of the body from the scene...."

Fiske and the OIC generally agree with the findings of Dr. James Beyer, who conducted the Foster autopsy, especially regarding the path of the bullet which entered "the soft palate inside the mouth... and exited from the center of the back of the head."[69]

However, even though the FBI concludes that the gun found in Foster's right hand was "operable" and that the spent cartridge inside the cylinder was fired inside this particular gun, it cannot confirm from any source that Foster had been in possession of this specific weapon prior to his death.[70] Nevertheless, the *Fiske Report*, like the USPP report, strongly suggests that the gun came from Foster's father's collection.

Opportunity

Although the *Fiske Report* generally agrees with the USPP's estimate that Foster had left the White House at about 1 PM, questions continue over the time Foster entered Fort Marcy Park. In fact, the *Fiske Report* admits:

> We have been unable to determine where Foster went
> following his departure from the Counsel's Office at about
> 1 p.m. We have also been unable to determine with cer-
> tainty when Foster entered Fort Marcy Park.... No one
> interviewed during this investigation had ever heard Foster
> mention the Park, or knew of Foster ever visiting the Park
> prior to the date of his death.

The Markland/USPP report had based its estimate of Foster's arrival at the park "at approximately 1445–1500 hours" on Hume's interview with Jim Ferris, the CIA employee who had been driving on the George Washington Memorial Parkway when a car similar to Foster's cut in front of him and entered the park. But, when interviewed during the OIC investigation, Ferris, who was shown photographs of Foster's car for the first time, believed that the car he saw had different license plates.[71]

And Patrick Knowlton, one of the two known people who stopped to urinate at the park while Foster was thought to be in the area, believed that the car he saw at or about 4:30 PM—in the space where Foster's Honda Accord was found—"appeared darker and more compact."

The other man to stop and urinate at Fort Marcy Park was Dale Kyle, who found Foster's body at or about 5:45 PM.

Regarding Judith Doody and Mark Feist, the picnicking couple, the *Fiske Report* states that "neither... observed anything unusual," even though Doody claimed to have seen, among other things, a "bare-chested" man behind the wheel of a tan or dark-colored Honda while Feist saw a long-haired man with a beard standing near this same vehicle with the hood up.

Ferris, Knowlton, Kyle, Doody, and Feist, as well as Jean Slade, the woman who owned the disabled Mercedes near the entrance to Fort Marcy Park, are *not* specifically named in the *Fiske Report*.

Further, as a general overview of the OIC investigation, the *Fiske Report* also confirms

- that the U.S. Park Police did have clear "investigative jurisdiction" in the Foster case;

- that Foster's body and clothing, as well as the surrounding crime-scene area, displayed no indication that a struggle had occurred, or that he had been "incapacitated by [drugs] or alcohol"; and

- that even though the 35 mm photographs of the crime scene taken by Simonello had been "underexposed and of little value,... the Polaroid photographs... clearly depict the condition of Foster's body shortly after the arrival of the Park Police."

The *Fiske Report* includes more new information, such as:

- the "ball-shaped gunpowder" found on Foster's white dress shirt and undershirt is consistent with the gunpowder found in the spent cartridge in Foster's gun;

- the eyeglasses found thirteen feet from Foster's body are consistent with the glasses he wore, and the gunpowder found on these glasses are consistent with the gunpowder in the spent cartridge in Foster's gun;[72] and

- the torn-up letter found in Foster's briefcase had, in fact, been written by Foster.

However, along with the mystery of the origin of the "transfer stain" on Foster's cheek,[73] the *Fiske Report* raises several problems with the evidence during their investigation. For instance:

- Neither the FBI nor the OIC's Pathologist Panel can determine the exact time of Foster's death, because "available information is insufficient."

- Like the USPP's earlier investigation, the OIC concedes that during the FBI's search of the crime scene at Fort Marcy Park, it could not find either bone fragments or the spent bullet that killed Vincent Foster.

- The FBI crime lab had found "one flattened ball-shaped gunpowder particle in scrapings from Foster's shoes and socks, and one disk-shaped particle on the paper that Foster's clothes were placed on at the Park Police Laboratory. The FBI Lab found that these particles did not originate from the fired cartridge in Foster's gun." However, the report adds, "These particles are believed to be the result of contamination some time after the clothing was removed from Foster's body."

- Although Dr. Beyer and, later, the FBI crime lab had found "large quantities of gunpowder" on the soft palate in Foster's mouth, the FBI "did not observe any burns caused by the muzzle blast." But the report explains that "such burns would not necessarily be expected under these circumstances."

- Although some of those at the crime scene and

certainly the crime-scene photographs show some black material on Foster's face, Dr. Beyer never analyzed this substance during or after the autopsy. The FBI concludes, "The question of whether there was gunpowder on Foster's face remains unresolved."

■ The FBI also states: "No ball-shaped gunpowder was identified on the tissue samples from the inside of Foster's mouth, when examined at the Office of the Medical Examiner for Northern Virginia."[74]

■ Although Dr. Beyer indicated that no drugs were found in Foster's blood, the FBI crime lab concludes that Foster's blood contained "small concentrations of [Trazodone], diazepam and nordiazepam. [Trazodone] is the antidepressant prescribed by Dr. Watkins.... Diazepam is commonly known as valium and nordiazepam is a metabolite of valium." The report notes that Lisa Foster had stated that she had valium in her home but was not aware that her husband had ever taken any.

■ Although confirming that the gun found in Foster's hand is, in fact, the gun that Foster had placed in his mouth, the FBI crime lab, based on a visual inspection, "did not reveal the presence of any blood" on the weapon.[75] However, further testing of the barrel of the gun does indicate the presence of DNA, which could have resulted from traces of blood or saliva. The DNA discovered on the barrel is consistent with the DNA in Foster's blood.

■ Although confirming the USPP's conclusion that
no fingerprints were found on the outside surface
of the gun in Foster's right hand, the FBI crime
lab discovered one fingerprint underneath one of
the grips on the handle of the gun. However, the
Fiske Report admits, "The FBI Lab determined
that this was not Foster's print."[76] In a footnote
to this revelation, the report added, "The ability
to recover prints varies due to a number of factors including the texture of the tested object and
characteristics of the person who came in contact
with that object. Latent prints can be destroyed
by exposure to certain elements, such as heat."

■ Even though Foster's body was found lying on the
ground of a public park, over two hundred yards
away from his car, the FBI crime lab concludes that
Foster's clothing "did not contain any *coherent*
soil.... However, the FBI lab found small particles
of mica on much of Foster's clothing, including his
shoes. This mica is consistent with the soil found in
the area where Foster's body was found."

Attached to the *Fiske Report* is an FBI report, dated May 9, 1994.
In it, the bureau's crime lab makes several other observations,
smacking of potential contamination, that are not included in the
main report:

■ "Semen was identified on Q10," which was the
evidence number assigned to Foster's shorts.

■ The report also reveals that "Foster's clothing

contained head hairs dissimilar from his own,
and carpet type fibers of various colors."

The FBI crime lab indicates:

> These colors include white, tan, gray, blue, red, and
> green.... It was also noted that a number of red/dark pink
> wool fibers were found in the debris from specimens Q9 [T-
> shirt], Q12 through Q15 [socks and shoes], Q31A and
> Q31C [the paper on which Foster's clothing was laid to dry
> in the USPP lab]. The sources of these wool and carpet
> fibers or their possible significance is unknown to the
> Laboratory.

> "Blonde to light brown head hairs of Caucasian origin
> which are dissimilar to the head hairs in the K2 known head
> hair sample from Vincent Foster were found in the debris
> removed from the Q9 T-shirt, the Q11 through Q11A pants
> and belt and the Q12 through Q15 socks and shoes."

Regarding the contamination issues that appear to plague the
investigation, the *Fiske Report* issues a blanket statement, specifically citing the conditions in the USPP's crime lab and indicating:

> Although the Park Police laboratory does take precau-
> tions to avoid contamination of evidence, it is a small facil-
> ity which was conducting a number of unrelated
> examinations in July 1993. Foster's clothes were laid out to
> dry for four days on the floor of a "photo lab room" adja-
> cent to the laboratory examination area. This room is regu-
> larly used by Park Police officers working on investigations
> and is equipped with an exhaust fan. It is possible that the
> clothes were contaminated while in this room.[77]

Despite the length of his investigation, Fiske reports that his probe of allegations that White House aides had attempted to obstruct the U.S. Park Police investigation by sabotaging efforts to search Foster's office has not yet been completed. Fiske hopes for completion by July 15.

On the same day as the release of the *Fiske Report*, President Clinton signs the Independent Counsel Act into law, which passed the U.S. House on June 21. Clinton says that the new law provides a "foundation stone for the trust between the government and our citizens."

22.

THE REACTION TO THE *Fiske Report* floods in.

Supporting the report, White House Counsel Lloyd Cutler scornfully tells reporters, "We hope these rumor-mongers and those parts of the media that published their rumors will now leave the Foster family in peace…. They were circulated, many of them, by prominent legislators of the Republican Party."

Less than enthusiastic about the report, Senator Alfonse D'Amato—who is preparing to hold hearings this month about Whitewater-related issues, including the Foster case—warns reporters, "There are many questions left unanswered and much that the American people need to know."

In a front-page article in the *Washington Post* about Fiske's work, reporters David Von Drehle and Howard Schneider write: "Fiske's report tells the story of a man stretched until he broke. As simple—and as mysterious—as that. In the months since Foster's body was found resting on a slope beside a Civil War cannon, the airwaves and printing presses have been filled with theories of conspiracy and intrigue....

"According to Fiske, the truth belied all the ugly glamour. Foster's death was a personal collapse, not a White House scandal."

Wesley Pruden of the *Washington Times* obviously disagrees, writing of the *Fiske Report*: "The explanation of how Mr. Foster died is more credible than the explanation of where he died. Some witnesses said he appeared to have been 'laid out,' as if for his coffin. (Arkansas boys are brought up to be polite and accommodating)....

"The [Fiske] report is a needed reminder that the Whitewater investigation is not ending, but just beginning."

Meantime, the day after President Clinton signs the Independent Counsel Act, Attorney General Reno asks a three-judge panel, designated by the new law to appoint independent counsels, to reappoint Robert Fiske as the independent counsel handling the Whitewater investigation.

That same day, Senators Donald Riegle and D'Amato of the Senate Banking Committee send a letter to Fiske, requesting "all records that are within your custody, control or possession, regardless of format," that relate to Whitewater and the Foster case.

Fiske responds by letter, attaching many of the requested materials.[78] Because he is still in the midst of his probe of the alleged mishandling of documents in Foster's office after his death, Fiske refuses to turn over those records. Fiske also withholds items that are potential evidence in his grand-jury investigation.

Over the next few days, Riegle and D'Amato send similar requests to other federal agencies involved in the investigation—the U.S. Park Police, the FBI, and the Department of Justice, among others—while subpoenas are sent to twelve witnesses:

Officer Kevin Fornshill, criminalist Peter Simonello, Investigator John Rolla, Captain Charles Hume, Investigator Cheryl Braun, Major Robert Hines, criminalist Eugene Smith, and Sergeant Robert Rule, all of the USPP; Richard Arthur, George Gonzalez, and Todd Hall, all of the Fairfax County Fire and Rescue Department; and Dr. James Beyer, who conducted Foster's autopsy. All twelve are ordered to sit for sworn depositions.

On Tuesday, July 5, after a remarkably long silence, Robert Bartley and the editorial board of the *Wall Street Journal* respond to the report of the independent counsel on the Foster case. Never big fans of Robert Fiske, the members of the board acknowledge that he has "performed a public service" by putting the question of whether Foster had committed suicide to rest.

However, once again, the *Journal* makes a defensive statement, saying that: "Mr. Fiske's report, too, provides a platform for shedding further blame on us, namely in interviews directed at dismissing the chance that Whitewater 'triggered' Mr. Foster's depression. We are accustomed to controversy, but this obscures the central point that depression is a disease. It is not caused by travel office scandals, press criticism or the normal stress of public or private life."

Seizing upon the direction of the two streams of blood that originated from Foster's mouth and nose, as well as the transfer stain from Foster's right shoulder to his right cheek—as described in the *Fiske Report*—Reed Irvine publishes a column in the *Washington Inquirer* on July 8, saying: "Obviously, for some time after Foster was shot, the head had to have been in a different position from that observed by those who found the body.... [I]t is clear that the blood stains are powerful, perhaps even irrefutable, evidence that Vincent Foster did not shoot himself in Fort Marcy Park and collapse in the supine, face-up position in which his body was found."

Irvine is among those conservative columnists and talk-show hosts who are complaining that the *Fiske Report* is nothing more than a whitewash and, possibly, part of wide-ranging cover-up.

Reverend Jerry Falwell, well known for his support of right-wing causes, is also busy. The religious leader is actively promoting a video, "The Clinton Chronicles," which contains thinly veiled charges that President Clinton has been involved in a series of murders, some of which appeared as suicides.[79]

Even the *Wall Street Journal* defended the president on this matter, writing in a July 19, 1994, editorial: "For our own part, we cannot for a minute imagine Bill Clinton knowingly involved, even tangentially, in plots of violence."

However, back on character, the *Journal*, in the same piece, publishes the 800-telephone number that readers may call to order the videotape.

23.

ON WEDNESDAY, JULY 13, a bitter exchange explodes in the U.S. House of Representatives between Representative David Bonior (D-Michigan), the majority whip of the U.S. House, and Representative Dan Burton, an Indiana Republican and star of C-SPAN, who, earlier in the day, had raised questions as to whether Foster had committed suicide. Congressman Burton and Senator Lauch Faircloth had written letters, independent of one another, asking federal appellate judges *not* to retain Fiske as the independent counsel, under the newly passed law.

After Burton's initial statement, Bonior angrily states, "Mr.

PART THREE ■ REVIEWING THE EVIDENCE

Speaker, the floor of this House is supposed to be a place where people exchange ideas. A place where we're supposed to work together to move this country forward and work out our differences with open and honest debate.

"It's not a place for sensationalism. It's not a place for rumor-mongering. And it's not a place for scandal-baiting.... Mr. Speaker, during a one-minute speech earlier this morning, we were treated to the same kind of scandal-mongering and gutter politics that's usually reserved for the cheap tabloids.

"Once again, we saw a member from the other side of the aisle take the floor and try to exploit the sad death of Vince Foster as something more than a tragic suicide. The fact is, Mr. Speaker, that this case has been closed...."

Immediately, the Speaker of the House recognizes Burton, who appears to speak for many of the critics of the *Fiske Report*, saying, "Mr. Speaker, I am very glad I was here to hear the remarks made by the majority whip, because I want to go into what I said this morning in more detail.

"I believe there is a real possibility that Vince Foster committed suicide. I do not believe, after reading that report in some detail with about seven other people, that he committed suicide at Fort Marcy Park. I believe his body was moved to that location, and I will tell this body why.

"I want to go into my remarks this morning, because I do not want to hurt the Foster family. But, at the same time, I believe that if there [were] some misdeeds done out there, the American people have a right to know; and this Congress has a right to know. And there should be a complete and full investigation if there are any irregularities.

"Let us go into this just a little bit. The man [who] found Vince Foster's body said his face was straight up, and yet if you read the report there was blood coagulated on the side of his face, and on the shirt. Forensics experts... say in the report that one of the people who worked on the investigation must have moved his head. The fact of the matter is before they even got out there the man that found him said his head was straight up. So the head had been moved before the experts went out there.

"Who moved the body? We need to find out who moved the body.

"There was blonde hair, not Mr. Foster's, on his T-shirt and other parts of his garments. Whose hair was it? It was not his. There were carpet and other wool fibers found on the body. Where did they come from?

"I do not like to talk about this, but there was semen found on his underwear, which would indicate there might have been a sexual experience that afternoon between one and five. If that is the case, it is hard to understand the state of mind of somebody who is thinking about committing suicide and having a sexual encounter at the same time.

"Here is something very damaging. They dug eighteen inches around the body, and they sifted all of the dirt, and they could find no skull fragments at the site,... and there was a three-inch [sic] hole at the back of the man's head from the gun.

"If he was killed at Fort Marcy Park, they would have found skull fragments at that site. Why were they not found there?

"I believe because he committed suicide or was killed someplace else and moved to that spot.

"All of the bullets that were found at the site, using modern technology, show that there were a number of bullets found but not the one which killed Vince Foster, and they were out there with grids and everything else for several days with sixteen people looking....

"Why did the man who found Foster's body say there was no gun in either hand, not once, not twice, but three times when he talked to Gordon Liddy, and that is the man the FBI investigated.

"My concern is for the facts and the truth. When people say I am down here trying to bring this body to a low ebb, I resent it."

Despite the criticism Congressman Burton receives for his remarks, he renews his attack on Tuesday, July 19.

On this day, however, instead of challenging the forensics of the crime scene, Burton, who is now being advised by David Bossie of Floyd Brown's Citizens United group, takes dead aim at the White House and asks nineteen questions:

1. When did White House Chief of Staff Thomas McLarty give the order to seal Foster's office? How was the White House staff informed of McLarty's order?

2. Why was the office not sealed until 11 AM the next morning?

3. Did Bernard Nussbaum, Patsy Thomasson, and Maggie Williams know about Thomas McLarty's order? How did they first learn about Foster's death?

4. Did somebody order Nussbaum, Thomasson, and Williams to search Foster's office, or did one of them make the decision to search the office?

5. If someone ordered them to search the office, what were they told to look for? If it was Nussbaum, Thomasson, or Williams's idea to search the office, what were they looking for?

6. Why would Hillary Clinton's chief of staff be in Foster's office, looking through files?

7. Why did they remove the Whitewater files, and what happened to them?

8. Were other documents taken? Were documents destroyed?

9. Where were the documents when they entered the office? Were they in locked files or a safe? If so, how were these opened?

10. Shouldn't they have left everything there for the police to examine?

11. Instead of keeping law enforcement from doing their job, shouldn't the White House staff have been giving them their full cooperation after their friend and colleague was found dead?

12. Why didn't President Clinton immediately order the FBI to take charge of the entire investigation, instead of allowing the Park Police to handle it?

13. Did White House officials purposely mislead the Park Police about the existence of Whitewater documents in Vince Foster's office?

14. How did the White House staff miss a note, torn into twenty-eight pieces, in the bottom of Vince Foster's briefcase during their first two searches of his office?

15. Why were there no fingerprints on the note?

16. What documents were given to Vince Foster's attorney, James Hamilton, and what was given to the Clintons' attorney, David Kendall? Were any destroyed?

17. Who were all the White House officials involved in the second search of Vincent Foster's office?

18. Did the White House staff have the legal right to prohibit law enforcement from searching Foster's office as part of an investigation into Foster's death?

19. Has the Senate Banking Committee requested the phone logs of Nussbaum, Williams, and Thomasson for the period immediately after · Foster's death?

Burton concludes by saying, "To the media, I would say, 'Start asking these questions.' These questions should not be left unanswered, and this body should be investigating [them]. [A]nd we will continue to do our best, but we are up against a stone wall right now with the special counsel."

24.

ON WEDNESDAY, JULY 20, the first anniversary of Foster's death and the same day as the first public release of a redacted set of the 1993 U.S. Park Police reports about its investigation of Foster's death, the Foster family, via their attorney, Jim Hamilton, releases their first official public statement since the *Fiske Report*, which they describe as "thorough and honest," indicating:

> Independent Counsel's Report on Vince Foster's death confirms what his family long has believed—that deep depression, which we never will fully understand, caused Vince to take his life. We also concur that the Whitewater affair had nothing to do with his death....

>   There is now no justification for painful, repetitious
> examination of those issues. The principal advocates for
> doing this appear chiefly motivated by mean-spirited parti-
> sanship.... We are particularly appalled by the shameful
> statements on the House floor by a legislator
> [Representative Burton] who, in our view, is purposefully
> employing outrageous innuendo and speculation for politi-
> cal ends.[80] It is so unfair for the family's privacy and emo-
> tions to be pawns in a partisan struggle.

On Friday, July 22, right-wing activist Floyd Brown, the chairman
of Citizens United, issues his group's latest assault on the White
House in its growing "ClintonWatch" series, *Whitewater: The
Conspiracy of Silence*, featuring an alphabetized list of principal
characters in the investigation and a chronology of key events in
the probe. In a cover letter to the report, Brown writes: "I hope
that you find this special report helpful as we draw closer to congressional hearings on the Whitewater matter. Citizens United
will continue to press for answers until the American people have
the whole truth about Whitewater—truth which the American
people both want and deserve."

In a response from the left on the *Fiske Report*, David Corn, a
columnist for *The Nation*, writes in its July 25 issue: "The issue
here is not the credibility of Fiske. It is the right's hatred of the
Clintons. Sure, during the Reagan days, leftists, liberals and pro-
gressives felt deep animosity toward the doddering president, but
the scandals they barked about were clear and present ones that
did not require elaborate speculation: Iran/Contra, Contra drug
dealing, the Bush family's unsavory business connections....

"Clinton is merely a mushy centrist. Yet to the right he is the
devil—quite literally to some."

On Tuesday, July 26, Reed Irvine of Accuracy in Media, after his op-ed piece about the Foster case is rejected by the *New York Times*, purchases a quarter-page ad in the *Times* for $16,800, titled "Fiske Shows His Hand." Irvine uses the findings of the FBI's crime lab in his attempt to discredit "two of Fiske's three major conclusions."

As he had earlier written, Irvine challenges the *Fiske Report*'s findings about the blood-transfer stain on Foster's cheek, as well as the semen, blonde hair, and carpet fibers found on Foster's clothing. Irvine chastises the media, particularly the *Times*, for failing "to subject Fiske's report to critical scrutiny."

Back in Washington, Representative Henry B. Gonzalez (D-Texas), the chairman of the U.S. House Banking, Finance and Urban Affairs Committee, opens his own hearings into Whitewater. However—out of respect for the family—Gonzalez decides *not* to address the issues spiraling around Foster's death.

In a June letter to House Speaker Thomas Foley, Gonzalez writes: "No congressional committee is in any way capable of acting as coroner or homicide investigator, even if there were some legislative purpose to be served in pursuing this issue.... I would urge that this subject be deleted, on the ground it lacks legitimate purpose. [T]he Congress is ill-equipped to undertake the task, and any congressional review would inevitably be criticized rightfully as inexpert."

25.

OPENING THE LONG-ANTICIPATED OVERSIGHT hearings into Whitewater-Madison Guaranty matters and the Park Police investigation of Foster's death on Friday, July 29, Senator Riegle announces that

the third area of inquiry—"the way in which White House officials handled documents in the office of White House Deputy
Counsel Vincent Foster at the time of his death"—will be delayed.

Riegle adds, "Mr. Fiske informed us on July 15—that's just two
weeks ago—that contrary to his earlier expectation, he had not
yet concluded his inquiry into the handling of Mr. Foster's documents. He, therefore, asked that we not address this issue at this
time, and, in deference to his request, we have put it aside until he
indicates his work in this area is completed."[81]

From the outset, the committee's hearings promise to be filled
with acrimony and partisanship.

FBI special agents William Colombell and Larry Monroe, as well
Dr. Charles Hirsch, New York City's chief medical examiner,
appear on the first panel to be questioned by the committee. All
three had worked closely with the Fiske investigation of Foster's
death.

Special Agent Monroe gives an opening statement on behalf of
his panel, recounting the conclusions of their investigation, saying, "After concluding that Mr. Foster's death was a result of a
suicide in Fort Marcy Park, our final task was to determine
whether there was any evidence to connect any Whitewater-
related issue to his suicide. We have found no such evidence.

"Those who worked in the White House, during the first half
of 1993, have all stated that Whitewater was not an issue of any
significance within the White House during that period. The issue
had received virtually no attention in the press since the spring of
1992 during the presidential campaign.

"As one person put it, Whitewater was not 'on the screen' at
the time of Mr. Vince Foster's death. It was not until October
1993, three months after Mr. Foster's death, when it was dis-

closed that the Resolution Trust Corporation had issued criminal referrals involving Madison Guaranty and Whitewater that the matter again received prominent public attention.

"Therefore, the timing of Mr. Foster's death does not suggest that Whitewater was a cause of any distress for him. Each of Mr. Foster's coworkers, friends, and family whom we questioned stated that Mr. Foster never expressed any concern to them about Whitewater-related issues.

"Obviously, the fact that Mr. Foster never expressed a concern about Whitewater to anyone does not mean that he did not, in fact, have such a concern. Thus, we cannot conclusively rule out such a concern as a possible contributing factor to his depression."

Senator D'Amato questions Monroe about Foster's possible knowledge of the warrant obtained to search the office of David Hale in Little Rock. Monroe replies that there is no evidence that Foster had any such knowledge.

D'Amato continues, "Mr. Hale's attorney called the White House or called Mr. Foster. There was some talk about that. If you have any information, I'd like to know about it."

Monroe, who appears somewhat baffled by the question, simply replies, "I do not, Senator."

"Has that been looked into?"

"Yes, sir."

"And we have no information with regard to that call from Mr. Hale's attorney?"

"I have no information in our investigation that there was any contact between Mr. Hale and Mr. Foster, Senator.... We have no information or evidence that Mr. Foster received any telephone call—"

"Did any White House personnel get a phone call from Mr. Hale's lawyer?" D'Amato continues to press.

"I'm not aware of that, sir, but, of course, we are still

continuing the investigation as to the follow-up in the White House after Mr. Foster's death, sir."

"You'll let us know, then?"

"Absolutely."

D'Amato, who merely appears to be fishing during this opening line of questioning, concludes, "I'll leave that an open question."

Later, Colombell, under questioning from Senator Christopher Bond (R-Missouri), comes to his partner's rescue on the matter of the Hale search warrant, saying that he had personally gone to Little Rock to inquire about a possible leak. During discussions with the supervising agent in the FBI's field office in Little Rock, the supervisor assured Colombell "that they could find no reason to believe that there was information leaked with regard to the search warrant."

Soon after, Senator Lauch Faircloth (R-North Carolina) takes over the questioning, saying, "Mr. Fiske claims... there's no evidence Whitewater played any role in the depression that led to the suicide. Were you made aware [that] before his death Vincent Foster had prepared and filed three years of delinquent tax returns for the Clintons' Whitewater partnership?"

Monroe replies, "I was not personally aware of that."

"Well, he did file three years' delinquent tax returns."

"Thank you, sir...."

"In 1992, the Whitewater issue surfaced in the Clinton presidential campaign and the Clintons hired an attorney who, of course, cleared them of any wrong. Later Whitewater resurfaced in the so-called Lyons report and was thoroughly discredited. Are you aware of the Whitewater report and the fact that James Lyons was to meet with Vince Foster the day after he died? Could that have affected his state of mind?"

"I was aware of his scheduled meeting with Mr. Foster the day after his death. Whether or not that had any impact on his state of mind would be mere conjecture on my part, Senator."

Clearly scoring some points, Faircloth attempts to ask about the documents discovered in Foster's office. Riegle rules that such questions are beyond the scope of the committee's mandate, because the issue was still under investigation by the OIC.

Senator Robert Bennett (R-Utah) asks Monroe about the "blond/light-brown hairs of Caucasian origin" that were found on Foster's clothing. "Has the FBI investigation determined the identity of those blond Caucasian head hairs?"

"No, we have not, sir...," Monroe replies. "The source of this hair could have been boundless. It could have been obtained at work. There was a White House ceremony that morning. It could have been from his residence. It could have been from his automobile, which was used quite often by his children. [It could have been] during the autopsy; during the period of time that the clothing was in the possession of the U.S. Park Police; [from] any blond-haired person at the death scene. [A]nd there's no way to determine whether or not those hairs were on those certain articles of clothing either on the day of his death or days previous to it. We are also very well aware, sir, that Mr. Foster's daughter... has blond hair."

Bennett continues, "The second one is in the same category. I'm curious. The FBI identified carpet-type fibers of various colors. They contain red, dark pink wool fibers on various pieces of his clothing. Does the FBI have any idea where [they] came from? Was there any attempt made to match that with any carpet in his home, car, or office?"

"No, sir," Monroe answers, "and for the same reasons I provided in response to your first question relative to the hairs. They were multiple colors. We had no way to match those particular carpets up, outside the fact that they most likely came from his residence or from his office."

26.

THE SECOND PANEL OF THE hearing features Dr. James Beyer, Sergeant Cheryl Braun, and Investigator John Rolla, all of whom take the oath. Not at their table but sitting in back of the sworn witnesses is Major Robert Hines, who has submitted a written statement.[82]

Chairman Riegle begins by asking what Braun and Rolla had observed at the crime scene. "Had the body been moved at all?" Riegle asks. "I mean, was the body in the position in which it was first found? [O]r had it been moved in any way by the time you arrived, to your knowledge?"

Rolla replies, "To my knowledge, the body had not been moved other than we do have this blood-transfer stain from the collar to the chin. Somebody either checked the carotid or whatever [and] may have moved the head; I do not know. [B]ut that is the only possible movement. Otherwise, no, the body had not been moved."

Senator Faircloth takes his turn and, once again, immediately begins skating along the forbidden territory, asking, "Ms. Braun, the Park Police did not seal Foster's office, but you did instruct David Watkins to secure Foster's office until the Park Police could secure it?"

"That's correct," Braun answers. "Before I left the death notification, I asked that Mr. Watkins take care of having that office secured...."

"But he didn't," Senator Faircloth replies. "That evening, Bernard Nussbaum, Maggie Williams, and Patsy Thomasson made an unauthorized entry into Foster's office and took the Whitewater files. They kept the Whitewater documents out of the hands of law-enforcement authorities."

Riegle begins to interrupt Faircloth's line of questioning, which has been forbidden in deference to Robert Fiske's investigation, when Senator Christopher Dodd (D-Connecticut) jumps in and

objects to it. After Dodd makes his point, Riegle politely asks
Faircloth to move on to something else.

Faircloth protests, "You know, it is my understanding that
[Fiske] was saying you cannot get into what was in the files. My
question is merely the handling of the material itself. I am not pursuing what was in them. I just want to know how it was handled."

Supported by an interpretation of their mandate by Senator
Paul Sarbanes (D-Maryland), Riegle rules Faircloth's line of questioning out of order.

Faircloth then turns his sights on Dr. Beyer, asking, "Dr. Beyer,
your autopsy report indicates that you took X rays of Mr. Foster."

"I had anticipated taking them," Dr. Beyer responds, "and I
had so stated in one of my reports."

"Your autopsy report says you took X rays of Mr. Foster. Did
you?"

"No, sir."

"Why did you say you did if you didn't?"

"As I indicated, I made out that report prior to actually performing the autopsy. We'd been having difficulty with our equipment, and we were not getting readable X rays. Therefore, one
was not taken...."

Faircloth asks, "Why didn't you call Fairfax Hospital and
arrange for a portable X ray machine to be brought in for your
use in such an important occasion?"

"...If it had been a penetrating gunshot wound, then an X ray
would have been a requirement."

"Well, was it not 'penetrating'?"

"No, sir. It was perforating."

"What did it do?"

"It was in and out."

Riegle interrupts, "Do I understand you to say that the termi-
nology you use when it is done in that way is it is a perforating

wound, as opposed to a penetrating wound? Is that what you are saying?"

Dr. Beyer explains, "'Perforating' indicates a wound of entrance and exit.... 'Penetrating' is a wound of entrance with retention of the missile...."

Faircloth continues, "The Park Police officers who were present at the autopsy said you told them not only was an X ray taken, you also told them the results of the X ray. How do you account for the contradiction?"

"I have no explanation," Beyer replies, "because I did not take an X ray."

Beyer adds that he had no X rays in his files that were taken between July 6 to July 26, 1993—while the X ray machine was broken or being repaired.

Senator Dodd asks, "You did not know the condition of your X ray machine at the time you filled out that form?"

"We were having trouble with it. Some days we would get a partial readable X ray. Other days, we wouldn't.... My error was not removing the 'yes' [on the gunshot chart] when I finalized the autopsy."

When Senator Patty Murray (D-Washington) takes over the questioning, she wants to discuss the circumstances of the death notification with Braun, saying, "There have been some hints that there may have been some kind of obstruction to your access to information the night of the Foster suicide, and I just want to walk back through that with you for a minute. When you arrived at the Foster home and informed Mrs. Foster that her husband had apparently committed suicide, what was her reaction?"

Braun replies, "It was a normal reaction of grief. She was hysterical, visibly shaken.... [S]he collapsed on the stairs. It wasn't an unusual reaction for somebody being told that their husband was dead."

"Then over the next hour, other people showed up at the scene. And, Sergeant Braun, you testified that Webster Hubbell pushed you out of the way at the Foster home. Do you think he did that in an attempt to cover something up?"

"As I said previously, I really hadn't gotten far enough with any kind of questioning. I was trying to build rapport. I really don't know what his purpose was in pushing me away. I think it was, in and of itself, rude, but I think it was done to comfort Sheila Anthony [to whom I was speaking at the time of the push]...."

Murray concludes, "I would think that most people would not be thinking about a police investigation the moment they have heard about a death of someone they loved. They would be thinking about the tragedy and how they are going to deal with it...?"

"Yes," Braun simply replies.

"So, from your perspective, do you feel that anyone was trying to obstruct you in trying to get information that night?"

"No, I wouldn't say they were."

The hearing ends peacefully shortly thereafter; the officers and officials of the U.S. Park Police can anticipate a wait of several months before the Senate Banking Committee decides for or against the way in which they handled the Foster case.

On August 1, in the wake of the hearing, Senator Bond publishes an op-ed piece in the *Washington Times*, which appears to set the stage for the future of the Foster investigation. Bond writes: "In my mind, the issue is not, nor has it ever been, that Mr. Foster committed suicide. That is what I believed happened. Rather, it is whether Whitewater issues played a part in his death and whether the White House made a conscious effort to withhold information relevant to Mr. Foster's state of mind."

27.

ON TUESDAY, AUGUST 2, just days after the Clinton White House appeared to have survived the latest Republican assault, the *Washington Post* reports that Bernard Nussbaum had removed a Whitewater file from Vincent Foster's office and given it to Maggie Williams, Hillary Clinton's chief of staff, on July 22, 1993. Worse yet, the file had been passed at the specific request of the first lady.

Reporter Ruth Marcus reveals: "A White House official said Williams, after being asked by Nussbaum to take charge of the documents, checked with the First Lady in Little Rock, Ark. Hillary Clinton told Williams to check with another White House employee 'about a safe place in the residence to store the documents,' the official said."[83]

Marcus adds that the file wound up in a "locked closet on the third floor of the White House residence," to which Williams had a key. The documents remained in the White House residence for five days until Robert Barnett, then the Clintons' personal attorney, picked them up on July 27.

Marcus quotes David Kendall, Barnett's law partner who took over as the Clintons' counsel, saying, "Neither the president nor Mrs. Clinton examined or reviewed the documents from Mr. Foster's office."

In December 1993, when the White House first confirmed published reports that a Whitewater file had been removed from Foster's office, the president's spokesperson insisted that Nussbaum had *immediately* turned over the file to the Clintons' attorney. Now, it turns out, that might not have been true.

At her daily press briefing, Dee Dee Myers confirms Marcus's story in the *Post* and admits, "I think, in hindsight, we should have been more clear about exactly what the chain of custody on those documents was. And I think that was a mistake."

But Myers's statement will not haunt the Clintons as much as a prior declaration made by Mrs. Clinton on April 22, 1994, during her press conference on Whitewater. At that time, the first lady, in response to a question about whether Maggie Williams had taken any documents from Foster's office, said: "I don't think that she did remove any documents. After Mr. Nussbaum reviewed the documents, and after he did so, as I recall—I was not here, I was in Arkansas—but I believe that that was done in the presence of officials from the Park Police and maybe some other agencies. Then Mr. Nussbaum distributed the files according to whom he thought should have them."[84]

That same night, Representative Burton returns to the floor of the U.S. House, speaking for nearly forty-five minutes on C-SPAN, which covers his speech live. One of the centerpieces of his latest attack on the *Fiske Report* is Marcus's report earlier that day in the *Washington Post*. He even reads a portion of it into the *Congressional Record*, adding:

> Well, the bottom line is the *Fiske Report* is inaccurate;
> the *Fiske Report* has glaring holes in it; the *Fiske Report*, as
> it is presently constituted, is not worth the paper it is
> written on.

The following day, Wednesday, August 3, John V. Esposito, a private investigator in Marlboro, New York, sends his reply to an earlier request from Reed Irvine of AIM to examine the *Fiske Report*.

Obviously knowledgeable, Esposito agrees with many of Irvine's concerns about the inadequacies of the *Fiske Report*—but only up to a point.

For instance, Esposito has some problems:

- no one in Foster's family could identify the gun

- no one had ever conducted a "dermal nitrate" test, which detects trace metal, on Foster's hands to determine whether he had actually fired a gun

- the two cartridges loaded into Foster's gun were never examined for latent prints

- no one ever obtained the fingerprints of the members of Foster's family—for elimination purposes—in order to determine the source of the latent prints in the car and on the gun.

But Esposito also throws cold water on two of the biggest controversies on the case, saying:

- the two unknown gunpowder particles found on Foster's socks and shoes—which were inconsistent with the gunpowder contained in the bullets in the gun—had most likely resulted from crime-lab contamination. Esposito continued: "Evidence contamination frequently occurs to evidence stored long term in police facilities," and

- the blood stains on Foster's clothing, including, presumably, his right shoulder—and, consequently, the mysterious "transfer stain"—"can be best explained by post mortem movement of the body by the police and ambulance people."

Esposito then lumps together evidence of the semen, hair, and carpet stains discovered by the FBI on Foster's clothing, saying, "Assuming Foster changed his shorts daily, as most men I know do, [t]he semen stains on his shorts, assuming he did not have sex with anyone at the White House, probably occurred at an unknown location between the time he left his White House Office and before his arrival at Fort Marcy Park, which could explain the carpet fibers and blond hairs found on his clothing."

On Thursday, August 4, the *Washington Times* publishes a full-page ad: "A Special Report on the Fiske Investigation of the Death of Vincent W. Foster, Jr.," prepared by Christopher Ruddy. The ad is paid for by the Western Journalism Center (WJC), a California-based, "non-profit, tax-exempt foundation promoting journalism education and investigative reporting."

Actually, Ruddy has not published a single article in the *New York Post* about the Foster case since March 11. Noting this, the July issue of the *AIM Report* states: "Fiske's report validating the White House line on Vincent Foster's death was, as we expected, accepted without question as gospel by all the media. The *New York Post*, which had done so much to expose the flaws in the investigation by the Park Police, found no fault with Fiske's blessing of the Park Police's findings. When Fiske leaked word to ABC News and the *New York Daily News* last March that his report would do just that, the *Post* took flight. The editors pulled investigative reporter Christopher Ruddy off the story. When the report was finally issued,... the *Post* reported it without any critical analysis."

Accompanying the spectacular full-page promotion for Ruddy's report is a pitch for a biweekly newsletter, *Dispatches*, founded and edited by Joseph Farah, the executive director of the WJC. Farah, the former editor of the defunct *Sacramento Union*, had created the WJC with James G. Smith, the *Union's* publisher, in 1991. The *Union's* owner was Richard Scaife, the chief financial backer of the

Western Journalism Center, who also contributes heavily to Reed Irvine's AIM, as well as *The American Spectator*.

According to the WJC's promotional literature: "The first major national investigative project was reporter Christopher Ruddy's full-time examination of the death of White House Deputy Counsel Vincent W. Foster.... [T]he center provided him with additional expense money, funding for Freedom of Information Act requests, legal support and publicity."

In the ad on August 4, Ruddy and Farah write: "To accept the Fiske–White House line of the Foster death, a person must accept the following scenario of inconsistencies":

> Mr. Foster, a devoted family man, decided to commit sui-
> cide, but left no note for his family, made no good-bye or
> final arrangements; went to a little known Virginia park he
> had no history of visiting; walked several hundred yards to
> the rear of the wooded park without getting soil on his
> shoes or clothes; sat down amid dense foliage and brush on
> the side of a hill; took out an 80-year-old gun his family
> can't positively identify; fired the gun with only two bullets
> in it, used his right hand when he was left-handed [sic]; after
> firing the gun, it remained in his hand, and fell neatly at his
> side; no visible blood was on the gun or on the front of his
> white shirt; he fell back into a neat position; despite having
> placed the gun deep into his mouth, no powder burns were
> evidenced nor were any teeth broken; and his heart stopped
> pumping immediately after the shot was fired.

Highlighting Ruddy's report is his claim that officials of the U.S. Park Police had falsified their own reports and staged a cover-up of the actual crime scene by moving Foster's body to another area within Fort Marcy Park. According to Ruddy, Foster's body was taken from a position closer to the first cannon in the grove near-est the parking lot, to the denser forest area by the second cannon.

Ruddy bases this charge on his interview with paramedic

George Gonzalez, who supposedly claimed that he, not USPP Officer Kevin Fornshill, had found Foster's body near the first cannon—even though Gonzalez had stated in a July 20 sworn deposition, "Officer Fornshill and Todd Hall had already found the body at the second cannon. And I followed seconds later."

Ruddy insists that a map Gonzalez had drawn for him supports this stunning but dubious allegation, and that an anonymous Park Police officer,[85] as well as the crime-scene photograph revealed by ABC News, confirmed it.

Instead of cooling down, the controversies over Foster death—real and imagined—are just heating up.

PART FOUR
Reality Unravels

"It seems to be entirely conceivable that they managed to throw substantial suspicion over no wrongdoing. You have to wonder in any such situation whether it's just clumsiness and paranoia, or whether there's some other reason. My own experience is: never underrate clumsiness and paranoia."

—PHILIP HEYMANN ON THE CLINTON WHITE HOUSE
AUGUST 2, 1995

1.

ON FRIDAY, AUGUST 5, 1994, *New York Times* columnist Anthony Lewis writes a defense of Robert Fiske and his controversial fifty-eight–page report, which Lewis describes as "massive." Insisting that Fiske has "exhaustively investigated" all of the remaining issues in the case, Lewis complains, "[T]hat did not stop the partisan conspiracists. They turned on Mr. Fiske, a highly respected former federal prosecutor, and charged that he had sold out."

This is the last public tribute Fiske will receive while serving as independent counsel.

That same day, as per the new law providing for the appointment of independent counsels, a three-judge panel, handpicked by Chief Justice William H. Rehnquist of the U.S. Supreme Court, removes Fiske as independent counsel and replaces him with another highly respected attorney, forty-eight-year-old Kenneth Starr, the former

U.S. solicitor general under President Bush and a partner in the prestigious law firm of Kirkland & Ellis. The three judges, who come from three separate appellate jurisdictions, give Starr, who has never before served as a prosecutor, broad responsibilities, including the authority to reinvestigate the death of Vincent Foster.

In appointing Starr, the judges state:

> It is not our intent to impugn the integrity of the
> Attorney General's appointee, but rather to reflect the intent
> of the Act that the actor be protected against the percep-
> tions of conflict. As Fiske was appointed by the incumbent
> administration, the Court therefore deems it in the best
> interest of the appearance of independence contemplated by
> the Act that a person not affiliated with the incumbent
> administration be appointed.[1]

Reed Irvine of AIM wastes no time communicating with Starr, sending him a letter on the day of his appointment. Irvine, who, along with Robert Bartley of the *Wall Street Journal*, has become a spiritual leader among the anti-Fiske forces, writes: "Mr. Fiske had demonstrated with his superficial report on the death of Vincent Foster that he could not be trusted to do a thorough, objective investigation of Whitewater....

"Unfortunately, the Republicans on the Senate Banking Committee chose to ignore the most serious flaws in Fiske's report, and they ostentatiously endorsed his findings. I believe that most of them did this not because they found the evidence he presented convincing, but because they believed they would damage their own credibility if they went counter to the establishment media's nearly unanimous endorsement of Fiske's findings."

In the wake of the Starr appointment, the *New York Times*

editorial page states on August 6 that through the selection of Starr, a conservative Republican, "the court has enhanced the appearance of an even-handed investigation."

Catherine S. Manegold, in her profile of Starr in the *Times*, writes: "Supporters of Mr. Starr, and they are many, say the former solicitor general and federal appeals court judge will be able to rise above both politics and his own inexperience [as a prosecutor of any kind] to cast a balanced eye on a difficult inquiry."

2.

REPRESENTATIVE WILLIAM CLINGER OF PENNSYLVANIA, the ranking Republican on the U.S. House Committee on Government Operations, had been looking into the Foster case since February. Although he complained about Robert Fiske limiting his investigation—with regard to the degree in which the White House staff had allegedly impeded the official USPP probe—Clinger had already announced in April that he believed that Foster had committed suicide.

On Friday, August 12, Clinger releases the results of his investigation in an eight-page report that includes two pages of endnotes. Despite his brevity, Clinger successfully puts several lingering controversies to rest, doing so, in some cases, more clearly and concisely than the *Fiske Report* did. For instance:

■ Regarding the allegation of a lack of blood at the crime scene: "Because Mr. Foster was lying [on his back and at] an angle, the blood drained downward instead of encompassing his entire body."

■ Regarding the lack of bone fragments: "The scene was not searched for bone fragments...

until approximately nine months after Mr.
Foster's death."

■ Regarding the lack of fingerprints on the gun:
Firearms experts "have suggested... that fingerprints are not always identifiable. Other factors,
such as the amount of oils on the decedent's fingers, the humidity, and the temperature, may
result in fingerprints not remaining on an object."

■ Regarding the semen found in Foster's shorts:
"Those who suggest that the presence of semen
demonstrates that a sexual liaison occurred on
the afternoon of Mr. Foster's death ignore the
testimony of medical experts who suggest that it
is not uncommon for an individual, at the time of
death, to defecate, urinate, or even ejaculate."

However, like everyone else, Clinger seems to be baffled by the
transfer stain on Foster's cheek, writing that the "bloodstain on
the right shoulder of Mr. Foster's shirt is admittedly difficult to
explain.... Regardless of what caused the bloodstain, however, it
cannot be disputed that if the body was moved into the park additional signs would support that conclusion."

In his conclusion, Clinger writes:

Perhaps the unexpected death of any high government
official will needlessly bring cries of conspiracy from many in
our society. That is unfortunate. The death of Mr. Foster has
been reviewed in detail by the experienced professionals at
the U.S. Park Police, who were performing their tasks under
extremely difficult circumstances. Special Counsel Robert
Fiske took that investigation one step further by establishing
a panel of noted forensic pathologists who reviewed all of the
available evidence and reached the same conclusion as that of

the Park Police. I reviewed the work of these two organizations and, with this report, support their findings.

Reed Irvine writes Clinger a letter on August 16, expressing his
disagreement, to which Clinger responds on September 7.

Three days later, Irvine sends Clinger another letter once again
strongly advocating the theory that Foster had died at a location
other than Fort Marcy Park, and that his body had been moved,
saying: "The presence of the semen, the hair and carpet fibers
could be clues to where Foster was and what he was doing on the
afternoon of July 20."[2]

To Irvine, the real questions about the Foster case have not
only not been answered, but they have never even been
addressed—because of the overwhelming determination by public
officials to confirm that Foster had committed suicide.

Meantime, another full-page ad, paid for by the Western
Journalism Center and promoting Christopher Ruddy's response
to the Fiske Report, is published. This ad appears in the Sunday,
August 28, edition of the New York Times and raises over forty
questions, which, to many inside the investigation, have already
been answered.[3]

Nevertheless, to those seeing the issues in the case for the first
time in the Times, serious problems still appear to exist in the official explanations of Foster's death.

One person who disagrees is U.S. Park Police Officer Kevin
Fornshill, who feels that he has been defamed, by implication, in
Ruddy's special report. Fornshill believes that Ruddy accused him
of lying about where he had discovered Foster's body while implying that he might have participated in a general cover-up.

Consequently, Fornshill, represented by Philadelphia attorney Philip Stinson, files a $2 million libel suit against Ruddy and the Western Journalism Center, as well as a Baltimore-based newsletter, *Strategic Investment*, which is offering Ruddy's special report for sale and publishing excerpts. Fornshill, who is mentioned five times in Ruddy's publication, files the case on August 31.[4]

In his sworn affidavit, Fornshill writes:

> The allegations of the defendants regarding me and other members of the United States Park Police are not true. Specifically, I found Mr. Foster's body in front of the "second cannon" in Fort Marcy; I did not change the location of Mr. Foster's body; I did not participate in any cover-up; I did not place a drop gun in Mr. Foster's hand; I did not lie to members of the media; I did not lie to the F.B.I., the Independent Counsel, or Congress; and, I did not obstruct justice or commit any federal offenses during the course of my involvement in the Foster case.

Ruddy's attorneys reply that Fornshill's suit lacks merit, because—although Ruddy does accuse the Park Police of, among other charges, a massive cover-up—the reporter does not accuse Fornshill, specifically, of being among those involved, even though Fornshill is only one of three Park Police employees named in Ruddy's special report.

In his own sworn affidavit, Ruddy insists:

> At points in my Special Report, I suggest that the Park Police may have engaged in a cover-up of evidence. In expressing this opinion, I did not name any specific park official or police officer. The references in the Special Report to Officer Fornshill do not in any way charge him with a cover-up, and I did not intend to charge him with a cover-up.

The *New York Post*, which had published Ruddy's earliest stories about the Foster case, is not named in the suit. Ruddy had left the *Post* in early September.

In his September 21 issue, James Dale Davidson, the editor of *Strategic Investment* and the chairman of the National Taxpayers Union, appears particularly bitter over being named in the suit, especially since Fornshill was never mentioned in the excerpts from Ruddy's special report published in his newsletter.[5]

Along with Davidson, another new name in the Foster investigation appears: Hugh H. Sprunt, a successful Texas-based businessman. Sprunt, who had received his bachelor and master's degrees in Earth and Planetary Science from MIT and his MBA and law degree from Stanford, has taken up a new hobby: to become an independent sleuth on the Foster case.[6]

On October 23, Sprunt faxes a memorandum to Reed Irvine and Joe Goulden at AIM, giving his detailed analysis of the note with the four columns of abbreviations and dates that was found by the Park Police among Foster's possessions and that appeared to be his worksheet on the Clintons' blind trust.

Later, in another memorandum, Sprunt appears to annihilate Ruddy's claim in his special report that Foster's body had been found by the first cannon instead of the second. Comparing a map of the area around Fort Marcy Park with the sketch-map of the crime scene that Ruddy had published in his special report, Sprunt reveals that Ruddy had erred by failing to confirm the north-south-east-west configuration in the sketch-map, which was based on a map paramedic George Gonzalez had earlier drawn for the reporter.

"[I]t appears to me at this point," Sprunt writes, "that the cumulative effect of these errors in the sketch map may well mean that Mr. Ruddy's hypothesis about the body being at cannon one instead of at cannon two (official position) is not correct. That is, we appear to have a total error approaching 90 degrees.... I would hate to see Chris Ruddy lose general credibility if the 'cannon one' versus 'cannon two' issue turns out to have been a canard. I think it important for all independent investigators of Whitewater-related matters not to burn bridges needlessly and to evaluate all the evidence objectively."[7]

In fact, in the next edition of his special report, Ruddy dramatically modifies his north-south-east-west configurations in his text, publishes a new crime-scene map with a 90-degree variation, and adds an acknowledgement to Sprunt—without ever relenting on his claim that Foster's body had been moved from the first cannon to the second or admitting the errors in his previous edition.[8]

On November 8—perhaps due in part to the continuing scandals that seem to be stemming from Foster's death—the Democrats have their heads handed to them in the midterm elections, losing both the House and Senate in a devastating political bloodbath, which appears to be a public repudiation of President and Hillary Clinton.

With this dramatic power shift, the Clinton White House suddenly realizes that everything old is new again—including the Foster case.

3.

IN ITS TUESDAY, JANUARY 3, 1995, report about the Park Police investigation of the death of Vincent Foster, the Senate Banking Committee, in its final hours under control of the Democrats, concludes:

The evidence overwhelmingly supports the conclusion of
the Park Police that on July 20, 1993, Mr. Foster died in
Fort Marcy Park from a self-inflicted gun shot wound to
the upper palate of his mouth. The Department of Justice,
the Federal Bureau of Investigation and the Office of the
Independent Counsel reached the same conclusion after
conducting their own investigations of Mr. Foster's death.
Although some aspects of the Park Police investigation
varied from standard procedures for conducting a death
investigation, the committee found no evidence that any
variances in the Park Police investigation affected the ultimate conclusion that Mr. Foster committed suicide at Fort
Marcy Park....
The committee finds no evidence of "improper conduct"
in the Park Police investigation.

But, now, the minority has become the majority, and the
Republicans promise to reopen the hearings into Whitewater and,
specifically, the manner in which the White House handled the
search of Vincent Foster's office in the aftermath of his death.

All speculation, moreover, about whether Kenneth Starr will
reinvestigate the Foster case ends when the OIC subpoenas several fire and rescue workers and police officers who were at the
Foster crime scene to appear before a federal grand jury in
Washington, D.C.

Although attorney Mark Tuohey directs the Foster investigation for Starr, another attorney, Miquel Rodriguez, a Harvard-
trained assistant U.S. attorney in Sacramento, has been brought in
to conduct the interrogations before the grand jury. In California,
Rodriguez, a short, thin man with a ponytail, had developed a
reputation as a prosecutor who is tough on cops.[9]

Or, at least, some cops. Just prior to his work before the grand
jury, Rodriguez calls Sergeant Cheryl Braun, who is slated to testify, at her home and asks her out on a date. Braun, who is in a

long-term relationship with another police officer, kindly rejects the offer—but is taken aback by the call.

Rescue workers Richard Arthur and Todd Hall are first to be questioned before the grand jury by Rodriguez on Thursday, January 5; and they will be followed to the stand by paramedic George Gonzalez.

As he had already told the FBI, Arthur of Fairfax County's Medic One claims to have seen an unreported gunshot wound on the right side of Foster's neck and restates his belief that Foster was holding either a .45 or 9-mm automatic in his right hand, not a .38 revolver.

Hall, also of Medic One, had said in his first interview with the FBI that he had seen a "red" flash in the woods after he examined Foster's body. During a second interview with the FBI, Hall appeared to concede that the red flash had come from Chain Bridge Road and was probably a car.

Rodriguez, who is also interested in the theft of some brightly colored vests from a National Park Service equipment room, questions Hall at length about whether he believes the red flash was a person or a car, and Hall appears to give some ground on this matter, suggesting that the red object might have been a person after all.

Apparently, Rodriguez is trying to make a case that Foster's alleged killer was running from the scene—wearing a bright-red vest.

Rodriguez's questioning is furthermore hardly routine and his aggressiveness agitates the Park Police, in particular, to the extent that they demand that their attorneys raise objections to his inquiries.

Officer Kevin Fornshill, who completes five hours of intense questioning from Rodriguez on January 10, during which time he is read the federal perjury statute, complains to his attorney, Philip Stinson, that the prosecutor is, essentially, accusing the officer of actually being involved in the murder of Vincent Foster and the subsequent cover-up of that murder. And Fornshill believes that Rodriguez wants him indicted.

Among other things, Fornshill tells Stinson, who has been standing and sitting outside the grand-jury room during his client's ordeal, that Rodriguez had suggested that Fornshill had been seen at Fort Marcy Park in an unmarked car earlier on the day of Foster's death. Rodriguez, who asked about the carpet fibers in the trunk of Fornshill's car, also grilled the officer on the whereabouts of his .38-caliber revolver, his previous sidearm of choice before switching to a 9-mm automatic.[10] And, of course, Rodriguez made clear to all of the grand jurors that prior to responding to the dead-body radio call at Fort Marcy Park, Fornshill had been working at the CIA, which adds an additional layer of intrigue to Rodriguez's scenario.

Clearly, to Fornshill and Stinson, Rodriguez is trying to make the case before the grand jury that the charade of a Foster suicide had been choreographed as part of a real-life murder conspiracy: that the gun had been placed in Foster's hand by his real killers, and that the federal government was in the midst of a massive cover-up.

But, the word coming out of the hearing room from those witnesses testifying is that the grand jurors are not buying into Rodriguez's theories, and that they are uneasy at his treatment of the police.

Nevertheless, Stinson, on behalf of Fornshill, calls Mark Tuohey in the OIC office and angrily asks for a letter officially notifying him that his client is a target of the grand-jury investigation. When Tuohey replies that he doesn't know what Stinson's talking about, Stinson explains that Rodriguez is trying to accuse Fornshill of murder.

Alarmed by this news, Tuohey tells Stinson that he is en route to the grand-jury hearing. Within minutes, Tuohey arrives and calls Rodriguez into a closed-door meeting.

When Fornshill returns to the grand-jury room—in the wake of Tuohey's conversation with Rodriguez—the tone is quite different; Rodriguez appears docile.

Seizing the opportunity to fan the flames, Reed Irvine sends Rodriguez a letter on Tuesday, January 17, encouraging him to push even harder in the Foster case. Irvine writes: "The fact that you are now doing what Mr. Fiske should have done, i.e., have testimony given under oath to a grand jury, is a clear indication that you know that both the Park Police and the Fiske investigations were inadequate. Obvious lies have gone unchallenged, and serious questions have gone unanswered."

Irvine has found additional reasons to challenge some of the basic conclusions by the Park Police, the *Fiske Report*, the *Clinger Report*, and the Senate Banking Committee. Other than his perennial questions about the transfer stain on Foster's cheek and his theory that Foster might have died at a location other than Fort Marcy Park, Irvine comes up with other problems about the case.

- Irvine has interviewed an employee of the company that had installed the X ray machine in the autopsy room at Fairfax Hospital, which Dr. Beyer insisted wasn't working. But the employee says that a new X ray machine had been placed in that location five weeks before Foster's death—and that a call for service did not come to the company until October 29, 1993, over three months after Foster had died. In other words, according to the employee, a working, well-functioning X ray machine was present during the Foster autopsy—contrary to what Dr. Beyer had said under oath.

■ Joe Purvis, a former prosecutor in Little Rock, has told Irvine's deputy that he had been permitted by Foster's mortician to view the body. According to Irvine's letter to Rodriguez, which was based on Purvis's observation, "[T]here was a dime-sized wound at the back of the neck just above the hair line. The mortician himself has refused to make any comment."[11]

■ Irvine continues to believe Ruddy's assertion that Foster's body had been moved from near the first cannon to the location near the second cannon, as paramedic George Gonzalez had allegedly told Ruddy during their first conversation. The Ruddy-Irvine theory is buoyed when Robert Morton of the *Washington Times* claims that Gonzalez had told him the same thing. And, although Gonzalez has since supposedly changed his story, Irvine receives a statement from Dr. Donald Haut, the Fairfax County medical examiner who pronounced Foster dead at the scene, in which Dr. Haut had allegedly claimed that Foster was found fifty feet from the only cannon the doctor saw in the park.[12]

■ Irvine challenges the "depression" motive for Foster's alleged suicide, pointing out the statements by Foster's family, friends, and White House colleagues during the immediate aftermath of his

death, denying that Foster was depressed. Irvine
also makes an issue of Dee Dee Myers's July 27,
1993, press briefing at which she first began to
claim that Foster had been depressed. White
House correspondents Brit Hume and Sarah
McClendon called Myers on this discrepancy.

In other words, Reed Irvine appears hellbent on proving—without saying it outright—that Foster was murdered.

Not surprisingly, on Friday, January 27—in the wake of the official Republican takeover in Washington—R. Emmett Tyrrell, Jr., the editor-in-chief of the conservative monthly, *The American Spectator*, publishes a column in the *Washington Times*, stating: "Mr. Starr has his work cut out for him. Yet there is plenty of evidence to work with. Twenty or more people came upon Mr. Foster's body at one point or another. If some are lying, and some seem to be, surely Mr. Starr can find out. Then perhaps he can find out why they are lying."

Also returning to the action is Christopher Ruddy, who, after his departure from the *New York Post* in early September, had been hired in November by the *Pittsburgh Tribune-Review*, which is owned by banking heir Richard Scaife, who contributes heavily to *The American Spectator* and the Western Journalism Center, AIM, and Jim Davidson's National Taxpayers Union.

Ruddy begins publishing about the Foster case again on Sunday, December 18, 1994, with a story about the mistakes Dr. Beyer had supposedly made in other autopsies, which Ruddy had detailed in a previous story for the *Post*. The following day, he publishes an article, really more of an editorial, urging Starr to launch an even more aggressive reinvestigation of the Foster case.

On January 12, Ruddy revisits his already discredited theory, which had highlighted his special report about the *Fiske Report*, that Foster's body had been moved from near the first cannon to the second cannon. But the Western Journalism Center then republishes Ruddy's *Tribune-Review* article in a full-page ad in the *Washington Times* on Friday, January 13, and in the *New York Times* on Thursday, January 19.

An order form appears in both ads, offering readers an opportunity to purchase Ruddy's revised special report and to contribute to the Western Journalism Center "to help the Western Journalism Center sponsor an independent investigation into the Foster case, as well as help defray the cost of ads like this one in newspapers across America."[13]

On Sunday, January 29, the Western Journalism Center publishes yet another full-page ad in the *New York Times*, promoting a forty-minute documentary on home video titled "Unanswered: The Death of Vincent Foster." Readers can purchase the videotape for $35 by calling a toll-free telephone number.[14] The ad states: "You will watch this full-color, 40-minute video documentary over and over again. You will want to show it to your friends. Once you see this tape, you will never think about the Foster case in the same way again."

4.

AS MORE QUESTIONS, LEGITIMATE OR NOT, are raised about the Foster case, the wider the parameter for criticism becomes.

On or about Thursday, February 9, the first book on the Foster case is published, *The Murder of Vince Foster*, written by Michael Kellett. In his 119-page book, Kellett tries to be as cute as possible with his section headings, like "The Explanation That Sucked," "Where Is the Bozo When You Really Need Him?" and

"Liberals Beware! The *Deadly* Editorials Are Coming to Get You! (*Ya ha haaa haaahhhh*)."

The book is nothing less than a complete defamation of the president and Mrs. Clinton in which he flat-out accuses them of the murder of Vincent W. Foster, Jr. In short, Kellett believes that Foster had been whacked, because he intended to reveal incriminating information about the Clintons.[15]

But, among the wild conspiracy theories on the Internet and in the tabloid press about the Foster case, Kellett's is only in the moderate range. Here are some others:

- Through the use of electromagnetism, Foster was murdered by drug-runners in Arkansas who were working in concert with government officials to inflate the price of Wal-Mart stock.

- In the February 20 issue of the *New York Post*, columnist John Crudele promotes a theory that Foster's death might have been connected to a long-standing political fight over a revolutionary computer program for tracking criminals, called "Promis," developed by Inslaw, Inc., an innovative Washington-based computer company, which claimed that its creation had been stolen by the Reagan Justice Department and then used, among others, by the National Security Agency (NSA).[16]

- The Citizens for Honest Government—chaired by Patrick Matrisciana, who is also the owner of Jeremiah Films—released a videotape titled *The Death of Vince Foster: What Really Happened?* The group's most recent production was *The Clinton Chronicles*, which had been heavily

promoted by Rev. Jerry Falwell.[17] Essentially, the
new film featured the work of three people:
Christopher Ruddy, Reed Irvine, and Gene
Wheaton, a former military-intelligence agent.

Among other things, this videotape casts additional suspicion
about Foster's death based on the blonde hair and carpet fibers
found on his clothes, as well as the semen in his shorts.

Without outright making the claim, the obvious implication of
the tape is that Foster was off at some secret hideaway on the
afternoon of July 20, 1993, having sex with an unidentified
blonde. There, he died—either by suicide or by murder. Then
some unknown persons wrapped Foster's body in a carpet and
dumped him and his car at Fort Marcy Park, leaving behind misleading evidence of a suicide.

After demonstrating some of his outstanding research abilities
with his analyses of flaws in the official and unofficial investigations, independent investigator Hugh Sprunt of Texas momentarily turns to the dark side in two memoranda. The first is faxed to
Irvine and Joe Goulden at AIM on Friday, March 10; the second
goes to British correspondent Ambrose Evans-Pritchard of the
Sunday Telegraph on March 13.

In these memoranda, particularly the second to Evans-Pritchard,
Sprunt puts forth a wildly speculative scenario about how Foster's
body could have been moved into Fort Marcy Park by his killers.
Sprunt, who has already annihilated Ruddy's theory about the
movement of Foster's body from cannon one to cannon two, now
appears to revive and embrace it, telling Evans-Pritchard that he has
posted his latest Foster theory on an Internet Newsgroup site.

Clearly disagreeing with his boss, Irvine deputy Joe Goulden,

who has also received copies of the two memos, replies in a letter
to Sprunt on Tuesday, March 14, saying:

> My feeling is that the Foster death indeed was a suicide,
> and that the scandal will arise from (a) where he was dur-
> ing the time he left the White House and his body was
> found; (b) why he killed himself and (c) what the Clinton
> crowd was so eager to conceal afterwards.... Ruddy and
> others have done good work in keeping the pressure on for
> the truth. We've lived with various Grassy Knoll conspiracy
> theories since Nov. 22, 1963, and we do not need another.
> That is why the investigation of the Foster death should be
> thorough and leave no avenues unpursued.

On Thursday, March 23, reporter Ellen Joan Pollock of the *Wall
Street Journal* publishes a front-page article titled "Vince Foster's
Death Is a Lively Business for Conspiracy Buffs," which details
the work of the Western Journalism Center and Joseph Farah,
Strategic Investment and James Davidson (who is also the chair-
man of the National Taxpayers Union), and Citizens for Honest
Government and Patrick Matrisciana.

Pollock continues: "Indeed, as it turns out, all three of the
major groups spreading conspiracy theories are linked to conservative activists, whose agendas include campaigning for a balanced budget and against gay rights. For some of them, the drive
to portray Mr. Foster's death as something nefarious is also an
opportunity to suggest that President and Mrs. Clinton may be
responsible for a cover-up—or worse."

Pollock adds that since leaving the *New York Post*, Christopher
Ruddy "has been all but adopted by some right-wing groups. He
now covers the Foster case for a conservative Pittsburgh paper
owned by [Richard] Scaife, and has also received financial support from WJC [Western Journalism Center]."[18]

Noticeably missing from Pollock's article is Reed Irvine of AIM. So Irvine calls Pollock on the same day as the article and tapes their conversation.

"How come you left us out of the story?" Irvine asks.

"I don't know, I'm sorry, " Pollock replies, somewhat puzzled by the question.

"I really feel hurt. Could it be that maybe we made too much sense?"

"No, sir," she replies.

Irvine toys with Pollock for a few minutes, then allows her to get off the hook by getting to the point. "We've done several reports on the Foster case," Irvine explains. "In fact, I was the one who first interested Chris Ruddy into looking into this story. And I think perhaps if you had gone a little deeper into the critique of what's wrong with the Foster investigations, that you might have written a very different story. Because I think the *Wall Street Journal*, like the *New York Times*[19] and others in the media, have really failed to do their job, which is to take a critical look at the *Fiske Report*."

When Pollock replies that she has done several stories about the *Fiske Report*, Irvine presses her on specific items of evidence—the blood-transfer stain, the supposed general lack of blood, and the manner in which Foster had supposedly held the gun. However, Pollock resists getting into the specifics of the case, trying to avoid an argument with Irvine, who is extremely well versed on the issues of the case and just itching for someone to debate.[20]

After this conversation, Irvine, Farah, and Davidson all write letters to the editor of the *Wall Street Journal*, defending their work, as well as the reporting of Christopher Ruddy. Irvine writes: "A cursory reading of Mr. Ruddy's stories should have shown you that rather than weaving conspiracy theories and generating scurrilous rumors about Mr. Foster's death, Mr. Ruddy did what you and other journalists should have done. Hearing charges that the Park Police investigation had been bungled, he did his own investigation."

Once again, the schizophrenia of the *Wall Street Journal* is clearly evident, especially since the newspaper had given Ruddy's reporting legitimacy from the outset with its January 31, 1994, editorial, citing his work.

5.

CONTINUING HIS ATTACK ON THE *FISKE REPORT* in another article on Wednesday, April 5, Ruddy returns the following day to report that the controversial Miquel Rodriguez, who had given Officer Fornshill such a hard time during his grand-jury appearance, had left Kenneth Starr's staff on Monday, March 20, after four months. Ruddy also claims to have a source, whom he does not name, who has told him that "Rodriguez left because he believed the grand jury process was being thwarted by his superior," who was Mark Tuohey, one of Starr's top deputies.[21]

In his April edition of the *AIM Report*, Reed Irvine calls the news of Rodriguez's resignation "most distressing," but he appears to fix the blame on Starr, whom he doesn't want to criticize *too* much. Irvine writes: "A former colleague of Starr's commented that Starr is a fine man but he suffers from a desire to please everyone. It appears in this case that he decided to please Mark Tuohey and sacrifice Miquel Rodriguez, whose determined efforts to learn the truth were making some people in Washington very nervous."

The critics also claim that Rodriguez had allegedly obtained the underexposed 35 mm crime-scene photographs taken by USPP criminalist Pete Simonello and submitted them to a private laboratory. There, they were supposedly enhanced, revealing scenes not consistent with the known Polaroid pictures. Supposedly in sync with what paramedic Richard Arthur and former prosecutor

Joe Purvis claimed to have seen, at least one of the photos, Rodriguez believes, shows a dime-sized neck wound midway between Foster's chin and ear, which indicates a tattooing of Foster's skin that might have been caused by a contact gunshot.

Inspired by the tactics of the defense team in Los Angeles during the O.J. Simpson murder case, which is still engrossing the media, Irvine writes an essay in his *AIM Report* titled "The Trial of Vincent Foster": "Simpson's lawyers are making heroic efforts to overcome an avalanche of evidence pointing to their client's guilt. They have left no stone unturned in their effort to create reasonable doubt in the minds of the jurors and the public. They have challenged the competence and integrity of the detectives and charged that their investigation was flawed.... No matter how outlandish their arguments, they have captured the media's attention."[22]

Irvine's strategy, as well as that of Farah, Davidson, and even Ruddy, is now easier to understand: Much of their attack concentrates on exploiting the recollections of people who have different versions of a particular incident, especially among those in the law-enforcement community. Through these contradictions, reasonable doubts about whether Foster had committed suicide may be posited.

For instance, on May 9, 1994, Lisa Foster told the FBI that she remembered that the only gun her husband had sent from Little Rock to Washington was silver in color. But the gun found in Foster's right hand was black, indicating that he had another gun that she didn't know about. Nevertheless, to the critics of the Foster case, this discrepancy places the FBI in direct contradiction with the U.S. Park Police, which did not mention this matter in its final report.

Thus, the critics can accuse the Park Police of incompetence or obstruction while blaming the FBI for failing to come up with evidence that Foster owned a black gun and how that black gun wound up in his right hand on the day of his death.

In another example: If Foster has no coherent soil on his shoes—as stated in the *Fiske Report*—he could not have walked through the park; thus, his body must have been placed there by persons unknown.

Such discrepancies are the principal staple of the critics' case.

On April 9, 1995, Ambrose Evans-Pritchard of London's *Sunday Telegraph* suggests that Foster might have left his office and killed himself in the White House parking lot. Then, according to the writer's sources, the White House lied about the time it was notified of his death—which had been officially set at 8:30 PM when the Secret Service received the call from Lieutenant Gavin of the Park Police.

Evans-Pritchard's information is based on a March 28, 1995, sworn affidavit signed by Roger Perry, an Arkansas trooper on duty at the governor's mansion in Little Rock, who had received a telephone call from Helen Dickey, a White House staff assistant, on July 20, 1993, allegedly telling him that Foster "had gone out to his car in the parking lot and had shot himself in the head." According to Perry's statement, he received the call between 5:30 and 8 PM, Washington time. Perry indicated that he passed this information on to Governor Jim Guy Tucker, via his wife.

Even though Evans-Pritchard's report is nonsense, many people on the Internet and elsewhere begin to believe it.[23]

On Thursday, April 27, Joseph Farah and the Western Journalism Center, Reed Irvine of AIM, and James Davidson of *Strategic*

Investment hold a joint press conference at 11 AM at the International Club on K Street in downtown Washington. There, Farah announces the release of the WJC's *Independent Report in re: The Death of Vincent Foster*, which has been compiled by two former members of the New York Police Department, Vincent Scalice and Fred Santucci, as well as Dr. Richard Saferstein, the former chief of the New Jersey State Crime Lab.

Scalice is the executive director of Forensic Control Systems; Santucci, a longtime forensic photographer for the NYPD, now works for Scalice at FCS. Although their report is forty-four pages long, only ten pages cover their analysis of the evidence.[24]

On the basis of much of the same evidence featured in Patrick Matrisciana's most recent videotape, the Western Journalism Center's forensic experts, saying that "homicide has not been ruled out," conclude that "a high probability exists that Foster's body was transported to Fort Marcy Park from an outside location."[25]

Both the Associated Press and Reuters cover the press conference and file stories on their wire services, which are picked up by newspapers and magazines, as well as radio and television stations throughout the country and, of course, the Internet. In England, a page-one article, written by Washington correspondent Ambrose Evans-Pritchard of the *Sunday Telegraph*, trumpets the headline: "White House aide was murdered, say experts."

Trying to nail the critics of the *Fiske Report*, especially Ruddy, reporter David L. Michelmore of the *Pittsburgh Post-Gazette*, the *Pittsburgh Tribune-Review's* nemesis, publishes an article, "Right wingers claim Clinton lawyer's death is a cover-up: Groups bankrolled by Richard Mellon Scaife still believe that Vincent Foster's suicide report is a lie."

Michelmore writes: "Feeding all these suspicions with new

theories and new testimony is a small band of writers on journalism's right wing, who, like Irvine, are not so far out of the mainstream that they can be dismissed as kooks.

"They share a dislike of President Clinton and a contempt for what they see as the media's liberal elite bias and their failure to pursue the story.

"They also share a benefactor in Richard Mellon Scaife, the Pittsburgh philanthropist and publisher of the *Tribune-Review* of Greensburg, the only daily newspaper in the country that is making a major effort to show that Foster did not die by his own hand."

6.

BACK AT THE U.S. CAPITOL, Senate Republicans don't need to muscle through approval of another Whitewater investigation. In fact, on Wednesday, May 17, by a bipartisan vote of 96–3, the full Senate approves Senate Resolution 120.

The legislation establishes a Special Committee to Investigate Whitewater Development Corporation and Related Matters, which will be administered by the Senate Banking Committee. Along with the continued investigations of Whitewater and Madison Guaranty, the resolution "authorized investigation into whether White House officials engaged in improper conduct in handling papers in Deputy White House Counsel Vincent Foster's office following his death."

The previous month, on April 22, Kenneth Starr, unlike Robert Fiske, had given the committee his blessing to proceed with its full and unencumbered investigation of the Foster case, saying that it would not interfere with his probe.

After the July 1994 hearings, a number of key issues have been left hanging, mostly because of the prohibition from Fiske, who lost his job the following month. They include:

- interference from the White House into the Park Police search of Foster's office;

- the presence of the staff of the White House Counsel's Office during the routine interviews of White House personnel by the Park Police; and

- the decision to deliver the torn-up note written by Foster to the Park Police nearly thirty hours after its discovery.

Two days later, Wesley Pruden of the *Washington Times* writes in his column: "Senate hearings on the order of the Watergate example are just what the Clintons hoped against reasonable hope to avoid. These are hearings that became inevitable with the final returns of the congressional elections of November '94, and the pressure on the dynamic duo to consider new lines of employment will become considerable as the consequence of running on a ticket with the Clintons sinks in on hundreds of Democratic congressmen, governors, land commissioners, sheriffs, county assessors, auditors and even collectors of deeds, from sea to shining sea."

Now eyeing the presidential election in 1996, the Republicans want it all; and the special committee's hearings—which will begin on Tuesday, July 18, and, once again, feature the Foster case—might just help their cause.

On Sunday, May 21, Ambrose Evans-Pritchard of the *Sunday Telegraph* publishes an article, "Secret Swiss link to White House death," claiming that between 1991 to 1993, Foster had booked three trips to Geneva, Switzerland, for reasons unknown. The first trip, in which he allegedly stayed in Geneva for less than a day, occurred in November 1991. The second trip supposedly took place during President-elect Clinton's 1992 transition period. Evans-Pritchard continues: "Finally, on July 1, 1993, [Foster] purchased a ticket through the White House Travel Office from Washington to Geneva on TWA and Swiss Air, reimbursing the White House from his personal American Express Card. But he never made the trip and was refunded by Swiss Air on July 8."

The reporter notes that twelve days after the refund, Foster was dead, adding that "there are no Swiss stamps in [Foster's] passport, but this would not necessarily be unusual."

On the Fourth of July, reporter Susan Schmidt of the *Washington Post* publishes her own take on the conspiracy theories revolving around Foster's death. One target is Ambrose Evans-Pritchard. Schmidt writes: "Sources with access to Foster's American Express receipts—including some during the period cited by Evans-Pritchard—say they show no purchases of airline tickets to Switzerland."

In a remarkable counterattack in which he exclaims "*J'accuse*" to "the powers of the *Washington Post*," Evans-Pritchard publishes his bitter reply in the *Sunday Telegraph*, which is reprinted on page one of the *Washington Times*. Evans-Pritchard accuses the *Post* of being nothing more than a shell of its former self since its landmark work on Watergate, suggesting that the newspaper has been sitting on or spiking stories in its new role—"wittingly or unwittingly—as a mouthpiece and a subtle tool of disinformation for the ruling regime."

Schmidt—who was actually no favorite of the Clinton White House because of her ground-breaking articles on Whitewater and the Resolution Trust Corporation, among other matters—stands by her story.[26]

As the hearings of the Special Committee on Whitewater approach, the critics of the previous official investigations of Foster's death case begin to publicize their own road maps about the case, hoping that the Republican majority will address their concerns. For instance:

- Christopher Ruddy, in his continuing series of articles in the *Pittsburgh Tribune-Review*, publishes a story on Wednesday, June 14, charging that other people spotted in Fort Marcy Park by Judith Doody, Mark Feist, and Patrick Knowlton had never been found, especially the "bare-chested" white male spotted behind the wheel of the Honda described by Doody and the intimidating-looking Hispanic man seen by Knowlton.[27] (Ruddy does not name the three witnesses in his article.)

- To emphasize other points of view about the Foster case, AIM hosts a conference, "The Vincent Foster Affair—Many Questions and Few Answers," on Thursday, June 15, at the Ramada Plaza Hotel on Thomas Circle in Washington. In the announcement, Reed Irvine writes: "Are those who criticize the investigations of the death of White House aide Vincent Foster irresponsible conspiracy theorists as some in the media have charged? Or are they level-headed skeptics who have refused to be taken in by an orchestrated cover-up?"

- In a Tuesday, June 20, article in *Investor's Business Daily*, Thomas McArdle offers a series

of reasons for the sudden resignation of prosecutor Miquel Rodriguez, the deputy to Kenneth
Starr who had angered the Park Police, among
others, because of his harsh questioning before
the grand jury. Along with Rodriguez's alleged
personality conflict with his immediate supervisor, Mark Tuohey, McArdle adds:

1. "Tuohey insisted that witnesses before the
   Foster grand jury be allowed to review evidence before testifying. Rodriguez is said to
   have feared this would allow witnesses to
   rehearse or alter their testimony."

2. "Rodriguez was not allowed to bring expert
   witnesses from outside the FBI before the
   grand jury."

3. "Tuohey interfered with Rodriguez's wish to
   use non-FBI lab and forensic analysis."

The critics plan to have a clear presence during the Special
Whitewater Committee's investigation.

7.

THE INCREASINGLY COMPLICATED and tangled web that the Foster
case has already become is now, rightly or wrongly, deeply inter-
twined with Whitewater-related activities.

On Sunday, July 9, Associated Press reporter Pete Yost publishes a wire story, stating that Henry O'Neill, a Secret Service
uniformed officer, has told Kenneth Starr's grand jury that he had
seen Maggie Williams "carrying papers either directly out of

Foster's office or from the suite of offices" on the night of his death. O'Neill had come into the White House Counsel's Office suite with the cleaning crew that night. While they were present, Williams had entered Foster's office, along with Bernard Nussbaum and Patsy Thomasson.

However, Williams, upon earlier hearing O'Neill's accusation against her, had taken a polygraph test, administered by Starr's office, which she passed. No deception was detected when she denied O'Neill's charge, which was also made during his June 23, 1995, sworn deposition before committee attorneys.

Regardless of whatever Williams has or has not done, the allegation fuels the Whitewater investigation.

Previously, the White House first revealed in December 1993 that a Whitewater file had been removed by Nussbaum from Foster's office on July 22 and that the White House counsel had turned the file over to the Clintons' personal attorney, Robert Barnett.

Then, on August 2, 1994, the White House confirmed that, two days after Foster's death, Nussbaum gave Williams a cardboard box that contained the Whitewater file from Foster's office. She arranged for it to be placed in a locked closet in the Clintons' residence on the third floor of the White House on orders from Hillary Clinton; Williams had kept the key to the closet. Five days later, on July 27, Barnett received the file from Williams.

AP reporter Yost adds that Mark Fabiani, a deputy White House counsel, had been authorized to give him and other journalists access to a seventy-two–page "Whitewater Development" file taken from Foster's office on July 22, 1993, which the reporter describes as "routine documents chronicling the first family's attempt to file belated tax returns for the unsuccessful real-estate venture they half owned. Among the contents was a

1990 letter to Mrs. Clinton from an accountant describing Whitewater records as being in chaotic condition."[28]

Yost also adds that the three White House aides who entered Foster's office on the night of his death are potentially legally vulnerable because of their conflicting stories:

- Thomasson says that she and Nussbaum arrived at Foster's office together, followed later by Williams.

- Nussbaum says that he arrived after both Thomasson and Williams, adding that all three of them left together.

- Williams says that she and Nussbaum left the office together, leaving Thomasson behind, alone, in Foster's office.

Thus, the White House's sudden cooperation in this matter is viewed as an apparent effort to neutralize the impact the documents might receive when introduced by the Republican majority during the upcoming hearings of the new special committee.

In fact, committee chairman D'Amato charges the White House with "spin control" by releasing these "selective" records to the media, adding, "Those documents do not give the total picture."

In a July 14 article about an additional one hundred pages of files regarding the Clintons' 1992 tax return, also released by the White House, reporters Susan Schmidt and Charles R. Babcock reveal that Foster—who had earlier finalized the December 1992 sale to Jim McDougal of the Clintons' interest in Whitewater for a mere $1,000—had been concerned about a possible audit of the

Whitewater Corporation by the Internal Revenue Service. In a handwritten note, Foster describes the situation as a "can of worms you shouldn't open."[29] Foster had feared that the Clintons would have difficulty explaining their losses.

Consequently, Foster had recommended to the Clintons' personal attorney, Robert Barnett, that the president and first lady claim a $1,000 capital gain on the December 1992 sale of their interest in the corporation to McDougal and simply pay the required tax.

In response to Foster's advice, Barnett warned against doing as Foster had suggested, saying in an April 7, 1993, letter: "This treatment bolsters the opponents' position. The president said he incurred a significant loss—this return shows no loss."

However, the Clintons decided to go with Foster on this matter, telling the media that they didn't claim their legitimate losses, because the corporation's "records were in disarray and they could not fully document them," according to Schmidt and Babcock.[30]

Meantime, in the July 17 edition of *Newsweek*, former *Washington Post* reporter Michael Isikoff publishes his own pre-Senate-hearings report on the Foster case.[31] Isikoff reveals that after the now-infamous Nussbaum-controlled search of Foster's office on July 22, 1993—during which Nussbaum supposedly emptied Foster's briefcase—Assistant White House Counsel Clifford Sloan had allegedly noticed scraps of paper still at the bottom of the briefcase.

According to Isikoff, Sloan, who is said to have made the discovery after the Park Police and FBI had left the White House, informed Nussbaum, who reportedly "brushed Sloan off."

Isikoff cites Michael Spafford, the law partner of Foster-family attorney Jim Hamilton, as the committee's source for this report.

Spafford, who represented the Foster family when Hamilton was unavailable, was present during the Nussbaum search on July 22.[32]

Isikoff writes: "Nussbaum and Sloan say they don't recall the incident. It wasn't until four days later that another White House lawyer, Stephen Neuwirth, discovered the shreds and assembled them into the note investigators now believe offers the clearest clue about Foster's state of mind."

8.

ON THE MORNING OF TUESDAY, JULY 18—the opening day of the Special Committee's hearings—the *New York Times* publishes an editorial, stating: "The first stage of the hearings concerns the White House's clumsy handling of the papers of Vincent Foster.... At the time of his death, he was trying to help his friend Bill Clinton clean up old Arkansas business without running afoul of new investigations. The theories that Mr. Foster died under suspicious circumstances seem cracked, but there is plenty of room for embarrassing testimony."

Nine Sony video screens—resembling those being used to display autopsy photographs and bloody footprints at the O.J. Simpson trial in Los Angeles—are set up in the U.S. Senate hearing room. They will be used to feature Whitewater documents and the torn-up note written by Foster and found in his briefcase, among other visual aids.

"Today, the Senate Whitewater Committee begins its first round of public hearings," says Senator D'Amato, the committee's chairman, presiding over its seventeen other members.[33] "The Senate has authorized the committee to ascertain the full facts about Whitewater and its many related matters. We intend to conduct fair, impartial and thorough hearings. That's what the American people want, expect and deserve....

"I will now briefly outline the three major areas the committee will look at during this round of Whitewater hearings: First, what happened in Vincent Foster's office on the night of July 20, 1993?...

"The next major episode, to which this round of hearings will turn, occurred on Thursday, July 22nd, two days after Vincent Foster's death [when his White House office was searched by Bernard Nussbaum]....

"Finally, the hearings will address the discovery by White House officials of a torn, undated page of writing by Vincent Foster that was eventually located in his briefcase in the White House office."

In the midst of other opening statements, Senator Frank Murkowski (R-Alaska), in a classic photo-op, grabs Foster's black-leather briefcase and holds it high in the air for all in the Senate hearing room to see, saying, "I have the briefcase in question here.... As anyone can plainly see, it would be pretty difficult not to see twenty-seven pieces of paper from a legal notebook.

"Had the Park Police or the FBI been examining this briefcase, there's no doubt they would have found the note and provided the president and the American people with the rationale for the Foster act. But the professionals did not handle the investigation; the White House handled the investigation."[34]

On July 23, Susan Schmidt of the *Washington Post* writes in a page-one story that White House Assistant Counsel Steve Neuwirth had told Senate investigators that Hillary Clinton—via New York attorney Susan Thomases, a personal friend of the Clintons—had relayed a message to Nussbaum, fearing full and unlimited access to Foster's office by law-enforcement officials prior to Nussbaum's July 22, 1993, search.

During the Fiske investigation, Susan Thomases had been named by Denver attorney James Lyons as being among the three known attorneys Foster had considered retaining for his defense in the Travel Office matter. And during her own telephone interview with the FBI on June 14, 1994, Thomases discussed her twenty-year friendship with the Clintons. Mrs. Clinton and Thomases served as members of the board of directors of the Children's Defense Fund; Maggie Williams had been its director of communications.

According to Schmidt's story: "Thomases, who worked on the Whitewater controversy during the campaign, was in communication with Hillary Clinton and her chief of staff, Margaret Williams, in the hours after Foster's death and came down to Washington in the days afterward.

"Nussbaum's attorney, James Fitzpatrick, said Thomases called Nussbaum on July 22 [about the search of Foster's office].... He said he could not explain why Thomases would have inserted herself into the issue, but said Nussbaum 'doesn't have any recollection [about] her saying anything about the First Lady.'"

The obvious question raised by the Schmidt article is: Exactly what was Susan Thomases doing, and what, if any, impact did she have on Nussbaum's decision to change the rules of the search of Foster's office?

On Tuesday, July 25, during a breakfast meeting with reporters, U.S. House Speaker Newt Gingrich, responding to a question about the Foster matter, says, "There's something that doesn't fit about this whole [Foster] case, and the way it's been handled.... I'm just not convinced he did [commit suicide]."

Soon after, Speaker Gingrich asks Representative Steven H.

Schiff, a Republican from New Mexico and an ex-prosecutor, to conduct his own probe of the Foster case in concert with Representative Clinger and his U.S. House Government Reform and Oversight Committee. Clinger is beginning his own investigation into the White House Travel Office matter.

Asked to reply to Gingrich, Assistant White House Counsel Mark Fabiani declares, "We regret that any elected official would put his weight behind a conspiracy industry that continues to exploit Vincent Foster and his family for political gain."

Interestingly, the longtime Gingrich-controlled GOPAC fund has been heavily financed by Richard Scaife, who has already made his presence felt, over and over again, among the critics of the Foster case.[35]

After the appearances before the Senate panel of Major Hines, Cheryl Braun, and John Rolla of the USPP, followed by David Watkins and Patsy Thomasson of the White House staff, the first anticipated clash of the testimonies between two witnesses occurs on Thursday, July 26, featuring Maggie Williams, Hillary Clinton's controversial chief of staff, and uniformed Secret Service officer Henry O'Neill.

During her sworn testimony, Maggie Williams, who says that she had received the news of Foster's death during a telephone call from Hillary Clinton, is tearful but adamant: "I took nothing from Vince's office. I didn't go into Foster's office with anything in mind concerning any documents that might be in his office. I did not look at, inspect or remove any documents. At no time was I instructed by anyone nor was there any suggestion from anyone that I go into Foster's office on the evening of July 20. I disturbed nothing while I was there."

The forty-one-year-old Williams offers committee members the results of one of two polygraphs she has taken, which have been arranged by her attorney Edward Dennis, a former top attorney in the Department of Justice under Presidents Reagan and Bush. As previously reported by Pete Yost of the Associated Press, the polygraph tests indicated no deception in response to her statements that she had neither removed nor carried anything out of Foster's office on the evening of July 20.

Although the challenges to Williams's credibility are minimal on that issue, they became more intense as Senator Connie Mack, a Florida Republican, tries to lay the groundwork for a conspiracy among Williams, Hillary Clinton, and Susan Thomases in the wake of Foster's death.

Mack reveals that Thomases had telephoned the White House several times on July 21, the day after Foster's death, beginning at 12:01 AM.

Although Mack alleges that several of Thomases's calls were made to Williams, the first lady's chief of staff acknowledges receiving only one call from Thomases, adding that the New York attorney often called the White House; thus, the list of calls revealed by Mack don't necessarily mean that "something sinister is going on here."

Williams adds in response to the charge of conspiracy, "Everything that happened was not some big plot. This list [of telephone calls from Thomases] does not suggest to me what it apparently suggests to you."

Two days after Williams's testimony, Paul Bedard of the *Washington Times* reveals that, according to his sources, Foster had kept a "diary" other than the diary about the postelection, preinaugural activities viewed by USPP Investigator John Rolla in James Hamilton's office in July 1993.

This document, written in a spiral notebook and leaked to Bedard, is Foster's detailed account about the Travel Office matter; Foster had written, "Privileged in anticipation of litigation," on the first page. The handwritten account concentrated on his concerns over the alleged involvement of the first lady in the firing of the seven Travel Office employees. He had begun making entries on May 30, 1993—just eleven days after the dismissals.

Bedard writes: "Mr. Foster wrote of discussing the scandal with First Lady Hillary Rodham Clinton. His notes say she was not satisfied with the administration's handling of the affair; conducted mostly by Mr. Foster; David Watkins, then head of administration; and Mr. Watkins' deputy, Patsy Thomasson, now director of personnel." Bedard adds that Foster had written in his diary: "Defend/HRC role whatever is, was in fact or might have been."

But Foster's notes also state: "HRC is perceived as being involved in the decision and events in which she has no participation."[36]

Meanwhile, as if there wasn't already enough public discussion about—and even comparisons between—the Vincent Foster and O.J. Simpson investigations, Kenneth Starr retains the services of criminalist Dr. Henry Lee, the head of the Connecticut State Police Forensic Science Laboratory since 1980, who had been hired by the Simpson defense team and is slated to put on a blood-spatter and shoe-print–pattern show for the jury at the Simpson trial.

Starr has asked Lee to review a portion of the crime-scene evidence in the Foster case.[37]

On July 31, the August 7 edition of *Time* is released and reveals the results of a *Time*/CNN telephone poll—taken between July 19 and 20—showing that 35 percent of those asked believe that

Vincent Foster committed suicide; 20 percent think he was murdered; and 45 percent aren't sure.

9.

CLEARLY, THE CHARACTER ALREADY CAST for role as villain in the Special
Committee's hearings about the handling of documents in Foster's
office is former White House Counsel Bernard Nussbaum. Stephen
Labaton of the *New York Times* interviews Nussbaum, who isn't
thrilled about this depiction, at his Manhattan office on July 28 and
publishes his story on Monday, July 31.

Labaton reports that on July 26, 1993, Mrs. Clinton, according to Nussbaum, had come into his office, where he showed her
Foster's torn-up note for the first time. Nussbaum told the
reporter, "She had a strong emotional reaction. She got up and
said, 'Bernie, I can't deal with this,' and with that, she walked out
of the office."

Since Maggie Williams's testimony, the Special Committee has heard
the testimonies of, among others, presidential aides Mack McLarty,
Bill Burton, David Gergen, and Bruce Lindsey, as well as staffers in
the White House Counsel's Office—Steve Neuwirth, Clifford Sloan,
Deborah Gorham,[38] Linda Tripp, and Tom Castleton. The Special
Committee has also heard the testimonies of those involved in the
controversial search in Foster's office two days after his death—
including Michael Spafford, Scott Salter, Roger Adams, Charles
Hume, Pete Markland, Dave Margolis,[39] and Philip Heymann.

On Tuesday, August 8, Susan Thomases responds to questions
about her contacts with Hillary Clinton, Maggie Williams, and
Bernard Nussbaum. Perhaps the most shocking revelation is that
Thomases had called either Mrs. Clinton or the White House no

fewer than seventeen times during the forty-three–hour period following Foster's death.

At 10:13 PM on July 20, 1993, after speaking with her husband about Foster's death, Mrs. Clinton talked to Maggie Williams for sixteen minutes. Then, at 11:19 PM, the first lady called Thomases and spoke to her for twenty minutes.

At 12:15 AM on July 21—fourteen minutes after her first call to the White House at 12:01—Thomases called Maggie Williams on her pager. At 11:03 AM, Thomases called an unknown person at a now-nonworking White House number.[40] At 11:06 AM and again at 4:30 PM, Thomases called Williams. At 5:50 PM, Thomases called Mrs. Clinton.

The following day, Thomases paged Nussbaum at 8:01 AM; she left a message for Williams at 9 AM. These calls were followed by others to McLarty (10:48 to 10:51 AM), Williams (11:04 to 11:10 AM), two more to McLarty (11:11 to 11:14, and 11:16 to 11:17 AM), and two more to Williams (11:37 to 11:48, and 11:50 to 11:54 AM).

That afternoon, at about 1 PM, Nussbaum began his search of Foster's office, with twelve others sitting and standing nearby, including Captain Hume and Detective Markland of the Park Police.

At 4 PM, Nussbaum and Williams did a final search of Foster's office, looking for documents dealing with the Clintons. Afterward, Tom Castleton reportedly took a box of documents— which, he told the Special Committee, the first lady "needed to review"—to the Clintons' residence in the White House and locked it in a closet.

From 5:13 to 5:22 PM, Thomases called and talked to Williams again. That call was followed by another to Bruce Lindsey from 5:23 to 5:26 PM.

From 7:12 to 7:13 PM, Thomases called the home of Hillary Clinton's mother.

Circumstantially, the timing and sheer volume of the calls appear extremely damning.

Majority Special Counsel Michael Chertoff, who had served as minority counsel during the 1994 Senate Banking Committee investigation, asks the fifty-one-year-old Thomases, "Did you have conversations with [Nussbaum] on July 21 or July 22, 1993, after [Foster's] death?"

"Yes," Thomases replies, "I had a conversation with Bernie Nussbaum...."

"And tell us what the conversation was concerning: the handling of a review of records in Mr. Foster's office?"

"I was not looking for... Bernie Nussbaum to talk about the review of documents in Vince Foster's office. I was really trying to reach him to talk about how he was feeling and how he was doing. I had known that he and Vince had grown to be very good friends, and that it was a very difficult thing for him to have lost his trusted deputy at this particular time."

"And what did he say about the documents?"

"He obviously was very focused on the documents at that time, where I was not. And he proceeded to tell me not to worry, that he had a plan, that he was going to take care of them.... He seemed to have a very clear sense that he was on top of it. He was going to handle it. He was going to give Vince's documents to Lisa [Foster's] lawyer, and that he was going to give the Clintons' documents to the Clintons' lawyers, and that he was going to protect all the presidential papers."

"He brought up the subject of the documents?"

"Yes, he did...."

"Did you know there were documents that were in the office that were personal to the Clintons?"

"I think I did...."

"Did he say he was going to take documents up to the [Clintons' White House] residence?"

"He did not...."

Chertoff continues, "And did you indicate in any way whatsoever, any view about the course that he was proposing to take?"

Thomases responds, "I indicated that it made sense to me. He had clearly thought long and hard about it, and he seemed to feel very sure of the course that he was taking. And I was not predisposed to disagree with him.... If I thought he was doing something terrible, I might have raised an objection. But it all sounded very well thought out to me."

"Did he tell you that he had had previous discussions with the Department of Justice about how the Department of Justice wanted to do this?"

"No, he did not...."

"You did share his view that there should not be 'unfettered access' to the documents by police?..."

"His focus was that he was going to do it his way...."

"Did you express in any way a view that in any way there should be a limitation placed upon the ability of law enforcement people to look at documents in the office?"

"No...."

"Well, we have evidence in the record that Mr. Nussbaum expressed to [Neuwirth] that you had the view in substance—I'm not saying it's a quote—that the police should not have 'unfettered access' to the papers in Mr. Foster's office. Is it your testimony that you never expressed any view like that to Mr. Nussbaum?"

"Yes, it is."

Chertoff then asks, "Did you talk to Hillary Clinton about the documents in Mr. Foster's office?"

Thomases answers, "I don't remember ever having a conversation with Hillary Clinton during the period after Vince Foster's death about the documents in Vince Foster's office."

10.

DRUM ROLL.

Bernard Nussbaum takes the hot seat on Wednesday, August 9, preparing to defend himself in a written statement and to field questions about his activities and decisions regarding his handling of the Foster case. Everyone seems to sense that, considering his op-ed piece in the *Times* the previous day, Nussbaum will be defiant. Meantime, Senate Republicans are expected to attempt to rip his testimony apart.

In his opening statement, Nussbaum declares, "This committee is looking into the following question: Did improper conduct occur regarding the way in which White House officials handled documents in Mr. Foster's office following his death? I have an answer to that question, Mr. Chairman. It is a categorical no....

"I did not nor, to my knowledge, did anyone else in the White House destroy, mishandle, or misappropriate any document in Vincent Foster's office."

Nussbaum goes on to say that, upon hearing of Foster's death, he was "stunned and deeply depressed." He returned to his office at the White House when he was struck by the thought that Foster might have left behind a suicide note. When he entered Foster's office, he found Patsy Thomasson, who was also looking for a note, sitting behind Foster's desk; Maggie Williams was crying on the couch.

"Patsy and I checked the surfaces in Vince's office. We opened a drawer or two, looking for a note. No one, *no one*, looked through Vince's files."

After failing to find a note, "the three of us then left the office. Nothing was removed by any of us. We were there no more than ten minutes."

The following day, Nussbaum says that he received a request from the U.S. Park Police. "They asked me to review the contents of Mr. Foster's office to see if there was a suicide note, an extortion note, or some other, similar document."*

Nussbaum believed that the request by the USPP would be the first of many, so he contacted Philip Heymann at the Department of Justice. After discussing the situation, they agreed the department would "coordinate the investigations of Foster's death."

Nussbaum continues, "In the late afternoon, I met with representatives of the Park Police, the Department of Justice and others. We agreed... after some discussion that a search of Vince's office would take place the next day."

Nussbaum insisted, "It is important to understand what we were being asked to do,... to understand what the search was for and what it was not for. The search was for a suicide note, an extortion note or some similar document which reflected depression or acute mental anguish. That is the request law-enforcement officials made of me. They did not ask to read every piece of paper in Foster's office, every official White House record there, every personal file there to see if there was any indication of concern about any matter Vince had been working on."

Defending himself against charges of his participation in the alleged Hillary Clinton–Susan Thomases–Maggie Williams cabal, Nussbaum continues, "I did not speak to the president or the First Lady about this matter, nor did Susan Thomases or anyone else

---

* There is no record of anyone at the U.S. Park Police ever *asking* Nussbaum to review the contents of Foster's office. The police wanted to do it themselves.

convey a message to me from either of them. Susan Thomases did not discuss the First Lady's views with me, but I should say I assumed from the outset of this tragedy that the First Lady, who's a very good lawyer, like every other good lawyer in or out of the White House, would believe that permitting unfettered access to a lawyer's office is not proper. That was my assumption. It was not the result of any conversation with her."

On July 22, 1993, according to Nussbaum, everyone involved in the "search" entered Foster's office together. "The agents were with me at all times during the search in Vince's office," Nussbaum explains. "As the agents watched, I personally pulled out each of the files in that office. I briefly reviewed the files. As I was doing so, I gave the agents a general description of the documents, and I checked to see if there was a suicide note or an extortion note or other similar document in those files.... But the agents did not sit as cigar-store dummies as I conducted the search.

"I also accepted requests from the agents to read for themselves any document I was describing.... They did ask to see and read certain documents. I set those documents aside. Subsequently, after we reviewed them, every document the agents asked for was, within a matter of days, given to the law-enforcement officials....

"During the office search on July 22nd, I saw a number of files that concerned personal matters of the Clintons.... I said, 'These were Clinton personal files.... These involve investments, taxes, other financial matters and the like.' Included was a file on the Clintons' Whitewater real-estate investment.... I believed the Clinton personal files belonged in the hands of the First Family or their personal lawyers."

Finally, regarding the discovery of Foster's torn-up note, Nussbaum stood firm on what he had told Captain Hume and Detective Markland of the Park Police: "During the July 22 search, I had removed files from this briefcase. I had not noticed scraps at the bottom of the case, nor do I recall any conversation on that date referring to scraps in the bottom of the case with Cliff Sloan or anyone else. On July 26, as soon as the scraps were found, they were pieced together by Steve [Neuwirth] in my office with my help.... The [note] was given to the Park Police the next day, on July 27, after Mrs. Foster and the president were given a chance to review it."

In short, Nussbaum insists that he has no regrets—except "I wish I had looked more carefully into the bottom of the briefcase."

Senator Orrin Hatch, a Republican from Utah, asks Nussbaum, "Mr. Margolis and Mr. Adams, they stated here that they thought there was an agreement that the Justice lawyers would review at least the title page and the first page of each document and then make a determination with respect to privilege...."

Nussbaum answers, "I never agreed to it...."

Hatch then asks, "Mr. Nussbaum, Roger Adams's notes of the meeting state that you reached an agreement. Mr. Neuwirth objected to the agreement, but you overruled him. Now, your testimony here is that he's mistaken, that that just didn't happen?"

"He has a different memory than I. I think he's mistaken, yes...."

"Did you talk to Ms. Thomases on July 22nd?"

"Yes...."

"You say that Ms. Thomases called you and said that she had heard about the discussions with Justice. She said that you brought it up, and that she did not really have an opinion about the search arrangements...."

"Senator, you're right. There is a difference in recollection...."

"The point is, did you tell her or did she tell you about these concerns?..."

"My memory is that she initiated... [a] discussion about whether or not there was a concern about a procedure...."

Senator Richard Shelby, now an anti-Clinton Republican who switched parties in November 1994, later continues the interrogation, asking, "Your idea of coordinate was not Mr. Heymann's idea of coordinate...."

Still standing firm, Nussbaum replies sharply, "No, I think our idea of coordinate was the same; our idea of how to conduct a search in the office is not the same, Senator Shelby."

"It was your idea for you to conduct the search, and they to be window dressing?"

"No, that's not what happened.... The fact is, Senator, they weren't window dressing. They were participating.... [As] I was describing documents, we were talking. And they would say, 'Mr. Nussbaum, even though we're looking for a suicide note, we'd like to see that document.'... I'd say, 'Fine, here, I'll put it in a pile, and I'll take a look at it later.'... That's what we were doing, Senator. That's participation. That's not sitting like a cigar-store Indian. That's not being [frozen]."

"But that's not what really happened though, was it?" Shelby persists.

"Oh," Nussbaum responds defiantly, "that is exactly what happened, Senator. And I was there, and I know it."

"That's your selective memory."

"No, sir, Senator. It's my accurate memory...."

"Do you remember the deputy attorney general, Mr. Heymann—and his testimony was that he was very, very angry—called you—"

As Nussbaum attempts to interrupt, Shelby admonishes him, "Let me finish. Just let me finish my question.... Did he say: 'Are you hiding something?' Mr. Nussbaum? Could he have said that?"

"Yes, he could have said that, but I don't remember that. I think it's something I would remember, but I don't remember it...."

"Mr. Nussbaum, did you basically not trust the Justice Department?"

"No, I trusted the Justice Department, Senator Shelby."

"And Mr. Heymann?"

"I trusted the Justice Department, Senator."

To the chagrin of the Senate Republicans, Nussbaum leaves the Senate hearing room later that day in one piece.[41]

11.

THE SEPTEMBER 11 ISSUE OF *THE NEW YORKER* features a lengthy and fascinating article about Lisa Foster, "Life After Vince," by Peter J. Boyer. Boyer had obtained the first media interview with the widow of the late deputy counsel.

Just the previous week, she announced that she had accepted the marriage proposal of fifty-five-year-old attorney Jim Moody of Wright, Lindsey & Jennings in Little Rock, a widower who had been nominated by President Clinton and recently confirmed by the U.S. Senate to serve on the federal bench in Arkansas.

In his remarkably revealing article, Boyer provides previously untold details about Lisa Braden Foster's background. For instance, she is the daughter of an insurance broker in Nashville, who, along with his wife, had six children. They lived a good life of country clubs and high-society debutante balls. A Roman Catholic, Lisa Braden went to a high school operated by Dominican nuns, then to Sweet Briar, an all-women's college in Virginia, majoring in mathematics.

As a sophomore, she had met her future husband, who was a sophomore at Davidson. They were married in April 1968 at St. Henry Catholic Church in Nashville. Boyer notes that at the time of the wedding Vincent was in his first year of law school at Vanderbilt. Later, Foster transferred to the University of Arkansas School of Law.

After graduation, Vincent Foster began his rise to local legal stardom. Meantime, the most important thing in Lisa's life was to have children and to raise a family. "I didn't really want to have a career," she told Boyer.

Boyer details the events leading to Foster's selection by President-elect Clinton as deputy White House counsel. Foster's appointment, which came on Christmas Eve 1992, was clinched after the Fosters learned that Mack McLarty, another lifelong friend of Vincent, had taken the job as Clinton's chief of staff. According to Boyer, Foster wanted to play second-in-command to Nussbaum—even though Clinton had asked Foster, who was already wildly successful at the Rose Law Firm, "Are you sure you want to do this?"

Boyer writes that Lisa told her husband, "I'm afraid if you don't do it you'll always be sorry."

But, immediately after he moved to Washington while Lisa remained in Little Rock with their youngest son, the couple began bickering during their long-distance telephone conversations. "I was angry at Vince about 90 percent of the time... for ignoring us and leaving us behind," she told Boyer.

The couple even had trouble on the president's inauguration day when Foster left his wife during the inaugural parade to go to work. Mrs. Foster, who was visiting from Little Rock, was so angry that she refused to accompany him to the inaugural ball.

Then, when she finally moved to Washington, he was already talking about quitting his job. "He didn't want to go out. He didn't want to do anything fun. He wanted me to stay home and cook. He never came home until nine or ten o'clock at night, then went straight to bed.... [I]t was basically awful."

Their trip to the Eastern Shore the weekend before his death appeared to be an opportunity to launch a new beginning in their relationship. However, according to Lisa, on the first night of their getaway, "I asked him if he felt trapped, and tears came to his eyes, and he cried."

On the night before her husband's death, Mrs. Foster asked him if he would "go on a date with her the following night." Foster, who seemed to be in a better mood, said that "he would try," adding that he had to attend a birthday party.[42]

But the next morning her husband did not "kiss her goodbye" before leaving for work. She told Boyer, "[H]e just had his back to me, so stiff. And he just walked out."

Boyer reports that Lisa completely accepted Investigator Rolla's account that her husband had committed suicide with a .38, saying that her mind immediately went to the guns she had brought up from Little Rock. She also told Boyer that she asked Rolla whether Vincent "had shot himself in the mouth or at the temple."

Explaining this odd remark, she mentioned that her husband had recently seen the movie, A Few Good Men, in which one of the characters had taken his own life by placing a gun in his mouth and pulling the trigger.

Angry in the wake of her husband's death, she called friends and colleagues of her husband, asking them if they knew why he had killed himself. She even telephoned Nussbaum and asked if he had fired her husband; he replied that he had not.

Lisa told Boyer that her husband had a life-insurance policy, which had remained in force even though he had taken his own life. He had also created trust funds for his children's educations. Everyone in the family seemed secure.

Regarding the much-discussed alleged affair between Hillary Clinton and her husband, Lisa Foster said that a segment on a tabloid-television show that explored the rumor in December 1993 had sent her fleeing from her own house in tears—even though she had discussed the rumor with her husband during the 1992 presidential campaign. He assured her that it was gossip and nothing more, insisting that he had never had an affair with Mrs. Clinton.

Although Lisa said she never talked with Mrs. Clinton about it, Boyer makes it clear that Lisa really didn't believe the rumor. "I just have faith in Vince and faith in Hillary that they did not have an affair," she tells Boyer. "If they did, who cares now?... Vince is dead."

On Tuesday, September 12, another team of FBI investigators and a National Park Service archaeologist—upon the orders of Kenneth Starr and the OIC, and led by Richard K. Graham, an expert at metal detection—reenter Fort Marcy Park en masse and seal off the entire area. At or about 11:30 AM, a half hour after their arrival, firearms experts shoot a .38-caliber revolver as part of a sophisticated ballistics test, in an effort to estimate the trajectory of the bullet that killed Vincent Foster and in hopes of finding this elusive slug.

While agents in cherry-pickers search the treetops for the bullet from the gun found in Foster's right hand, others use metal detectors on the ground within a 175-yard perimeter of search grids marked with orange stakes.

But, once again, they find no bullet.

12.

REED IRVINE AND AIM, Joseph Farah and Western Journalism Center, Jim Davidson and *Strategic Investment*, Christopher Ruddy and the *Pittsburgh Tribune-Review*, and Ambrose Evans-Pritchard and the *Sunday Telegraph*, as well as independents like Hugh Sprunt, continue to fire away at the verdict that Foster had committed suicide in Fort Marcy Park.

Paul Harvey, the influential radio commentator known for his folksy, commonsense approach to the news, also joins the chorus of skeptics about the Foster case by raising doubts about the official investigations in his widely heard radio reports on September 26 and 27.

Meantime, CBS's 60 Minutes prepares for an upcoming broadcast about the Foster case, and Irvine finds out about it on October 5, just three days before its scheduled air date and two days after O.J. Simpson's acquittal in his murder trial.

Irvine immediately writes a letter to Phil Scheffler, a senior producer for 60 Minutes, saying: "60 Minutes could perform a great service by making this an important part of your program and demanding the release of the records. If, on the other hand, your program ignores these questions and confirms the findings of the Park Police and Fiske investigations, you may be acutely embarrassed when Congress pries the records loose and delves into the reasons for the cover-up. That could happen in a few weeks."

The following day, Irvine tapes his telephone conversation with Mike Wallace, who reveals that his production team has been working on the piece for the past two months. Almost immediately, Irvine and Wallace clash on the sourcing in the 60 Minutes segment.

Still complaining about not being informed about the broadcast, Irvine says, "I didn't know anybody who did know about it."

Wallace replies, "Very good. Well, are you familiar with Congressman Clinger?... He will appear here: a Republican congressman."

"Well, sure," Irvine responds, knowing much more about the case than Wallace, "he bought the Park Police and the Fiske Report line."

"Yeah. Well, he's on. He's on. So it occurs to me that—Why don't you take a good look and then do what you think?"

Already sensing the theme of the program, Irvine shoots back, "Well, I'm sorry to see that you're going to use Clinger, because I asked twenty questions of—"

Wallace interrupts, "He's a Republican congressman. He's chairman of a committee. He is a very intelligent and highly regarded man of great experience."

Irvine explains, "Mike, let me tell you my experience with Bill Clinger. I posed twenty questions to Fiske, which he didn't answer. And then Clinger came out with his report, endorsing the *Fiske Report*, so I sent over the questions [to Clinger]. I said, 'Fine, since you think... the report stands up, well, perhaps *you'll* answer these questions.' And his staff said that he would do so. And, of course, I didn't hear from him for some time. I went back to them, and they finally said, 'Well, he's not going to answer.' That was it. So he can't answer the questions either."

Brushing that off, Wallace replies, "Well, perhaps some of the questions will be answered for you on Sunday."

Actually, what Irvine and the other critics, especially Christopher Ruddy, do not realize is that they never had a prayer of being taken seriously.

After hearing that *60 Minutes* was preparing a segment on the Foster case, Phil Stinson, Kevin Fornshill's attorney, wrote a letter to Don Hewitt, the program's executive producer, complaining that the Western Journalism Center had sent out a mailing, alleging that the center was working with *60 Minutes* on the Foster case. Soon after, Stinson received a call from Robert Anderson, a segment producer for the popular show, who requested a copy of what Western Journalism Center had been sending out. Stinson faxed Anderson the mailing. According to Stinson, Hewitt was furious. Almost immediately, Stinson received another call from an associate producer, who allegedly told him, among other things, "We just want to nail Ruddy."

With Stinson agreeing to cooperate, Anderson and the associate producer, who had already started working on their own Foster probe, came to the attorney's office in Philadelphia where they met with Fornshill and discussed the case. Obviously, they wanted Fornshill on camera; Fornshill had received written permission from Chief Langston's office to cooperate.

After a subsequent meeting in Washington—which included an on-camera walkthrough of Fort Marcy Park with Mike Wallace, who had come to the park in a limousine—Fornshill agreed to fly to New York later that day with Stinson. CBS put them up at the Le Parker Meridien Hotel on West 56th Street in midtown Manhattan.

The plan was simple: Ruddy was going to be interviewed by Wallace the following day, and the *60 Minutes* people wanted Fornshill and Stinson in the next room. At some point during the interview, Wallace was going to ask Ruddy, "What questions do you have for Fornshill? And, if you had the opportunity to talk to him, would you talk to him?" When Ruddy replied that he would, Fornshill was going to emerge from the room—with his attorney—and confront Ruddy.

But instead of being placed in another room, Fornshill and Stinson were seated in the bathroom, listening through the door and waiting for their cue. They knew Wallace was in on this, because he had said hello to them before Ruddy walked in.

After Ruddy arrived and the interview began, however, something unexpected happened: Wallace started buying into what Ruddy was saying about the problems with the Foster case. For over two hours, Fornshill and Stinson listened with stunned disbelief as Ruddy appeared to be persuading Wallace, who, according to Stinson, seemed "confused and unprepared."[43]

After Ruddy and Wallace went their separate ways at the lunch break, Fornshill and Stinson received the all-clear to come out of the bathroom. Anderson, who was very upset, came up to the two men, allegedly lamenting, "It's not going well. The story's dead. I can't believe this: Mike is blowing it!"

Then, Anderson asked Fornshill and Stinson to return to the *60 Minutes* office—apparently to deprogram Wallace. Anderson also requested that they come up with five to seven talking points for Wallace.

When they met with Wallace in his office during the lunch break, Fornshill and Stinson, with Anderson present, started to prep him. But Wallace stopped them, with such questions as: "Why is there no soil on Foster's shoes?"

After a lengthy conversation, Wallace relented and agreed with Anderson to ask Ruddy the hardball questions Fornshill and Stinson had prepared. Soon after, they all returned to the hotel; Fornshill and Stinson went back into the bathroom.

When the interview with Ruddy resumed, Wallace was obviously more aggressive with him—even though Fornshill and Stinson were upset by Wallace's lack of good follow-up questions. But, in the end, it was enough. The drama of seeing Fornshill and Stinson emerge into the room where Ruddy was being interviewed never became necessary.

It was a shoe-string catch—but at Ruddy's expense.

That night, Mike Wallace's segment on the Foster case travels right down the line with the previous official investigations: Foster, a man who placed the highest premium on honor and integrity, had been compromised by Travelgate and exposed in the *Wall Street Journal*. Depressed over these matters, as well as the failed nominations of Zoe Baird and Kimba Wood, Foster, who feared professional destruction had he been caught seeing a psychiatrist, saw no other way out but suicide.[44] The most forceful of Wallace's on-camera guests is attorney James Hamilton, who speaks on behalf of Lisa Foster and expresses their common belief that Vincent Foster had killed himself.

Instead of the weak sister that Fornshill and Stinson had seen in person, Wallace, on the edited film, is forceful in his delivery, lecturing viewers on crime-scene issues, and taunting those who disagree with the official version of events.

This leads, of course, to Christopher Ruddy, whom Wallace mercilessly attacks. But, while attempting to respond to Wallace's accusations, Ruddy is, on several occasions, cut short by the film editor, who, instead, shows Wallace snickering and laughing at him. Wallace actually cackles at one point during his interview with Ruddy, "Give me a break!"

For instance, Ruddy had written an article on January 12, 1995, stating that Dr. Donald Haut, the medical examiner who came to the Foster crime scene, told him that he had not seen "a lot of blood on the ground."

When interviewed by Wallace during the program, Dr. Haut denies ever saying that to Ruddy, who had already explained to Wallace that he had taped the conversation with Haut and offered to share it—an offer Wallace rebuffed.

Nevertheless, this is one of the issues that Wallace—who even misquotes what Ruddy had written about Dr. Haut—uses to nail the reporter.

Wallace's unprofessional, heavy-handed, and vindicative performance infuriates even those who believe the official reports about Foster's death and disagree with Ruddy and the other critics.[45]

Once again, a golden opportunity to annihilate the minutiae

peddlers of the Foster case is reduced to a mere exercise in name-calling and shabby journalism.

Predictably—and, perhaps, justifiably—the critics go ballistic in the wake of the *60 Minutes* broadcast. And they appear strengthened by Wallace's low-ball attack.

On Wednesday, October 11, Ruddy, appearing on Reed Irvine's weekly television show, "The Other Side of the Story," angrily accuses Wallace of a "[reckless] disregard for the truth." And, in the October issue of the *AIM Report*, Irvine describes the *60 Minutes* report as "dishonest and unfair."

On Friday, October 13, R. Emmett Tyrrell, the editor-in-chief of *The American Spectator*, continues the angry reaction to the *60 Minutes* program. In November, *The American Spectator* publishes Ambrose Evans-Pritchard's article, "The Death That Won't Die," a summary of the current state of evidence on the Foster case.

On Sunday, October 15, the Western Journalism Center publishes a full-page ad in the *New York Times*, defending Christopher Ruddy's work while lambasting Mike Wallace's program. The headline reads:

Mike Wallace, Can You Pass the Cover-Up Test?
Special Counsel Robert Fiske Flunked It.

Meantime, seemingly provoked by the *60 Minutes* program, an avalanche of questionable data and wild speculation about the Foster case finds its way onto the Internet, demonstrating the best and worst of the new information superhighway. President Clinton, one of the Internet's greatest supporters, is accused of everything from weapons trafficking to murder, among many other groundless allegations.

On Sunday, October 22, Ambrose Evans-Pritchard, who is almost keeping pace with Ruddy in published articles about the Foster case, resurrects the controversy over Patrick Knowlton, who was written about but not named by Ruddy on June 14 in the *Tribune-Review*.

In his article in the *Sunday Telegraph*, Evans-Pritchard writes that Knowlton—whom the reporter publicly names for the first time—is accusing the FBI and Fiske investigators of trying "to persuade [Knowlton] into changing his story" about, among other things, the rust-brown color of the older Honda with Arkansas plates he had supposedly seen, as well as his sighting of a Hispanic-looking man with a threatening demeanor who was in a blue car at Fort Marcy on the day of Foster's death.[46]

Knowlton, whom the British journalist identifies as a "construction consultant," also insists that he could pick this man with the intimidating glare out of a lineup. Evans-Pritchard's story includes a sketch of the man Knowlton claims to have seen in the parking lot.

On Wednesday, October 25, Jim Davidson of *Strategic Investment* calls another press conference at the Willard Hotel in Washington, announcing that he has retained the services of a panel of three forensic handwriting experts—all of whom now declare that the torn-up note found in Vincent Foster's briefcase is a forgery.[47] The panel consists of:

■ Reginald E. Alton, dean of degrees at St. Edmund Hall at Oxford University in England.[48]

- Ronald Rice, the head of New England
  Investigation of Boston, as well as a qualified and
  board-certified documents examiner. He had
  reviewed documents in several previous high-
  profile cases, including those involving the
  Boston Strangler, Ted Bundy, and O.J. Simpson.

- Vincent Scalice, a former homicide detective and
  identification expert with the New York Police
  Department, who had filed an earlier statement dis-
  puting the findings of the *Fiske Report* on behalf of
  the Western Journalism Center. Scalice has also
  been a key source for Christopher Ruddy.

All three experts had compared the torn-up note supposedly
written by Foster with twelve other known samples of his writing;
all three conclude that the torn-up note had been written with
numerous differences in lettering and overall style by someone
other than Vincent Foster.

Davidson immediately provides his panel's findings to independent counsel Kenneth Starr, insisting that the allegedly phony note
was torn up to disguise the forgery. He also claims that the forgery
explains why there are no fingerprints on the torn-up note.

13.

ON WEDNESDAY, OCTOBER 25, a July 21st tentative agreement between
the White House and the Special Committee regarding the release
of previously redacted documents stemming from the Foster case
collapses, causing Chairman D'Amato to announce bitterly that
the committee has "been misled and that there has been an obvious pattern of delay."

D'Amato adds, "The Clinton White House cannot play games with this congressional oversight committee. The heart of our democracy depends on our ability to perform our constitutional duty. We will not let the Clinton White House toy with this committee any longer."

Actually, one of the architects of Clinton's legal strategy is the former chief of staff for Vice President Gore, forty-five-year–old Jack Quinn, who has replaced Abner Mikva as White House counsel. Clinton appreciates Quinn for his hard-line stands regarding investigations of Foster's death and Whitewater-related activities.[49]

Under political duress, however, the White House has already revealed more telephone calls, indicating that on July 22, 1993, the day of the controversial search of Foster's office, Maggie Williams called Hillary Clinton at 7:44 AM at the home of Mrs. Clinton's mother in Little Rock. The two women spoke for seven minutes, hanging up at 7:51.

Six minutes later, at 7:57, the first lady called Susan Thomases in Washington. They spoke for three minutes until 8:00.

At 8:01, Thomases called Nussbaum's pager—shortly before the Park Police and the FBI arrived at the White House.

Finally, at 12:55 PM, twenty minutes before the 1:15 search of Foster's office officially began, Williams called Mrs. Clinton, who had just paged Williams at 12:47 PM.[50]

The following day, Thursday, October 26, the *Washington Times* publishes an editorial about these latest telephone-call revelations, stating what most people seem to be thinking: "It doesn't take a very suspicious mind to construct an interpretation of this string of calls that puts Mrs. Clinton in the driver's seat. Could it be that Ms. Williams called the first lady to warn her that Mr. Nussbaum was going to let investigators into Mr. Foster's office, and that Mrs. Clinton in [turn] called Ms. Thomases so that she could deliver instructions to Mr. Nussbaum?"

That same day, the Special Committee, as earlier threatened, issues forty subpoenas for a variety of Whitewater-related documents.

On Thursday, November 2, Maggie Williams and Susan Thomases make their second appearances before the Special Committee with Thomases telling the senators from the outset, "My recollection of those events [after Foster's death], and my overall memory of what happened at that time, remain essentially the same as when I appeared before you last August."

Indeed, plagued by memory lapses and discrepancies in their testimonies, both women continue to insist that neither they nor Hillary Clinton had ever attempted to impede the Foster-death investigation.

The committee also reveals a Secret Service log, showing that Thomases had spent nearly six hours at the White House on July 27, 1993—the same day that the documents Williams had arranged to be placed in the Clintons' personal residence had been transferred to the Clintons' personal attorney, Robert Barnett. This was also just hours before the White House notified the Park Police about Foster's torn-up note, nearly thirty hours after finding it.

Thomases claims to have no recollection about any of this, including spending six hours on that particular day at the White House.

Although concerned with the partisan atmosphere hovering over the Special Committee's hearings, the New York Times appears impressed with the committee's latest revelations, stating in a

December 6 editorial: "At the very least the hearings have reinforced the impression that the White House and its loyalists in key government agencies went to puzzling lengths to hobble legitimate investigations into those long-ago events in Arkansas and the death of Vincent Foster, the White House counsel.

"The hearings have also reaffirmed that Hillary Rodham Clinton's associates seem incapable of producing candid answers to questions about the events following the Foster suicide and the handling of the Whitewater documents in his office."

14.

On Wednesday, January 3, 1996, the White House releases a 1993 memorandum to the Special Committee written by David Watkins—who had resigned in 1994 after being discovered using a presidential helicopter to attend a golf outing and had to reimburse the federal government over $13,000 for doing so. The memo is addressed, but was never sent, to Mack McLarty. A copy had been found in Patsy Thomasson's files.

In this document, Watkins speaks about the Clintons' earlier displeasure with their Secret Service guards, all of whom had worked for President and Mrs. Bush. Inspired by Harry Thomason, Hillary Clinton had come to view these guards as unfriendly toward the new residents of the White House. Consequently, Mrs. Clinton allegedly asked Vincent Foster whether she should push to have the guards replaced. After conferring with Watkins, Foster returned to the first lady and insisted that such action was not necessary; that the guards had been trained to appear detached from the personal lives of the first family, whom they were there to protect. Mrs. Clinton accepted Foster's explanation, and none of the White House guards was replaced.

However, after a February 19, 1993, news story in the *Chicago Sun-Times*, claiming that Mrs. Clinton had smashed a lamp

during an argument with her husband in their private residence at
the White House, she blamed Foster and Watkins for not replacing the guards, whom she believed had leaked the story, which she
insisted was inaccurate.[51]

In his 1993 memo to McLarty, written after the firings in the
Travel Office, Watkins states:

> As you recall, an issue developed between the Secret
> Service and the First Family in February and March requir-
> ing resolution and action.... [T]he First Lady in particular
> was extremely upset with the delayed action in that case.
>   Likewise, in this case, the First Lady took interest in hav-
> ing the Travel Office situation resolved quickly.... Once this
> made it onto the First Lady's agenda, Vince Foster became
> involved, and he... regularly informed me of her attention
> to the Travel Office situation—as well as her insistence that
> the situation be resolved immediately by replacing the
> Travel Office staff....
>   We both knew there would be hell to pay if, after our
> failure in the Secret Service situation earlier, we failed to
> take swift and decisive action in conformity with the First
> Lady's wishes.[52]

Needless to say, the release of this memo—even though written by
a man who had given conflicting stories about the alleged involvement of the first lady in Travelgate—causes a sensation among the
Republicans, especially those on Representative William Clinger's
Committee on Government Reform and Oversight, which is looking into Travelgate.[53]

The memo also reaffirms speculation that Foster had taken his
own life because of his despair in the wake of Travelgate.

Two days after the release of the Watkins memorandum, on Friday,
January 5, 1996, the White House releases more documents:

Hillary Clinton's billing records from the Rose Law Firm for her work on behalf of Madison Guaranty, which had been subpoenaed by the Resolution Trust Corporation two years ago. They had been discovered the previous August and then rediscovered on Thursday night by Carolyn Huber, a White House aide and the former office manager of the Rose Law Firm, who found them in the Book Room of the Clintons' third-floor residence.[54]

Just the previous Sunday, the statute of limitations for potential lawsuits against those who had advised collapsed savings and loan institutions expired—which coincided with the termination of the Resolution Trust Corporation.

As soon as investigators for the Special Committee receive the long-sought records, they notice numerous handwritten notations, which had been made by Vincent Foster in red ink. Many wondered if these documents had been removed from Foster's office on July 22, 1993.

They also show that Mrs. Clinton had worked on Castle Grande, a bogus real-estate project that is at the center of the current fraud case against Jim McDougal and Arkansas Governor Jim Guy Tucker, both of whom had been indicted along with McDougal's wife, Susan, on August 17, 1995. Jim McDougal had also shared the Castle Grande partnership with Seth Ward, who was Webb Hubbell's father-in-law. The complicated scheme helped lead to the downfall of Madison Guaranty, McDougal's savings and loan.

According to the newly discovered billing records, Mrs. Clinton had logged in fifty hours of work for Castle Grande over a fifteen-month period. But, in a sworn statement to the Resolution Trust Corporation in May 1995, Mrs. Clinton had "represented that she knew nothing about Castle Grande," according to the Special Committee.

How much did Foster know about the Castle Grande prior to

his death? Apparently something. Soon after, Susan Schmidt of the *Washington Post* writes that Foster had received "letters from Arkansas' two senators questioning the RTC's treatment of former Madison insider Seth Ward. In early July [1993] Foster told Nussbaum he would have to recuse himself from those congressional inquiries."[55]

On Monday, January 8, 1996, columnist William Safire of the *New York Times* throws a roundhouse punch at Mrs. Clinton, writing: "Americans of all political persuasions are coming to the sad realization that our First Lady—a woman of undoubted talents who was a role model for many in her generation—is a congenital liar.

"Drip by drip, like Whitewater torture, the case is being made that she is compelled to mislead, and to ensnare her subordinates and friends in a web of deceit."

White House spokesman Mike McCurry replies that if her husband weren't president, he would "deliver a forceful response to the bridge of Mr. Safire's nose."

But apart from this kid's stuff between the president and Safire, Mrs. Clinton is clearly being shoved against the ropes.[56]

In another editorial extremely critical of the Clintons on January 21, the *New York Times* insists that Hillary Clinton should testify before the Special Committee. Among several reasons cited, the *Times* states: "Mrs. Clinton might be able to shed light on the late Vincent Foster's migrating files. These files may have included the billing records, since his handwritten notations are all over them. In testimony last year, Mrs. Clinton's chief of staff, Margaret Williams, and her close confidante, Susan Thomases, suffered astounding memory lapses when asked about missing files."

The day after the *Times*'s editorial, Kenneth Starr subpoenas Mrs. Clinton to appear before his federal grand jury investigating Whitewater-related crimes. It is the first time in American history that the first lady has been called to testify under oath before a grand jury investigating criminal misconduct.

15.

JIM DAVIDSON OF *STRATEGIC INVESTMENT* has grown weary of what he insists has been bad faith in the official investigation of the Foster case, and publishes an article in his February 14 edition, "Kenneth Starr, the Pontius Pilate of the Potomac."

Davidson, who compares Starr to Robert Fiske, now believes that Starr has abandoned the search for the truth and sold out, continuing the alleged cover-up of Foster's supposed murder. Specifically, Davidson cites Starr's failure to pursue several key leads as his evidence that the independent counsel has been pulling his punches. Davidson is particularly upset that Starr doesn't appear to be taking seriously, among other things, the alleged forgery of the torn-up note found in Foster's briefcase and the supposed presence of other possible co-conspirators at Fort Marcy Park as identified by such people as Patrick Knowlton.

Many of Davidson's complaints against Starr come from Christopher Ruddy's ongoing investigation, which now reveals that White House aide Thomas Castleton had seen Foster leaving his office *with* his briefcase. This, to Ruddy and Davidson, adds to the credibility of witnesses, like Knowlton, who claim to have seen a briefcase in the Honda parked in the lot at Fort Marcy.

Ruddy has also received information from a source involved in the Special Committee's investigation, informing him that an unidentified woman who applied makeup to President Clinton before his appearance on *Larry King Live* on the evening of July 20,

1993, had supposedly overheard a conversation between the president and an unidentified aide.

According to Ruddy's February 14, 1996, story in the *Pittsburgh Tribune-Review*, the woman stated that just prior to going on the program at 9 PM, President Clinton received a message from the aide that "a note had been found in Foster's office."

The woman, Ruddy writes, had given her story to Robert Fiske in 1994 during his investigation. However, there is no mention of her account in his report, and her statement was not passed on to the Senate Banking Committee.

According to the White House's version, the president received the tragic news about Foster's death at about 10 PM from Mack McLarty, whom the makeup artist added was present during the alleged 9 PM conversation.

Asking what the president knew and when he knew it in the wake of Ruddy's latest story, reporter Dale Hurd of the Christian Broadcasting Network airs his own report about the Foster case on February 29, provoking Pat Robertson of the *700 Club* to charge, "It was overwhelming, but there is a massive cover-up in the media [about the Foster case]. The media will not touch it. It is just amazing.... It is very frightening. And, ladies and gentlemen, if you think Watergate was a bad cover-up, this is worse."

On the same day as the CBN report and in the midst of the presidential primaries, the official life of the Special Committee on Whitewater comes to an apparent end, needing another Senate vote in order to complete its work. In response to the Republicans' demands for an open-ended deadline and an additional $600,000 in funding, the Democrats threaten a filibuster in an attempt to prevent Senate action.

The minority have countered with an offer of an April 3 deadline and $185,000 budget. When the Democrats are rebuffed, the filibuster commences; the Republicans need 60 percent of the full Senate, sixty members, to end the filibuster and force a vote.

On March 11, the *Wall Street Journal* publishes an editorial, accusing the Democrats of participating in the White House cover-up of Whitewater, adding: "[P]resumptive GOP nominee Bob Dole carries the burden of an insider image. But as Senate majority leader he has the power to make Democrats pay dearly for a filibuster joining the Whitewater cover-up. If he wants to be a 'comeback adult,' one of the best things he could do is to make sure dirty linen is appropriately washed."[57]

But, regardless of the merit of the Republicans' case on Whitewater, the fact that Senator D'Amato has become the co-chairman of Senate Majority Leader Bob Dole's presidential campaign does not add to the illusion of a fair and impartial investigation.

Despite the relentless beating the Clintons are receiving from the *New York Times*, Reed Irvine continues criticizing the newspaper for failing to challenge the official version of how Foster actually died.

Unable to persuade the *Times* to launch its own independent investigation, Irvine and AIM purchase space in the newspaper for a five-part series discussing the unanswered questions about the Foster case. For the first three segments, they buy three quarter-page ads at $19,825 each; the final two installments are contained in a single full-page ad on April 7.

Each of Irvine's articles has a special point:

> *Part One* (on March 18): Regarding the crime scene, Irvine summarizes the evidence as "no bullet, no bone, no brains, no blood." Irvine also revisits the issue of the person

spotted by Patrick Knowlton at Fort Marcy Park while Foster's car was parked in the lot.

Part Two (on March 22): Irvine revisits the issues of the lack of dirt on Foster's shoes, that Foster's eyeglasses were found nineteen feet from his body, that no one heard a gunshot, about the transfer stain on Foster's cheek, and about the two people seen near Foster's car by Judith Doody and Mark Feist, whom Irvine does not name.

Part Three (on March 29): Irvine revisits the sudden reversal on July 27, 1993, by White House spokeswoman Dee Dee Myers to claim that Foster had been depressed—after seven days of denials that he was. Irvine also continues to insist that the torn-up note found in Foster's briefcase might have been a forgery.

Part Four (on April 7): Irvine challenges the identification of Foster's gun, saying that Lisa Foster had told the FBI she had brought a silver-colored gun to Washington from Little Rock. The revolver found in Foster's right hand was black.

Part Five (on April 7): Irvine revisits the issues of the underexposed 35 mm pictures and missing Polaroid photographs, as well as the allegedly missing X rays from the autopsy. Irvine also resurrects the hair and fiber evidence on Foster's body, the semen in his shorts, and the question whether Foster had left the White House with his briefcase.

In the full-page ad, which contains the fourth and fifth segments of the series, Irvine includes a statement "To Readers of the *New York Times*," saying: "Our big media—the national newspapers, news magazines, wire services and TV networks—have all refused to report that the official investigators have ignored, concealed and misrepresented evidence discussed in this series of ads that runs counter to their theory that Vincent Foster committed suicide in Fort Marcy Park. They have now been joined by James B. Stewart, author of *Blood Sport*, who abets the cover-up and ignores all the evidence that exposes it, including the failure to find a bullet, bone fragments, brain tissue, and blood spatter in the park."

Stewart, a Pulitzer Prize-winning journalist and a former front-page editor of the *Wall Street Journal*, has just published a widely respected chronicle of the Clinton administration, focusing on Whitewater-related scandals and "the Clintons' political trial by combat."

On April 10, *Dispatches*, the publication of Joseph Farah and the Western Journalism Center, runs a review of Stewart's book, written by Christopher Ruddy, who attacks the author for his reporting on the Foster case.

Using the now-familiar "gotcha" technique of book reviewing, Ruddy, who is also attacked in the book, tries to discredit Stewart's work because of a half-dozen minor errors in the Preface.

For instance, Ruddy condemns Stewart for misspelling the last name of USPP Officer Franz Ferstl and for writing that the medical examiner arrived at Fort Marcy Park at "around 7 PM" instead of at 7:40.

Ruddy continues with the predictable result of this form of book reviewing: "Can a book that contains so many casual errors make any reliable conclusions? That's a good question for the reader to answer."

Being a victim of this same cheap-shot tactic, Ruddy should know better than to use this shabby device.[58]

Nevertheless, *Blood Sport*, a well-researched and important book, soon climbs to number one on the *New York Times* best-seller list.

One reason for the book's success is Stewart's penetrating interview with Susan Thomases, who told him that she had met with Foster on Wednesday evening, July 14, 1993, just six days before

his death, at a private rooming house at 2020 O Street, where
Thomases occasionally stayed while in Washington.

During their conversation that night, Foster lamented that he felt
he had "let the president and Hillary down" during Travelgate.
Thomases also claimed that Foster had expressed his distrust of
David Watkins, whom he feared would turn on anyone to protect
himself, including Hillary Clinton. And Foster spoke of his desire
for "the quieter, predictable life" he once had in Little Rock.

But, according to Stewart, Thomases said that her conversation
with Foster "took a curious turn":

> One thing he had not missed about his life in Little
> Rock was Lisa, his wife. The marriage had not been
> what he'd hoped for, and it hadn't been for years. He
> had to make all the decisions in the family. She was com-
> pletely dependent on him, and this had become a burden.
> He found he couldn't confide in her. Lisa's recent arrival
> in Washington had brought this to the fore, just when
> Foster himself needed someone to lean on.
>
> Thomases didn't know what to say. Foster seemed
> calm, dignified—but infinitely sad.[59]

Stewart has now introduced another possible cause for Foster's
depression.

16.

WITH THE DEMOCRATS ON THE OFFENSIVE by placing the Special
Committee's work in jeopardy with their filibuster, they also turn
their wrath on Kenneth Starr. Since his appointment as independent counsel, it seemed that Starr had donated a mere $1,750 to
a political action committee controlled by Kirkland & Ellis, his

law firm, which contributed $2,000 to Bob Dole's 1996 campaign for the presidency, among other bipartisan contributions.

The Democrats also accuse Starr, who has maintained his million-dollar-a-year private legal practice even while serving as independent counsel, of a variety of other conflicts of interests.[60] For instance, Starr, who had earlier offered to assist Paula Jones in her sexual-harassment case against President Clinton, represents Brown & Williamson Tobacco Corporation, a major target of President Clinton and his antismoking crusade.

With the support of his ethics advisor, Sam Dash, the former majority counsel for the Senate Watergate Committee, Starr replies that he sees nothing wrong with his outside work, noting that sixteen of the seventeen previously appointed independent counsels did not give up their private practice to perform their public service.

Not swayed by this rationale, the *New York Times* publishes an editorial on Wednesday, April 17, saying: "After listening to Kenneth Starr's narrow, legalistic reasons for his continued representation of wealthy, politically active clients while serving as independent counsel, we have concluded that Mr. Starr is not the person to deliver.... It is time for him to step aside and let the investigation go forward under a replacement from the senior staff."

Defiantly, Starr refuses to resign, replying curtly, "We are continuing on with the important work of this office."

Meantime, Starr appoints Steve Parker, an assistant U.S. attorney in Memphis who specializes in homicide cases, to head the final phases of the Foster-death investigation. Starr's deputy, W. Hickman Ewing, Parker's former boss, makes the announcement and says in a statement: "There remain questions about Foster's death. Was it murder? Or was it a suicide? Either way, why?"

On the same day as the *Times*'s demand for Starr's resignation—and after D'Amato's threat to return the Whitewater investigation to his Senate Banking Committee—Senate Republicans and Democrats finally compromise after a seven-week deadlock, extending the Special Committee on Whitewater's hearings until June 14 and agreeing that a final report will be issued three days later. To complete the task, the Senate allocates $450,000 for the committee.

This decision is made just eleven days before President Clinton's scheduled videotaped deposition in the federal trial in Little Rock of Jim and Susan McDougal and Arkansas Governor Jim Guy Tucker, who have been charged with bank fraud and conspiracy. The prosecution's star witness in that trial, which began on March 4, is David Hale, who, as part of his plea-bargaining agreement, claims that Clinton, as Arkansas governor, had pressured him and Capital Management Services to make an illegal $300,000 loan to Mrs. McDougal.

In previous reports, the president had denied any involvement in the loan.

The conventional wisdom in Washington is that if Kenneth Starr, whose prosecution team is handling the trial, fails to gain convictions in Little Rock, his investigation of Whitewater is doomed. In other words, in view of the president's continuing favorable polls, the relentless assault on him and his administration would appear to be partisan and punitive.

On the other hand, convictions in Little Rock will give Starr tremendous momentum to continue his probe of the Clintons, Whitewater, and the White House handling of the Foster case.

On Tuesday, May 14, as James Stewart's book, *Blood Sport*, continues to receive widespread attention, Susan Thomases is recalled before the Senate Whitewater Committee for the third time.

Asked to explain her comments to Stewart about Foster's personal problems, she says that on the evening highlighted by Stewart in his book, she had met with Foster for twenty minutes to a half hour. During this time, he expressed concern over a possible congressional probe of Travelgate, as well as his fear that Hillary Clinton might become an "unfair target." Specifically, Foster believed that the source of this information would be David Watkins, whom he apparently no longer trusted. Ironically, Watkins had accompanied USPP Investigators Braun and Rolla to the Fosters' home on the night of his death.

Senator Faircloth asks Thomases about her telephone interview with an FBI special agent on June 14, 1994, in the midst of the Fiske investigation, "Did you tell the FBI about your conversation with Mr. Foster...?"

"[The FBI special agent] didn't really ask about it," Thomases replies after earlier admitting that she had discussed the matter with the first lady.

"And you didn't think this was pertinent information that you ought to tell and something the FBI would be very interested in—but it was important enough to tell to James Stewart later when he was writing a book that you thought was friendly to the Clintons? Is that right?"

"Is that a question?"

"Yes, that's a question...."

"I thought it was okay to share that with James Stewart...."

"Before this committee, from day one, [you have told us] 'I don't know.' 'I don't remember.' 'I don't know.' Would you tell us, are you trying to mislead the committee?..."

"Senator," Thomases responds defiantly, "I have no intention of misleading anybody."[61]

Interestingly, the senators do not ask Thomases about Foster's lament on his wife and their marriage, which she had passed on to Stewart.

Whether the Democrats like it or not, Kenneth Starr is here to stay. On Tuesday, May 28, despite President Clinton's four-hour testimony for the defense on videotape the previous month, a federal jury, apparently believing the testimony of David Hale of Capital Management Services, convicts Jim and Susan McDougal, as well as Arkansas Governor Jim Guy Tucker, of bank fraud and conspiracy.

17.

UPON THE COMPLETION OF THE SPECIAL COMMITTEE'S thirteen-month investigation on Friday, June 14, 1996, which has been the longest-running congressional probe of a sitting president in American history, the major media receive the committee's long-awaited 673-page final report.

Although the White House tries to spin the conclusions of the Special Committee with "So what?" the findings cannot be dismissed so easily.

Specifically regarding the Foster case, a majority of the Special Committee, alleging a "pattern of obstruction," issues the following sixteen findings:

1. At the time of his death, Vincent Foster was intimately involved in two brewing scandals—Travelgate and Whitewater—touching on President and Mrs. Clinton.

2. Senior White House officials were aware that the president and Mrs. Clinton faced potential

liability over Whitewater and their relationship
with the McDougals.

3. Senior White House officials ignored repeated
requests by law-enforcement officials to seal Mr.
Foster's office on the night of his death.

4. White House officials conducted an improper
search of Mr. Foster's office on the night of his
death.

5. Margaret Williams may have removed files from
the White House Counsel suite on the night of
[Foster's] death.

6. Bernard Nussbaum agreed with the Justice
Department officials on July 21, 1993, to allow
law-enforcement officials to review documents in
Mr. Foster's office.

7. Margaret Williams and Susan Thomases, in consultation with Mrs. Clinton, took part in formu-
lating the procedure for reviewing documents in
Mr. Foster's office on July 22, 1993.

8. Bernard Nussbaum failed to conduct a meaningful
review of Mr. Foster's office and did not describe
to law-enforcement officials sensitive files pertain-
ing to the Clintons and the administration.

9. An index of documents in Mr. Foster's office is
missing and other indices were revised following
his death to conceal possible references to
Whitewater.

10. Bernard Nussbaum knew about yellow scraps of

paper in Mr. Foster's briefcase prior to Stephen
Neuwirth's apparent discovery on July 26, 1993.

11. Margaret Williams, in consultation with Mrs.
    Clinton, removed files from Mr. Foster's office to
    the White House residence to be reviewed by the
    Clintons.

12. Senior White House officials did not provide
    complete and accurate information to the Park
    Police and FBI with respect to the handling of
    Mr. Foster's note.

13. Mr. Hubbell probably knew about the discovery
    of Mr. Foster's note on July 27, 1993.

14. Margaret Williams provided inaccurate and
    incomplete testimony to the Special Committee in
    order to conceal Mrs. Clinton's role in the
    handling of documents in Mr. Foster's office
    following his death.

15. Susan Thomases provided inaccurate and incom-
    plete testimony to the Special Committee in order to
    conceal Mrs. Clinton's role in the handling of docu-
    ments in Mr. Foster's office following his death.

16. Bernard Nussbaum provided inaccurate and
    incomplete testimony to the Special Committee
    concerning the handling of documents in Mr.
    Foster's office following his death.

Clearly, the Senate Republicans—heavily influenced by their
Special Counsel Michael Chertoff—view Hillary Clinton as a sinister force in what they believed to have been the White House
cover-up in the wake of Foster's death.

The majority report concludes:

> From the moment that she was notified of Mr. Foster's
> death, Mrs. Clinton and her key agents—Margaret
> Williams and Susan Thomases—were engaged in the subse-
> quent handling of documents in Mr. Foster's office....
> The evidence strongly suggests that Mrs. Clinton, upon
> learning of Mr. Foster's death, at least realized its connec-
> tion to... [the] Travelgate scandal, and perhaps to the
> Whitewater matter, and dispatched her trusted lieutenants
> to contain any potential embarrassment or political
> damage....
> Taken as a whole, the events described in this report and
> summarized in this conclusion, reveal a concerted effort by
> senior White House officials to block career law-enforce-
> ment investigators from conducting a thorough investiga-
> tion of a unique and disturbing event—the first suicide of a
> very senior U.S. official in almost fifty years.

The committee Democrats—led by Special Minority Counsel
Richard Ben-Veniste, a former Watergate prosecutor—respond in
their section of the final report, defending the White House's handling of the Foster matter. For the most part, the Democrats' explanations stand in direct contrast to the Republicans' findings,
insisting that an innocent answer can be found for every question
raised in the majority report.

In other words, according to the Senate Democrats, the White
House and Mrs. Clinton, although occasionally erring in judgment, did nothing nefarious or illegal during the Foster case.

According to the Democrats on the Special Committee, on the
night of Foster's death, David Watkins had asked Patsy
Thomasson to enter Foster's office to search for a suicide note, as
did Bernard Nussbaum. In spite of the sworn statement of USPP
Investigator Cheryl Braun, neither Watkins nor anyone else from

the White House ever received a request from the Park Police to seal Foster's office.

After a brief search that evening, Nussbaum and Thomasson found no note and left—along with Maggie Williams, who had entered Foster's office purely out of grief. Despite uniformed Secret Service Officer Henry O'Neill's testimony, Williams did not remove anything from the office on July 20; he probably confused that date with the subsequently approved removal of documents two days later.

On July 21, the Democrats continue, Nussbaum forthrightly informed representatives from the Park Police, the FBI, and the Department of Justice that they had entered Foster's office the night before to search for a suicide note but did not find one.

According to the committee's minority report, the Park Police were interested only in those documents that reflected Foster's state of mind prior to his death. Regardless of what they considered relevant to that end, the Democrats claim, officials from the Park Police had absolutely no authority to review or take anything they wanted from Foster's office; nor did the USPP ask to see Foster's substantive files.

Further, despite statements by representatives from the Department of Justice and the USPP, Nussbaum had never agreed to any arrangement with them about the manner in which Foster's office would be searched. Specifically, the Democrats insist, Nussbaum never agreed to allow attorneys from the Justice Department to screen the documents, contrary to statements by Philip Heymann, Dave Margolis, and Roger Adams.

In short, according to the committee's minority report, neither Nussbaum nor any other White House official, including Hillary Clinton and "her trusted lieutenants," interfered with, hindered, or sabotaged the Foster investigation by the Park Police.

Regarding the torn-up note found in Foster's briefcase, the

Democrats conclude that Nussbaum had simply overlooked it during his search on July 22, 1993. However, after discovering its existence, Nussbaum acted properly, notifying key White House officials and Foster's family about the note. After those notifications, he turned the note over to the Justice Department, which, as the designated intermediary, then offered it to the Park Police.

Similarly, the Democrats maintain, Nussbaum acted properly by removing specific Foster documents and giving them to attorneys for either the Clintons or the Foster family.

In its conclusion, the minority states:

> The venom with which the Majority focuses its attack on Hillary Rodham Clinton is surprising, even in the context of the investigation.... Every act is portrayed in its most sinister light, every failure of recollection is treated as though the standard for human experience is total recall and photographic memory.
>
> Perhaps the most sensationalized conclusions of the Majority involved the handling of Vincent Foster's papers. The crux of the disagreement between White House Counsel Bernard Nussbaum and Deputy Attorney General Philip Heymann was whether Nussbaum's insistence on being the one to review Foster's files in the presence of Justice Department lawyers and law enforcement officials would create an unfortunate appearance problem for the White House. Heymann agreed that, legally, the Park Police investigators had no right to enter the office and search the files, nor could Justice Department lawyers obtain a search warrant or subpoena. While Heymann was clearly prescient about the public and political fallout from Nussbaum's decision, who is to say that Nussbaum wasn't right also in believing that even if the Justice Department lawyers had taken part in the search, critics of the administration would simply charge a broader conspiracy?

Responding herself to the charges, Mrs. Clinton dismisses the entire GOP-inspired investigation by the Special Committee on Whitewater as "the politically preordained verdict of a partisan kangaroo court."

Predictably, the *Washington Times* says in a June 18 editorial: "The Republicans' report on the Senate Whitewater Committee investigation does an admirable job of laying it all out and summing up the whole catalog of dishonest, unethical and likely illegal behavior that make up the Whitewater scandal."

But the *New York Times*, which has been equally rough on the White House for its handling of the Foster case, states in its own editorial on June 19: "Neither side delivered a knockout legal punch, although the Republicans scored more debating points. They have at least laid down a paper trail of suspicious behavior that the Democrats have been unable to explain away....

"Mr. Starr must eventually report to a court and the public on whether the Clintons and their allies have engaged in illegality or regrettable but non-criminal lapses of judgment and duty. His report may come closer to the kind of full accounting that could not emerge from the political whirlpool of the Senate."

Apparently, after earlier calling for Starr's resignation, the *New York Times* supports him once again.

18.

ON JULY 24, 1996, U.S. DISTRICT JUDGE Alexander Williams, Jr., of Maryland dismisses Officer Kevin Fornshill's $2 million libel suit against Christopher Ruddy, Jim Davidson and *Strategic Investment*, and the Western Journalism Center. In this anticlimactic end, Judge Alexander's written opinion agrees with the defense attorneys that Ruddy, who had attacked the Park Police as part of his criticism of the *Fiske Report,* had not *specifically* charged Fornshill with any wrongdoing.

After the release of the Special Committee on Whitewater's final report, Reed Irvine continues his assault on the official Foster investigations.

On Wednesday, August 7, Irvine writes a letter to Hickman Ewing, Starr's deputy, who has been based in Little Rock during the investigation. In his letter, Irvine encourages Ewing to utilize the grand-jury process, as Miquel Rodriguez had previously attempted, "to persuade certain individuals to tell the truth" in the Foster case.

Irvine, who still suspects a forgery, asks Ewing to put the torn-up note to another independent handwriting examination, insisting that the manner in which Steve Neuwirth claimed to have found the scraps of paper in Foster's briefcase defies belief.

In addition, Irvine claims that the "D'Amato committee's report chose a cop-out, saying they did not submit the note for independent examination because the Foster family attorney and the White House would not provide them with... original samples of Foster's handwriting."

Further, Irvine continues to claim that the "evidence that the White House has lied about the time that it learned of Foster's death makes a strong case that it is hiding something."[62]

On October 25, Patrick Knowlton files a million-dollar harassment suit in federal court against the United States Government, including FBI Special Agents Larry Monroe and Russell Bransford and two named citizens of "the country of Jordan," as well as twenty-four

John Does, whom he claims had targeted him for surveillance. Knowlton was the driver of the Thrifty Rental truck who stopped at Fort Marcy Park to urinate and saw an Hispanic-appearing man behaving suspiciously on the afternoon of Foster's death.

Knowlton's cause had already been detailed and embraced by journalists Christopher Ruddy and Ambrose Evans-Pritchard.[63]

The American public doesn't appear too concerned about the findings of the Special Committee on Whitewater or the lingering questions about the Foster case, given the president's rising personal popularity, perhaps due, in part, to the incredible growth of the American economy, as well as the astounding rise of stock prices on Wall Street.

On Tuesday, November 5—as a result of his amazing ability to survive all of the probes of his administration and a growing belief that they have been politically motivated—President Clinton defeats Bob Dole and Ross Perot of the Reform Party, winning 379 electoral votes but only 49 percent of the popular vote. Clinton is the first Democratic president to be reelected since President Franklin D. Roosevelt.

In the January 1997 issue of *The American Spectator*, David Watkins becomes the first prominent mutineer against President Clinton, once his close friend. Earlier, Watkins and his wife had tried but failed to market their tell-all book about their relationship with the president. The project generated little interest among New York publishers.

In lieu of a book deal, Rebecca Borders, who was to have written the Watkins' book, publishes a stunning article, "Hell to Pay," in *The American Spectator*.

In this story, which is based on her interviews with Watkins and his wife, Borders reveals that:

- Vincent Foster believed that he was being monitored via electronic and physical surveillance.[64]

- Lisa Foster had confided to Watkins's wife that she had come to Washington to join Vincent Foster in order to save their marriage.

- Hillary Clinton and Vincent Foster *were* having an affair. "In Little Rock," Watkins told Borders, "we had not been aware of Vince and Hillary's so-called relationship, and I never saw anything personally that would confirm the gossip about them. But [my wife] was told soon after we arrived in Washington that Vince and Hillary were involved in a love affair. She was told by someone who was very close to Vince. And they said it was not idle speculation—everyone in Vince's family knew about it."

- Mrs. Clinton was kept away from Lisa Foster at the funeral.

- President Clinton was having an affair with Marsha Scott, the director of White House correspondence, who had met with Foster the day before his death. Watkins told Borders that his wife had said, "Marsha is pretty pumped up about the whole thing and she's bragging about it. She told me, 'I spent the night with Bill in his bed. I had my head in his lap and we reminisced all night long. I'm wearing the same clothes as yesterday

and I'm going to have to wear them the whole day
again.'"

- Watkins "fell on [his] sword in an effort to
  protect Hillary" during the Travel Office
  investigation.

- Regardless, Watkins believes that he had been set
  up when a photographer snapped his picture
  while getting on a White House helicopter to
  attend a golf outing. Watkins, who lost his job as
  the director of White House administration as a
  result of this incident, believes that the White
  House decided to use him as the ultimate fall guy
  for Travelgate and wanted him out of the way.

- After their return to Arkansas in August 1996,
  Watkins and his wife placed a new bumper sticker
  on their car—supporting Bob Dole for President.[65]

19.

IN MID-FEBRUARY, KENNETH STARR creates a furor when he announces
that he is leaving his job as independent counsel on August 1 to
head the Pepperdine University School of Law and its new School
of Public Policy in Malibu. Almost immediately, information surfaces, indicating that Richard Scaife, a member of Pepperdine
University's Board of Regents, had contributed $1.1 million for
the creation of the new school.

On Friday, February 21, amidst widespread criticism, Starr, calling his decision to leave his post as independent counsel "a mistake," announces that he has changed his mind and will stay on.

Two days later, on Sunday, February 23, the *Los Angeles Times* reports that after an "exhaustive inquiry," Starr has concluded that Foster committed suicide. The *Times* quotes an unnamed source, saying, "It puts [an end] to that bunch of nuts out there spinning conspiracy theories and talking about murder and cover-ups."[66]

That same day, the *New York Times Magazine* publishes a cover story, "The Clinton Haters," written by Philip Weiss, a contributing writer to the magazine. Hugh Sprunt, "prominent Vincent Foster cover-up theorist," graces the cover, sitting on the tourists' side of the south-lawn fence of the White House and looking deadly serious.

Also featured on the cover are the words:

> No president has been put at the center of more conspiracy theories, nor been the object of more virulent accusations. What is it about Bill Clinton—and the nation he leads?

Weiss identifies the radical sect of Clinton haters the "Clinton crazies," a term first coined by Ambrose Evans-Pritchard, whom Weiss counts as "one of them." Weiss also includes the usual suspects—Sprunt, Nichols, Matrisciana, and Ruddy, among others—adding: "The number of influential Clinton crazies is probably no more than a hundred, but their audience is in the tens of millions. The percolation of questions about the Foster case from Web sites to newsletters to talk radio to newspapers like the *New York Post* and the *Wall Street Journal* motivated the White House counsel's office to draft its report on conspiracies just before the Senate Whitewater hearings in the summer of 1995....

"Those fingered in the report characterize it as a Nixon-style enemies list aimed at delegitimizing Clinton's critics. But on a central point the administration and its enemies are in perfect agreement: because of new forms of communication—talk radio, newsletters, the Internet, mail-order videos—a significant portion of the population has developed an understanding of Bill Clinton as a debased, even criminal politician."

The White House report Weiss refers to is the *Communication Stream of Conspiracy Commerce*, a 331-page document in which the White House and the Democratic National Committee piece together the "media food chain," which has haunted the Clinton administration since the rumors began that Vincent Foster had been murdered. The report, prepared in July 1995, has since been circulated to reporters in the mainstream media.[67]

In its opening "Overview," the report states:

> The Communication Stream of Conspiracy Commerce refers to the mode of communication employed by the right wing to convey their fringe stories into legitimate subjects of coverage by the mainstream media. This is how the stream works. First, well-funded right-wing think tanks and individuals underwrite conservative newsletters and newspapers such as the Western Journalism Center, *The American Spectator* and the *Pittsburgh Tribune Review.* Next, the stories are reprinted on the Internet where they are bounced all over the world. From the Internet, the stories are bounced into the mainstream media through one of two ways: 1) The story will be picked up by the British tabloids and covered as a major story, from which the American right-of-center mainstream media (i.e., the *Wall Street Journal, Washington Times* and *New York Post*) will then pick the story up; or 2) The story will be bounced directly from the Internet to the right-of-center mainstream American media. After the mainstream right-of-center American media covers the story, congressional committees will look into the story. After Congress looks into the story, the story now has the legitimacy to be covered by the remainder of the American mainstream press as a "real" story.

The White House report concentrates its attack on Richard Scaife, Christopher Ruddy, James Davidson of *Strategic Investment* and the National Taxpayers Union, former Lauch Faircloth staffer and current Dan Burton staffer David Bossie, Joseph Farah and the Western Journalism Center, and Floyd Brown and Citizens United.

Although the White House report is easily dismissed by most in the establishment press as the equivalent of a paranoid's paradise, the fact is that the forces against the Clinton administration are, as they have been all along, formidable, well financed, and out for blood—just as others were against President Nixon, who resigned while facing impeachment.

20.

ON FRIDAY, MARCH 7, REED IRVINE hosts a fascinating media symposium, featuring Ted Koppel of ABC, NBC's *Meet the Press* host Tim Russert, and Christopher Ruddy. The discussion, which is broadcast nationwide on C-SPAN, concentrates on the mainstream media's coverage or, according to Irvine and Ruddy, the *lack* of coverage of the Foster case and the scandals revolving around the Clinton administration.

"Our job at NBC," Russert explains, "is to cover the news and, when reports come from Robert Fiske or Ken Starr or from the White House or congressional committees, we cover them the very best we can...."

Ruddy declares, "What disturbs me most about this administration is that they have engaged in a pattern of abuse of power. And this abuse of power is, I believe, very threatening to all our civil liberties. More than that, I think it also exposed the fact that the press has been unwilling to hold the current administration accountable...."

In response to a question from the audience, Koppel, who does-n't make an opening statement, indirectly replies to Ruddy's concerns, saying, "It seems to me that [Irvine and Ruddy are] under the impression that if there was a great, dramatic and indeed shat-tering story..., those of us in the media have anything to gain by not broadcasting it. You give me the evidence; I'll be delighted to broadcast it. I call it one of the great misconceptions that exist in America today...."

Responding to Koppel, Ruddy says, "My particular experience was the story of Vince Foster, which Mr. Koppel did a program on, and I laud him for having Reed on [as his sole guest]. The opening segment, done by [ABC reporter] Chris Bury, is something that comes right out of that White House conspiracy file. It starts off by saying that the publisher of my newspaper, Richard Mellon Scaife, is behind this big conspiracy against the Clintons and names the Western Journalism Center and Reed Irvine's group.

"They had all these photographs or diagrams with Richard Scaife at the top and all the money and the interconnections. It's the [wildest] conspiracy theory that I've ever seen reported, and there was really very little discussion of all the overwhelming details in the forensic, circumstantial, physical case in the Foster death, not to mention the really serious questions about the han-dling of the matter by Robert Fiske and Kenneth Starr. The whole point of the program was a White House hit-job on those people [who] were asking legitimate questions."

Attacking Ruddy directly, Koppel fires back, "I think that you have shown yourself in the past two years to be one of the great experts in building up a conspiracy theory. To the degree that those gathered here believe that Vincent Foster was killed directly or indirectly on the orders of people in the White House, first lady, or the president, all I can tell you is that I think you are sadly mistaken. There is no evidence.

"There are questions, as there are in relation to almost every murder involving a public figure or suicide of a public figure. There are always going to be some questions that cannot be answered. I believe you have taken those questions and blown them up to such a degree that perhaps you have succeeded in leaving doubts in the minds of some Americans. But, at some point or another, I hope and pray that you are going to let that poor man rest in peace."

Defending himself, Ruddy replies, "Please tell me where I've ever insinuated that Vince Foster was murdered. Please tell the public now that you have made this charge that I have said there's a conspiracy that began in the White House or anywhere else to murder Vince Foster."

"Let me use a little simple logic here," Koppel says. "If the man didn't kill himself, someone else had to have killed him."

Ruddy retorts, "I didn't say that he didn't kill himself. I said, 'There's a question.' Are we allowed to—"

Koppel interrupts, "To the degree that you are raising questions about it, you are implying or suggesting that what so far has been the consequence of every inquiry—namely the conclusion that he committed suicide—that you have doubts about that. If you have doubts about that, you are suggesting that he did not commit suicide. If he did not commit suicide, then he was murdered. I don't know what other logical inference to draw...."

Soon after, Russert continues, "Reed, may I ask a question? I'm curious about this. The Fiske investigation by a former Republican U.S. attorney concluded the death was a suicide. If Ken Starr, a man who accepted a position as dean of a law school and school of public policy funded by the Scaife Foundation, concludes that Vincent Foster's death was a suicide, will you accept that?"

"Absolutely not," Irvine responds. "One of the first things Ken Starr did was hire a prosecutor [Miquel Rodriguez] who started to investigate the Foster case as a possible homicide, and he was let go. They got rid of him. One thing Ken Starr should have done... was exhume the body and have another autopsy made."

Russert asks, "What was Starr's motive?"

"I can't read his mind," Irvine continues. "All I can read are his actions...."

In response to another question, Koppel says, directly to Irvine and Ruddy, "It seems to me that the definition of a conspiracy here is anyone who finds an answer you don't want to hear."

On Tuesday, July 15, Kenneth Starr announces, once again, that his office has concluded that Vincent Foster committed suicide. This latest announcement, accompanied by a report privately given to Federal Appellate Judge David Sentelle of the D.C. Circuit, and his panel of appellate judges, is "based on investigation, analysis and review of the evidence by experts and experienced investigators and prosecutors."

But, even though Starr has not released his report or a single piece of evidence from his investigation, Peter Jennings, the anchor on ABC's World News Tonight, permits himself to tell his viewers, "Kenneth Starr put to rest any doubts, except among real conspiracy theorists, that Deputy White House Counsel Vince Foster committed suicide."

21.

AFTER ALL OF STARR'S PREVIOUS LEAKS that indicate that he will conclude that Foster killed himself, this latest announcement comes as no surprise to his critics, like Reed Irvine, Hugh Sprunt, Patrick Matrisciana, and Christopher Ruddy.

In the July issue of the AIM Report, Irvine writes: "Has Ken Starr discovered some startling new evidence since then that answers all those questions and proves that Foster killed himself in Fort Marcy Park? We know of only one big investigative effort that he has made since Rodriguez resigned. That was the seven-week search of Fort Marcy Park for the bullet that killed Foster. That was in September-October 1995. It was made because the expert he had hired to analyze the forensic evidence in the case, Dr. Henry Lee, told him that he needed some forensic evidence that would prove that Foster died in the park. The bullet was the only thing they could hope to find, but... they came away empty-handed."

On Saturday, July 19, Hugh Sprunt, with the help of Patrick Knowlton, uncovers an incredible document in the National Archives from Dr. Donald Haut, the medical examiner who had pronounced Foster dead at the crime scene.[68] This document contains a "narrative summary," which appears to indicate that he had seen an exit wound on Foster's neck!

Specifically, Dr. Haut, in part, had allegedly written in his official report:

> After anonymous call was received at 18:04 hours, US Park Police officers found 48 yrs Caucasian male with self-inflicted gunshot wound *mouth to neck* on a foot path in [Fort Marcy] Park. (Emphasis added)

Instead of appearing as "mouth to head," as it should, Dr. Haut's alleged notation completely contradicts the autopsy report prepared by Dr. James Beyer, as well as the observations of every police officer and investigator at the crime scene who saw Foster's wound.

Unfortunately—or more importantly, depending on one's point of view—it seems to confirm the claims of a neck wound by Fairfax County paramedic Richard Arthur and Little Rock attorney Joe Purvis who had received permission from Foster's mortician to view the body. Moreover, according to Ruddy, Miquel Rodriguez discovered a photograph that showed a wound or trauma to Foster's neck.

If this notation is genuine, Dr. Haut contradicted it in the report that resulted from his April 12, 1994, interview with the FBI during the Fiske investigation—during which he said that he had seen a wound in the back of Foster's head. The only controversy Dr. Haut—who had wrongly stated his time of arrival at the crime scene at 6:45 instead of 7:40 PM—had stirred during his interview with the FBI was when he said he only saw a small volume of blood from this wound, which he thought had been caused by a "low-velocity weapon." Still, the FBI report stated: "Haut did not feel Foster's demise was anything out of the ordinary."*

In his July 21 article about Starr's still-undisclosed report, Ruddy—who describes Starr as "Barney Fife, prosecutor"—writes in what appears to be more of an op-ed piece than a news report: "Since some of Starr's investigation took place before a grand jury, much, if not all, of the report could remain hidden, shrouded under federal rules assuring that grand juries can operate in secrecy....

"My hunch is that Starr is not so comfortable with the findings of his office. When and if all the documents of his case are released, we may find that most of his investigation was finished some time ago, but Starr sat on the evidence and stalled his report.

"Starr is well aware of what happened with Fiske."

The following month, on Friday, August 29, the U.S. Court of Appeals for the D.C. Circuit rules, 2 to 1, that Foster-family attorney Jim Hamilton is required to turn over to Kenneth Starr at

---

* During my interview with Dr. Haut about this document, he said, "I don't specifically remember writing this notation. But, as a practical matter, I saw and have stated ever since that the only wound was in the back of Foster's head."

least a portion of a set of notes, memorializing his final conversation with Vincent Foster just nine days before his death. According to the OIC, Foster had come to Hamilton, one of three attorneys he was considering retaining, to discuss his potential legal problems.

Earlier, a lower court had quashed Starr's subpoena for the notes, accepting Hamilton's argument that an attorney-client privilege continued to exist between Hamilton and Foster, even though Foster is dead. The appellate court disagreed, setting the stage for a battle before the U.S. Supreme Court.[69]

Widespread speculation circulates that Hamilton's notes might contain the real motive behind Foster's suicide, as well as possible evidence of the Clintons' alleged complicity in Travelgate and Whitewater-related activities.

Actually, Hamilton had written to President Clinton on January 5, 1994: "The White House should not forget that attorney-client and executive privileges are legitimate doctrines in proper contests.... Bernie initially acted properly in protecting the contents of Vince's files."

Perhaps, instead of hiding some deep, dark secret, Hamilton is simply practicing what he preaches.

In mid-September, *Pittsburgh Tribune-Review* correspondent Christopher Ruddy—now also a Media Fellow at the Hoover Institution on War, Revolution and Peace at Stanford University—publishes his long-awaited book, *The Strange Death of Vincent Foster: An Investigation*, which is released by Free Press, a subsidiary of Simon & Schuster. At once, Ruddy's work is heavily supported and promoted by his longtime supporters: Joseph Farah of the Western Journalism Center, Reed Irvine of AIM, and Patrick Matrisciana of the Citizens for Honest

Government, as well as Ruddy's boss, Richard Scaife. Former FBI Director William Sessions also provides a glowing quote for the book on its back cover.

The hero of Ruddy's book is Miquel Rodriguez, the controversial one-time prosecutor for the Starr team, who had suggested to a federal grand jury that members of the Park Police, such as Officer Kevin Fornshill, might have been involved in a massive cover-up, if not the actual murder of Vincent Foster. Ruddy implies that Rodriguez was the only attorney on the Office of the Independent Counsel staff who really tried to get to the bottom of Foster's death; and, for trying to do so, was suppressed by corrupt parties.

But, back to reality, Ruddy actually misses a great opportunity to set the record straight and to legitimize his own motives, as well as his important role as a reporter on this case. Although he is quick to criticize others, especially the Park Police, for not maintaining high performance standards, he, once again, lowers the bar for himself. He still insists, among other things, that paramedic George Gonzalez discovered Foster's body near the first cannon, and that there was no soil on Foster's shoes, stubbornly refusing to back down on anything he had previously written.

In the end, he reduces his hard work to nothing more than a carnival sideshow.

The *New York Times Book Review* assigns Richard Brookhiser, a senior editor at William Buckley's conservative magazine, *National Review*, to write a lengthy review of Ruddy's work. The review is published on September 28 and concludes: "You don't have to believe in murder in high places to be unhappy with the way the Foster case has been handled.... [S]o many loose ends suggest that the initial Park Police investigation was sloppy and that all subsequent ones—which essentially began by accepting its conclusions—have been lazy. Zealous colleagues may have rifled Foster's office; why not his body?"

Buoyed by the *Times*'s review, the Ruddy book is now accepted by many as a serious piece of journalism. But the immediate problem for Ruddy and his publisher is that their hot book might become cold coffee after the release of the *Starr Report*.

22.

ON FRIDAY, OCTOBER 10, after a three-year $30 million investigation, the three-judge panel finally releases Kenneth Starr's 114-page report on the death of Vincent Foster, which, to all intents and purposes, concurs with the general findings of the U.S. Park Police, the *Fiske Report*, the U.S. Senate Banking Committee, the *Clinger Report*, and the Special Committee on Whitewater: Foster took his own life at Fort Marcy Park.

But the report, which is, of course, immediately embraced by the mainstream media, includes a candid statement by Dr. Henry Lee, the OIC's chief criminalist on this matter:

> [A] perfect reconstruction of the circumstances of Mr. Foster's death was not possible at the time of the OIC's investigation. The reasons include the lack of complete documentation of the original shooting scene; the lack of subsequent records and photographs of each item of physical evidence prior to examination; the lack of X rays of Mr. Foster's body, tissue, and bone fragments in the areas at the scene under and around Mr. Foster's head; the lack of close-up photographs of any definite patterns and quantity of the bloodstains found on Mr. Foster's clothing and body at the scene; and the unknown location of the fatal bullet, which makes complete reconstruction of the bullet trajectory difficult.

Along with Dr. Lee and pathologist Dr. Brian Blackbourne, the OIC has retained the services of Dr. Alan L. Berman, the executive director of the American Association of Suicidology and the former director of the National Center for the Study and Prevention of Suicide.

Among their findings in the *Starr Report* are the following:

Motive

As in all the other previous investigations, the *Starr Report* concludes that Vincent Foster's personal depression had led to his decision to take his own life. But Dr. Berman declares that Foster wasn't merely depressed; rather, he suffered from "clinical depression." Dr. Berman adds:

> **Mistakes, real or perceived, posed a profound threat to [Foster's] self-esteem/self-worth and represented evidence for a lack of control over his environment. Feelings of unworthiness, inferiority, and guilt followed and were difficult for him to tolerate. There are signs of an intense and profound anguish, harsh self-evaluation, shame, and chronic fear. All these on top of an evident clinical depression and his separation from the comforts and security of Little Rock. He, furthermore, faced a feared humiliation should he resign and return to Little Rock.[70]**

Noting Sheila Anthony's attempts to get her brother to call Dr. Hedaya and Foster's own call to Dr. Watkins, Dr. Berman adds that Foster had been "overwhelmed," adding that he was "under an increasing burden of intense external stress, a loss of security, a painful scanning of his environment for negative judgments regarding his performance, a rigid hold of perfectionist self-demands, a breakdown in and the absence of his usual ability to handle that stress primarily due to the impact of a mental disorder which was undertreated."

Declaring that most people who commit suicide do not leave a note, Dr. Berman explains that Foster, at the time of his decision to end his life, was "intensely self-focused;... overwhelmed and out of control."

Regarding the undated, torn-up note found in Foster's briefcase, the *Starr Report* indicates no doubt that he had written it, according to another analysis by the FBI's handwriting analyst, as well as that by Gus R. Lesnevich, a respected independent expert who had served in the Questioned Document Section of the U.S. Army's Criminal Investigation Division and later the Secret Service.[71]

A fingerprint analysis of Foster's note by the FBI also reveals—for the first time—that the palm print found on the note had been left by Bernard Nussbaum.

Further, the OIC repeats a previously reported fact: that, just prior to Foster's death, Nussbaum had come to believe that "Mr. Foster's work product had deteriorated and that Mr. Foster had seemed distracted." Just four days before he died, "he cried at dinner with his wife" and discussed resigning from the White House staff.

Starr's investigators also spoke to Foster's mother, Alice Fae Foster, who had said that her son had called her "a day or two" before he died and complained that his job had become "such a grind."

However, the *Starr Report* adds:

> The OIC, like other investigations before, is not aware of
> a single, obvious triggering event that might have motivated
> Mr. Foster to commit suicide.... In short, the OIC cannot
> set forth a particular reason or set of reasons *why* Mr.
> Foster committed suicide.

Consequently, the *Starr Report* begins a recitation of Foster's known problems at the White House: the controversial selections of nominees to federal posts, health care, and Hillary Clinton's Health Care Task Force, the Travel Office matter, the Clintons' tax returns and the sale of their interest in Whitewater to James McDougal, and the Clintons' blind trust, among others.

And, of course, the *Starr Report* reminds readers of the editorial criticism received by Foster and the Clinton White House from the *Wall Street Journal*, as well as Foster's haunting commencement address at the University of Arkansas's School of Law about the need to safeguard one's reputation.

In another new piece of evidence, Starr's investigators have discovered a March 4, 1993, letter Foster wrote to an unnamed friend in which he stated:

> I have never worked so hard for so long in my life. The legal issues are mind boggling and the time pressures are immense.... The pressure, financial sacrifice and family disruption are the price of public service at this level. As they say, "The wind blows hardest at the top of the mountain."

Consequently, Dr. Berman concludes:

> In my opinion and to a 100% degree of medical certainty, the death of Vincent Foster was a suicide. No plausible evidence has been presented to support any other conclusion.

Means

As with the other investigations, Starr and his staff cannot conclude absolutely that the gun found in Foster's right hand had once been part of his father's gun collection.[72] But Foster's sister, Sharon Bowman—who had previously remembered that her father kept a black revolver by his bed—found five .38-caliber cartridges at the family's home in Hope, Arkansas.

According to the *Starr Report*:

> FBI Laboratory examination revealed that four of the cartridges were of the same manufacture (Remington) as in the revolver found in Mr. Foster's hand; they were manufactured at a different time than the cartridge and casing found from Mr. Foster's gun.

Furthermore:

- The OIC adds that the type of ammunition found in the gun had not been manufactured since 1975.

- Noting that Lisa Foster had not been able to identify the gun, the *Starr Report* continues: "She stated to the OIC in November 1995, when viewing the gun recovered from Mr. Foster's hand, that it was the gun she unpacked in Washington but had not subsequently found, although she said she seemed to remember the front of the gun looking lighter in color when she saw it during the move to Washington."

    (This is the *Starr Report*'s explanation for Lisa Foster's controversial statement to the FBI on May 9, 1994, about the "silver-colored gun.")

- Dr. Lee confirms the finding in the *Fiske Report* that Foster's DNA appears on the barrel of the gun—where he also found "brownish-colored deposits" that are consistent with blood. Lee then goes a step further, analyzing the brown paper in which USPP criminalist Pete Simonello had originally wrapped the gun—item number 38 on the USPP property report. Dr. Lee discovered "the presence of reddish-colored particles" on the paper, which "gave positive results with a chemical test for blood." Dr. Lee also identifies "[b]lood spatters and tissue-like materials... on the finger-print lift tape from the weapon."

■ Equally remarkably, Dr. Lee finds a small bone chip among the debris on another piece of brown paper, on which Foster's clothing had dried while in the USPP crime lab. This bone chip also contains Foster's DNA. The report states: "Dr. Lee concludes that 'This bone chip originated from Mr. Foster and separated from his skull at the time the projectile exited Mr. Foster's head.'"[73]

■ Starr's investigators had found "a kitchen oven mitt... in the glove compartment in Mr. Foster's car," which is present in the photographs taken of the car's interior. Dr. Lee, analyzing this oven mitt, as well as the front-left pocket of Foster's pants, discovered traces of lead and a portion of a sunflower seed husk in each. "The presence of these trace materials could indicate that they share a common origin," Dr. Lee reports. "These materials in the pants pocket clearly resulted from the transfer by an intermediate object, such as the Colt weapon."

According to the *Starr Report*, members of Fosters' family have identified the oven mitt. But none of them can explain how it went from their kitchen to the car.

In other words, Foster had probably placed the gun in the oven mitt at his home, taken the gun out of the mitt, placed the mitt in his glove compartment, and then put the gun in his front-left pocket. Investigator Cheryl Braun found Foster's keys when she turned his front-right pocket inside out. Had she done the same to the front-left pocket, this evidence probably would have been lost.

- Dr. Lee discovered bloodstains on *both* sides of the lenses of Foster's eyeglasses, and, thus, concludes that Foster had been wearing his eyeglasses—which were found thirteen feet below his body—at the time he fired the gun into his mouth.

- In crime-scene photographs of Foster's body and the surrounding area, Dr. Lee detected "[r]eddish-brown, blood-like stains... on several leaves of the vegetation in this area."[74]

- Regarding the OIC's inability to find the bullet that killed Foster, the *Starr Report* concludes, "[T]here is a distinct possibility the bullet's trajectory was altered due to its striking or ricocheting off a natural or man-made obstruction," adding that "Foster's head could have been turned to one side or the other when the shot was fired," causing an unknown bullet trajectory.

Opportunity

Like the other investigations, the *Starr Report* cannot pinpoint or even give a ballpark estimate about the time Foster actually entered Fort Marcy Park—or whether he had gone anywhere after leaving the White House. But the *Starr Report* does conclude:

- That Foster's shoes did, in fact, contain "soil materials and vegetative matter," as well as the mica identified in the *Fiske Report*. Dr. Lee notes that the earlier FBI analysis of Foster's shoes had merely found no "coherent soil," which could be compared with soil samples from Fort Marcy Park. *Traces* of soil were present.

- Dr. Blackbourne also insists that Foster shot himself at the location where his body was found, adding:

  "Movement of the body, after the gunshot, by another person(s) would have produced a trail of dripping blood and displaced some of his clothing. If he had been transported from another location, such movement would have resulted in much greater blood soilage of his clothing (as was seen when he later was placed in a body bag and transported to Fairfax Hospital and later to the Medical Examiner's Office). No trail of dripping blood was observed about the body on the scene. His clothing was neat and not displaced. The blood beneath the head and on the face and shoulder is consistent with coming from the entrance and exit wounds."

With regard to the observations of the six known people at or near Fort Marcy Park at or around the time Foster may have been present, either alive or dead, Starr refers to them as C1 through C6.[75] Acknowledging their claims to have seen other people in the area, the *Starr Report* states:

There is no evidence that any of those unidentified persons (or any unidentified persons, for that matter) had any connection to Mr. Foster's death; and the totality of the forensic, circumstantial, testimonial, and state-of-mind evidence contrasts with any such speculation.*

In other relevant findings, the *Starr Report* determines:

■ Of the thirty-five carpet fibers found on Foster's clothing, twenty-three are white, and have been found to be consistent with a white carpet in the Fosters' home. Four of the remaining twelve non-white carpet fibers are found to be consistent with the carpets found in the White House and Foster's car. (The origin of the eight remaining colored carpet fibers cannot be found.)

Thus, the *Starr Report* concludes: "In sum, therefore, the carpet fiber evidence—the determination that the white fibers were consistent with a carpet from the Fosters' house and the variety and insignificant number of other fibers—does not support speculation that Mr. Foster was wrapped and moved in a carpet on July 20th."

■ Regarding the controversial blood-transfer stain on Foster's cheek, the *Starr Report* insists, as had the other investigations, that an unknown person had simply nudged Foster's head—before any photographs were taken.

---

* Identified as C2 in the *Starr Report*, Patrick Knowlton, via his attorney, John H. Clarke, requested that his response "be appended" to the final report. Against Starr's objections, the three-judge panel with jurisdiction over the OIC ruled that Knowlton's statement be made part of the record.

   USPP Officer Kevin Fornshill's attorney, Philip M. Stinson, and White House Staff Assistant Helen Dickey's attorney, John R. Tisdale, also published addenda on behalf of their clients.

■ In addition, Dr. Blackbourne addresses the repeated sighting of a possible neck wound on Foster's right side, saying that Dr. Hirsch, who led the forensic team during the Fiske investigation and reviewed the autopsy photographs, saw "flecks of dried blood" in that location, which could have been mistaken for a possible wound. Dr. Blackbourne concludes: "[T]here certainly is nothing described in the autopsy to make me suspect that there is in any way any trauma to the side of his neck."

■ Regarding Foster's black briefcase, Thomas Castleton, during the Fiske investigation, had told FBI special agents that he remembered Foster carrying a briefcase out of his office on the day of his death, adding that it "looked very much like the one" that was searched by Nussbaum on July 22. The *Starr Report* notes, however, that Linda Tripp was sure that Foster did not have his briefcase, and Betsy Pond had answered "[n]ot that I recall" when asked whether Foster left with his briefcase.

■ Starr's investigators found the previously unidentified assistant to Dr. Beyer during the autopsy and interviewed him. He stated that he "recalled moving the [X ray] machine over Mr. Foster's body in the usual procedure and taking the X ray. He said that he did not know until near the end of the autopsy that the machine did not expose the film."

The *Starr Report* concludes that, based on the autopsy report and its subsequent analysis by the OIC, along with the photographic evidence, Foster had been killed by a mouth-to-head gunshot wound, and that no other wounds were present.

The cited evidence that Foster had shot himself includes the following:

- Foster was found with the gun in his right hand, with his thumb, which had a visible indentation, trapped in the trigger guard;

- the evidence "tends to show" that the gun was Foster's property;

- "gunshot residue-like material" was discovered on Foster's right hand—in a manner confirmed by comparison testing with the revolver found in Foster's hand;

- similar residue was found on the soft palate of Foster's mouth;

- traces of lead were detected on Foster's clothing;

- an examination yielded evidence of Foster's DNA on the barrel of the gun;

- blood consistent with Foster's was found on the paper in which the gun had been wrapped by USPP criminalist Peter Simonello;

- blood spatters were discovered on the fingerprint lifts from the revolver;

- there were no signs of a struggle at the crime scene, nor on Foster's body or clothing;

- a small bone chip, containing Foster's DNA, was discovered in the trace evidence collected from Foster's clothing;

- there was no evidence that Foster had ingested either drugs or alcohol;

- traces of gunshot residue were discovered "in a sample of the soil from the place where Mr. Foster was found;"[76]

- additional blood spatter was found in photographs on the vegetation around Foster's body at the crime scene;

- there was no indication that Foster's body had been wrapped or cleaned; and

- no one saw Foster, conscious or unconscious, with anyone else at Fort Marcy Park.

To Kenneth Starr and his associates in the Office of Independent Counsel, this case is dead bang. In the final paragraph of their report, they state:

> In sum, based on all of the available evidence, which is considerable, the OIC agrees with the conclusion reached by every official entity that has examined the issue: Mr. Foster committed suicide by gunshot in Fort Marcy Park on July 20, 1993.

After the release of the *Starr Report*, Sheila Foster Anthony releases a statement to the Associated Press: "I have read Mr. Starr's report and agree with its conclusions, just as I agreed with Mr. Fiske's, that Vince died by his own hand in Fort Marcy Park.

However, I believe that the investigation could have been completed and the report issued months, if not years, sooner.

"Certainly, a more expeditious handling of this matter by the independent counsel would have spared the family further anguish and the public further uncertainty caused by the ridiculous conspiracy theories proffered by those with a profit or political motive. In my view, it was unconscionable for Mr. Starr for so long to allow the American people to entertain any thought that the President of the United States somehow had complicity in Vince's death."[77]

23.

WORRIED ABOUT THEIR OWN CREDIBILITY after clinging too long to insignificant details of the Foster crime scene, many conservatives begin to distance themselves from the likes of Christopher Ruddy and Ambrose Evans-Pritchard, who has published his own book, *The Secret Life of Bill Clinton*, one-third of which concerns the Foster case. Like Ruddy's, Evans-Pritchard's work is released without the author having had the opportunity to see and respond to the *Starr Report*. Like Ruddy, Evans-Pritchard's hero is Miquel Rodriguez.

But, unlike Ruddy, Evans-Pritchard virtually declares that Foster was murdered, saying: "I do not know whether Vincent Foster was depressed before his death. It is irrelevant anyway. The hard evidence indicates that the crime scene was staged, period. Even if Foster was depressed, somebody still put a gun in his hand, somebody still inflicted a perforating wound on his neck, his body still levitated 700 feet into Fort Marcy Park without leaving soil residue on his shoes, and he still managed to drive to Fort Marcy Park without any car keys."[78]

Such disputable claims lead to not only a distancing but a virtual bloodletting among right-wing activists.

One of the first shots fired within the right-wing sanctuary over the Foster case is from Byron York, an investigative reporter for *The American Spectator*, who writes an October 27 article in the Rupert Murdoch-backed and William Kristol-edited neo-conservative *Weekly Standard*, "Vince Foster, in the Park, with the Gun."[79] In his review of Ruddy's book, York declares: "Judging by their writing, speeches, and fund-raising appeals, the conspiracy theorists simply have too much invested in their murder scenarios to conclude that the evidence proves them wrong. But in the end, it does just that."

Even though Richard Brookhiser, a senior editor for *National Review*, had written a good-as-it-can-get review for Ruddy in the *New York Times Book Review*, the *National Review* publishes its own critique of Ruddy's book by Jacob Cohen, a professor of American studies at Brandeis University, in the November 24 issue, saying: "In the name of simple good sense, will people like Christopher Ruddy never let go and make way for the investigation of legitimate suspicions about possible obstructions of justice connected with the removal from Foster's office of papers perhaps touching on Whitewater [and] Travelgate...? That is where the story is."

The *Wall Street Journal* assigns Ruddy's book to Micah Morrison, a *Journal* editorial page writer who had written several columns critical of President Clinton, including one called "The Mena Coverup" in October 1994.

Morrison writes on November 25: "Mr. Starr's refutation has unleashed a torrent of criticism of Mr. Ruddy, especially from conservative magazines anxious to divorce themselves from allegations of conspiracy-mongering. Having declared our own view back in 1994, we'll still decline to join the current orgy of Ruddy-bashing. Yes, he and a few allies are obsessive in refusing to accept the answers Mr. Starr now provides. But that does not mean his questions never should have been asked."

But the real battle had begun in October after R. Emmett Tyrrell, the editor of *The American Spectator*, which is heavily backed by Richard Scaife, fired Ronald Burr, the *Spectator's* publisher, who, according to an October 20 article by Howard Kurtz of the *Washington Post*, "objected to spending the bulk of the Scaife funds on reporters poking around Arkansas and hiring investigators to examine Clinton's past."

This flap over Burr's firing is followed by another when the *Spectator*, which had earlier run a major story about the Foster case by Ambrose Evans-Pritchard, publishes its own opinion of Ruddy's book by senior correspondent John Corry, who renews the Ruddy-bashing with a remarkably bad review in the December issue.

Soon after publication of Corry's scathing attack, Scaife informs Emmett Tyrrell that he is not renewing his annual six-figure grants to the publication, which have totaled more than $2 million over the past seven years.

Commenting on all this, Reed Irvine of AIM, who has always openly and honestly acknowledged the money he has received from Scaife, issues a press release, criticizing the *Spectator* for Corry's review of Ruddy's book, insisting: "Ruddy has been a highly-valued employee of Scaife's paper since 1994. Since Scaife believes that his work on the Foster case has been very important, the *Spectator's* attack on Ruddy was an attack on Scaife as well."

But, more than anything else, Irvine's innocent comment speaks volumes about the dilemma of those who are dependent on Richard Scaife's money: They *cannot* back down without his permission.

Meantime, life in Washington continues. The big-time politicians, the partisan special-interest groups, and the high-priced journalists—most of whom have masters of their own—continue to be judged by the quality of people they seek and destroy: The bigger the target, the greater the reward. But, in this particular case, Vincent Foster was never a major target, and no one—including the Republicans and the *Wall Street Journal*—deserved or wanted a trophy in the wake of his death.

Still, when Foster ended the bitter note found in his briefcase with, "Here ruining people is considered sport," he spoke a final truth before committing his desperate act. In doing so, however, he failed to recognize that, in Washington, the sport is best played with tolerance, as well as dignity and finesse. In this town, the real survivors are the bridge and chess players, not the brawlers who skate on the thin ice upon which the game of politics has always been played.

Perhaps, for a moment after writing the note, Foster remembered this and took his own best counsel: He tore it up.

But, in the end, unable to balance the rules of the sport with his own problems, Vincent Foster drove to Fort Marcy Park on that hot summer day and took his own life.

EPILOGUE
Revisiting Motive

WHAT STRIKES ME MOST ABOUT THE CASE of Vincent Foster's suicide is that there are really no bad guys in this tragic story—only a handful of people who did their jobs badly. The problem with this case, as with many others, is that unexpected complications often arise for people who are doing their jobs well, which cannot be easily resolved or explained.

For instance, USPP Officer Kevin Fornshill told me that when he located Foster's body, the victim's head was resting on the right shoulder of his shirt—which investigators later saw was bloodstained from the two streams of blood flowing from his mouth and nose.

During my interview with John Rolla, the lead investigator at the crime scene, he said that he saw Foster's head "straight up, looking at the sky." On Foster's right cheek, Rolla saw "a transfer stain. It was not a heavy stain; it was a light stain."

Seeing Foster's head and face in the same position as Rolla,

USPP criminalist Pete Simonello told me, "It was obvious that Foster's head, at one point, had been resting on his shoulder. We just didn't know how it went from that position to face up—except that, somehow, his head moved or was moved."

The critics of the Foster case used the transfer stain on Foster's cheek as a major argument that Foster's body had been moved to the area near the second cannon—or that the stain had actually come from the phantom neck wound that no fewer than three witnesses had supposedly seen.

But, during my interview with USPP Lieutenant Patrick Gavin, a former paramedic, he said that, when he first viewed Foster's head face-up, he noticed a "hyperextension" of his neck, "which is a standard procedure for clearing a victim's airway and providing easy access to the carotid pulse."

Indeed, Michael Regan, the spokesman for the Fairfax County Fire and Rescue Department, told me, "With CPR, one of the acronyms we use is 'ABC.' You put an ear close to the person's mouth and listen to see if there is air coming out of the airway. That's 'A.' 'B' is for breathing. As you are listening to the airway, you are looking down the line of the chest to see if there is any movement. The third step, is 'C,' check for circulation, which is the carotid pulse in the neck. Those are what we call the ABCs."

Regan also noted that, although rescue workers must have consideration for the preservation of a crime scene, that task is always secondary to saving a life. Consequently, crime scenes are often disturbed during the life-saving process.

Trying to resolve the long-standing question of how Foster's head was moved, I received permission to interview Fairfax County rescue worker Todd Hall, knowing that he had already testified under oath on two separate occasions that he had not moved Foster's head. I was the first reporter he had ever spoken to about the Foster case.

Now a lieutenant, Hall, who specializes in the handling of hazardous materials and had driven Medic One on the day of Foster's suicide, recounted that he, along with Fornshill and paramedic George Gonzalez, had split off from the other rescue workers and gone into the main grove, past a large cannon. At the end of the grove, Fornshill separated from them and went into the smaller second grove to the north. Moments later, Fornshill, after finding Foster's body, called out.

Also consistent with the official reports, Hall said that he arrived first, just ahead of Gonzalez, and saw Foster lying on the hill in the midst of a great deal of foliage in front of a second cannon.

I then asked Hall, "When you were standing over the body, looking down on his right side, could you see the gun, or did you have to get down to see it?"

"You could have seen it standing," Hall replied, "if that was the first place you looked. But my first glance was at his upper body."

"Then what did you do?"

"I was carrying a bag that contained my emergency equipment, and I dropped the bag. Then, I crouched down to check his carotid pulse on the left side of his neck."

"Which side were you on?"

"The right side, up by his shoulder."

"So, from the right side, you were leaning over to check the left side?"

"Right. I was performing my ABCs. I was looking down at his chest to see if it was moving as I was checking the pulse. And that's when I noticed the gun. That shocked me, and I sprang up to my feet."

During the proper performance of his duties, Hall now admits, he might have moved Foster's head when he jumped up after seeing the gun in Foster's right hand while checking the carotid pulse on the left side of his neck.

He never realized that his innocent reaction could have caused so many problems.

Giving him the benefit of the doubt, the same could be true of White House Counsel Bernard Nussbaum, who might have simply performed in this case as would any good attorney, protecting the privileges and privacy he felt were entitled to his clients. After all, Foster's office was not a crime scene, and there are legitimate legal issues as to the degree of access the Park Police were entitled to have to Foster's files, if any at all—just as there would be if, for instance, the director of the CIA or a newspaper editor committed suicide. In these hypothetical cases, it is doubtful that the police would have "unfettered access" to the deceased's personal records without legal challenge.

Many critics have suggested that, instead of being dependent on Nussbaum's goodwill, the Park Police should have simply obtained a subpoena for all of the relevant documents in Foster's office. But, even if a subpoena had been issued, Nussbaum, as White House counsel, would have wound up going through the documents and complying with the subpoena—unilaterally. Nothing would have been different. In fact, while being questioned by Richard Ben-Veniste, the special minority counsel of the Special Committee, Philip Heymann conceded, "We didn't have any legal power to demand in court what I was insisting on."

Unfortunately for Nussbaum, he threw himself on a live grenade by defying Heymann and his two trusted men, Dave Margolis and Roger Adams. Nussbaum aroused suspicion because, after apparently agreeing to allow others to participate in the search, he suddenly changed his mind. And that—along with the loose talk and unfounded assertions by Major Robert Hines of the Park Police to the media, as well as the subsequent revelations about the telephone calls among Hillary Clinton, Maggie Williams, and Susan Thomases—led to the multidimensional spiraling of charges, ranging from obstruction of justice and perjury to such peripheral issues as the president's womanizing, all of which could have led or still may lead to the downfall of the Clinton White House.[1]

Meanwhile, five years after Foster's death, the "triggering event" that led him to take his own life continues to be a mystery. And there are others.

Official investigators say that there are four key issues that still beg answers as to the extent of Foster's knowledge. The first is the criminal referrals from the RTC that were being shuffled between the Department of Justice in Washington and the U.S. Attorney's Office in Little Rock. The second is the search warrant on David Hale's office, which was issued on the afternoon of Foster's death. The third is the bogus Castle Grande real-estate scheme and related charges, which led to the fraud and conspiracy convictions of Jim and Susan McDougal and Jim Guy Tucker. Finally, there are the overbilling problems at the Rose Law Firm, which led to the downfall of Webb Hubbell—the number-three person at the Department of Justice. How much did Hubbell know about and influence the RTC referrals, the Hale search warrant, and the Castle Grande affair, in which his father-in-law, Seth Ward, had been implicated?

The long-claimed but widely disputed affair between Vincent Foster and Hillary Clinton also continues to be "in play" and worthy of serious consideration, according to several official investigators. But, among those who have access to sworn statements and other evidence, no one seems to be able—or willing—to define the exact parameters of their relationship.

For instance, there are dozens of alleged witnesses, especially

Arkansas state troopers, who are prepared to attest that the affair had occurred; and Ileene Watkins, David Watkins's wife, has insisted that Lisa Foster was well aware of this, even though Mrs. Foster denied it in Peter Boyer's revealing article in *The New Yorker*. But most, if not all, of these sources, including Mrs. Watkins, have some provable ax to grind against the Clintons.

We do know, however, that Foster idolized Hillary Clinton, as is demonstrated in Foster's "diary" of the postelection, preinauguration period that Jim Hamilton showed to Investigator Rolla. And Webb Hubbell doesn't hesitate in his own book to note that Lisa Foster was extremely jealous of her husband's relationship with Mrs. Clinton.

But there is still no proof that her relationship with Foster went beyond anything more than a close friendship.

By the end of Foster's life, that relationship, whatever it once had been, had changed dramatically from his country-club days in Little Rock where he was a high-powered local attorney. In the White House, he faced problems he had never seen before. And as those close to him have confirmed, Mrs. Clinton, once Foster's legal protégé, blamed him for not protecting her against the hostile forces of Washington. During the final weeks of his life, he began referring to Mrs. Clinton as "the client."

On the night of his death, Foster had only two known commitments: a birthday party at the White House and a "date" with his wife, Lisa.

Even accepting the fact that Foster's decision to take his own life was the culmination of a multitude of problems, laying the entire motive on his work-related troubles is giving short shrift to other matters that were affecting his state of mind.

Regarding Foster's personal life, one cannot help but consider the taboo subject of the relationship between Vincent and Lisa Foster, which was in serious trouble—according to what Susan Thomases, who had spoken to Foster less than a week before his death, told James Stewart for his book, *Blood Sport.* And, although Mrs. Foster didn't concede the depth of their problems in her interview with Peter Boyer of *The New Yorker*, she did admit that she and her husband were both unhappy with the state of their marriage since his move to Washington. According to Mrs. Foster, these troubles were present as early as the day of the president's inauguration when she became so angry with her husband that she refused to attend the inaugural ball with him.

Yet, according to the FBI's report of its interview with Mrs. Foster: "There were no domestic problems between Lisa Foster and [Vincent] Foster during the entirety of their twenty-five–year relationship."

The fact that Vincent Foster committed suicide instead of keeping a "date" with his wife that night, which was agreed would mark a new beginning in their relationship—as well as his coldness toward her that morning and his decision not to leave behind a suicide note—reflects on Lisa Foster more than anyone else. No doubt this weighed heavily on Mrs. Foster, who, from all indications and sources, was a loyal and devoted wife.

Incredibly, the *Fiske Report* and *Starr Report* steered away from this extremely delicate matter and refused to discuss it.

For the record, I made two attempts to interview Lisa Foster via her attorney, Jim Hamilton; but he referred me to the record of the case—even though I insisted that it contained her glaring contradictions and clear evidence of a troubled marriage.

Reviewing what was happening in Foster's life at the time of his death: Whitewater wasn't on the public's radar screen, the anticipated investigations of Travelgate were not materializing because of the control of Congress by the then-Democratic majority, and the editorials attacking Foster in the *Wall Street Journal* were really not that bad, compared to the treatment that others in the Clinton administration were receiving.

Professionally, although he was facing potentially serious difficulties, there didn't seem to be anything on or under the surface that Foster, an experienced attorney, didn't have time to forestall or to maneuver around.

But not everything that happens inside the Beltway is political; there is human drama here as well. And the body of evidence indicates that the "triggering event" that led to Vincent Foster's decision to commit suicide occurred within his private life, not his public career.

NOTES

Part Two

1. Fort Marcy is an earthen fort with a 338-yard perimeter, built on the southern bank of the Potomac River in 1861 during the Civil War to protect against assaults on Washington's Chain Bridge. It was named in honor of Brigadier General Randolph Barnes Marcy, General George B. McClellan's chief of staff and father-in-law.

2. The United States Park Police operates under the National Park Service (NPS) within the Department of the Interior. Founded in 1791, the USPP is the oldest uniformed police agency in the country, exercising full law enforcement and investigative authority in those areas under the jurisdiction of the NPS, including America's national monuments and parks.

   The chief of the USPP reports directly to the director of the NPS's National Capital Region.

   On January 13, 1982, the U.S. Park Police received international acclaim when officers in its Aviation Unit courageously and dramatically rescued a handful of survivors after Air Florida Flight 90 left National Airport in the midst of a snowstorm, crashed into

Washington's Fourteenth Street Bridge, and plunged into the frozen Potomac River.

3. On January 25, 1993, a gunman stepped out of his white utility vehicle, parked near the CIA entrance on Route 123, raised an assault rifle, and began firing at drivers who were turning into CIA headquarters. The gunman killed two people and wounded three others.

   Since this tragic incident, the U.S. Park Police has provided a uniformed presence at the entrances to CIA headquarters.

   Fornshill told me that he was in an unmarked car on July 20, 1993, because no marked cars were available on that particular day.

4. In the second FCFRD unit, Sergeant James A. Iacone was the officer-in-charge; his technician/driver was Ralph Pisani, and the other firefighter was Jennifer M. Wacha, a rookie with the department. The presence of a fire truck crew in response to an emergency dispatch was standard operating procedure—to aid, if necessary, with traffic control and to operate extraction and recovery equipment.

5. In his official report, Gonzalez described the gray Honda as brown in color—although he would later say during a July 20, 1994, sworn deposition that the car was "a darker color, charcoal gray or brown."

   Franz Ferstl, the USPP reporting officer, and Renee Abt, one of the three police investigators at the scene, described it as gray-brown. However, in several official reports, the Honda would simply be described as gray.

   The actual color of the Honda would become significant as the investigation proceeded.

6. During my interview with Fornshill, he admitted that he had erred when he didn't check to see the gun in Foster's right hand. Specifically, Fornshill told me, "The mistake I made was I said that 'It's an apparent suicide' over the air. I shouldn't have said that without confirming the gun. The second I said it, I knew that I shouldn't have said it."

7. Officer Fornshill heard the report about the couple in the woods but had been told by either another police officer or a member of

the fire and rescue team that they were "volunteers" working in the park.

In fact, they were private citizens having a picnic.

8. Hodakievic was driving a blue 1991 Honda Civic hatchback.

9. An official May 2, 1994, USPP report describes the five scenes depicted in Ferstl's photographs:

    1 - Rear of cannon
    2 - Heavily foliaged area
    3 - VF's body - looking down from top of berm
    4 - VF's body - focusing on face
    5 - VF's body - focusing on rt. side shoulder

During my research for this book, I was shown these five photographs, among others, and confirmed the depictions listed in this USPP report.

However, there was a controversy over the number of photos taken by Ferstl. In his May 2, 1994, interview with the FBI, Ferstl said that he took "approximately seven photos."

When I interviewed Ferstl, he told me that he never knew for sure just how many pictures he had taken, adding that there could have been as many as eight or as few as five. All he remembers is taking photographs and then giving them to Sergeant Edwards.

10. Sergeant Edwards told me that, although he had given Ferstl the responsibility of photographing the crime scene, he might possibly have taken one or two of the pictures he signed—although he has no specific recollection of doing so.

During my interview with Ferstl, he agreed that it was possible that Edwards took a picture or two—but he, too, doesn't remember that happening.

Regardless of who took some or all of these pictures, they are all in the same group that were signed by Edwards.

11. Without a crime-scene log, I have re-created the appearances of the police personnel based on official reports, sworn depositions, and my own interviews with *all* those officers and investigators present.

I have also given USPP personnel—as well as the key rescue workers—the opportunity to approve what I have written about their individual roles at the crime scene.

12. Rescue worker Jennifer Wacha, who was on the Engine One crew with Iacone, told me that *none* of the paramedics knew either Vincent Foster's name or that he worked at the White House by the time they left Fort Marcy Park at 6:37 PM. She did remember some joking in the parking lot that he *might* have worked for the Clinton administration because of his Arkansas tags.

13. Soon after her arrival at Fort Marcy Park, Investigator Abt checked the hood of the Mercedes and indicated in her notes that it was still warm.

Officer Hodakievic ran a check on the disabled blue Mercedes with Virginia tags near the entrance to Fort Marcy Park and learned that it was registered to Jean Slade of McLean.

Slade, a Washington lobbyist, later told the police that after her car broke down at about 5:55 PM, fifty to sixty feet short of the entrance ramp to Fort Marcy, she walked into the parking lot, looking for a telephone, and noticed two parked cars. One was dark blue; the other was gray or silver.

Finding no phone, Slade continued, she walked north on George Washington Memorial Parkway. As she approached the McLean/Chain Bridge Road exit, she heard sirens and saw emergency vehicles speeding southbound, without realizing that they were heading for Fort Marcy Park.

At or about 7 PM that night, a tow truck met Slade at her car.

14. An official May 2, 1994, USPP report describes the five scenes depicted in Braun's photographs:

1 - Driver seat
2 - Rear seat - driver side
3 - Rear seat - passenger side
4 - Ft. seat - passenger side
5 - Rear of vehicle

During my research for this book, I was shown these five

photographs, among others, and confirmed the depictions listed in this USPP report.

15. During my interview with Investigator Abt, she explained that before Foster's White House identification was found in his car, she had suspected that Foster worked at the White House after seeing the letters "WHCA," meaning White House Communications Agency, on his pager. She added this reference in her crime-scene notes.

16. Simonello wears cotton gloves while collecting evidence—unless he is handling hazardous materials, which would call for latex gloves. However, Simonello explained, a person wearing latex gloves can leave fingerprints if the ridges on their prints are thick enough to protrude through the latex.

17. During my interview with Rolla, he mentioned that he had smelled alcohol on Dr. Haut's breath. Seeing Rolla hesitate after saying that, I switched off the tape recorder, asking Rolla if he wanted to discuss this matter on or off the record. Rolla shrugged and said he wanted it on the record, so I restarted the recorder. Rolla said, "Speaking with [Dr. Haut], I could smell... what I believe was an odor of alcohol on his breath." Moments later, Rolla added, "He didn't seem shaky. He didn't slur his speech. And he didn't do very much on the scene."

Knowing that Dr. Haut later made several controversial statements about his observations at the crime scene, I asked both Pete Simonello and Renee Abt whether they had smelled alcohol on Dr. Haut's breath. They said that they had not.

I then interviewed Officer Christine Hodakievic and asked her the question. She replied, "I wouldn't go so far as to say that I got the impression that he was drunk."

But, Hodakievic, like Rolla, had smelled alcohol on Dr. Haut.

Finally, I went to Cheryl Braun, who, without any prompting, told me that she, too, had smelled alcohol on Dr. Haut's breath.

During my interview with Dr. Haut, he told me that he had a glass of dry Spanish sherry prior to dinner and a glass of red wine while he ate. Almost immediately after, he received the call to go to Fort Marcy Park.

18. Rolla and Investigator Renee Abt, as well as criminalist Pete
    Simonello, remember Rolla taking pictures of Foster's body *after*
    he had been turned over upon the arrival of Dr. Donald Haut, the
    medical examiner.

    But these pictures of Foster's body are not part of the inventory.
    What happened to them?

    During my tape-recorded interview with Rolla, he suddenly
    remembered that he had given the photographs to Dr. Haut. "You
    know, I don't know why I never thought of this before. It just
    rolled off my tongue. That's standard procedure. Every medical
    examiner on the scene requires one or two Polaroids to take with
    them to stick with their report...."

    Discussing which photographs he might have given to Dr. Haut,
    Rolla said that he had probably given him a picture of the back of
    Foster's head, as well as "a back shot, because I know I took a shot
    of [Foster] on his back."

    However, the FBI's May 14, 1994, interview with Dr. Haut
    stated that he "does not recall the body being photographed while
    he was at the death scene."

    During my interview with Dr. Haut, he said he did see the police
    photographing the body "with a Polaroid"; however, he denies
    that anyone gave him any photographs.

19. The Truck One crew consisted of Lieutenant William Bianchi, dri-
    ver Victoria A. Jacobs, and apprentice technician Andrew
    Makuch. They arrived five minutes behind Ambulance One.

20. Ashford told me that he said that he never discussed his conclusion
    with any of the USPP investigators at the scene. And they never
    told him that a gun had already been recovered, and that Foster
    was a suspected suicide victim.

    But, according to numerous rescue workers and police officers,
    lack of communication between rescue workers and police officers
    at a crime scene is not uncommon.

21. Other miscellaneous possessions in this category included credit-
    card receipts from local restaurants, an unsigned blank check from
    the Worthen Bank in Little Rock, a business card from attorney
    Bernard W. Nussbaum of Wachtell, Lipton, Rosen & Katz in New

York, a note on White House stationery that contained the names of three doctors, and a personal calendar, which contained no appointments for the afternoon of July 20, 1993, and only a notation of his regular 9 AM staff meeting for July 21.

22. Cheryl Braun told me that the map was folded in a square, apparently indicating that Foster—or someone else driving the car on some earlier date—had tried to find his way somewhere. She observed that the map was opened to "a generalized map of the Washington metropolitan area with the beltways," which included Fort Marcy Park.

    There were no marks or notations on the map.

23. While at Fort Marcy Park, Abt received a radio call requesting CIB's assistance in a car-jacking incident. Abt volunteered to remove herself from the Foster case to investigate the car jacking.

24. Blowback occurs when a weapon fires and the hot gases expand out of the barrel, causing a slight vacuum that sucks air back into the barrel. After a shot from contact range, trace evidence, such as tissue and blood spattering from the wound, might also be sucked onto and into the barrel of the gun, as well as possibly onto the shooter.

25. Dr. Haut told me that it was impossible to say whether Foster was sitting or lying down; that one guess was a good as the other.

26. Officer Watson told me that he was with Braun when she discovered Foster's White House identification. But Watson insisted he never heard her make any request to him about contacting Lieutenant Gavin or anyone else.

    As soon as Foster was identified as a White House employee, Watson took the young intern who had accompanied him to Fort Marcy Park and left the area.

27. Investigator John Rolla told me that he had called the general number of the Secret Service's Uniform Division from his cellular phone in the parking lot after Foster's body had been taken to the morgue, and spoken to the man who answered the telephone. He informed this officer that they had found a man with a White

House identification who might have committed suicide.

In Rolla's handwritten notes, he wrote the name of a "Lieutenant Walter," who was with the Secret Service. However, according to available Secret Service records, there is no notation of Rolla's call—only Lieutenant Gavin's.

28. Created in 1820, the Rose Law Firm was founded by Judge Uriah M. Rose, who was among the original founders of the American Bar Association. The firm's top clients included Stephens, Inc. (a major investment banking firm operated by Jackson Stephens, a top Clinton backer), the Federal Savings and Loan Insurance Corporation (FSLIC), TCBY (the frozen-yogurt company), Tyson Foods, and Wal-Mart, among other corporate giants.

29. Kennedy and Livingstone viewed Foster's body, through a glass window, between 9:45 and 10:30 PM. They were accompanied by a Fairfax County police officer and a hospital nurse. Neither White House aide was ever alone with the body.

30. On the USPP property report, Item #14 was described as "one key ring marked 'Cook Jeep Sales'"; Item #15 was "one key ring, marked 'Vince's Keys.'"

31. A July 20, 1993, internal U.S. Secret Service memorandum to Special Agent Scott Marble includes a couple of obvious mistakes:

> On 7/20/93, at 2130 HRS, Lt. Woltz, USSS/UD— WHB, contacted the ID/DD and advised that at 2030 HRS, this date, he was contacted by Lt Gavin, US Park Police, who provided the following information:
> On the evening of 7/20/93, unknown time, US Park Police discovered the body of Vincent Foster in his car [sic]. The car was parked in the Ft. Marcy area of Va near the GW Parkway. Mr. Foster apparently died of a self-inflicted gunshot wound to the head. A .38 cal. revolver was found in the car [sic]. [Emphasis added]

During my interview with Lieutenant Gavin—who had earlier been at the crime scene and viewed Foster's body in the woods, as well as the gun in his right hand—he insisted that he *never* told anyone, particularly the Secret Service, that either Foster's body or gun had been found "in the car."

Clearly, this mistake was made by the Secret Service, not Lieutenant Gavin.

32. Per the official chain of command, Chief Langston reported to Robert Stanton, the director of the Capital Region of the National Park Service of the Department of the Interior. Upon receiving Lieutenant Gavin's report of Foster's death, Langston telephoned Stanton and gave him the news.

33. The Fosters' home was just two blocks from Montrose Park, another heavily wooded recreational area operated by the National Park Service.

34. According to a May 1994 report of the U.S. General Accounting Office, the White House Travel Office, among other responsibilities, "provides travel arrangements for members of the press corps who accompany the president on trips. The Travel Office also provides ticketing and travel services for [the president's] staff traveling on official business.

"In assisting the press on presidential trips, White House Travel Office staff arrange for or coordinate such services as chartered air transportation, ground transportation services, and working space and telephone services."

Amidst allegations of wrongdoing by White House Travel Office employees, which had been collected by David Watkins, Foster had assigned William Kennedy—the same man who was en route to identify his body at Fairfax County Hospital—to probe the situation. Immediately, Kennedy had recruited an outside accounting firm, Peat Marwick, to conduct an internal audit of the Travel Office; Kennedy also approached the FBI about a possible criminal investigation.

After Peat Marwick issued its findings—which alleged a degree of mismanagement that could justify a complete housecleaning—the White House fired all seven Travel Office employees on May 19, 1993, claiming evidence of embezzlement and the receipt of kickbacks. But, after the story broke in the *Washington Post*, the

White House was widely criticized for overplaying its hand. In fact, the charges against the seven fired employees could not be proven.

On June 1, the FBI submitted its own report to Attorney General Janet Reno. In that report, Kennedy was charged with pressuring the FBI to investigate the matter and threatening to go to the Internal Revenue Service if the FBI refused. The FBI also claimed that Hollywood producer Harry Thomason, a personal friend of the president and Hillary Clinton, had a financial interest in a charter-airline company and could have benefited financially from the Travel Office firings.

Kennedy—who, as an associate counsel in the White House, dealt with the FBI on nearly a daily basis—denied any wrongdoing.

As a result of the FBI report, the White House conducted its own internal inquiry and released its report on July 2. Among others, including Watkins, Kennedy was reprimanded for his alleged improper actions, which he continued to deny. The White House report also indicated that Vincent Foster had no fewer than two conversations with Hillary Clinton, who had allegedly asked him how he was handling the "problems" with the Travel Office.

In the wake of the White House report, Foster became angry that Kennedy, his longtime friend, had been among those punished. Rightly or wrongly, many believed that Foster, who was not reprimanded, might have allowed Kennedy to take the fall for him. Foster was also reportedly upset that the first lady had, in fact, been placed in the line of fire as a result of their conversations about this matter.

35. Mrs. Anthony headed the Office of Legislative Affairs for the Department of Justice.

36. Another presidential advisor, George Stephanopoulos, had called Hubbell at the restaurant. Stephanopoulos, who had heard the news from White House Chief of Staff Thomas F. "Mack" McLarty, informed Hubbell that Foster had been found dead, and that he might have committed suicide. He added that William Kennedy had gone to identify the body. Moments later, Hubbell and his wife, Suzy, left the restaurant with Scott, who had driven them to the restaurant. They drove to the Hubbells' home, so that Hubbell could pick up his address book before they went to the Fosters' home.

Hubbell knew that he had notifications of his own to make.

Soon after, he went to Sheila Anthony's house, which was just across the street, where he found Sharon Bowman as well. Hubbell broke the sad news to Foster's sisters.

Together, they went to Vincent and Lisa Foster's home.

37. Watkins later denied ever receiving this request from Investigator Braun.

38. John Rolla did not include this conversation in either his notes or his written report. He admitted to me that this was a mistake, saying that he should have memorialized her response.

Lisa Foster, however, later confirmed to Peter Boyer of *The New Yorker* that she had made the remark.

39. Lisa Caputo was with Hillary Clinton when she received McLarty's telephone call. She said in a July 10, 1995, sworn deposition that Mrs. Clinton began to cry upon receiving the call, saying, "It just can't be true."

40. Rolla mentioned nothing in his report about President Clinton's presence at the Fosters' home that night.

41. In fact, after this particular model of Motorola Bravo pager is switched off, all of the memory contained in the device is automatically erased. Even if Rolla had turned on the device, he would have found nothing.

42. Lindsey, who was legal counsel to the Democratic Party in 1992, was not a partner in the Rose Law Firm. He was with Wright, Lindsey & Jennings in Little Rock, which Clinton had joined after his 1980 defeat for governor of Arkansas.

The Rose firm, specifically Vincent Foster, represented Lindsey's firm as corporate counsel prior to January 1993.

43. On June 17, in "Who Is Vincent Foster?" the *Journal* complained about Foster's apparent refusal to supply the newspaper with his photograph, as well as the White House's "most disturbing... carelessness about following the law." The *Journal*—which filed a

Freedom of Information Act request for Foster's picture that the
White House ignored—continued: "No doubt Mr. Foster and
company consider us mischievous (at best). Of course the Clinton
administration has little reason to love us.... Does the law mean
one thing for critics and another for friends? Will we in the end
have to go to court to get a reply, or will even that work? Does it
take a $50,000-a-day fine to get this mule's attention?... Who
ensures that this administration follows the law, or explains why
not? A good question. While constitutional law may not have been
the big part of the Rose firm's practice, it seems to us that a good
man for the job would be deputy counsel Foster."

In the place where Foster's picture would have appeared, the
Journal simply ran a question mark backed by a silhouette profile
of a man's head.

On June 24, in "Vincent Foster's Victory," the *Journal*, which
did publish Foster's picture, commented on the recent ruling by a
U.S. appellate court, declaring that Hillary Clinton's role with the
Health Care Task Force made her the "functional equivalent" of a
federal employee under the Federal Advisory Committee Act
(FACA)—as Foster had argued. The *Journal* added sarcastically:
"As we say, for achieving these outcomes we think Mr. Foster
deserves a salute from conservatives. With one mighty sweep he
has struck a blow for separation of powers.... As for Iran-Contra,
we suspect that Vincent Foster and Ollie North might hit it off."

On July 14, the *Journal*, in "FBI Director Rose?" again attacked
the Rose Law Firm's alumni at the White House, picturing Foster,
Hillary Clinton, Webster Hubbell, and William Kennedy in the
same editorial. But the only mention of Foster was: "Vincent
Foster, the deputy White House counsel, serves as all-purpose advisor to Hillary Clinton on health reform thickets and other matters.
(His sister, Sheila Foster Anthony, is slated to run Justice's legislative offices.)... We now know Mrs. Clinton inquired about the
travel office affair with Mr. Foster, and that she was prominently
carboned on copies of crucial memos."

On July 19, the day before Foster's death, in "What's the
Rush?" the *Journal* questioned why the White House had been in
such a big hurry to get rid of William Sessions, who would be fired
that day as FBI director. Comparing the White House's handling of
Sessions to its management of the Travel Office matter, the

Journal, noting Foster's role in Travelgate, charged: "The mores on display from the Rose alumni are far from confidence-building." Foster was named in the editorial, along with Hillary Clinton, William Kennedy, and Webster Hubbell. Simonello normally worked four ten-hour days and then received three days off. A week before Foster's death, his supervisor, Sergeant Danny Lawston, had approved a fourth day off on this particular week for Simonello, who needed to take care of some personal business.

44. Simonello normally worked four ten-hour days and then received three days off. A week before Foster's death, his supervisor, Sergeant Danny Lawston, had approved a fourth day off on this particular week for Simonello, who needed to take care of some personal business.

45. Major Hines told me that the request for an earlier autopsy was his and his alone. He did not discuss the matter with anyone else, including White House personnel.

46. In his official report, dated July 28, 1993, Dr. Beyer did not list any of the USPP personnel, except Morrissette, as being present during the autopsy.

    When Sergeant Rule asked for the name of his assistant, Dr. Beyer snapped, "You are dealing with me here. You don't need his name."

    Dr. Beyer, through his secretary, refused to speak with me.

47. All four of the USPP officers present at the autopsy—Sergeant Robert Rule, Investigator Jim Morrissette, identification technician Shelly Hill, and then-ID trainee Wayne Johnson—told me during my separate interviews with them that there were *no* other wounds or trauma to Foster's body.

    Specifically, there was no wound of any kind on Foster's neck, as others would later claim.

48. Morrissette told me that, later that day, after he returned to his office, he received a telephone call from a man who claimed that Foster had been having a homosexual affair with the son of a prominent Arkansas banker. Although Morrissette placed this

information in the "gossip" file, he did contact the coroner's office and requested that Foster's blood be checked for AIDS. Another unproven rumor linked Foster to a male hairdresser in Little Rock.

49. That same morning—during a discussion with two of his associate counsels, Stephen Neuwirth and Clifford Sloan—Nussbaum at first balked at the idea of sealing Foster's office, challenging that it could be considered a crime scene.

50. Nussbaum had earlier received considerable criticism for the poor work of his staff in the previous nominations of Zoe Baird, Kimba Wood, and Lani Guinier—all of whom failed to receive Senate confirmation.

    However, the successful confirmation of Janet Reno as U.S. attorney general, the excellent prospects for the respected Ruth Bader Ginsburg as a U.S. Supreme Court associate justice, and Judge Louis Freeh as FBI director appeared to be helping rebuild the waning public confidence in the Clinton administration's nomination process.

51. In late June 1993, the Arkansas Bar Association named Foster as its Outstanding Lawyer of the Year. But he could not attend the dinner at which the award was to be presented, because he had been asked by Nussbaum to interview Stephen G. Breyer in Boston, whom President Clinton nominated to the U.S. Supreme Court in 1994.

52. During the evening of July 20, 1993, Nussbaum had received a call on his pager from Mark Gearan, who was with Mack McLarty and George Stephanopoulos at the White House during the president's appearance on *Larry King Live*. At the time, the White House counsel was having dinner at Galileo's restaurant in Washington with his wife Toby and another couple.

    Excusing himself from dinner, Nussbaum went to a telephone to respond to the page from Gearan who gave him the bad news.

    Within minutes, Nussbaum arrived by cab at the White House, in the midst of Larry King's interview with the president, who still didn't know about Foster's death.

53. According to the Secret Service log kept by the guard stationed at

Foster's door, Nussbaum had, once again, entered Foster's office at 11:10 AM on July 21, 1993.

54. The items found in Foster's wallet were not fingerprinted.

55. Reporter Thomas V. DiBacco quoted this verse in his article about the Forrestal suicide in the July 22, 1993, edition of the *Washington Times*.

56. In 1987, Robert McFarlane, President Reagan's National Security advisor, attempted but, fortunately, failed to commit suicide after he was implicated in the Iran-Contra scandal.

57. In fact, the *Washington Times* published an editorial on July 23, 1993, titled: "There was no Vincent Foster story."
    The editorial stated: "The *Washington Times* had nothing on Mr. Foster and was not in the process of developing anything. Zero."

58. Captain Hume erroneously stated on his report that his interview with Betsy Pond had taken place on "August 22, 1993." In fact, it occurred on July 22.

59. Among the myths about the search is that Nussbaum had actually picked up Foster's briefcase and declared that it was empty after shaking it upside down or flattening it out on the desk. In fact, Nussbaum had only picked up the briefcase to place it against the wall behind Foster's desk. There was no shaking or flattening.

60. An official May 2, 1994, USPP report describes the eight scenes depicted in Rolla's photographs:

    1 - Right hand showing gun & thumb in guard
    2 - Glasses on ground
    3 - VF's body - taken from below feet
    4 - VF's body - focusing on right side & arm
    5 - VF's body - focus on top of head thru heavy foliage
    6 - VF's body - focus on head & upper torso
    7 - VF's body - looking directly down into face
    8 - VF's face - taken from right side

During my research for this book, I was shown these eight photographs, among others, and confirmed the depictions listed in this USPP report.

This inventory does not include the two photographs that Rolla told me that he had allegedly given to Dr. Haut at the crime scene.

61. During my interview with Larry Romans of the USPP photo lab, who had processed Simonello's film, I asked him for an explanation for what had happened. Romans replied, "Pete is a qualified photographer. Evidently, something in this semiautomatic camera went haywire. It just didn't record as it should have at a correct exposure. For some reason, the camera underexposed everything. Little or no image appeared in the negative material. Later, I just turned the negatives over to the FBI, and I never saw them again."

When I asked him whether modern technology could save the pictures, he explained, "Computers can enhance them to some degree, but you can't correct something that's not there to begin with."

62. During his April 18, 1994, interview with the FBI, Ferris contested the statement in the USPP report about which state had appeared on the license plate.

63. This report in *Newsweek* was emphatically denied by John Brummett, the author of *High Wire: The Education of Bill Clinton* (Hyperion, 1994). Based on a statement by Donna McLarty, Brummett wrote on page 174: "For about an hour, from 1:30 to 2:30 PM, the two White House wives and old friends from Arkansas talked. Lisa Foster said that Vince seemed a little more chipper and that they had thoroughly enjoyed their weekend on the eastern shore, where they had played tennis."

Brummett specifically quoted Mrs. McLarty saying, "[H]onestly, we had an upbeat conversation."

Brummett revealed that a third unnamed woman at the Four Seasons had sat down with Lisa Foster and Donna McLarty for a few minutes. Later that night, after hearing the news of Vincent Foster's death while at a party, she had told the other party-goers of her brief encounter with Foster's wife and Mrs. McLarty that afternoon and "speculated" about that conversation.

Convinced that the *Newsweek* story was derived from her party chatter, she later called Donna McLarty to apologize, according to Brummett.

64. Specifically, Foster was concerned about a possible congressional probe of Travelgate, which, in fact, was stalled in both houses of Congress *before* Foster's death.

65. During my interview with Megby, he referred to his notes of the July 27 meeting, saying that Nussbaum had told him that the note had been found at 5 PM *that day*. He added that the Foster family was notified an hour later. Actually, the note had been found the previous day.

66. The Ushers Office consisted of a chief usher, who was Gary Walters, and three assistants. The office manages the White House eighty-seven–member staff, who maintain and care for the Executive Residence, as well as its furnishings and the First Family's household. The office also arranges and prepares for official and ceremonial presidential events.

67. Kaki Hockersmith, an interior designer from Little Rock, was the official White House decorator; HRC is Hillary Rodham Clinton. The White House decorator is selected by and works for the First Family. The initial estimate for the renovation of the Clinton White House was set at $250,000 in March 1993 but was increased to $337,000 in June. The final cost in November wound up at $396,429. None of this money came from public funds; all of it was raised through private donations.

68. USPP Detective Joe Megby used the word "legal" instead of "loyal" in his notes, which were taken as Nussbaum read the note aloud on the night of July 27, 1993.

69. Foster's 1989 Honda Accord remained at this location for about two weeks before being housed in the basement of the New Executive Office Building for several more weeks. After Lisa Foster finally retrieved the car, she sold it to a member of her family.

70. The writing sample given to Rolla and Kass was a June 18, 1993,

handwritten letter signed by Foster to the American Exploration Company, with which the Foster family had been doing business.

71. In a July 30, 1993, article in the *New York Times*—with a July 29 dateline—reporter Jehl wrote that Dee Dee Myers "questioned an account in the *New York Times* today in which a person close to the Fosters said Mr. Foster had spent reclusive weekends working at home in bed."

72. Mrs. Foster, who saw the note when she and Hamilton came to Nussbaum's office on the afternoon of July 27, identified her husband's handwriting.

73. Detective Markland told me that the USPP's interview with Lisa Foster almost didn't happen. After her husband's funeral, Mrs. Foster had remained in Little Rock while Hume and Markland were making requests to Hamilton to interview her. As the investigation rolled on without the interview being scheduled, the police investigators told Hamilton that they were going to fly to Arkansas to interview her. At that point, Hamilton arranged for Mrs. Foster to come to Washington to meet with the police in his office.

74. Hubbell had come to the Eastern Shore on Saturday after attending a meeting at which the decision was made to fire FBI Director William Sessions, who officially lost his job on Monday, July 19, the day before Foster's death.

75. En route to the White House, Foster dropped off his daughter, Laura, at her summer job, and his son, Vincent III, at the Metro. Consequently, Foster arrived at the White House later than usual.

76. Hume and Markland both told me that they wanted to speak with Foster's children, but Hamilton refused to make them available.

77. In the August 9, 1993, issue of *U.S. News & World Report*, reporters Kenneth T. Walsh and Matthew Cooper interviewed President Clinton and asked him about the Foster note. Clinton told them, "I was notified that there was some sort of note he'd written to himself that he had torn up that may shed some light on

his state of mind. The minute I heard about it, I said, 'Certainly that has to be turned over to the authorities. Let them read and evaluate it.'"

78. *NBC Nightly News* was first to report details of the FBI investigation that night.

    Among those interviewed by FBI Special Agents Dennis Condon and Scott Salter were: Roger Adams, Bill Burton, Donald Flynn, David Gergen, Deborah Gorham, Philip Heymann, Charles Hume, Paul Imbordino, Thomas McLarty, David Margolis, Pete Markland, Joe Megby, Steve Neuwirth, Bernard Nussbaum, and Clifford Sloan.

79. In an August 7, 1995, prepared statement to the Senate Whitewater Committee, Mack McLarty explained that Collier had called David Gergen, complaining about the lack of cooperation the White House Counsel's Office had been giving the U.S. Park Police. Gergen discussed the matter with McLarty, who then spoke with Nussbaum, who then talked to Clifford Sloan.

80. The USPP never received any e-mail messages sent or received by Foster. And the USPP never attempted to get Foster's long-distance calls from his home.

81. Pincus wrote an op-ed article, "Vincent Foster: Out of His Element," which was published on August 5, 1993, in the *Washington Post*. Pincus, who had last seen Foster at their lunch on July 9, wrote, in part: "From afar in Little Rock, before he came to... Washington, he was an admirer of the *Post*, the *New York Times* and the *Wall Street Journal*. Up close and in the White House, that view changed....

    "His composure sometimes broke when he would discuss what he considered wild assertions in one paper that would be denied but then picked up blindly by others. He would have been amazed and extremely disturbed by the rumors that have accompanied his own suicide and found their way into print."

82. Dr. Watkins had called Morgan Pharmacy at the corner of P and 30th Streets, in northwest Washington, which is a few blocks from

Foster's home. The pharmacist filled the prescription with thirty 50-mg tablets of Desyrel. The pharmacy then delivered the medication to the Fosters' home by 6 PM.

83. After the December 31, 1992, physical, Dr. Watkins prescribed Restoril, a mild sleep aid, for Foster. But Foster refused to take the drug, fearing that he could become addicted.

84. Captain Hume interviewed Gordon Rather on August 5, 1993.

85. The USPP had made the request directly to the ATF's crime lab and not through its Washington Field Division, which was standard operating procedure. This caused some later confusion among the ATF's high command, which had not been notified of the USPP's request but had received several media requests for information about the testing.

86. On Friday, October 22, 1993—over ten weeks after the results of the investigations by the Park Police, the FBI, and the Department of Justice—the Alcohol, Tobacco and Firearms Bureau filed its "closing report" on the agency's examination of the .38 revolver found in Foster's hand, which corroborated the final results from the other law-enforcement groups.

    Respected firearms examiner Carlo J. Rosati headed the investigation.

    That same month, Treasury Secretary Bentsen, in the wake of evidence of the botched February 1983 federal assault on David Koresh's compound in Waco, Texas, selected Secret Service Director John Magaw to replace Stephen Higgins as the chief of the Bureau of Alcohol, Tobacco and Firearms.

87. During her sworn testimony before the Senate Whitewater Committee on July 25, 1995, Thomasson said that while looking for a possible suicide note she opened the drawers in Foster's desk, checking to see if anything was on top. "My thought process was if someone left a suicide note, they would leave it where it could be easily found," she testified.

88. Also, in September 1993, Hale alleged that James Guy Tucker,

who succeeded Clinton as the governor of Arkansas, was also an alleged beneficiary and among those applying the pressure for him to make the loan.

Subsequent to Hale's charges, President Clinton met with Tucker no fewer than two times: at the White House on October 6 and in Seattle on November 18.

89. As negotiated by Foster, McDougal bought the Clintons' investment in Whitewater for a mere $1,000 in December 1992.

90. A Japanese-language officer for the Marine Corps during World War II and a former Fulbright Scholar at Oxford, Irvine, an economist for the Federal Reserve Board from 1951 to 1977, was already deeply involved in anticommunist activities by the time he founded AIM in 1969. Three years later, Irvine created the *AIM Report*, a newsletter that still serves as the voice of his media-watchdog organization.

Goulden, a respected award-winning journalist and the former Washington bureau chief of the *Philadelphia Inquirer*, was also the bestselling author of sixteen books. Many in the world of journalism and publishing were shocked when Goulden joined Irvine and the right-wing AIM group in January 1989. But the fifty-nine–year-old Goulden, who had all the money he needed from the success of his books, believed that his generation had made a mess of journalism, and that serious media criticism had been lacking.

91. Among other services, AIM syndicated its radio commentaries, *Media Monitor*, and produced a syndicated television program, *The Other Side of the Story*.

Charles Seib, a former ombudsman for the *Washington Post*, a perennial target of AIM, once said of the organization, "It sticks in my craw, but I'll say it: Irvine and his AIM are good for the press."

92. Richard Scaife controlled three principal philanthropic organizations, the family's Allegheny, Carthage, and Sarah Scaife Foundations.

In 1972, he gave a million dollars to President Nixon's Committee to Re-Elect the President and had contributed heavily to such conservative think tanks as the American Enterprise

Institute, the Heritage Foundation, and the Center for Strategic and International Studies.

Reportedly, in Scaife's view, the similarities between the deaths of his one-time mentor, Pittsburgh attorney Robert Duggan, and Vincent Foster were remarkable, making the Foster case a matter of particular interest.

93. Before joining the *Post*, Ruddy, the son of a Nassau County police officer, had studied at St. John's University in Queens, as well as the Hebrew University in Jerusalem, and earned a master's degree from the prestigious London School of Economics. After a brief career as a high-school teacher in New York, Ruddy, while editing and writing for the *New York Guardian*, debunked a highly acclaimed documentary on public television, which claimed that prisoners at the notorious Buchenwald and Dachau concentration camps had been liberated by two heroic black combat units in the wake of bloody battles with the Nazis. After prominent Jewish publications, as well as *New York* magazine and the *New Republic*, conducted their own investigations, Ruddy's work was confirmed: The story was false.

94. On August 25, 1993, Hamilton sent a letter to Attorney General Reno, asking her for the original of Foster's torn-up note. In his letter, Hamilton wrote: "The family, of course, understood the need for the Park Police and the FBI to obtain and analyze the note. Now, however, the investigations into Vince's death are concluded and family members see no good reason why the note should not be returned to Mrs. Foster."

Reno politely turned down Hamilton's request.

95. As described by Isikoff: "The apparently unfinished list, identified as written in Foster's hand, was divided into four columns. One listed three dates: '2/80' and '3/80,' both listed twice, and '12/83.' Another had different combinations of three capital letters: 'C or H,' 'C or B,' 'C or B or H.' In the third and fourth columns, across from the 2/80 and 3/80 dates, were the numbers '1000,' '100' or '50,' and apparent references to cities in Arkansas: 'LR,' 'N,' 'Bentonville,' and 'Hot Spr.'"

Part Three

1. On January 31, 1994, Attorney General Janet Reno—citing the U.S. Code, specifically 5 U.S.C. 301 and 28 U.S.C. 509, 510, 543 as her authority—published a statement in the February 4 *Federal Register*, designating Robert Fiske as "independent counsel."

2. Born in Brooklyn and educated at Yale and the University of Michigan School of Law, the sixty-three–year-old Fiske—a respected moderate Republican and attorney with the law firm of Davis, Polk & Wardwell—had been chosen by President Bush for the position of deputy attorney general in the Department of Justice. However, Fiske backed away from the job when he began having problems with conservatives during the Senate confirmation process, because of his membership on a committee of the American Bar Association that screened judges and was critical of several nominees made by President Reagan.

   One of Fiske's former law partners, Lawrence E. Walsh, had been serving as the controversial independent counsel in the Iran-Contra case.

   According to press reports, Walsh had been Fiske's longtime mentor.

3. Christopher Ruddy later claimed that paramedic George Gonzalez, not Officer Kevin Fornshill, found Foster's body. But in his January 27, 1994, article, the reporter simply wrote that Gonzalez "says he was the first rescue worker to see Foster's body."

   Actually, this, too, was wrong. The first rescue worker to reach Foster's body after it was discovered by Fornshill was Todd Hall, according to my own interviews with both Fornshill and Hall in 1997, which corroborated their previous sworn statements.

4. During my interview with Corey Ashford, he confirmed what Ruddy had written about him: He saw neither blood nor an exit wound. In fact, remarkably enough, Ashford told me that he didn't even remember seeing a cannon.

   But he added that it was getting dark by the time he arrived at Fort Marcy Park, that he handled Foster for "less than five seconds" while hoisting him into the body bag, and that he never saw the back of his body where the exit wound and the major concentration of blood were.

More puzzling was the fact that Ashford, who was wearing latex gloves and a long-sleeve shirt, said that there was no blood on him or his clothing after he handled Foster. However, he explained that he picked up Foster by the armpits, where there were no reported blood stains.

5. On January 31, 1994, Reed Irvine and Joe Goulden, who had filed an FOIA request for the police and FBI reports, published another op-ed piece in the *Washington Times*. Irvine and Goulden wrote: "On Jan. 14, Maj. Robert Hines, the Park Police spokesman, told us that there was no exit wound in Mr. Foster's head. He also said a ballistics test had proven that the bullet that killed Mr. Foster came from the gun in his hand.

"A week later, Maj. Hines told Mr. Ruddy exactly the opposite—that indeed there was an exit wound, and that the bullet had not been found.... Maj. Hines also told us and Mr. Ruddy that the D.C. Metropolitan Police Department laboratory had done the ballistics test, but a D.C. police ballistics expert told Mr. Ruddy that was untrue."

In its January-B 1994 *AIM Report* newsletter, Irvine and Goulden added: "After the *Washington Times* published an AIM column in which we discussed what Ruddy had learned and cited the discrepancies between that and what Hines told us, Hines finally returned our calls and apologized for having given us erroneous information. He said there was a small exit wound, very little blood, and that the gun and powder residue tests had been done by the Bureau of Alcohol, Tobacco and Firearms, something the BATF had denied but now confirms."

6. The *Wall Street Journal*, January 31, 1994.

7. Jim Morrissette and Robert Rule of the USPP did go to the Saudi compound and also spoke to construction workers in the area. But they did not talk to others in the neighborhood.

8. Actually, there are no fewer than four entrances to Fort Marcy Park: the main entrance off George Washington Memorial Parkway;

through a gap in a fence, which is less than three feet wide, on Chain Bridge Road; a path, further up on Chain Bridge Road, on the side of a small home; and another gap in the fence on the side of an upscale housing subdivision off the northwest portion of the park.

9. On March 4, 1994, following up on the earlier report in the *Washington Times*, the *New York Times* revealed that Jeremy Hedges, a college student who worked as a courier for the Rose Law Firm in Little Rock, had told a federal grand jury that he and another aide had shredded a box of Vincent Foster's files.

    A Rose spokesman issued a short statement to the *New York Times*, saying: "No files of Vincent Foster's have been destroyed. In the process of a lawyer changing offices, a box of old files containing internal Rose firm materials, such as copies of notes of firm committee meetings, was destroyed earlier this year."

10. In the March-B 1994 issue of the *AIM Report*, Reed Irvine and Joseph Goulden published a lengthy article, "The Foster Death: Case Still Open," in which they wrote: "Major Hines told us the Park Police believe the shot was fired into the open mouth with the barrel a few inches away."

    Once again, Hines had erred. The official conclusion of the Park Police was and continued to be that Foster had placed the gun in his mouth.

11. According to Ruddy's own definition: "A 'drop gun' is an old, nondescript and untraceable revolver that can be 'dropped' by someone at a staged suicide or crime."

12. Clinger made his announcement on February 24, 1994, over the objections of U.S. House Government Operations Committee Chairman John Conyers, a Michigan Democrat—and in defiance of Robert Fiske's ongoing investigation.

13. Two other attorneys, William S. Duffey, Jr., and Carl J. Stich, Jr., were also retained to aid during the Little Rock phase of the Foster investigation. Fiske also hired respected Houston prosecutor Russell Hardin, Jr., as the special trial counsel in the prosecution of David Hale.

14. On February 25, 1994, Fairfax County Attorney David P. Bobzien, at the request of Fiske and the FBI, supplied the OIC with a list of the eleven fire and rescue personnel who responded to the July 20 call at Fort Marcy Park, along with the "computer traffic that was generated by [the Foster] event." The county attorney also offered to give the FBI a copy of the original 911 tape, which had been preserved as evidence.

15. Hubbell resigned from the Department of Justice on March 14, 1994.

16. On March 8, 1994, President Clinton named the distinguished seventy-six–year-old Lloyd Cutler, who had pursued President Nixon during the Watergate scandal, as his new White House counsel, replacing the embattled Nussbaum who resigned three days earlier. Cutler, who had served in this same role under President Carter, promised President Clinton that he would stay in the position until September.

17. The Senate vote took place on March 17, 1994.

18. The next day, Tuesday, March 8, 1994, Ruddy revealed that Dr. James Beyer, the deputy chief medical examiner who performed the autopsy on Foster, had been proven wrong in a previous suicide ruling and was in the midst of being challenged on a second.

    On the same day as Ruddy's article, reporter Michael Hedges of the *Washington Times* published his own independent story about Dr. Beyer's mistakes.

19. I interviewed *all* of the USPP investigators who worked on the Foster case. All of them denied having any evidence that a hideaway apartment existed.

20. David Smick, Johnson's partner, was a former top aide to one-time Republican Congressman Jack Kemp of New York.

    According to an article in the March 17, 1994, edition of the *Washington Times*, written by John M. Doyle about the impact of the Foster hideaway rumor in Johnson's publication: "Within hours after the rumor hit the trading rooms Thursday [March 10], bond and stock prices fell, the dollar weakened and gold prices shot up $8 an ounce."

The March 21, 1994, issue of *Newsweek* published its own story about the "flow of lip-smacking stories" about the Foster matter, including the gossip published in Johnson's newsletter. However, reporter Russell Watson gave credit for the twenty-three–point drop in the Dow on March 10 to conservative broadcaster Rush Limbaugh, who had "embellished that report... [claiming] that Vince Foster was murdered in an apartment owned by Hillary Clinton."

21. In his book, *Friends in High Places*, Webb Hubbell wrote on page 255 that Hillary Clinton had asked him to investigate a report about "a Navy hit squad that murders people and makes their deaths look like suicide."

22. The security official was Luther "Jerry" Parks, the security chief for a building in which the Clinton campaign leased space. He was shot and killed while driving his van on September 26, 1993. His killer had apparently pulled up next to him in another vehicle and opened fire.

23. Floyd Brown caused a major controversy during the 1988 presidential campaign when his political-action group produced the now-infamous Willie Horton ad, which portrayed Democrat Michael Dukakis as being soft on crime and criminals.

24. On March 20, 1994, the *New York Times*, which laughed on the sidelines while the *New York Post* and the *New York Daily News* warred with each other, published an article by Tom Kuntz, who wrote: "For a change, the parties in this round of the Tabloid War are getting outside help. The *Post*, which under the ownership of Rupert Murdoch has developed a reputation for stirring up trouble for the Democrats, got a boost when the no-less-partisan editorial page of the *Wall Street Journal* referred to *Post* articles in an unusually long editorial [on January 31] raising questions about Mr. Foster's death."

25. On Friday, April 29, the FBI reinterviewed Arthur. This time, he was taken to Fort Marcy Park and asked to give federal agents a walkthrough of the area while recalling what he had seen and done. Arthur, who said he "did not trust [George] Gonzalez's

judgment" about the Foster case, still seemed to believe that Foster had been murdered, right there at Fort Marcy Park.

26. Prepared statement of Michael Shaheen, Hearing before the Committee on Government Reform and Oversight, U.S. House of Representatives, October 24, 1995, page 127.

27. After completing the search, the FBI inspected the area, adding, "[I]t was returned to its natural condition as closely as possible."

28. The FBI interviewed Gorham on April 19 and April 26, 1994.

29. The FBI interviewed Skyles on April 20, 1994.

30. The FBI interviewed Ferris on April 18, 1994.

31. After the Ferris interview, the FBI interviewed two security officers at the Saudi Arabian ambassador's residence, which is located on Chain Bridge Road, across the street from a walk-in entrance—with an opening less than three feet wide in a long chain-linked fence—to Fort Marcy Park. (The Saudis have a security camera pointed directly at this entrance.)

    The security men, Robert Arthur Denning and Roger George Bailey, neither heard nor saw anything out of the ordinary.

32. The FBI first interviewed Knowlton on April 15, 1994.

33. In an attempt to clarify some of these issues, the FBI reinterviewed Knowlton on May 11, 1994.

    But, even after the FBI showed Knowlton photographs of Foster's gray Honda—which had been described by Investigator Renee Abt as gray-brown in her crime-scene notes—Knowlton stood firm, insisting that he had seen an older model of Honda that was rusty brown, adding that its license plate contained a different configuration of letters than a photograph of Foster's tag. Knowlton also maintained his description of the second blue car and its driver who had acted in a threatening manner toward him. In short, Knowlton was unmovable.

34. The FBI report also added:

> [U]pon exiting Fort Marcy Park, [Knowlton] did view
> in the right hand lane of the [northbound] George
> Washington Parkway a Ford passenger van which was
> slowing down and possibly could have made a right
> hand turn into Fort Marcy Park.

According to the FBI, Knowlton said that he couldn't provide
any further details about this passenger van or its driver. However,
Knowlton later denied ever saying that, insisting that he could pick
the man out of a lineup.

35. The FBI interviewed Feist on April 5, 1994.

36. Feist told the FBI that he and Doody remained in her car for about
fifteen minutes before going into the woods for their picnic, adding
that he had seen a jogger, "an older man with graying hair, thin
built, wearing red shorts."

37. The FBI interviewed Doody on April 7, 1994.

38. According to Doody, after the mystery man in the white van left, "an
old, dirty and run down large 4-door sedan (color unknown)" pulled
into the parking lot. The driver of this car—"a white male with long,
shaggy hair with a large build"—made a U-turn and exited.
    While out in the woods, she saw another "big and burly" man
with dark-brown hair and blue jeans walking "towards the parking lot."

39. Lankler received this package from Liddy on April 6, 1994.

40. In a December 30, 1994, memorandum, Reed Irvine told Kyle
about the original 911 call, in which he was described by Francis
Swann as being "queery." Irvine continued: "There was speculation that [Kyle] was 'cruising,' not looking for a place to urinate. I
raised this with Dale. He said he was not gay and that he had gone
to the park with girl friends. He said Marcy is favored by hetero-
sexuals and that the gays congregate at Turkey Run."

41. The FBI's first interview with Marsha Scott was on May 12, 1994.

42. In his book *Friends in High Places*, Webb Hubbell wrote on pages 40–41: "Marsha Scott tells me that after [Foster] went to Washington, an informal poll was taken at the White House asking the women there whom they would most like to have an affair with. Vince won going away."

43. The FBI's second interview with Scott took place on June 9, 1994.

44. The OIC-FBI team interviewed Kennedy on May 6, 1994.

45. Curious about the Foster-Carroll relationship, the FBI interviewed Carroll on Tuesday, May 17, 1994. Carroll, who admitted to having been extremely disappointed by Foster's decision to leave the Rose Law Firm, described the suicide as "a complete mystery."

46. The FBI interviewed Hubbell on April 13 and 14, 1994.
    The previous month, on March 14, Hubbell had resigned from the Justice Department after becoming the target of an internal review by the Rose Law Firm for alleged overbilling and expense-account abuses—and in the midst of the Senate Banking Committee's investigation of the RTC and the "heads-up" warnings to the White House.

47. In his book, *Friends in High Places*, Hubbell wrote on page 250 that he "wrapped the gun in a towel and gave it to Beryl [Anthony] for safekeeping."

48. The second interview with Hubbell occurred on June 7, 1994.

49. The FBI interviewed Sheila Anthony on April 28, 1994.

50. The FBI interviewed the three psychiatrists who had been recommended to Foster by his sister, Sheila Anthony: Dr. Martin G. Allen, Dr. Stefan A. Pasternack, and Dr. Robert Hedaya. They confirmed that they had never spoken to Vincent Foster.
    However, on May 17, 1994, Dr. Hedaya gave the FBI a chronology of events, leading up to his discussion with Mrs. Anthony, which confirmed her statement to the FBI.

NOTES 419

Through a mutual friend, Mrs. Anthony received an introduction to Dr. Hedaya, who had been told that she knew someone in "a crisis situation." She explained to him that her brother "was extremely depressed and in need of psychological counseling," and that he held "a very sensitive position at the White House." She explained that "his depression was directly related to highly sensitive and confidential matters." In consideration of this, Mrs. Anthony asked Dr. Hedaya if he could see her brother "'off the record' for one counseling session."

The doctor agreed, hoping to provide "basic education therapy regarding the causes of depression and suggested ways to cope with this disease." Upon hearing this, Mrs. Anthony revealed her brother's name to him, adding that she would have him call that day.

But Foster never called, and Sheila Anthony received confirmation of that two days after her brother's death when she called Dr. Hedaya. Two to three weeks later, Mrs. Anthony visited Dr. Hedaya at his office for a general discussion about depression. During that meeting, Mrs. Anthony explained to him that "there was something going on in [Foster's] life," but that it was "not [as] sinister as being reported in the media."

51. At the time of his December 31, 1992, physical, according to Dr. Larry Watkins, Foster weighed 194 pounds, which appeared to dispute claims by his wife, among others, that he had been losing weight. At the time of his autopsy, Foster weighed 197 pounds.

   However, it was likely that Foster, who was eating more junk food while exercising less, gained weight during the early months of the Clinton administration and then began to lose it as his depression set in during the latter weeks of his life.

52. Mrs. Foster told the FBI that she was aware that Senator Bob Dole "had written a letter on July 15, 1993, requesting a congressional investigation of the Travel Office matter." Also, the Fosters' oldest son, Vincent III, an aide to Senator Dale Bumpers, had attended a meeting of the Senate Judiciary Committee, where a resolution for an official probe had been proposed but tabled.

53. After checking records at the White House, the OIC learned that Foster's blood pressure had actually been 132/84, which was normal for the forty-eight–year-old Foster.

54. On May 16, 1994, the FBI interviewed Foster's personal physician, Dr. Larry Watkins, who had previously talked to Captain Hume on August 2, 1993. During that earlier interview, Dr. Watkins said that Foster had called him on the day before his death, and he had returned the call that same day. During their conversation, Foster admitted that he was depressed, so Foster prescribed a mild antidepressant.

    According to the FBI, Dr. Watkins said that even though Foster's call was "unprecedented," he didn't believe that Foster was "significantly depressed nor had Foster given the impression that he was 'in crisis.' From what Foster told him, Foster's condition sounded mild and situational."

55. Mrs. Foster also told the OIC-FBI team that her husband had decided not to go jogging that morning, "because it would take him too long to cool off."

56. According to Mrs. Foster, her husband had parked his car in slot 16 on Executive Boulevard West while working at the White House. "Lisa Foster knows," the FBI report stated, "that the trunks of vehicles are checked when the vehicles are driven onto the White House grounds."

    However, there has never been any official confirmation that Foster actually parked on the White House grounds that day.

57. FBI agents canvassed Foster's Georgetown neighborhood, searching for anyone who had seen Vincent Foster return to his home on the afternoon of July 20, 1993. No one had—although several did see Lisa Foster come and go, consistent with Mrs. Foster's statement to the FBI.

58. Mrs. Foster did say that her sister-in-law, Sharon Bowman, had received the elder Foster's shotguns and "one handgun," and "that Beryl Anthony has one of the handguns from the estate here in Washington, D.C." This was probably the gun that Hubbell took from the Fosters' home on the night of the suicide.

    In what appeared to be a last-ditch effort to get a positive identification that the gun found in Foster's right hand once belonged to Foster's late father, the FBI visited Foster's nephew, Lee

Bowman, a gun enthusiast who worked for Barclays Bank in New York on June 28, 1994. Bowman told the FBI that he had often gone shooting with his grandfather and had seen many of his guns.

But this was another dead end. Although the gun found in Foster's right hand seemed familiar to him, Bowman could not positively identify it.

59. During my interviews with Hume and Markland, as well as Braun and Rolla, they were all upset that Lisa Foster had concealed her knowledge of guns in the house. Markland, in particular, told me that had he known this, he would have attempted to get a search warrant for the Fosters' home.

60. FBI special agents spoke to Acting U.S. Attorney Pence about his knowledge of the search warrant on May 19, 1994. The FBI reported: "[Pence] said that he was made aware of the search warrant, about one or two days before the warrant was to be executed, due to his position.... After having been told about the search warrant, he spoke with no one else about it until he heard from AUSA Jackson that the search had gone smoothly."

61. The FBI's second interview with Lyons took place on June 27, 1994.

62. Another witness interviewed by the FBI about Foster and Whitewater was Ricki L. Seidman, an assistant to President Clinton, on June 23, 1994. "She said," according to the FBI report, "the only Whitewater issue she could recall was in April 1993 in connection with the Clintons' tax returns. The tax returns show that the Clintons had divested themselves of their interest in Whitewater.... [I]t was believed the tax returns would bring the Whitewater issue into the 'public domain again.'"

But Seidman added that Foster was "agitated" over Travelgate but "not upset by Whitewater."

63. Interviewed by the FBI on June 14, 1994, Thomases was an attorney with the New York law firm of Willkie, Farr & Gallagher, which had a Washington office for which she was the managing partner. She spent Wednesdays and Thursdays in D.C. and the rest of her time in New York.

64. To review and independently confirm the OIC's evidentiary findings, Fiske retained the services of a distinguished four-man panel
of forensic experts. This pathologist panel included Dr. James L.
Luke, who had aided in the interviews of medical personnel during the investigation; Dr. Charles Hirsch, New York City's chief
medical examiner; Dr. Donald T. Reay of Seattle, King County's
chief medical examiner; and Dr. Charles J. Stahl, medical examiner
for the Armed Forces Institute of Pathology in Washington, D.C.

65. In his report, Fiske wrote: "We have reviewed all of the
Whitewater-related documents from Mr. Foster's files that were
delivered to the [Clintons'] personal attorney after his death.
However, Rule 6 (e) of the Federal Rules of Criminal Procedure
precludes us from disclosing the content of these documents since
they were obtained by grand jury subpoena."
   The report added:

> It was not until October 1993, three months after Foster's
> death, when it was disclosed that the Resolution Trust
> Corporation had issued criminal referrals involving
> Madison Guaranty and Whitewater, that the matter again
> received prominent public attention.... Obviously, the
> fact that Foster never expressed a concern about
> Whitewater or Madison to anyone does not mean that he
> did not, in fact, have such a concern. Thus, we cannot
> conclusively rule out such a concern as a possible con-
> tributing factor to his depression. What we can conclude
> is that there is no evidence that he did have such a con-
> cern against a background in which Whitewater/Madison
> issues were neither a matter of expressed concern in the
> White House, nor the subject of media attention.

Regarding the possibility that Foster had, somehow, found out
that a search warrant had been authorized against David Hale's
Capital Management Services, Fiske concluded:

> The search warrant was issued by the Federal
> District Court in Little Rock, Arkansas, on the after-
> noon of July 20, 1993, the date of Foster's death.
> However, the search warrant was not made public until

it was executed, on July 21, after Foster's death. We
have investigated to determine whether Foster learned
of the search warrant prior to his death and have found
no evidence that he did.

66. Ninty-one of the 138 pages of attachments were the curriculum
vitae of each of the consultants/experts retained by the OIC.

67. The *Fiske Report* noted, "Calls of less than one minute are
reflected on a telephone bill as one minute in length."

68. The *Fiske Report* did not mention rescue worker Corey Ashford's
coding of Foster's death as a homicide.

69. Even though Dr. Beyer had stated on his autopsy form that X rays
had been taken of Foster's head, the *Fiske Report* corrected this,
saying: "The office X ray machine was inoperable at the time of
Foster's autopsy, and as a result no X rays were taken."

70. Regarding the two serial numbers on the gun, the *Fiske Report*
stated that this indicated "that it was assembled with parts from
two different guns. The only available records indicate that guns
bearing those serial numbers were purchased in 1913."

Further, in the report's discussion of the gun, Fiske indicated
that Lisa Foster had twice asked her husband to remove a gun that
was part of a shipment of items from Little Rock to Washington.
However, the report also noted that the gun she had found in their
home on the night of her husband's death was not the same gun
that she had previously seen.

The *Fiske Report* did not address the fact that the gun Mrs.
Foster had identified was silver, not black—which was the color of
the gun found in Foster's right hand.

71. During my interview with Ferris, he said that he was familiar with the
Arkansas license plate, and that the tag he saw was not from
Arkansas, adding, "It just struck me that the plate was from a mid-
western state."

Later, during our conversation, he added, "Also, if the pictures
the FBI showed me were actually the pictures of Vincent Foster's car,
then it was *not* the same car I saw pull in front of me on that day."

At the time of Foster's death, Ferris was an "imagery analyst" for the CIA. "I have an eye for detail," Ferris told me.

According to the *Fiske Report*, the only license plate that fit Ferris's description was from Montana.

72. Explaining how Foster's eyeglasses wound up so far from his head, the *Fiske Report* speculated: "One obvious scenario is that the eyeglasses were dislodged by the sudden backward movement of Foster's head when the gun was fired, after which the glasses bounced down the hill."

73. Regarding the transfer stain, the *Fiske Report* stated: "The FBI Lab concluded that the pattern of the blood on Foster's face and on Foster's shoulder is consistent with Foster's face having come into contact with the shoulder of his shirt at some point. Because Foster's head is not in contact with his shoulder in the photographs, the FBI Lab Report concludes that Foster's head 'moved or was moved after being in contact with the shoulder.' The Pathologist Panel endorsed this conclusion, stating that 'a rightward tilt of his face was changed to a forward orientation by one of the early observers before the scene photographs were taken.'"

74. However, the FBI added, "Inasmuch as these tissue samples were prepared in a way which is not conducive to retaining unconsumed gunpowder particles, these findings are not unexpected. Also, unconsumed gunpowder particles are different from residue of gunpowder. The FBI Laboratory findings are not inconsistent with the Pathologists' Report relating to a suicide finding in which the muzzle of the firearm was in Foster's mouth."

75. USPP criminalist Pete Simonello had said repeatedly that he saw "one small speck or droplet of blood on the barrel." However, the gun was processed for fingerprints by E.J. Smith, Simonello's partner, during Simonello's four-day leave, which began the day after Foster's death. Smith did not report seeing any blood on the barrel.

76. During my interview with Simonello, he told me that he believed that *his* fingerprint was found under the grip of Foster's gun.

Simonello said that he had probably left it there while engraving his initials on the handle for identification purposes.

77. This statement about contamination was based on a June 1, 1994, FBI interview with USPP criminalist Pete Simonello.

78. Fiske sent his response on July 11, 1994.

79. Narrating the videotape was Larry Nichols, an ex-state official in Arkansas who had been forced out of his job by Governor Clinton and then filed a lawsuit against the governor in 1990, alleging that Clinton had used state funds to woo five separate women—one of whom was Gennifer Flowers, who, during the 1992 presidential campaign, claimed to have had an affair with Clinton. The suit was later dismissed. (Clinton reportedly admitted the affair during his January 17, 1998, sworn testimony in the Paula Jones case.)

    On tape, Nichols also tried to connect Clinton to an alleged narcotics-trafficking operation revolving around an airstrip in Mena, Arkansas.

80. On July 28, 1994, Burton, along with John Mica (R-Florida) and Dana Rohrabacher (R-California), took the sworn deposition of Dale Kyle, who repeated that he had not seen a gun in Foster's hand. Burton and the other congressmen attempted to use this statement as a means to discredit the *Fiske Report*.

81. Other senators who participated in the hearing included Paul Sarbanes (D-Maryland), Phil Gramm (R-Texas), Christopher Dodd (D-Connecticut), Christopher Bond (R-Missouri), Jim Sasser (D-Tennessee), Connie Mack (R-Florida), Richard Shelby (D-Alabama), Lauch Faircloth (R-North Carolina), John Kerry (D-Massachusetts), William Roth (R-Delaware), Richard Bryan (D-Nevada), Robert Bennett (R-Utah), Barbara Boxer (D-California), Pete Domenici (R-New Mexico), Ben Nighthorse Campbell (D-Colorado), Orrin Hatch (R-Utah), Carol Moseley-Braun (D-Illinois), and Patty Murray (D-Washington).

82. In the statement he submitted to the committee, Hines wrote: "After Mr. Foster's death—and even after we reported our

finding—there were some reports in the media alleging—with absolutely no supporting evidence—that he was murdered, that his body was moved after death to Ft. Marcy, that there was a conspiracy involved in his death. These fraudulent and twisted allegations have, among a host of other things, called into question the competence and professionalism of the United States Park Police."

83. Actually, a portion of this story appeared in the "Periscope" section of the August 8, 1994, edition of *Newsweek*, which hit the newsstands on August 1, the day before Marcus's story. Marcus acknowledged *Newsweek*, a subsidiary of the Washington Post Company, in her article.

84. In a published letter to the editor of the *New York Times* on August 18, 1994, David E. Kendall wrote: "[Hillary Clinton's] press conference response dealt with claims of improper conduct on the part of Ms. Williams (that is, the reported unauthorized removal of documents from Mr. Foster's office on the night of his suicide). Mrs. Clinton's response then and now is that no such conduct occurred. Mrs. Clinton proceeded to explain that Bernard W. Nussbaum, then White House counsel, had reviewed the files (two days later, in fact) in the presence of law enforcement officials and then had distributed the files as he thought appropriate and that personal legal files 'went to our lawyer.'"

85. USPP Officer Franz Ferstl told me that he believes that he is the unnamed officer in Ruddy's report. Ferstl claimed that Ruddy had exploited his vague recollections about the crime scene, which might have contradicted some established facts. When Ferstl sensed that Ruddy was locking him into statements he was not sure were correct, he stopped talking to the reporter, realizing that he had been speaking to him without authorization from the USPP. This made Ruddy more suspicious that Ferstl was hiding something—which, Ferstl insisted to me, he was not.

Part Four

1. Before Starr became Bush's solicitor general in 1989, President
   Reagan nominated him to the U.S. Court of Appeals for the
   District of Columbia.

   Also appointed to that same court by Reagan was Judge David
   B. Sentelle, who headed the three-judge panel that selected Starr.
   The other two judges were Joseph T. Sneed of the U.S Court of
   Appeals for the Ninth Circuit in San Francisco and John D.
   Butzner, Jr., of the U.S. Court of Appeals for the Fourth Circuit in
   Richmond, Virginia.

   Sentelle, who was known as a protégé of Senator Jesse Helms
   (R-North Carolina), had cast the deciding votes in the appeals of
   Oliver North and John Poindexter, two principals in the Iran-
   Contra scandal; Sentelle's votes overturned their convictions.

   Just prior to Starr's appointment, Lauch Faircloth, the other
   Republican senator from North Carolina and a member of the
   Senate Banking Committee, had written a letter to the Department
   of Justice, asking for Fiske's dismissal.

   A controversy later erupted when Sentelle reportedly was seen
   having lunch with Helms and Faircloth in the Senate dining room
   on July 14—just two weeks after Attorney General Reno had
   asked Sentelle and the other two judges to reappoint Fiske. This
   luncheon was followed by a private conversation between Sentelle
   and Faircloth on the tram that runs below the U.S. Capitol.

   After these meetings became public, three private citizens filed
   charges against Sentelle for professional misconduct. These complaints, filed separately and supported by five former presidents of
   the American Bar Association, were received by Harry T. Edwards,
   the chief judge of the U.S. Court of Appeals for the District of
   Columbia.

   Edwards became chief judge of the appellate court after the former chief judge, Abner Mikva, was selected to replace Lloyd
   Cutler as White House counsel on August 11, six days after Starr's
   appointment; Mikva would not begin his new job until October 1.

   In his ruling on Sentelle's behavior, Judge Edwards later wrote:

   > There may be some members of society who would
   > question the actions of the accused judge, for they have
   > a pristine (albeit arguably naive) view of the appoint-

ment process. But this is irrelevant. The simple point
here is that, even accepting the complaints as true for
purposes of this analysis, the judge who has been
accused in this case would have violated no provision
of law or ethical canon. There is no basis whatsoever
for proceedings against this judge.

To the citizen-activists who filed the initial complaint, it was
very relevant. During an interview with the *Washington Post*, one
citizen group leader asked, "Would [Edwards] consult with the
head of the Mafia before he makes a decision on organized crime?
It leaves the door wide open for anybody to consult with anybody
on anything."

The *New York Times* added on November 9, 1994: "The
behavior of Judge David Sentelle, which put a cloud over the
appointment of a new independent prosecutor in the Whitewater
case during August, was bad in itself. But the justification for that
behavior now offered up by Chief Judge Harry Edwards of the
U.S. Court of Appeals is equally appalling."

2. Irvine appeared to believe the theory that Foster was a partner in
an apartment in northern Virginia, specifically the Lincoln Towers
in Arlington. Irvine wrote to Clinger: "This is the same apartment
building where RTC official Jon Walker went to commit suicide a
few weeks after Foster's death.... Was there some connection
between Foster and Walker, who is said to have been involved in
processing the Madison S & L criminal referrals?"

3. A similar ad, also paid for by the Western Journalism Center, appeared
in the *Washington Post* on Wednesday, November 16, 1994.

4. The libel case was initially filed in Maryland's Circuit Court for
Montgomery County. Later, the litigation was kicked up to the
United States District Court for the District of Maryland, Southern
Division (Civil Action No. AW 94-2723).

Actually, Fornshill's attorney, Philip Stinson, told me that he
had precipitated the case after a friend showed him a copy of
Strategic Investment, in which Ruddy's special report was discussed. Stinson saw a reference to a "drop gun" that had allegedly

been placed in Foster's hand. In Stinson's reading, he believed that the implication was that Fornshill had placed it there. Up to that point, Stinson had advised Fornshill to ignore Ruddy's work.

While drafting his legal complaint against Ruddy and *Strategic Investment*, Stinson received a copy of the full-page ad, touting Ruddy's special report, in the *New York Times*, which had been paid for by the Western Journalism Center. Consequently, Stinson added WJC to the libel suit.

5. In late July 1994, Davidson and *Strategic Investment* agreed to pay Ruddy $1,000 in return for the right to distribute his special report.

6. Sprunt, who had grown up in Arkansas, told me that he had been drawn to the Foster case because of its similarity to a major tragedy he had suffered on Christmas Day 1968 when his grandfather, who was terminally ill, shot himself in the head with a .38-caliber revolver at his home in Memphis. He died in front of his grandson, who had heard the shot.

7. Memorandum from Hugh Sprunt to Joe Goulden and Reed Irvine, February 8, 1995.

8. Future editions of Ruddy's special report, which continued to be sold by the Western Journalism Center, were clearly changed. For instance, in the first edition of Ruddy's report, the text about the locations of the two cannons on his map read:

    > The first sits in the *southwest* corner of the square closest to the park's parking lot. The other rests in the opposite, *northeast* corner.... [Emphasis added]

    In a later edition, the text was changed to read:

    > The first sits in the *southeast* corner of the square closest to the park's parking lot. The other rests in the opposite, *northwest* corner.... [Emphasis added]

9. I twice spoke to Rodriguez, who said that he could not answer any questions without the permission of Starr's office.

10. Fornshill replied that he didn't own the sidearms he used in the line of duty; the U.S. Park Police did. Fornshill added that he returned his .38 to the department when he switched to the 9 mm.

11. Claiming that there was a misunderstanding during his conversation with Irvine's deputy, Purvis has since denied seeing this neck wound.

12. During my interview with Dr. Haut, he confirmed his statement to Irvine. Even after I explained the position of the cannon relative to Foster's body, Dr. Haut didn't remember the cannon so close to the body.

13. Ruddy's two other articles in the *Tribune-Review* that same month, also dealing with previously discussed crime-scene issues, receive similar treatment in two more separate ads in the *Washington Times*.

14. In another full-page ad in the *Washington Times* on February 22, 1995, James Davidson and his publication, *Strategic Investment*, also advertised the forty-minute videotape for $29.95 instead of $35.

    Speaking on the Foster case, Davidson dramatically stated: "Strong evidence exists that a crime took place and that officials engaged in a cover-up. This is not only important because of its effect on the financial markets, but because it puts a cloud over our whole economic, political and social system."

15. Kellett published a 287-page update of his book in 1996, which was advertised in a full-page ad in the *Washington Times*'s National Weekly edition on March 30, 1997.

16. A more detailed version of this theory was later written by James R. Norman, a senior editor at *Forbes*. His extremely complicated article, "Fostergate," had supposedly been set to run at *Forbes* but was withdrawn by his magazine at the eleventh hour. Norman then published his story in the August 1995 edition of *Media Bypass Magazine*, an alternative publication for articles not embraced by the mainstream media.

    Briefly, Norman had received information from several sources in the intelligence community, many of whom he refused to name, who stated that Foster was under investigation for espionage, along with his connections to Systematics, Inslaw, the National Security Agency, BCCI, and Banca Della Svizzera Italiana in Chiasso, Switzerland, at the time of his death.

Specifically, according to Norman, "The CIA had Foster under serious investigation for leaking high-level secrets to the State of Israel.... Vince Foster a spy? Actually, it is much worse than that, if the CIA's suspicions are confirmed by the ongoing foreign counterintelligence probe. He would have been an invaluable double agent with potential access to not only high-level political information, but also to sensitive code, encryption and data transmission secrets, the stuff by which modern war is won or lost."

In the October 2, 1995, issue of *Fortune*, *Forbes*'s major competitor, reporter Linda Grant published a brief article about the controversy between Norman and *Forbes*'s editor James W. Michaels, who killed Norman's story about the Foster case because "many of the story's sources were not credible," according to Michaels.

After Norman's piece appeared in *Media Bypass*, he continued to lobby Michaels to publish his article, including an appeal in the form of a memorandum, which wound up on the Internet. However, in this document, Norman, who had "advanced" his story, now made the claim that former Reagan Defense Secretary Caspar Weinberger, also *Forbes*'s chairman, had been among those officials linked to the scandal Norman discussed.

After seeing this memo, Michaels, according to *Fortune*, gave Norman an ultimatum, which led to Norman's resignation from the staff of the magazine.

Interestingly, Deborah Gorham of the White House Counsel's Office told the Special Whitewater Committee that Foster was in possession of two top secret files from the National Security Agency, which he had asked her to place in the office safe. The September 11, 1995, issue of *Newsweek* reported that "sources say Foster's files dealt with legal questions about national emergencies, such as the outbreak of war."

17. In or about early June 1995, Falwell also sent out a mass-marketing letter, promoting the new video on the death of Vincent Foster. For $38, contributors to Falwell's Liberty Alliance received a copy of the video.

18. Ruddy published two more stories on March 22 and March 29, 1995, about the Fiske investigation. In his March 22 article, Ruddy set the record straight that Foster was right-handed after previously writing that he was left-handed.

Apparently, everyone who claimed that Foster was left-handed had received this erroneous information from a March 16, 1994, article in the *Boston Globe*.

19. Along with conversations with Dean Baquet, a reporter with the *New York Times*, Irvine had an exchange of letters between Irvine and Joseph Lelyveld, the executive editor of the *Times*, who defended his newspaper's coverage of the Foster case.

On April 6, 1995, Irvine and Joe Goulden met with *Times* Chairman and CEO Arthur O. "Punch" Sulzberger, Sr. This conversation, which was tape-recorded with Sulzberger's approval, was quite friendly.

On May 9, after Irvine continued to complain about the lack of coverage the Foster case was receiving, Sulzberger sent him a letter, saying: "Believe me, we will continue to search out every lead and follow every reasonable trail that might shed light on the Foster case. As I have said to you before, and I repeat, the *New York Times* is not in the business of suppressing the news and we have no axes to grind. You may not believe this, but it is true."

20. That same day, on March 23, 1995, Irvine wrote a letter to Micah Morrison, a member of the *Wall Street Journal's* editorial page staff who had formerly worked for *The American Spectator*, criticizing Pollock's reporting and defending Ruddy's. While with the *Journal*, Morrison had written several columns critical of President Clinton, including one called "The Mena Coverup" on October 18, 1994.

Irvine sent copies of this letter to Pollock and Ruddy, as well as Davidson, Scaife, Farah, Matrisciana, and Kenneth Starr.

21. In his book, *The Strange Death of Vincent Foster* (Free Press, 1997), Christopher Ruddy quoted Rodriguez on page 216 as saying: "As an ethical person, I don't believe I could be involved in what [Starr's OIC team] were doing."

Ambrose Evans-Pritchard in his book, *The Secret Life of Bill*

Clinton: The Unreported Stories (Regnery, 1997), wrote on pages 149–150: "The word was put out that Rodriguez was unstable. It was whispered that his conduct was becoming unprofessional.... Rodriguez was, of course, being roasted slowly on the Beltway spit."

Rodriguez, who returned to his job as an assistant U.S. attorney in Sacramento, was portrayed as a hero in both of these books.

22. Irvine ran full-page ads about this edition of the *AIM Report* in the May 23, 1995, issue of the *Washington Times* and the June 18, 1995, issue of the *Washington Post*.

23. Another Arkansas trooper, Larry Patterson, who also knew Helen Dickey, corroborated Perry's recollection in his own March 28, 1995, affidavit, saying that he remembered Perry's call to him coming in before 7 PM, Washington time. (Both Perry and Patterson had been assigned to protect the Clinton family while Bill Clinton was the governor of Arkansas.)

However, in her own sworn affidavit, executed on September 13, 1995, Dickey stated that she didn't hear about Foster's death until after 10 PM on July 20, 1993—after the conclusion of CNN's *Larry King Live*, featuring President Clinton, which she watched "on a television in a room on the third floor of the White House Residence.... Shortly thereafter, John Fanning, an employee of the White House Usher's Office, told me that Mr. Foster had been found dead. I had no knowledge of Mr. Foster's death until I learned the news from Mr. Fanning."

Dickey added that she called the governor's mansion in Little Rock to inform her friends of Foster's death, and that Trooper Perry had answered the phone. "I told [Perry] that Mr. Foster had killed himself and that his body had been found in a park," not in a parked car.

During her sworn testimony before the U.S. Senate's Special Committee on Whitewater on February 14, 1996, Dickey stood by her affidavit.

Near the conclusion of her testimony, Chairman D'Amato said, "I apologize to you for bringing this up, but the Majority and the Minority thought that it was important. I think we thought it was important that we get a clarification, and we're not going to go any further."

24. Nine pages are biographical sketches of Scalice, Santucci, and Saferstein. Another twenty-five pages are articles written previously by Christopher Ruddy.

25. Perhaps the most interesting—or dubious—observation made by Scalice and Santucci is their identification of a *magnolia acuminata* leaf in the Polaroid crime-scene photo revealed by ABC News. When they searched the second-cannon site where the Park Police insisted that Foster's body had been found, Scalice and Santucci could not identify that particular form of plant life. However, they did find *magnolia acuminata* near the first cannon where Ruddy claims that Foster's body had been found by paramedic George Gonzalez.

Scalice, Santucci, and Saferstein conducted their investigation at Fort Marcy Park on Saturday, March 4, 1995, which was in the midst of the second winter since Foster's death on July 20, 1993, and *after* the FBI dug up the area during its search on April 4, 1994. The three investigators arrived at the park at 2 PM when the temperature was forty-one degrees, and were gone before the sun set.

26. Evans-Pritchard didn't mention anything about Foster's alleged trips to Switzerland in his 1997 book, *The Secret Life of Bill Clinton*, which included a lengthy section about Foster's death.

27. Reed Irvine appeared on ABC's *Nightline* on July 18, 1995, after the first day of hearings by the U.S. Senate's Special Committee on Whitewater. Irvine made an issue out of the other people seen at Fort Marcy Park, including those allegedly in and around Foster's car, and was critical of the *Fiske Report* for misreporting or ignoring what the eyewitnesses—especially Patrick Knowlton, Judith Doody, and Mark Feist—claimed to have seen.

28. The accountant, Yoly Redden, wrote: "The [Whitewater] corporation has no set of books and there were no work papers to back up the ending balances on the previous tax returns.

"We piece-mealed the information from bank records, the records we received from you," among other documents. Yost added the Redden's letter also stated that the corporation's "state charter was revoked in March 1984 for non-payment of franchise taxes."

29. On Friday, July 21, 1995, the *Wall Street Journal's* editorial staff published another editorial titled "Call Fiske," which again challenged the *Fiske Report's* conclusion that no evidence exists that the issues swirling around Whitewater and Madison Guaranty were troubling Foster.

    Building on the story in the *Washington Post* the previous week about Foster's fear of opening a "can of worms" with the Clintons' income-tax return, the *Journal* used this and other handwritten notes from the late-deputy counsel to conclude: "Anyone whose mother tongue is English, we should think, would conclude that Whitewater was very much a concern to Mr. Foster in the weeks before his death."

30. The Clintons were deposed—once again, separately and under oath—by Whitewater prosecutor Kenneth Starr on April 22, 1995. Abner Mikva and David Kendall represented the president and first lady during their depositions. Accompanying Starr were his deputies, Mark Tuohey and William Duffey, as well as senior counsel Hickman Ewing.

31. Isikoff reportedly had a falling out with editors at the *Washington Post* over the *Post's* refusal to publish an exclusive story about Paula Jones and her sexual-harassment charges against President Clinton. After some drama in the newsroom, Isikoff wound up at *Newsweek*, a subsidiary of the *Post*.

    On May 6, 1994, Jones had filed suit in Little Rock against President Clinton.

32. Spafford's version was boosted by the testimony of Deborah Gorham, who said that she had seen "something yellow" in the briefcase; Linda Tripp confirmed that Gorham had mentioned seeing "little yellow sticky notes" in the briefcase.

    After the torn-up note was later discovered, Nussbaum allegedly questioned Gorham aggressively about what she had and had not seen in the briefcase.

33. The other members of the Special Committee on Whitewater included the following Republicans: Richard Shelby (Alabama), Christopher Bond (Missouri), Connie Mack (Florida), Lauch

Faircloth (North Carolina), Robert Bennett (Utah), Rod Grams (Minnesota), Bill Frist (Tennessee), Orrin Hatch (Utah), and Frank Murkowski (Alaska).

The Democrats included: Paul Sarbanes (Maryland), Christopher Dodd (Connecticut), John Kerry (Massachusetts), Richard Bryan (Nevada), Barbara Boxer (California), Carol Moseley-Braun (Illinois), Patty Murray (Washington), and Paul Simon (Illinois).

On October 12, 1995, Pete Domenici of New Mexico replaced Frist on the Senate panel; Richard Shelby, who sat with the Democrats during the Senate Banking Committee's July 1994 investigation of the Foster case, had switched parties and became a Republican on November 9, 1994.

Also, the same month as the hearings began, Faircloth had hired David Bossie of Floyd Brown's Citizens United as a personal aide.

34. The committee's first witness was former Associate Attorney General Webster Hubbell, who, on December 6, 1994, had pleaded guilty before a federal court in Little Rock to fraudulent billing practices at the Rose Law Firm.

35. On August 13, 1995, reporter Tim Weiner of the *New York Times* published an article about Scaife and asked him about his interest in the Foster case. Scaife replied, "The death of Vincent Foster: I think that's the Rosetta Stone to the whole Clinton administration. There are just too many questions that have no answers."

36. Michael Shaheen, the head of the Department of Justice's Office of Professional Responsibility, was reportedly "stunned" that Foster's detailed account of the Travel Office matter had been withheld from him during his investigation of Travelgate.

An attorney for Bernard Nussbaum replied that the White House never supplied it, because "the Justice Department never followed up and never asked for that Travel Office file," according to a September 19, 1995, report in the *Washington Post*.

Robert Fiske, who had subpoenaed Travel Office documents while serving as the independent counsel, never received this material either.

37. In September 1995, Dr. Brian Blackbourne, San Diego's chief medical examiner since 1990, joined Lee in the reexamination of forensic evidence in the Foster case. Before moving to San Diego, Dr. Blackbourne had served as the chief medical examiner for the Commonwealth of Massachusetts from 1983 to 1990.

   The OIC had also retained the two FBI special agents who worked on the Fiske investigation: William Colombell and Larry Monroe.

38. Gorham testified that two days after Foster's death, she noticed that the index she kept about the personal financial records of the president and Mrs. Clinton was missing from a drawer in Foster's office. She made the discovery after Nussbaum and Maggie Williams had asked her for Foster's files on the Clintons' finances.

   The Special Committee had located a file on a computer in the White House Counsel's Office that appeared to contain the index. However, Gorham was not certain that it was the same list.

39. David Margolis of the Department of Justice, who had remained loyal to the U.S. Park Police throughout the investigation, faced quadruple bypass heart surgery and testified on August 10, 1995, after his recovery.

40. The telephone number dialed was 202-456-7194. It is possible that Thomases simply dialed an incorrect number.

41. Nussbaum returned for further questioning from the Senate panel the following day, August 10, 1995.

42. A birthday card was found by the police in Foster's Honda on the day of his death and became item number 25 on the USPP property report. It was simply addressed to "Tom," who was a White House staffer, according to Peter Boyer.

43. During a discussion about this matter, Ruddy told me that Wallace, who "didn't know very much about the case at all," had agreed with him that mistakes had been made by the Park Police and in the *Fiske Report*, which Ruddy was led to believe would become a major theme during the segment.

   Clearly, Ruddy was misled and lured into a trap.

44. In recent years, Mike Wallace had been extremely forthright about his own bouts with clinical depression.

45. On July 28, 1996, *60 Minutes*, with only minor editing, repeated its segment about the Foster case.

46. The color of the Honda in the parking lot at Fort Marcy continued to stir controversy. In the November 27, 1995, issue of *Insight*, the magazine of the *Washington Times*, reporter Jamie Dettmer reported his interview with Jean Slade, the woman whose Mercedes broke down near the entrance to the park on the afternoon of Foster's death. According to Dettmer, Slade told him that the FBI had erred in its report about her identification of the Honda. Confirming that one of the cars she saw was blue, as she told the FBI, she added that the other car was not gray or silver, but "light tan or brown."

    This appeared to agree somewhat with the color of the Honda Knowlton claimed to have seen.

    Dettmer also noted that Judith Doody had told the FBI that she had seen what she believed to be a Honda "either tan or dark in color." And the reporter added that Doody's companion, Mark Feist, had described the car to the FBI as a "small station wagon or hatchback, brown in color."

    Both Doody and Feist were publicly named, for the first time, in Dettmer's article.

47. Christopher Ruddy first broke the story of the panel's conclusions earlier that same day in the *Pittsburgh Tribune-Review*.

    The Western Journalism Center co-sponsored the analysis by the three experts.

48. Professor Alton might not have been completely nonpartisan and detached from this case. The *Sunday Express* published an article on October 29, 1995, quoting him as saying: "The forgery is as nothing compared to the evidence of all sorts of dark deeds and jiggery-pokery bubbling under the surface. When the truth comes out it will be totally shocking if it appears the state has just done away with an inconvenient man. If Clinton's administration fails because of this, it won't only be because of our findings.

"Some of the people I met [in the U.S.] believe it will be as damning as Watergate."

49. According to Matthew Cooper in his January 8, 1996, article in *The New Republic*: "On August 7, Bill Clinton was, as is his habit, channel surfing late at night in the residence of the White House. When he got to C-SPAN and its rebroadcast of the Senate Whitewater Committee's hearings, he quit clicking, say insiders. That day, several White House officials had testified, including Jack Quinn.... Clinton, sources say, was transfixed and delighted by Quinn's forcefulness.

    "Quinn had argued that Bernard Nussbaum, far from being overzealous in his handling of the investigation following the suicide of Vincent Foster, was at first too accommodating."

50. Three other calls on July 22 interested the committee. According to the November 3, 1995, edition of the *New York Times*, the first came at 3:05 PM from Bill Burton, who left a message for Maggie Williams; at 3:25, Steve Neuwirth also left a message for Williams. Then, at 11:19 that night, Hillary Clinton called the White House switchboard; but no record exits as to whom she spoke.

51. Author James B. Stewart wrote on page 248 in his book, *Blood Sport* (Touchstone, 1997): "Watkins accepted the reprimand, but Foster seemed stunned. In all their years together, years in which he had so often acted as Hillary's mentor and protector, she had never spoken to him like this. The encounter drove home the fact that he was now working for her—from that point on he almost invariably referred to Hillary, but not Bill, as 'the client.'"

52. On November 16, 1995, Billy Dale, the former head of the White House Travel Office, who had been indicted for his alleged abuses in the White House Travel Office, was acquitted.

    Dale was lauded by members of the U.S. House Committee on Government Reform and Oversight during his January 24, 1996, appearance.

53. Watkins testified before the U.S. House Committee on Government Reform and Oversight on January 17, 1996.

54. On Thursday, January 18, 1996, Carolyn Huber testified before the Special Committee, indicating that the billing records she had discovered in the Book Room of the Clintons' private residence in the White House the previous August had "just appeared there.... I thought they had been left there for me to take down to put in the file."

Just a few days earlier, she had been in the same room but had not noticed the documents, which she later found in plain view. After discovering the documents, she placed them in a storage box without reading them. She didn't realize their significance until she reviewed the files in the box in January 1996.

Hillary Clinton continued to deny any knowledge of the billing records found in her residence or how they got there. The Clintons insisted that numerous members of the White House staff also had access to the Book Room.

On June 4, 1996, the FBI sent a letter to the Special Committee, indicating that the bureau's crime lab had discovered six different sets of fingerprints on the billing records found in the Clintons' private residence in the White House.

In addition to those of Mrs. Clinton and Vincent Foster, the FBI found the fingerprints of Carolyn Huber; Huber's assistant, Mildred Alston, who, like Huber, had worked at the Rose Law Firm; and two paralegals, Sandra Hatch of the Rose firm and Marc Rolfe at Williams & Connolly. Rolfe worked for David Kendall, the Clintons' personal attorney.

55. *Washington Post*, January 30, 1995.

56. Simultaneously, in the midst of her promotion tour for her new bestselling book, *It Takes a Village*, Hillary Clinton was hounded with questions about the discrepancies in her previous statements about, among other subjects, the Foster case, Whitewater, Madison Guaranty, her commodities trades, and the Travel Office matter.

During an appearance on National Public Radio, Mrs. Clinton spoke of her family's financial situation, saying, "It's a little bit odd that here we are, both my husband and I, nearly fifty years old, which is hard to believe. We don't own a house; we own half of the house that my mother lives in, in order to help support her. He has his 1968 Mustang. I have my 1986 Oldsmobile Cutlass. A recent magazine said that with our legal bills, we are bankrupt."

57. Actually, the *Wall Street Journal* speculated that the Democrats' filibuster was to prevent hearings about convicted drug dealer Dan Lasater, Patsy Thomasson's former boss who had ties to Governor Clinton's administration in Arkansas.

58. Ruddy had just taken another hit in the March/April edition of *The Columbia Journalism Review* in an article, "The Vince Foster Factory," written by Trudy Lieberman. In her story, Lieberman appeared to make light of Ruddy's recent receipt of the Western Journalism Center's "Courage in Journalism Award," which was accompanied by a crystal trophy and a $2,000 check.

59. James B. Stewart, *Blood Sport* (Touchstone, 1996), pages 284–285.

60. The eighteen principal clients Starr represented included Apple Computer, United Airlines, Chiquita Brands International, Ronald Haft, and the National Football League Players Association.

61. On May 16, 1996, just two days after Thomases's final appearance before the committee, word of another suicide quickly spread through Washington. The victim was fifty-six–year-old Admiral Jeremy M. "Mike" Boorda, the chief of naval operations since March 1994, who had been under investigation by *Newsweek*, regarding his possession of decorations for valor that he had not earned. While in pursuit by two reporters, Boorda left his office at the Pentagon, drove to his home, placed a .38-caliber revolver to his chest, and pulled the trigger.

62. Actually, Irvine had taken that quote from his own, newly prepared analysis of the Foster case, "Farce and Fraud in Foster Findings."

    Later, Irvine wrote a memorandum to Representative Dan Burton on December 9, 1996, titled "How to Crack the Foster Case," which addressed the specifics of many of the issues raised in his report.

63. In fact, Knowlton had taken and passed a polygraph test on December 21, 1995, administered by Paul K. Minor, the FBI's respected former chief polygraph examiner.

64. In his book, *Friends in High Places*, Webb Hubbell wrote on pages 239–240: "[Foster] told me he no longer trusted telephones, even the ones in his office. He seemed to be buying into the growing belief that somehow the Secret Service or burrowed-in Republicans were monitoring phone calls. Once we were talking on the telephone and he told me, 'Hub, we do need to talk, but I can't on the telephone.' We agreed to 'go to a park bench and just talk' sometime soon."

In the October 16, 1995, issue of *Newsweek*, the "Periscope" section cited a Department of Justice report in which Foster believed that "the White House had been 'set up' by hostile FBI officials" after the Travel Office firings. In addition, Alice Sessions, the wife of the former FBI director, had warned Foster's sister, Sheila Anthony, that "there were people within the FBI who were trying to do in the administration. She also said bureau officials had planted 'listening devices' in her home." *Newsweek* added that Anthony told Foster about her conversations with Mrs. Sessions.

Nevertheless, *Newsweek* stated, "The Justice report found Foster's fears of an FBI plot were groundless."

65. In 1996, David Brock of *The American Spectator* wrote—and took a considerable amount of heat from other conservatives for a surprisingly sympathetic biography of the first lady, *The Seduction of Hillary Rodham*. On page 409, Brock wrote: "Ignored by the press were Watkins' serious credibility problems. Watkins himself admitted that he initially misled White House and congressional investigators about Hillary's role [in the Travel Office matter]."

66. *Newsweek* had reported in its December 2, 1996, edition that Starr had concluded that Foster committed suicide.

Similar reports had appeared as early as 1995 on the Scripps-Howard wire service, the *Wall Street Journal*, and on CBS's *60 Minutes*.

67. Joseph Farah and the Western Journalism Center believed that the White House report so resembled the infamous Nixon "enemies list," that WJC reprinted the report and sold it.

68. In papers filed by Knowlton and his attorney with the OIC, which

were published as an addendum to the *Starr Report*, Knowlton said that the Dr. Haut document was found on July 17, 1997, two days *before* Sprunt said they had found it.

69. U.S. District Judge John Garrett Penn was the lower court judge who ruled in favor of Hamilton. Ironically, Penn also had been assigned to hear the harassment case, *Knowlton v. U.S., et al.*

70. The *Starr Report* discussed a situation in May 1993 concerning Foster's country club in Little Rock, which had become embroiled in controversy after the discovery that it had no African-American members. That same month, Foster resigned as a member of the club, which had once been an important center of the Fosters' social life.

71. Lesnevich had twenty-three *original* samples of Foster's handwriting to help him conduct his analysis, including five pages of copy and eighteen checks.

72. Starr's investigators had interviewed Foster's mother, Alice Mae Foster. Neither she nor her longtime housekeeper could identify a photograph of the gun found in her son's right hand as one of the guns in her husband's collection.

The investigators also interviewed Vincent Foster's three children, but none of them could positively identify the gun—although all three had seen at least one handgun in the house.

73. The *Fiske Report* stated that the FBI crime lab had also examined the brown paper that had held Foster's clothing. However, the FBI attributed the materials they found on the paper—including "one flattened ball-shaped gunpowder particle in scrapings from Foster's shoes and socks, and one disk-shaped particle"—as having emanated from contamination in the USPP lab.

Obviously, Dr. Lee disagreed.

74. USPP Investigator Renee Abt told me that she, along with other police investigators at the crime scene, had specifically examined the foliage around Foster's body for blood but found none. However, Abt, a gardener, did observe minuscule raised brown spots on the leaves, which she described as a "leaf disease."

75. The following code identifies these witnesses in the *Starr Report*: C1/Jim Ferris, C2/Patrick Knowlton, C3/Mark Feist, C4/Judith Doody, C5/Dale Kyle, and C6/Jean Slade.

76. USPP criminalist Pete Simonello and Investigator Jim Morrissette told me that they were puzzled by this finding—since the Park Police didn't take a soil sample under Foster's head on either July 20 or July 21, 1993, when they were, separately, at Fort Marcy Park, conducting their investigations.

    The results of any soil-sample analysis taken after that, they believe, must be viewed with some skepticism.

77. Actually, though, Kenneth Starr has not yet closed the book on Vincent Foster, promising a further analysis of the events that took place in Foster's office during the week *after* his death, as part of his anticipated report on Whitewater-related activities.

78. *The Secret Life of Bill Clinton*, page 226.

79. Byron York wrote a hilarious exposé about the Clinton Investigative Commission for the August 1996 issue of *The American Spectator*. In one passage of his story, York quoted a fund-raising letter from the executive director of the Virginia-based commission, saying: "On that gruesome afternoon, Vince Foster was with a mysterious blond (his wife, Lisa, is a brunette). He ate a meal and engaged in adulterous sexual relations with this blond. A few hours later he was dead. By law, I am not allowed to make a conclusion here. The facts speak for themselves."

    York also noted a popular bumper sticker being promoted by a commission staffer: *If Vince Foster Had A Gun, He Would Be Alive Today.*

Epilogue

1. As this book was going to press, President Clinton was in the midst
    of the greatest crisis of his presidency, battling for his political sur-
    vival in the wake of revelations of his alleged affair with Monica
    Lewinsky, a White House intern in 1995.

    Linda Tripp, Nussbaum's former executive assistant and one of
    the last known White House staffers to see Vincent Foster alive,
    had left the White House in August 1994 and went to work in the
    Pentagon's press office—where Lewinsky was reassigned in April
    1996. The two women became acquainted; both were eventually
    subpoenaed to testify in Paula Jones's sexual-harassment suit. Prior
    to their testimonies, Lewinsky told Tripp about her alleged affair
    with the president.

    Tripp, who had considered writing a book about the Clinton
    White House, recorded several of these conversations and eventu-
    ally went to Kenneth Starr's office with the tapes. Also on tape,
    Lewinsky had alleged that Washington attorney Vernon Jordan, a
    close friend of the president, had encouraged her to lie in her testi-
    mony in the Jones case—a charge Jordan later denied. Starr was
    already in the midst of an investigation of Jordan's relationship
    with Webb Hubbell as part of his overall Whitewater investigation.

    Lewinsky had signed a sworn affidavit on January 7, 1998,
    declaring that she had not had any sexual relationship with the pres-
    ident, who, himself, was deposed in the Jones case on January 17.

    Four days before the president testified, Tripp lured Lewinsky to
    the Ritz-Carlton Hotel in Pentagon City. Wired for sound by
    Starr's staff, Tripp had another conversation about the alleged
    affair. (Michael Isikoff of *Newsweek* had the Lewinsky story, but
    Newsweek held back on printing it at the request of the Office of
    the Independent Counsel. The story was then broken by Susan
    Schmidt and two other reporters at the *Washington Post* on
    January 21.)

    In the midst of an unprecedented media assault, as well as calls
    for his resignation or impeachment, the president denied both the
    alleged affair and any effort to silence Lewinsky.

Index

C

Capital Management Services, 141

Capitol Police, 6

Caputo, Lisa, 47

Car keys: *See also* Honda Accord; discovery of, 42-43; search for, 31

Cardozo, Michael, 209

Career overview, 63

Carroll, John Phillip, 64, 205, 418n

Castle Grande, 333

Castleton, Tom, 75, 78

CBS television network, 152, 321

Central Intelligence Agency, 3, 390n

Chertoff, Michael, 310, 346

Chicago Sun-Times, 331

Chicago Tribune, 142

Children's Defense Fund, 304

Cholak, Phil, 49

Christian Broadcasting Network, 336

CIA. *See* Central Intelligence Agency

CIB. *See* Criminal Investigations Branch

Citizens for Honest Government, 286

Citizens United, 175, 251, 254

Clifford, Clark, 156

Clinger, William F., Jr., 165-166, 273-275, 322, 413n

Clinton, Bill: address to White House staff following Foster's death, 61-62; announcement that Whitewater documents would be turned over, 147; call to Vince Foster, 96, 97-99; comments on Foster's motive for suicide, 84; comments on *Larry King Live,* 156; comments on torn-up note, 406-407n; depositions, 224-229, 342; eulogy for Foster, 92; Lewinsky crisis, 445n; notification of death, 47-48, 335-336; partnership with McDougals, 139-142; press release about Foster's death, 49; reelection, 352; request for appointment of Whitewater special counsel, 152-153; *Washington Times* story on removal of Whitewater documents from Foster's office, 145-147; withdrawal from Nussbaum, 171

Clinton, Chelsea, 47, 153

Clinton, Hillary: billing records from Rose Law Firm, 333; business partnerships with Foster, 74-75; comments on financial situation, 440n; comments on Foster's state of mind, 123; conclusions of special Whitewater committee, 347, 349; connection to Madison Guaranty, 7; deposition to independent counsel, 229-232; dislike for Secret Service guards, 331-332; Foster's comments during commencement ceremony speech, 64; friendship with Foster, 5, 64, 109; notification of death, 47; as partner in Rose Law Firm, 42; partner-